T0293002

Junk Food Politics

Junk Food Politics

How Beverage and Fast Food Industries
Are Reshaping Emerging Economies

Eduardo J. Gómez

JOHNS HOPKINS UNIVERSITY PRESS   BALTIMORE

© 2023 Johns Hopkins University Press
All rights reserved. Published 2023
Printed in the United States of America on acid-free paper
9 8 7 6 5 4 3 2 1

Johns Hopkins University Press
2715 North Charles Street
Baltimore, Maryland 21218
www.press.jhu.edu

Library of Congress Cataloging-in-Publication Data

Names: Gómez, Eduardo J., 1973– author.
Title: Junk food politics : how beverage and fast food industries are reshaping
    emerging economies / Eduardo J. Gómez.
Description: Baltimore : Johns Hopkins University Press, 2022. | Includes
    bibliographical references and index.
Identifiers: LCCN 2021047164 | ISBN 9781421444284 (hardcover) | ISBN
    9781421444291 (ebook)
Subjects: LCSH: Nutrition policy—Developing countries. | Public health—Economic
    aspects—Developing countries. | Food industry and trade—Moral and ethical
    aspects. | Junk food—Developing countries.
Classification: LCC TX360.5 .G66 2022 | DDC 363.809172/4—dc23/eng/20220327
LC record available at https://lccn.loc.gov/2021047164

A catalog record for this book is available from the British Library.

*Special discounts are available for bulk purchases of this book. For more information, please
contact Special Sales at specialsales@jh.edu.*

To my dear father, Guillermo Leon Gómez,
who always listens, encourages, and supports
my big ideas and ambitions

Contents

Preface

I love London coffee shops—they welcome diverse groups of people, are always lively, and often are the best place to mingle, read, and generate big ideas. My idea for this book emerged in such a place. Sipping a dark *cafezinho* one afternoon in west London, I chanced upon an online news article discussing the power of food-based interest groups for influencing university research in ways that made US health care officials overlook the harmful health effects of sugar. I could not believe how influential these interest groups were. At the same time, I began to realize that many of the most innovative programs for preventing obesity and type 2 diabetes around the world were not working as well as expected. After several years of policy innovations in countries such as Brazil and Mexico, cases of obesity and type 2 diabetes were burgeoning; and even more worrisome, it was happening at an alarming rate among vulnerable populations, such as children and the poor. Why? Could it be that a major external force, such as the political and social prowess of major food industries, was hampering the design and implementation of these policies? A flame was lit. A big idea emerged. And I endeavored to find answers to this vexing question.

I soon realized that providing an answer to this question required an in-depth comparative historical analysis of how major food and beverage industries came to wield great influence; how these industries were shaping politics, policy, and society; and how or even *if* governments should work with these industries in response. I wondered—in emerging middle-income countries seeing a rapid increase in foreign direct investment and economic growth—whether recent transitions to democracy and electoral institutions could safeguard vulnerable populations from the industries' policy influence and their unhealthy products. Were politicians genuinely committed to protecting children and the poor from consuming these products too much and preventing their associated ailments? Were presidential, congressional, and bureaucratic institutions adapting by learning how to grapple with this new public health challenge? In my mind, writing a book was the only fitting way to address these concerns adequately.

Books require a lot of work, commitment, and support. Writing one is a marathon. I had the honor and privilege along the way of working with amazing colleagues. I would like first to thank my editor at Johns Hopkins University Press, Robin Coleman, as well as the Editorial Board at Hopkins for providing me with the opportunity to have this book published. Robin offered in-depth comments, support, and encouragement along the way. Robert Brown, a production editor at Hopkins, did a brilliant job of working with me on polishing the end product. I would also like to thank other colleagues and research assistants for their thoughts and suggestions at different stages of research and writing: Ally Wolloch, Nino Dzotsenidze, James McGuire, Joseph Harris, and Tara Kessaram.

Finally, my family and friends were there for me throughout the process. My father, Guillermo L. Gómez, never failed to offer a listening ear and encouragement. When I wasn't writing, my dear friends Patrick Crotty, Ash Hoque, Fathima Wakeel, and Robert Hargrove, along with my family away from home at the Roger Gracie Brazilian Jiu Jitsu Academy in west London, were always available for respite and support. It was a long haul, but my peeps helped push me across the finish line.

Junk Food Politics

Introduction

In 2016, Dr. Margaret Chan, who was China's first woman to serve as director general of the World Health Organization (WHO), delivered a keynote address to the National Academy of Medicine. She was a leader. She was a visionary. And she had an important message. Speaking to a captivated audience, Director Chan discussed the need to tackle the burgeoning epidemic of obesity and type 2 diabetes. Toward the end of her presentation, she argued that one of the primary reasons for the emergence of these epidemics was the lack of political will to tackle the interests and power of big industry. Specifically, she commented: "When crafting preventive strategies, government officials must recognize that the widespread occurrence of obesity and diabetes throughout a population is not a failure of individual willpower to resist fats and sweets or exercise more. It is a failure of political will to take on the powerful food and soda industries. If governments understand this duty, the fight against obesity and diabetes can be won. The interests of the public must be prioritized over those of corporations" (Chan 2017).

In essence, this book seeks to address why many of our most thriving emerging economies today have neglected to fulfill Dr. Chan's call to duty of taking on the interests and power of major junk food industries—defined here as multinational and domestic soda and ultraprocessed food companies. Achieving this requires policies that not only *effectively* inform consumers, such as by ensuring the provision of accurate and reliable food labels, but also effectively regulate the marketing and sale of their products, especially toward vulnerable populations, such as children and the poor. Unfortunately, for most countries in the developing world, governments have neglected to earnestly pursue these marketing and sales regulatory policies, instead allowing junk food industries to thrive and prosper, but at the expense of the deteriorating health of these vulnerable populations.

An intriguing puzzle emerges. Despite the absence of these much-needed regulatory policies, several of the world's biggest emerging economies, such as Mexico, Brazil, India, China, Indonesia, and South Africa, have done a commendable job of implementing a host of innovative obesity and type 2 diabetes prevention programs. Indeed, in these emerging economies, which are the focus of this book, governments have unleashed a myriad of innovative public awareness campaigns and funding for nutritional and exercise programs, and, in some instances, have even introduced controversial soda taxes. Mexico was a global leader in this last regard, being the first in the world to adopt a national soda tax in 2013. What's more, in 2010, Brazil was recognized by the international community, along with the United Kingdom, for its policy innovations in tackling obesity (Gómez 2015). Nevertheless, these governments have repeatedly neglected to take on the power of big industry by failing to enact effective regulatory policies circumscribing industry's ability to communicate, market, and sell their products, especially to vulnerable populations. These policy outcomes have emerged at a time when the majority of childhood obesity cases are soaring in these high-growth emerging markets, throughout the Americas, Asia, and Africa, and where type 2 diabetes is now prevalent among adults and adolescents. In fact, according to the WHO, "the vast majority of overweight or obese children live in developing countries, where the rate of increase has been more than 30% higher than that of developed countries" (2020, 1; see figure).

Addressing this puzzling situation requires an in-depth comparative historical analysis of the complex world of junk food politics. In this book, I argue that there is a context of fear and opportunity—that is, junk food industries continuously fear the prospect of losing revenue in the industrialized West and opportunities abound for investment in the emerging economies. With a rising middle-income class and increased consumer spending, more than ever industries have had incentives to engage in several political, institutional, and civil societal tactics facilitating their ability to stymie the creation and implementation of regulatory policies. From engaging in innovative policy partnerships with government to reshaping bureaucratic institutions and civil societal actors in their favor, these industries have garnered the political legitimacy and influence needed to achieve this policy objective.

But industries are only partly to blame. Governments are equally respon-

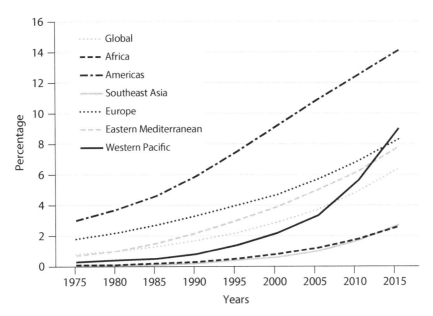

Prevalence of obesity among children and adolescents (ages 5–19). *Source*: WHO, 2020. Global Health Observatory data repository. https://apps.who.int /gho/data/view.main.BMIPLUS2REGv?lang=en

sible. Basically, junk food politics is a two-way street. While industries have worked hard to influence government, political leaders have had a historic track record of partnering with industry to achieve their alternative policy, and thus political, agendas. Powerful presidents in Mexico, Brazil, India, China, Indonesia, and South Africa have viewed these industries as necessary allies, helping these heads of state implement a host of economic and social welfare programs—and in the process, contributing to their nation's developmental prospects. But more importantly for these leaders, they have benefited politically, as partnering with industry has helped them to fulfill their economic and social welfare objectives, and thus achieve electoral promises. In this context, industry's political tactics have been *indirectly* supported by presidential partnership and political ambition.

To better understand and explain the complex world of junk food politics, this book introduces an analytical framework named Industry Politics and Complementary Institutions (IPCI). To my knowledge, this framework is the first to unify several theoretical schools of thought in political science and public health policy to guide our analysis and, more importantly, provide a more thorough explanation of the junk food industry's political and policy influence in several emerging economies. As I explain in chapter 1, this framework begins by focusing on the broader historical context of fear and opportunity, where, more than ever, industry fears of dwindling global profits, when combined with new investment opportunities in the emerging economies, have generated incentives for junk food industries to influence politics, society, and policy. In this historical context, IPCI emphasizes that industries have engaged in several political processes, ranging from the formation of health policy partnerships with government officials to industry lobbying, the provision of largesse, and the strategic infiltration of bureaucratic institutions. At the same time, IPCI underscores industry's efforts to restructure society in its favor—that is, by establishing civil societal partnerships and providing social services while strategically using these partnerships to generate divisions in society and, ultimately, to undermine collective opposition against industry. And finally, this framework introduces the important concept of *complementary institutions*. In other words, the historical and contemporary incentives that presidents have to partner with and use industry for political objectives. These partnerships ultimately serve to indirectly supplement the political tactics and influence of junk food industries while emphasizing the fact that governments and their political leaders are also to blame for industry's ongoing policy influence over noncommunicable diseases (NCDs).

When taken together, IPCI provides greater insight into why junk food industries continue to have the political legitimacy and influence needed to repeatedly undermine the introduction and effectiveness of NCD regulatory policies. Nevertheless, this approach also helps to explain why several of our biggest emerging economies have neglected to achieve Director Chan's call to duty of taking on the power and interests of big business. Sometimes it seems that political leaders benefit more from seeing these industries thrive and prosper, sadly, to the detriment of the health of our children and the poor.

Understanding Junk Food Politics

Applying my analytical framework to the cases of Mexico, Brazil, India, Indonesia, China, and South Africa helps to provide a thorough explanation of the junk food industry's political interference in NCD regulatory policy.

In Mexico, the presence and influence of these industries emerged shortly after the introduction of free market reforms—for instance, free trade and deregulation. This context allowed industries, such as Coca-Cola, to obtain an early foothold in the market, becoming important economic and political entities. As the public health challenges of obesity and type 2 diabetes emerged, however, the government was slow to respond. After several years of scientific warnings from Mexico's National Institute of Public Health, the government implemented national prevention programs focusing on NCD awareness and improved nutrition. While regulatory policies targeting the marketing and sale of junk food products were eventually introduced, they were poorly enforced and mostly ignored.

For the most part, these outcomes were the product of the junk food industry's apparent legitimacy and policy influence, facilitated through several political and social tactics. These tactics included working closely with Department of Health officials to create health and educational programs in schools, lobbying, and engaging in largesse (mainly via electoral campaign contributions) while infiltrating national bureaucratic advisory committees in order to safeguard industry's ideas and policy interests. These industries also engaged in several partnerships with academic researchers and nongovernmental organizations (NGOs), but to the detriment of civil society's ability to mobilize and hold industries accountable for their actions. Despite these challenges, activists continue to draw attention to the need to address Mexico's childhood obesity and diabetes problem. Though initially struggling to gain government recognition and influence, in recent years, activists and NGOs have highlighted the junk food industry's harmful effects and drawn greater attention to the need for more aggressive regulatory action.

Nevertheless, industry's political tactics and influence were also indirectly supported by Mexico's powerful presidents, such as Vicente Fox (PAN, 2000–2006), Felipe Calderón (PAN, 2006–2012), and Enrique Peña Nieto (PRI, 2012–2018). These leaders partnered with soda and ultraprocessed food companies in order to achieve their alternative economic and social welfare agendas, such as implementing popular anti-hunger campaigns. This kind of strong presidential support, what IPCI refers to as an example of complementary institutions, further emboldened industry's political legitimacy and, unfortunately, its ongoing policy influence.

Mexico's neighbor to the south, Brazil, faced similar challenges. There, major junk food industries emerged following the transition to democracy and free market reforms, a process facilitating and encouraging investment in the soda, snack food, and fast food sectors. Despite an increase in obesity and type 2 diabetes cases among Brazil's most vulnerable populations, the government was slow to respond. And when it did eventually respond, the Ministry of Health's (MoH) focus was first on providing innovative prevention programs, with an emphasis on information and awareness. While regulations restricting the marketing and sale of products were eventually introduced, they were either limited, ignored, or blocked by industry interests. And to this day, the government has not implemented—or even attempted to introduce—a tax on sodas and junk foods.

Similar to what we saw in Mexico, these outcomes were the product of several industries' efforts to engage in health policy partnerships with the MoH, lobbying and largesse (via campaign donations), while strategically infiltrating national regulatory agencies, such as Anvisa, Brazil's national regulatory agency for food, pharmaceutical, tobacco, and other health care services. Nevertheless, major industries, such as PepsiCo, Coca-Cola, and Nestlé, also provided several corporate social responsibility activities, ranging from the provision of community employment programs to supporting gay rights campaigns. Helpful in building social allies, these industry efforts nevertheless contributed to divisions in society between those that supported industry and those that did not, in turn hampering nutrition activists' ability to mobilize in opposition. Despite these challenges, the activist community continues to strive to address industry's harmful effects in society, and especially among children and the poor.

And yet, the onus of responsibility cannot solely be placed on junk food industries. The government has also been responsible for industry's ongoing policy influence. Indeed, Brazil's presidents, such as Luiz Inácio "Lula" da Silva (PT, 2002–2010), appear to have benefited from establishing a strong partnership with industry leaders, strategically using them to achieve popular anti-poverty measures. Lula even went so far as to create federal institutions that would sustain this partnership with industry. Strong presidential backing, or what I refer to as complementary institutions, indirectly contributed to these industries' political legitimacy and policy influence.

India, Brazil's counterpart in South Asia, is also experiencing similar challenges. Although junk food industries initially struggled to enter India's market due to the presence of a nationalist socialist government, free market reforms beginning in the 1990s generated new incentives and opportunities for several industries (mainly foreign) to capture and develop the market. India's government faced the dual burden of malnutrition, however, where ongoing undernutrition was soon accompanied by a high level of obesity and type 2 diabetes cases, surging in recent years among children and the poor. In this complex nutritional context, the Ministry of Health and Family Welfare (MHFW) was considerably delayed in providing several NCD prevention programs. While parliament eventually succeeded in adopting a "sin tax" on sodas and junk foods in 2017, ineffective regulations emerged in the area of food labeling; the marketing of these products has instead relied on ineffective industry self-regulation, sans government involvement, while to this day, not a single piece of legislation exists regulating junk food sales, especially toward children.

Industry politics has once again interfered, contributing to these policy outcomes. These outcomes were influenced by industry's efforts to partner with government on several innovative NCD prevention programs, aggressive lobbying, as well as industry's infiltration of federal regulatory agencies. At the same time, several companies, such as PepsiCo, Coca-Cola, and Nestlé, have invested in local communities by providing health and other social welfare services. While broadening their support base, these efforts have nevertheless divided society and its ability to mobilize against industry's political activities and policy influence. While new and emerging, nutritionist activists in India are nevertheless making excellent progress in drawing attention to these industry tactics, raising greater awareness about the need to improve children and the poor's nutrition and overall health while pressuring the government to adopt more aggressive regulatory policies.

However, once again, industry politics is only partly to blame. In India, the government has also done its part in contributing to industry's ongoing policy influence. Indeed, as seen in Mexico and Brazil, India's political leaders, such as Prime Minister Narendra Modi (2014–present) of the Bharatiya Janata Party, have relied on junk food industries as vital partners in achieving Modi's objective of increasing foreign direct investment, economic growth, and prosperity for all. By working with industry to achieve these alternative economic objectives, though, Modi has indirectly bolstered the political legitimacy and influence of these industries, while helping him maintain popular support. Here, once again, complementary institutions have only served to benefit industry, ultimately at the expense of improving the health of children and the poor.

Indonesia, India's neighbor to the south, also saw the gradual emergence of a thriving junk food industry, kindled by the expeditious transition to free market reforms and decentralization. Similar to India, the double burden of malnutrition contributed to delays in the MoH's policy response. While MoH prevention programs eventually emerged, efforts to introduce a soda tax were nevertheless short-lived. Few, if any, regulatory efforts were made in the areas of food labeling, marketing, and sales. And this has occurred amid the burgeoning growth of obesity and type 2 diabetes cases among the islands' most vulnerable populations.

But why did this occur? Industries and their supportive interest groups were successful mainly due to their aggressive lobbying efforts while incessantly pressuring legislators to refrain from adopting a soda tax. Although close policy partnerships were never pursued with government, several junk food industries engaged in a wide range of corporate social responsibility initiatives in order to establish social legitimacy and influence. Nevertheless, these activities contributed to growing divisions in society, where industry partnerships with nutrition scientists and NGOs reduced the number of allies that activists could work with to mobilize and confront industry's ongoing policy influence. In this challenging context, and despite the fact that civil society's presence in the area of nutrition has only recently emerged, activists are doing a commendable job of raising awareness about obesity and type 2 diabetes, and the double burden of malnutrition, while calling for more aggressive industry regulations.

At the same time, however, Indonesia's presidents have also indirectly contributed to the junk food industry's success. Recent presidents, such as Susilo Bambang Yudhoyono, commonly referred to by his initials (SBY; 2004–2014) and Joko "Jokowi" Widodo (2014–present), have established close partnerships with several major industries in order to help accelerate economic development, provide food security, and reduce poverty. But unfortunately, these complementary institutions once again appear to have indirectly contributed to industry's ongoing political and NCD policy influence.

By far Asia's largest economy, China has also seen the consequences of complex junk food politics. After several years of political isolation from the West and a closed-off economy, major multinational industries emerged to capture the market, instigate development, and establish a strong foothold in the economy. Amid an escalating increase in childhood obesity and type 2 diabetes cases, the MoH was slow to respond, and when it did, it emphasized a host of NCD prevention and awareness campaigns. In addition to highlighting sound nutrition, most of these prevention programs were focused on the importance of daily physical exercise, especially for children. Despite these impressive campaigns, a soda tax was never introduced. Worse still, no effort has been made to create effective food labels, while no legislation exists regulating the marketing and sale of these foods to children. This, in turn, has incentivized industries to aggressively market their products to children and the poor.

But why has this occurred? Once again, industries have been highly adept at influencing prevention and regulatory policy in their favor. As we saw in other countries, one key strategy has been these industries' policy partnerships with government, such as helping improve nutrition and exercise in schools. At the same time, industries have engaged in several lobbying tactics, though mainly through informal meetings with policy makers. Perhaps industries' most effective strategy has been its strategic infiltration of the China Centers for Disease Control and Prevention (CDC) and industry's ability to inculcate its policy ideas by establishing strong linkages with policy makers within the China CDC (Greenhalgh 2019a). This tactic has allowed major companies like Coca-Cola to work through supportive NGOs, such as the International Life Sciences Institute, to establish the importance of physical exercise for preventing childhood obesity within the China CDC (Greenhalgh 2019a). What's more, industries have engaged in a wide variety of corporate social responsibility (CSR) activities, in turn aiding industries in their ability to increase their community support and social legitimacy. The dearth of NGOs that are working on advocating for improved nutrition among China's most vulnerable communities means that these CSR activities have not contributed to divisions within society. And unfortunately, while civic awareness and interests in improving China's obesity and type 2 diabetes situation has increased, for a variety of political reasons, ranging from government suspicion of activist activities (especially those linked to foreign NGOs) and a reluctance to incorporate civil society's views, NGOs still have not had the space and opportunity needed to successfully hold industries accountable while pressuring government for NCD regulatory policies.

Once again, further complicating matters is the central government's efforts to partner with industry to help achieve the government's goal of advancing economic development and eradicating poverty. In fact, central and provincial governments have worked closely with major companies such as PepsiCo and Coca-Cola on eradicating poverty, especially in rural areas—a historic central government priority. All the while, political leaders, since the days of Deng Xiaoping (1978–1992) to the current president, Xi Jinping (2012–present), have viewed these industries, and the private sector in general, as vital to helping develop China's economic and social prosperity. In the end, it appears that these complementary institutions have helped to increase industry's broader political acceptability and policy influence.

Finally, South Africa, the African continent's largest economy, has also struggled with the two-way road of junk food politics. After several years of geopolitical and economic isolation due to Apartheid rule, eventually major soda and ultraprocessed food industries entered South Africa's market with gusto, flourishing and providing new opportunities, backed by the new democratic president, Nelson Mandela, in 1994. The burgeoning growth and consumption of these junk food products has nevertheless contributed to an ongoing increase in obesity and type 2 diabetes, afflicting not only children (who now lead the African region in overall obesity cases) but also the urban and rural poor. In a context of ongoing malnourishment, poverty, and HIV/AIDS, the Department of Health was slow to respond; when it did, it emphasized the introduction of public health prevention campaigns, such as improved nutrition, balanced diets, and exercise. While a soda tax was eventually introduced, it took several years to be passed by parliament, while the tax was substantially reduced. Even further disheartening has been the inadequacy of food labels, and the absence of any regulation for advertising and selling these products to children. Instead, the government has encouraged industry self-regulation through company pledges not to market products to children, especially near schools, but this, too, has been repeatedly ignored by these companies.

But why did these outcomes emerge? Once again, industry politics mattered. And this entailed a host of political tactics. For instance, several industries engaged in health policy partnerships with government officials, such as working with government to provide physical education programs in schools. At the same time, these industries and their interest group representatives, such as the Beverage Association of South Africa, aggressively lobbied the government to successfully delay and water down the 2018 soda tax. But several companies, such as Nestlé and Coca-Cola, also engaged in a host of CSR initiatives, ranging from the provision of health care to job training, in turn helping build social support and legitimacy. As we saw in several other countries, however, these activities have contributed to the emergence of a divided society, where industry's relationship with NGOs and academics has generated conflict and a lack of collaboration with other activists seeking to raise attention about NCDs and to hold these industries accountable. While the activist community in the area of nutrition is new, it is troubled by a lack of adequate resources and attention. Nevertheless, activist efforts continue and are gradually building greater attention and awareness to the need to improve the health of children and the poor.

But industry alone cannot be blamed for South Africa's ongoing efforts to introduce more effective NCD regulations and improve the health of its most vulnerable populations. Once again, the government is also to blame. Indeed, since the Nelson Mandela administration (1994–1999) to current-day president Cyril Ramaphosa of the ANC political party (2018–present), presidents have strengthened their partnership with junk food industries in order to achieve these politicians' priorities to improve the economy, provide jobs, tackle poverty, and ensure food security. In essence, these complementary institutions have once again served to indirectly support the junk food industry and its unrelenting efforts to influence policy and politics.

Thus, in sum, the countries of Mexico, Brazil, India, China, Indonesia, and South Africa have revealed that the political power and influence of junk food industries is strong, enduring, and obstructing the creation of NCD regulatory policies. Unfortunately, and as we will see in the following pages, it seems that most governments in these emerging economies still have not paid heed to former WHO director Margaret Chan's initial warnings and recommendations to take on the power and interests of big business. Regardless of how innovative these governments have been at introducing NCD policies, even those focused on childhood obesity and type 2 diabetes, for the most part, they are still far from willing to undercut the power and influence of industries through more aggressive regulatory policies. Junk food politics has interfered, and most importantly of all, it has interfered in ways that continue to impair the health and well-being of children and the poor in these thriving developing nations.

Methodological Approach

I adopted a qualitative methodological approach to comparative historical research in preparation for writing this book. The empirical evidence used for the country case study chapters were obtained from several qualitative sources, such as books, peer-reviewed journal articles, policy reports, and credible newspaper sources. In-depth interviews with several activists, academic researchers, and NGO experts were also conducted for many of the country case study chapters. This interview data was used to provide further empirical evidence of the causal and factual claims made throughout this book. Interviews were conducted via Skype and Zoom communications in 2019, 2020, and 2021.

With respect to case study selection, I selected and compared the countries of Mexico, Brazil, India, Indonesia, China, and South Africa for several reasons. First, these nations are arguably the largest emerging economies in their respective regions with high levels of obesity and type 2 diabetes, particularly among children and the poor. Second, I sought to obtain global regional representation—that is, selecting countries from Latin America, Asia, and Africa. Third, these case studies were selected due to the rich availability of published literature on these countries and on the issues of concern in this book. Finally, these cases were selected in order to illustrate the potential utility of IPCI, rather than striving to use these case studies to test and establish a generalizable theory through a deductive approach to causal inference (Imenda 2014). Instead, and as I explain in chapter 2, this analytical framework was inductive in its approach. That is, IPCI's concepts were developed based on existing concepts and theories in political science and public health policy as well as new theoretical concepts that I established, with the goal of better organizing and explaining complex causal events within countries rather than predicting them and establishing generalizable theoretical claims, which is a key distinction between analytical and theoretical frameworks (Stanley 2012).

But what was the purpose of my comparative analysis? The countries of Mexico, Brazil, India, Indonesia, China, and South Africa are different in many ways, seemingly incomparable. So why compare them? The goal was to illustrate and explain their unique politics, institutions, policies, and social movements and their distinctive experiences in dealing with junk food industries rather than treating them as similar generalizable cases, reflecting similar patterns of causality and outcomes over time. I therefore adopted Skocpol and Somer's (1980) notion of contrasts of contexts in comparative historical analysis for the purpose of highlighting unique causal mechanisms and outcomes between complex sets of cases (see also Collier 1993).

A Road Map

This book is broken up into several chapters. In the next chapter, I conduct a literature review and introduce readers to IPCI. Chapter 2, titled "Fear and Opportunity," then provides an explanation for why junk food industries are seeking to eagerly invest in emerging markets, setting the broader historical context for these industries' political and policy strategies in these countries. Chapter 3 closely examines the case of Mexico, followed by Brazil in chapter 4, India in chapter 5, Indonesia in chapter 6, China in chapter 7, and South Africa in chapter 8. The conclusion summarizes the key findings from these chapters, as well as the theoretical and empirical lessons learned, while providing recommendations for policy makers.

1

Interest Group Theory, Institutions, and Public Health Policy

The study of interest groups and public policy has a long tradition in the field of political science. This is particularly the case when it comes to studying health care policy in the United States. Indeed, one of the very first books to focus on interest group theory in American health care politics—and the field of political science in general—was Oliver Garceau's (1941) seminal discussion of the rise and policy influence of the American Medical Association. Over time, a phalanx of scholarly articles and books began to emerge exploring the various contexts under which interest groups successfully manipulate public health policy in the United States and Western Europe (Eckstein 1960; Marmor and Thomas 1972; Morone 1992; Navarro 1995; Oliver and Dowell 1994). By the 1990s, the field of comparative politics also began to see discussions of interest groups and their interaction with political institutions and health care in other Western European democracies (Immergut 1992).

Interest group theory has traditionally focused on the United States and Western European democracies. Little is known about how this theoretical approach informs the transformation of public health policy in developing nations. With this new scholarly topic only emerging in the past two decades, political scientists examining public health policy in developing nations have instead focused on other types of political and institutional issues as factors influencing health policy reform. Focuses include the impact of democratic consolidation on children's health (McGuire 2010); the importance of state capacity, government commitment, and leadership to eradicate HIV/AIDS and other diseases (Gauri and Khaleghian 2002; Johnson 2004); the formal design and impact of political institutional arrangements, such as federalism, decentralization, and intergovernmental relations (Rich and Gómez 2012); and even ethnic divisions and HIV/AIDS policy contestation (Lieberman 2009). Nevertheless, in the area of public health policy, it seems that political scientists have paid little attention to the role of professional interest groups in developing nations, their interaction with political institutions and civil society, and their ability to manipulate policy in their favor. This book strives to fill this lacuna in the literature.

To do so, we first need to understand the major schools of thought with respect to interest group theory and their political activities in the health policy–making process, as well as the recent public health policy literature addressing these issues. In what follows, I lay out the main arguments in the existing literature, along with their strengths and weaknesses, with the ultimate objective of proposing an alternative analytical framework based on the literature's theoretical and contextual limitations. Called Industry Politics and Complementary Institutions, or IPCI for short, the proposed analytical framework applies and builds on the existing literature in political science and public health policy to provide a more comprehensive picture and explanation of the complex interest group *and* institutional contexts facilitating junk food industries' ongoing ability to influence noncommunicable disease policy in the emerging economies.

Interest Group Theory and Policy Reform

In the field of political science, the study of interest group lobbying and political strategies for manipulating public policy has a long-standing tradition. Inspired mainly by the works of American politics scholars, several theoretical and methodological approaches have emerged to explain how private sector interest groups manipulate congressional voting and policy agenda-setting processes (Baumgartner and Jones 1993). Historically much of this literature has focused on two areas: that is, what Gais and Walker (1991) once referred to as "insider" versus "outsider" interest group political tactics; because of this, I focus on the literature addressing these particular legislative and bureaucratic tactics that interest groups take as well as their counterarguments.

Insider lobbying strategies have traditionally focused on the various tactics that interest groups use within government to manipulate policy agenda-setting processes. More specifically, this literature focuses on the efforts made by industry lobbyists to directly meet with presidents, congressional politicians, and/or senior bureaucrats to persuade them into taking a particular stance on a proposed piece of legislation. This art of persuasion, if you will, occurs when lobbyists meet with these government officials to provide information, such as scientific evidence supporting industry's policy interests, with the goal of changing these politicians' views through the dissemination of information and evidence (Berry 1977; McSpadden and Culhane 1999; Milbrath 1963). When the policy issue receives little media attention, thus dropping in its overall public and political saliency, and is more technical in nature, Culpepper (2011) claims that these lobbying activities often take place behind closed doors, dubbed "quiet politics." McGrath (2007) also discusses how these industries often employ strategies commonly used by marketing firms to alter their language and organizational titles to make them more appealing and persuasive to politicians. Finally, an ongoing, well-known strategy is the simple act of direct bribery and corruption. In this context, lobbyists' tactics have included using campaign contributions to ensure that their policy interests are maintained and that legislators vote in their favor, revealing a context where legislators and lobbyists act as agents engaged in a mutual beneficial exchange (Hall and Deardorff 2006; Klüver and Zeidler 2019; Morton and Cameron 1992).

Though not explicitly applying political science interest group theory to their research, recent health policy scholars have unearthed similar kinds of industrial insider tactics. For several years, scholars have addressed the corporate political activity literature (Hillman and Hitt 1999; Lawton, McGuire, and Rajwani 2012; Savell et al. 2014). In general, this literature focuses on the ways in which a variety of industries strive to influence policy through a myriad of political and social tactics. In recent years, Hillman and Hitt (1999) built on the existing CPA literature to put forth a more comprehensive approach explaining the various political tactics used by industry to influence policy. These tactics referred to what the authors described as *information* (i.e., industries engaging in various lobbying activities—as described earlier—as well as sponsoring supportive scientific research). Next, industries engage in what Hillman and Hitt (1999) refer to as *constituency building* (i.e., industries partnering with voters or local communities who, in turn, pressure policy makers in support of an industry's policy views), thus emitting "bottom-up" pressures. Hillman and Hitt (1999) also describe *fi-*

nancial incentives, which may take the form of industry-direct contributions to politicians and political parties: for example, providing speaking honorariums and paid travel expenses to influence votes and achieve industry's policy preferences. Savell and colleagues (2014) later developed a taxonomy of six strategies used by the tobacco industry to influence congressional votes on public health policy while also introducing us to the various narratives used by these industries to shape policy discussions and agenda setting. This was achieved by emphasizing the unintended economic consequence of policy reform, legal and regulatory redundancy, and the existence of insufficient credible evidence.

Savell and colleagues' (2014) six CPA strategies are as follows:

1. *Information*: that is, building upon Hillman and Hitt's (1999) discussion about lobbying while adding to this industry's effort to fund supportive scientific research, thus reformulating evidence and establishing policy partnerships with government, such as participating in government policy working groups and technical and advisory groups, as well as working with and providing advice to policy makers. Lima and Galea (2018) subsequently also referred to these kinds of information lobbying tactics, such as industry's usage of scientific information and expertise (though at times being biased / having incomplete information) when discussing the food industry's tactics, influence, and power.

2. *Financial incentives* are used by lobbyists to engage in the aforementioned insider tactics of policy influence via direct and indirect financial incentives to legislators (even the offering of employment).

3. *Constituency-building*: that is, building upon Hillman and Hitt's (1999) discussion of industry partnering with other sectors and communities in support of industry's policies, thus connoting broad support for industry's policy positions (see also discussions by Miller and Harkins [2010] and Moodie and colleagues [2013] of the food industry on these related issues) while extending this to include partnerships with other industries supporting their policy position.

4. *Legal*: that is, using the law either as a preemptive strategy or a threat (of legal action).

5. *Policy substitution*: that is, advocating for industry self-regulation in the area of marketing and sales.

6. *Constituency fragmentation/destabilization* encompasses strategies to discredit and prevent the emergence and influence of potential opponents
   in society.

Political scientists have also underscored the outsider tactics used by
industry lobbyists to sway agenda-setting processes. One strategy has been
lobbyists' efforts to engage in what Keller (2018) refers to as noisy politics,
or publicly sharing information about the proposed legislation through the
usage of the media and other public venues with the goal of increasing the
overall political saliency of the issue. In this process, the author emphasizes
the importance for industry lobbyists to carefully frame policy issues in ways
that the general public can easily understand. By raising public awareness
and the saliency of a policy issue, lobbyists exert external pressure and may
incentivize politicians to refrain from pursuing costly legislation. Alternatively, Berry (1977) highlights how industries can use the media to publicly
discredit existing policies, embarrass legislators, and, in the process, motivate the latter to support industry's views. West and colleagues (1996) have
also underscored that interest groups often use media ads not only to cri-
tique proposed health care policy proposals but also to generate negative
perceptions about the proposed legislation in society. This reveals the latter's distaste for policy proposals, ultimately motivating legislators not to
pursue the legislation.

Recent work in the CPA research illustrates the utility of participating
in what political scientists refer to as outsider tactics. As the work of Miller
and Harkins (2010) demonstrates, alcohol and food industries, for example,
have expanded their lobbying efforts to include strategic communication
strategies through their management of social media, civil society (NGOs),
and academics (the science). For example, these industries often work with
online magazines to convey their message about particular policies, publicly
discrediting critics and skewing scientific evidence while financing NGOs or
consulting firms (often working within government), even going so far as
to create NGOs, in essence capturing society in order to convey industry's
views and have influence over decision makers (Miller and Harkins 2010).

Finally, in addition to these insider and outsider tactics, it is important
to emphasize that interest groups have also strategically used their work
with local communities to further augment their reputation, legitimacy, and,
by extension, policy influence. While political scientists have focused on the

electoral legislative arena, sociologists and policy scholars have mainly addressed this issue through the literature on corporate social responsibility. Often surfacing in response to civil societal protests and demands on industries to act ethically and responsibly, CSR activities emerge when industries voluntarily engage in a host of social and community activities. This is done to enhance their reputation as industries conscious of societal needs, displaying that they are ethically and morally responsible, with the objective of increasing their social and, by extension, political reputation and influence. In the area of food and NCD policy, Moodie and colleagues (2013) have emphasized how industries often provide campaigns focused on preventing violence against women in order to reduce criticism of industry. Similarly, in the United Kingdom, Hastings (2012) has underscored the alcohol industry's efforts to empower women through midwife training programs, while working with NGOs to improve school education and other social services that will improve the alcohol industry's reputation as entities that are part of the solution to the alcohol problem. Alternatively, work by Fooks and Gilmore (2013) has highlighted the ways that major tobacco industries, such as the British American Tobacco corporation, have used philanthropy to increase access to politicians and bolster industry's reputation in providing important and trustworthy policy information. In particular, they reference how philanthropic efforts can increase the company's reputation and trust among legislators, in turn facilitating their ability to influence policy.

Yet another CSR tactic employed by industry has been voluntary self-regulation. As the work of Vogel (2008) discusses, typically, in response to social protests and demands, industries will voluntarily pledge to engage in activities that display their dedication to acting in an ethical and responsible manner. Moreover, Vogel (2008) maintains that industries often pursue these self-regulations as a strategy with the goal of incentivizing the government not to pursue additional policy regulations. As Vogel (2008) further points out, these self-regulations are soft laws, different from hard laws, in that they do not entail any enforcement mechanisms—an ongoing problem as we will soon see in the emerging economies. In the area of NCD policy, this tactic has been increasingly popular among major food industries. They do so mainly by engaging in public pledges or agreements with government to restrict the sale and marketing of their products toward children, or by improving the nutritional content of their foods (Sacks et al. 2013). The goal has not only been to increase the industry's political and social reputation but, rather, and following Vogel (2008, 2010), to convince government offi-cials that no further costly regulations on industry are required.

While I certainly break bread with these scholars in emphasizing the importance of these interest group tactics, such as the political science and CPA literature's emphasis on insider tactics, several limitations still remain.

First, in the area of junk food politics, more than ever, industries are re-luctant to engage in outsider policy tactics. Junk food industries and their supportive interest groups often fear the negative political, social, and pos-sible financial ramifications of publicly obstructing the creation of NCD pol-icies, such as obesity prevention, especially those geared toward children. In-stead, they prefer to be seen as solutions to the problem by openly working with government and civil society and engaging in supportive CSR activities to overcome the harmful health effects of their products (Hastings 2012). Second, this literature does not address the broader social consequences of interest group tactics, especially with respect to civil society's ability to ef-fectively mobilize in response to industry's obstruction of regulatory policy. Third, this literature pays essentially no attention to how interest groups strategically use institutions, such as federal bureaucratic agencies, to en-sure that their policy ideas are firmly in place to safeguard their interests. And finally, this literature does not address how industry's CSR activities supplement national insider political tactics to further increase industry's political legitimacy and policy influence; in accordance with Bernhagen and Patsiurko (2015) and Walker and Rea (2014), this research needs to explore how, when, and to what extent CSR supplements insider and outsider indus-try tactics.

However, some studies suggest that relying exclusively on interest group tactics is not enough. Sometimes interest groups engage in a variety of in-sider or outsider tactics but do not achieve their policy objectives (De Bruycker and Beyers 2019). On the other hand, industry's desired objectives may emerge in the absence of these interest group tactics, often due to policy makers' personal views, support, and unforeseen events, or what De Bruycker and Beyers (2019) refer to as "exogenous factors or even lucky coincidence" (59). De Bruycker and Beyers (2019) go on to explain that there is therefore no guarantee that lobbying tactics are sufficient for explaining policy influence. Alternatively, other interest group scholars have emphasized the importance of contextual conditions, rather than industry tactics, such as organizational or political contexts, that facilitate the emergence of effective insider and outsider tactics.

Indeed, other political scientists emphasize the organizational power and resources of interest groups, which, in turn, determine whether they can—and are willing to—engage in insider or outsider tactics in the first place. In this camp, Gais and Walker (1991) were among the first to claim that the lobbying industry's policy success rests on the cohesiveness and adaptability of its organizational structure; this includes the ability to overcome internal conflicts of interest, as well as having the financial resources needed to engage in the preferred lobbying activities. Moreover, the authors also highlighted the importance of possessing technical knowledge on particular sectors to improve their credibility and persuasiveness. As Hojnacki and colleagues (2012) explain, the amount of resources interest groups have shapes their legislative tactics: civic groups with access to fewer financial resources, when compared to business-based interest groups, had to be more careful and selective in where and how they were spending their money during advocacy campaigns, while considering the visibility of their efforts. In this context, moreover, findings by Figueiredo and Richter (2014) confirm that smaller lobbying firms are less likely than larger firms to engage in lobbying activities because they have fewer resources. Berry (1977) and, later, De Bruycker (2014) added the importance of these industries' ability to have strong internal communications structures and thus make decisions more quickly. However, what also mattered for Gais and Walker (1991) was *where* these financial and technical resources came from. That is, if these resources were acquired from NGOs or activists, industries were more likely to engage in the aforementioned outsider tactics of working with these groups to raise public awareness and confront lawmakers. Alternatively, when these resources were acquired from big businesses, lobbyists were more likely to engage in insider tactics. Binderkrantz and colleagues (2015) have nevertheless claimed that the reason some lobbyists are more successful than others has to do with their cumulative access to several political arenas—that is, the same interest groups having the same access to several arenas, over time, which, in turn, is shaped by a group's vast resources; this leads to a sense of "privileged pluralism" (p. 109).

However, research by Grossman (2012) finds that interest group organizational resource capacity was not a key factor in explaining their ability to

influence policy. Through an innovative historical policy analysis of 268 policy decisions in the United States from 1945 to 2004, across 14 policy sectors,
Grossman (2012) found that advocacy-based organizations with comparatively fewer resources (e.g., when compared to businesses and unions) were
the most influential with respect to policy change. These advocacy associations were more influential because of their strong reputation for representing particular constituencies. Similar to Grossman (2012), Lorenz (2019) also
discovered that the large size of interest groups, their homogenous status,
and massive campaign contributions does not necessarily guarantee their
ability to influence policy agenda-setting processes. Instead, what is more
important is the diversity of interests present within lobbying coalitions,
the information that they provide to congressional committees, and the latter's willingness to see these diverse interests as viable policies and interests
to pursue them, which, in turn, is shaped by a committee's perception of bills
supported by a party majority or divided government.

Finally, rather than focus on interest group tactics and their organizational capacity, political scientists have focused on the nature of political
institutions and their ability to determine *if* and to what extent these groups
can access politicians and bureaucrats, which legislative tactics they can take,
and if they will be successful. Here, the work of Ishio (1999), for example,
claims that industry's ability to participate in insider or outsider tactics is
shaped first and foremost by the design of political and bureaucratic institutions. For example, the United States' complex checks and balances system,
especially with respect to limited bureaucratic autonomy, which provides
lobbyists with several potential avenues of influence, as well as its direct
election of political candidates can encourage a combination of insider and
outsider tactics. By contrast, Japan's more consensual decision-making structure, greater autonomy in bureaucratic decision making, along with a political party system that is more cohesive in nature has encouraged the usage
of insider tactics. Alternatively, Heitshusen (2000) emphasizes how the US
congress' decision in the 1970s to increase the decentralization of policy
deliberations by introducing several subcommittees in the US House of Representatives has gradually forced interest groups to alter their insider lobbying tactics. As seen in the House on issues such as labor policy, this is especially the case when new committees introduce legislative representatives
with alternative ideological and policy views on labor policy, thus requiring
more convincing information from interest groups, such as the provision of

technical information. Conversely, when interest groups encounter legislative committees with more support, as seen with policy issues focused on the environment, representative interest groups need only provide less costly political information.

While this book certainly agrees with the importance of institutional designs, which includes access to politicians, bureaucratic committees, and the federal courts, and how this, in turn, influences interest group insider tactics, this literature is limited in several areas. First, following Gómez (2019), it does not underscore how interest groups' access to institutions, over a long period of time, amplifies their policy influence. Moreover, it does not address how interest groups strategically infiltrate institutions, such as the bureaucracy, with their policy ideas and interests, ultimately ensuring that their policy interests are sustained. Additionally, this literature does not address what I describe as the importance of *complementary institutions*—that is, important agenda-setting institutions, such as the office of the presidency, that can also serve to complement and reinforce interest group political tactics, legitimacy, and influence within government. While political scientists have acknowledged the importance of political context, such as legislative activity in being positively associated with interest group density and response (see Klüver and Ziedler 2019, though they also find a positive relationship between interest group density and legislative activity over time), supportive presidential contexts can also serve to *indirectly complement*, rather than compete with, interest group interests, tactics, and strategies— as I discuss in more detail shortly.

The New Politics of Junk Food Industries and Policy Manipulation

In explaining the rise and political influence of junk food industries in the emerging economies, this book comports with several aspects of the aforementioned political science (insider) interest group research, public health CPA, and social responsibility literature, while nevertheless addressing their theoretical and contextual shortcomings. More specifically, the analytical approach taken in this book applies and builds on the importance of interest group insider, CPA, and social responsibility tactics, as well as the importance of institutional design and industry manipulation of bureaucratic institutions, while also revealing an alternative complementary role that presidential institutions play in supplementing these industry activities.

My focus on the emerging economies introduces yet another limitation with the existing political science, CPA, and social responsibility literature. The first centers on the fact that this literature to date has focused mainly on consolidated democracies within the United States and Western Europe (Hojnacki et al. 2012). With the exception of recent studies addressing this topic in developing nations (Carriedo et al. 2021; Ojeda et al. 2020; Tangcharoensathien et al. 2019), to my knowledge essentially no research has been conducted on an in-depth comparative historical analysis of the junk food industry's political and policy tactics across several emerging economies, as well as their relationship with the bureaucracy, political leaders, and civil society. However, because of this, we do not know to what extent these efforts are present and help to explain NCD policy obstructions in the developing world. Furthermore, without an in-depth comparative historical analysis, we cannot discover and explain the alternative political and social tactics that these interest groups engage in, their broader policy and social consequences, and the vital role of political context—particularly at the domestic and international level—due to the developing world's increased global integration and the ongoing influence of international policy ideas and power.

This book argues that in this alternative domestic and international context, major junk food industries and their representatives have pursued several types of political and social tactics, becoming increasingly entrepreneurial and successful in their efforts to obstruct any and all NCD policies challenging their ability to conduct business. But why is this the case? Why have industries in these countries been more creative and aggressive in pursuing alternative approaches to NCD policy obstruction?

We must first understand the broader historical context generating these types of activities in the first place. In essence, it's all about *fear* and *opportunity*. Due to an increasingly health-conscious market in the West, industries fear a continued decrease in sales and profitability. As chapter 2 explains, in recent years, junk food industries have seen a precipitous decline in sales within their traditional Western markets, such as the United States and Europe. Though delayed when compared to these nations, the international wave of public awareness and interest in good nutrition and health is finding its way to emerging markets. This trend concerns these industries and makes them all the more eager to find creative political and social strategies to safeguard their NCD policy interests.

Interest Group Theory   25

At the same time, opportunity matters. These industries are taking advantage of a gradual rise in income among the middle class and poor in emerging markets, which is often the result of popular anti-poverty programs providing disposable cash to these members of the population. Furthermore, these industries are taking advantage of the excessive concentration of political power, at the highest levels of government, which often facilitates their ability to have an impact on the policy-making discussions of the political elite. As Gómez and Menedez (2021) have argued, in the realm of public health policy in Latin America, a very small concentration of political and bureaucratic elites often make the most critical policy decisions on their own, without adequately consulting civil society. These industries know this and have taken strategic advantage of this context. Indeed, unlike democracies in the advanced industrialized world, where, due to a longer history of democracy, vibrant political parties reflect strong social movements, it seems that big businesses in nascent democracies often face fewer countervailing political forces and credible threats to policy interests. Junk food industries in the emerging economies therefore appear to have considerably more power and influence than in mainly Western-based pluralist democracies where they may at times be forced to choose between policy adaptation and defeat due to staunch political party opposition (Paster 2018).

Establishing a New Analytical Framework: Industry Politics and Complementary Institutions

In order to provide a more comprehensive explanation of junk food industries' political and policy influence in the emerging economies, this book introduces an analytical framework titled Industry Politics and Complementary Institutions. IPCI builds on the theoretical and empirical limitations of the aforementioned political science and public health policy literature. The goal of IPCI is to better explain the NCD policy agenda-setting and implementation processes in these economies—that is, why and how NCD prevention and regulatory policies become a national priority, and why existing legislation may not be enforced. IPCI is used to explain the reasons why, for example, presidents and legislative institutions do not pursue specific NCD policies, such as soda taxes or marketing/sales regulations, or why they do not enforce these policies by means of monitoring and imposing penalties for noncompliance.

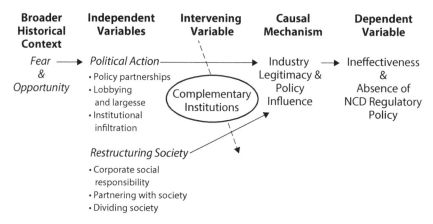

Industry politics and complementary institutions

IPCI combines an analysis of historical contextual backdrop and the causal mechanisms linking industry political activity and the role of institutions in policy outcomes (see figure). As previously mentioned, it begins with the broader historical context of fear and opportunity as explanations for why industries pursue the emerging economies and become political entities in the first place. Next, IPCI focuses on the specific processes that industries, as well as governments, engage in. In the area of industry called *political action*, IPCI applies the political science and health policy literature on insider lobbying and CPA (Culpepper 2011; Gais and Walker 1991; Hillman and Hitt 1999; Savell et al. 2014), the institutional infiltration and conversion literature (Falleti 2009; Goldfrank 2011; Klein and Lee 2019), and, in the area of *restructuring society*, industry strategies for shaping civil societal views and interests as well as their ramifications for civic mobilization (Gómez 2019a; Moodie et al. 2013; Walker and Rea, 2014). At the same time, however, IPCI maintains that domestic institutions also matter—that is, these industry tactics are greatly facilitated by the complementary role of presidents who are supportive of industry and seeking to work closely with industries to achieve alternative economic and social welfare policies and political objectives. As the figure illustrates, this process reflects the presence of complementary institutions as intervening variables both complementing and reinforcing the tactics of political action and restructuring society, in turn contributing to industry's legitimacy and policy influence and ultimately the ineffectiveness and absence of NCD regulatory policies.

Political Action

In the emerging economies today, interest groups representing junk food industries, as well as industries themselves, have employed a host of creative insider and CPA strategies to achieve their primary objective: they work to not only limit the creation of public health prevention programs discouraging the consumption of their products, such as a soda tax, but, perhaps more importantly, to prevent *any and all* legislation proposing to regulate the marketing and sale of their products.

The first political tactic that industries use is nothing new: they often seek to partner with politicians and government officials, often through government workshops/committees, to create innovative public health programs tackling NCDs (Miller and Harkins 2010; Savell et al. 2014). Industries may also work closely with government officials to improve the overall quality of ingredients in foods and food labeling. Moreover, these industries may also enter into formal agreements with governments to restrict the advertising of their products to children—also known as self-regulation (Vogel 2010). Through these crafty political tactics, as well as through CSR activities, industries want to ensure that they are viewed within government as the solution to the problem of industrial epidemics (Hastings 2012). Importantly, IPCI also builds on Vogel's (2010) position that these tactics are mainly used to avoid the creation of any further regulations harming industry's interests (on this note, see also Bernhagen and Patsiurko 2015). By partnering with government on NCD prevention programs and food reformulation initiatives, this generates trust and support from government officials toward industry, viewing them as genuine allies in the plight against obesity and type 2 diabetes among children, adolescents, and the poor, believing that industry is doing its part in helping the government stem the rising tide of NCDs. Consequently, politicians often have no interest and incentive to pursue alternative regulations that may jeopardize their relationship with industry.

And yet, industry's goal is not altogether altruistic in striving to safeguard these vulnerable populations from NCDs. Instead, industries' political activities are often used to establish enduring government allies, such as with politicians, who can be trusted to never cross the line in support of legislation restricting the marketing and sale of industry products.

As we will see in several countries discussed in this book, companies such as Coca-Cola, PepsiCo, Nestlé, and Unilever have been very proactive in seeking out government officials and local schools to work with and create programs focused on increased physical fitness and exercise while at the same time working with governments to adopt limited policy regulations, such as improving nutritional content and information about their foods (e.g., food labeling). To achieve these endeavors, industries and the interest groups or NGOs they work with are often proactive in organizing one-on-one meetings with health officials while involving themselves with national and local government committees, often co-organized with industry leaders (on China, see Greenhalgh 2019a).

In addition, IPCI applies the rich literature on interest group lobbying and largesse to influence public health policy (Hillman and Hitt 1999; Lima and Galea 2018; Morton and Cameron 1992; Savell et al. 2014). Building on this literature, IPCI reinforces the fact that these political strategies are also occurring in the emerging economies in response to proposed NCD prevention and regulatory policies. Indeed, industries in several countries discussed in this book have engaged in numerous lobbying tactics to obstruct the creation of these policies.

As IPCI emphasizes, yet another tactic that junk food industries engage in is the process of *institutional infiltration*. This process occurs when industries or their representatives (e.g., NGOs) strive to occupy bureaucratic institutions in order to ensure that their interests are represented, incessantly pressuring policy makers (in a sense, assuming an internal bureaucratic lobbying process), while establishing their policy ideas and interests within existing federal bureaucratic agencies to ensure that their views are safeguarded and maintained over time. Here, IPCI builds on the work of several scholars recognizing how external actors, for example, civil society, can purposefully infiltrate institutions in order to achieve their objectives (Falleti 2009; Goldfrank 2011; Klein and Lee 2019).

For example, through their analytical framework, Politics of Infiltration, Klein and Lee (2019) highlight the proactive efforts of civil societal actors to infiltrate institutions, what they refer to as the politics of forward infiltration and occupation. In an instance of institutional occupation, after ongoing bargaining with state actors, social movements gradually obtain a presence within state institutions to ensure that society's interests and agendas are established, thus reforming preexisting institutions to society's liking.

Ultimately, these reformulated institutions leave little choice for incumbent state actors but to adopt the institutional infiltrator's (civil society's) reformulated institutions. Similarly, Falleti (2009) claims that, after state intrusion into society, social movements may then infiltrate institutions with their interests and health policy ideas in order to build sustainable coalitions of support for these movements' ideas within bureaucratic institutions. Discussing the case of Brazil, Falleti (2009) asserts that social health movements, such as the prodemocratic Sanitarista social movement, dedicated to establishing universal health care as a human right during the transition to democracy, gradually established their own presence within federal agencies (as well as municipal governments and international health agencies), introducing and sustaining their particular policies, maintaining a strong network of societal and state government support, and redirecting health policy reforms established by the military to achieve new health care objectives. These objectives included achieving universal health care as a right and provided by the state in a decentralized, participatory manner through the new democratic constitution of 1988.

As IPCI explains, junk food industries may take a similar approach by infiltrating federal health care agencies *through* allied NGOs in society. As the seminal contribution of Greenhalgh (2019a) explains in the case of China, NGOs such as the International Life Sciences Institute often clandestinely infiltrate public health agencies, implant their ideas and policy prescriptions, and in the process transform NCD policies in industry's favor.

Restructuring Society

At the same time, IPCI emphasizes that industries are equally as committed to restructuring civil society in their favor. To this end, several strategies are pursued. First, applying and building on the aforementioned CPA strategy of constituency building (Hillman and Hitt 1999; Savell et al. 2014), industries work hard to create supportive allies within academia. Industries often seek out influential academics from prestigious universities that will conduct research and provide evidence supporting industry's policy views on nutrition, NCDs, and the effectiveness of existing policies, such as soda taxes. However, the process industries use to approach academics is often clandestine and indirect, such as funneling money through seemingly independent private foundations and philanthropies, who, in turn, provide

funding to academic researchers. Ultimately, the objective is to not only obtain scientific evidence supporting industry claims but also to alter the discourse surrounding the root causes of NCDs.

The second strategy that industries pursue is to establish strong, mutually reinforcing alliances with ideologically sympathetic NGOs and poor
communities. With respect to NGOs, industries often seek to support advocates who provide research and public campaign messages highlighting the
importance of individual liberty in food consumption, as well as the importance of physical exercise and overall happiness as an essential ingredient
for prosperous living. These NGOs also work with local communities—such
as schools and families—on behalf of these industries; in so doing, these
NGOs act as hired middlemen shaping community views through a variety
of tactics. These efforts resemble and build on Walker and Rea's (2014) discussion of corporations mobilizing society by hiring NGOs or think tanks
in support of industry's views, as well as hiring consulting firms to engage
grassroots lobbying campaigns that help to marshal supportive public opinion about particular policy issues.

With respect to poor communities, junk food industries may reduce
public criticism and build a strong support base by providing critical social
services, activities that build on the aforementioned CSR literature (Moodie
et al. 2013). An increasingly common strategy has been the provision of
community jobs. In return for helping sell and market food products, poor
families receive a monthly income and a sense of empowerment and independence. At the same time, industries build a strong social support base
by financing and organizing popular community events. For example, by
sponsoring local sports clubs, as well as providing T-shirts and equipment
in communities that cannot afford them, industries generate social support,
acceptability, and legitimacy for their products.

Thus, to further ensure that their various political and institutional tactics work and help to guarantee their legislative policy influence, junk food
industries supplement these efforts with additional tactics geared toward
civil society. De Bruycker and Beyers (2019) claim that legislative tactics, on
their own, are often insufficient for ensuring that interest groups achieve
their desired policy objectives. De Bruycker and Beyers (2019) further maintain that interest groups' creation of "heterogenous coalitions—which rely
on a diverse and representative constituency—can exert a more credible
and encompassing signal of societal support when compared to coalitions

consisting of a narrower set of organized interests (e.g., only environmental NGOs or only business interests)" (60). While the interest group social tactics described in this book do not fall in line with traditional outsider tactics (as mentioned earlier), the aforementioned IPCI tactics in society can help to further augment junk food industries' legitimacy and influence within government, in turn supplementing and further reinforcing their insider tactics. This view aligns with others claiming that business civic mobilization tactics can often complement and industry's lobbying activities within government (Bernhagen and Patsiurko 2015; Walker and Rea 2014).

Nevertheless, while industry strategies to restructure and mobilize civil societal support may often be successful, the scholarly literature to date has overlooked the broader social consequences of these efforts. As Gómez (2019a) maintains, a key area that the literature has failed to address is how these strategies contribute to increased division and conflict between those nutrition activists who defend the public's health and those academic researchers or NGOs working with industry, in turn hampering civil society's ability to create a unified voice and to engender an effective social movement in response to industry's activities. IPCI applies and illustrates the efficacy of Gomez's (2019a) claim that, by industries supporting those academic researchers or NGOs upholding industry's policy message, pitting these NGOs against activists who do not share these views and do not have nearly the same amount of resources, industries essentially divide society and hamper civic mobilization by generating conflicts of interests and disagreements between these actors. In the end, this reduces the number of potential allies in society that activists can potentially work with and that can mobilize with them to hold industries accountable for their actions.

Complementary Institutions

Nevertheless, industries' various political and social strategies are insufficient for explaining why they continue to have so much influence over NCD policy in the emerging economies. As IPCI explains, governments are also partly to blame. More specifically, I argue that a government's complementary institutions can serve to further increase junk food industries' political legitimacy and policy influence. Building on recent scholars' arguments that a politician's personal connections and rational electoral interests to support industry bolsters the latter's policy-making influence (Gómez 2019a), according to IPCI, complementary institutions are comprised of three components. First, these institutions emerge when a president's preexisting relationship and experiences with industries, either by way of previous working relationships or investments in them, cultivate a sense of loyalty and support from presidents for these industries' ongoing development and prosperity. In this context, industries are viewed with a favorable eye that then facilitates their ability to gain access to policy makers and have influence within government (Gómez 2019a).

The second component of these complementary institutions arises when presidents strategically partner with and use these industries to achieve alternative policy and, thus, political objectives, such as broader social welfare (e.g., anti-poverty) and economic policy goals (e.g., foreign direct investment and economic growth). Third, complementary institutions arise when presidents engage in institution-building processes in order to ensure that industries can sustain these partnerships and achieve these politicians' alternative social welfare and economic policy objectives. In the process, this institution-building exercise helps to secure a president's popularity and support in society and within government. For example, institution building may take the form of creating federal agencies or formal offices designed specifically to deepen these presidential policy partnerships with industry—as we'll see in the case of Brazil.

When these components are taken together, complementary institutions serve to further supplement and enhance junk food industries' political and social strategies. Guided by presidents' historical ties and broader political and policy objectives, complementary institutions generate incentives for the government to reach out to and use industries, which comports nicely with industries' aforementioned strategies to work with government and civil society. Seen in this light, government and industries' interests dovetail to engender a context that facilitates industry's NCD policy-making influence.

Conclusion

When taken together, the IPCI analytical framework applies the political science and public health policy literature to provide a more in-depth explanation for why and how junk food industries are having ongoing NCD regulatory policy influence in the emerging economies. More than ever, in these countries, industries are succeeding in avoiding costly policy regulations, such as marketing, labeling, sales, and, in some instances, soda tax legislation, in order to survive and thrive in a context where societies are becoming increasingly cognizant of good health and nutrition. IPCI's application of theories, especially from political science, to the context of NCD policy making in the emerging economies helps to unravel further details and additional insights into why industries have so much influence and are achieving these policy objectives. And unfortunately, why industries' political activities and policy influence is increasing at the expense of the health and prosperity of nations' most vulnerable populations: children and the poor.

But where did the general interest and impetus for these industry political activities come from in the first place? As the next chapter explains, and in accordance with IPCI, industry activities mainly emerged from industry fears and opportunities. Fears that they will not perform and earn well in their traditional home markets and opportunities to search for alternative markets where they can thrive and sustain their profitability and influence.

2

Fear and Opportunity

In recent years, major multinational soda and ultraprocessed food companies, or what I refer to in this book as junk food industries, have started to heavily invest in several emerging economies. These investments are worth billions of dollars and have gone into not only opening new food production and distribution centers but also restaurants, convenience stores, and even coffee shops. As nations throughout Latin America, Africa, and Asia embraced neoliberal economic reforms, including free trade, privatization, and market deregulation, junk food industries happily noticed and began to invest. A new opportunity emerged. An opportunity to expand in countries with a burgeoning middle class that was eager, in many instances, to consume foods that had been inaccessible in the past. As this chapter explains, however, the effort to invest in these countries was not just influenced by economic prospect and opportunity; it was also influenced by industry's ongoing fear of losing its financial stronghold in wealthier nations, markets that had become increasingly saturated by processed and fast food products (Stuckler and Nestle 2012). In countries such as the United States and Western Europe, there appeared to emerge an earlier wave of consumer awareness and consciousness regarding food consumption, good health, and nutrition; this was a product of these nations' longer history of consuming unhealthy foods and their gradual awareness of the health consequences associated with it.

A combination of industry fear and opportunity have therefore combined to lend insight into why these junk food industries have invested heavily in emerging economies. Furthermore, and as I explained in the previous chapter, understanding this broader historical context is the first step in our approach to explaining the rise and influence of junk food industries in the developing world. Indeed, understanding the context of fear and opportunity accounts for the genesis of these industries' unwavering interest in doing all they can to gradually influence the political and social context in their favor. In essence, and as we will see in subsequent chapters, this fear and opportunity has emerged to motivate industries into becoming political animals; to embed themselves within a complex web of presidential institutions, legislative institutions, and the health care bureaucracy; and, moreover, to embed themselves within society. Industries accomplish this by building support and creating new followers as well as by instigating division and hampering civil society's ability to mobilize and resist industries' ongoing policy influence—and often at the expense of nations' most vulnerable populations: children and the poor.

Fear

But why do junk food industries have so much to fear? For many years, companies such as Coca-Cola, PepsiCo, and Nestlé, and other popular restaurant chains such as McDonald's and Kentucky Fried Chicken (KFC) thrived throughout the United States and Western Europe. In this context, the root of industry fears stems from an ongoing shift in what consumers know and what they want when it comes to food. The first root cause of industry fears stems from the average consumer's increase in their knowledge, understanding, and awareness about healthy food and nutrition. In the United States, some have even argued that early failed attempts to introduce soda taxes in cities contributed to consumer knowledge about just how bad sodas are for your health. According to Margot Sanger-Katz (2015), while former Philadelphia mayor Michael A. Nutter fell short of introducing a soda tax in 2010, "in the course of the fight, they [i.e., polticians in favor of obesity prevention policies, like Mayor Nutter] have reminded people that soda is not a healthy product. They have echoed similar messages coming from public health researchers and others—and fundamentally changed the way Americans think about soda" (1). Even in Europe, due to the rise of social media, news, and information that is readily available, people are learning about the importance of food in determining their overall health and wellness (Martucci 2018).

In the United States, this change in consumer knowledge and awareness has led to a shift in consumer preferences in favor of heathier foods.

As Buchholz (2019) points out, "In a survey recently published by the International Food Information Council and the American Heart Foundation, 43 percent of Americans claimed to always be on the lookout for healthy options when shopping, while 52 percent said they were at least sometimes scouting for healthy foods" (1). Others claim that in the United States, it is the millennials who are being more proactive and prioritizing a change in their preferences for healthier foods and lifestyles in general (Gustafson 2017). More and more individuals are also becoming concerned with the consumption of sugar, a concern that analysts claim has been particularly challenging for companies such as Coca-Cola (Ballard 2018).

In this new consumer context, the demand for sodas has decreased significantly in the United States. Taylor and Jacobson (2016) claim that due to increased awareness and concern among scientists, activists, and the public at large about the scientific evidence underscoring the harmful effects of consuming sugar-sweetened beverages on individual health, that this "publicity in the United States about that evidence, for example, has helped decrease per-capita consumption of sugar drinks by 25 percent between 1998 and 2014" (vii). According to Jordan Weissmann of *The Atlantic* magazine, who interviewed John Sicher of *Beverage Digest* in 2012, Weissman (2012) claims that Sicher stated that "since 2006, Sicher said, the total volume of carbonated soft drink sales has fallen about 11 percent, from 10.2 billion cases to 9.3 billion. Some of that drop is the result of changing consumer preferences. Parts of the population are becoming more health conscious" (1). Sanger-Katz (2015) further claimed that "over the last 20 years, sales of full-calorie soda in the United States have plummeted by more than 25 percent" (1). In contrast, sales of healthier products, such as bottled water, have increased (Sanger-Katz 2015). Other analysts, such as Gary Hemphill, director of research for Beverage Marketing Corporation, shares a similar viewpoint, claiming that "consumer demand for healthier refreshment has negatively impacted the carbonated soft drink category. . . . Thirsty consumers still like soda but increasingly they have been reaching for healthier options like bottled water" (quoted in Jacobsen 2019, 1). What's more, Sanger-Katz (2015) maintains that far fewer children are consuming sodas in the United States. The author states that "from 2004 to 2012, children consumed 79 fewer sugar-sweetened beverage calories a day, according to a large government survey, representing a 4 percent cut in calories overall. As total calorie intake has declined, obesity rates among school-age children appear to have leveled off" (1). Additionally, according to the Beverage Marketing Corporation, in 2018, the market for carbonated drinks decreased from 13.3 billion gallons in 2012 to 12.5 in 2016 (Beverage Marketing Corporation 2018).

Opportunity

In response to these challenging environments in the United States and Europe, in recent years junk food industries have sought to diversify and expand their profits. The emerging economies have been particularly appealing in this regard, especially considering dwindling sales in richer nations and increased sales in less developed countries (Stuckler and Nestle 2012; Taylor and Jacobson 2016). In fact, by 2012, Stuckler and Nestle (2012) claimed that "virtually all growth in Big Food's sales occurs in developing countries" (e10001242). The introduction of free market reforms with ample opportunity for foreign direct investment, trade, and opportunity for business growth has incentivized industries to invest in economies such as Mexico, Brazil, India, China, Indonesia, and South Africa. Indeed, as Taylor and Jacobson (2016) nicely put it: "With soda executives drooling over the almost limitless opportunities for sales growth in Latin America, Asia, Africa, and the Middle East, their marketing onslaught involves everything from building bottling plants to buying a fleet of trucks to sponsoring celebrity-studded advertising campaigns" (1). But executives in the United States have also been excited about the absence of policy regulations in these emerging markets. As one analyst put it: "One of the reasons the US junk food industry has so aggressively targeted Mexico is because—while US companies certainly are not going hungry on the domestic scene—US restrictions on food advertisements for children means that 'corporations look around the world to see where the legal framework still allows them to market to children, and they double down'" (see Fernandez 2020, 1, and her quotation here of Alyshia Gálvez's *Eating NAFTA*). At the same time, and as we will see in subsequent chapters in this book, powerful and influential presidents have proactively encouraged this investment into their countries, viewing this not only as a way to accelerate economic growth and prosperity for their citizens but also to deepen their political influence.

The emerging economies of Latin America, Africa, and Asia have seen significant growth in the number of middle-class people with more disposable income and an insatiable desire for new foods and experiences. This context provides an excellent opportunity for junk food industries and other businesses to prosper and grow (Taylor and Jacobs 2016). According to some analysts, China and India alone will comprise approximately "43.3% of the global middle class by 2030" (European Commission 2020, 1). According to Signé (2019), rising incomes across Africa and the growing demand for goods and services should incentivize businesses to invest, particularly as "43 percent of Africans across the continent will belong to the middle or upper classes" (1). At the same time, a host of anti-poverty programs have provided additional income for the poor (Gómez 2019b). In turn, this leads to the poor having greater access to sodas and ultraprocessed foods—finding their way even as far as Brazil's vast Amazon basin, where Nestlé has, in the past, navigated narrow waterways to bring local residents delicious goods (Dantas and Mulier 2010).

Still, we must keep in mind that for many years consumers in these emerging markets were neglected Western-based foods because of their isolationist socialist governments—for example, India (during the 1960s and 1970s) and China. For many countries, especially in Asia, eating at popular Western fast food restaurants also brings with it the association of having a higher social status and more prestige, as emphasized by Andy Brennan, analyst at IBISWorld Industry, who also claimed that "it's a real status symbol to be eating in an American restaurant in Asia" (quoted in Schoen 2013, 1). With ample opportunity for investment, increased consumer demand, and individuals with the ready means to purchase their products, Western-based junk food industries, such as Coca-Cola, Pepsi-Co, Nestlé, McDonald's, and Kentucky Fried Chicken (just to name a few), have been eager to invest, expand, and take advantage of these new market opportunities.

Further incentivizing these industries to invest in emerging economies has been the substantial delay in consumer awareness and interest in the harmful effects of sugar and in eating healthier foods. Consumer knowledge and interest in good nutrition and healthy living is new in many of these developing nations. Ongoing cultures and beliefs, such as the physical, social, and economic benefits of being overweight within a historical context of poverty and malnutrition, have clashed with the arrival of new Western-based foods and diets, in turn making these societies even more susceptible to NCDs (Koopman et al. 2016). It appears that this cultural context has made it particularly difficult to adopt new ways of thinking about healthy eating, good health, and nutrition. At the same time, these industries are well aware of this and strive, in a sense, to take advantage of this complex cultural context.

The ongoing growth of soda and ultraprocessed food sales in emerging economies has provided further incentives and opportunities to invest and grow in them. As Gómez (2019b) maintains, the sale of snack foods "increased by 92% in developing nations in 2002, while soda sales recently quadrupled" (1). And as Hennis (quoted in Moubarac 2015, vii) points out: "While sales volumes remain higher in high-income countries, the rate of growth was faster in lower-income countries during the period 2000–2013." According to Moubarac (2015), while total volume sales (measured in kilotons) for drinks and ultraprocessed foods were highest in North America, increasing from 102,868 in 2000 to 105,276 in 2013, the rate of growth (as a percentage) was higher in Asia/Pacific (114.9 percent), Middle East and Africa (71.4 percent), Eastern Europe (73.3 percent), and Latin America (48 percent), versus North America (2.3 percent) and Western Europe's (18.5 percent) (15). Moubarac further contends that Latin America eventually surpassed North America in the total volume of sales in carbonated soft drinks by US$81 billion. In fact, Latin America's sales "doubled between 2000 and 2013," whereas sales plateaued and started to decline in North America after 2012 (15). Moubarac concluded that, "clearly, the potential market for this leading range of ultra-processed products is now greater in Latin America" (16). Furthermore, Moubarac found that when it came to the sales per-capita of ultra-processed foods and drinks, Latin America fell in fourth place behind Western Europe (third place), Australasia (second place), and North America (first place).

Today, analysts note that "Coca-Cola generates more than half of its revenue outside of the United States, where soft drink consumption is trending upward as a result of rising disposable incomes in many developing economies" (Sanchez 2019, 1). That said, it appears that Coca-Cola is certainly not out of the game. Despite soda sales wanning in recent years in the United States and Europe, the company is still seeing profits due to several factors, such as price adjusting, structural downsizing, and entering new types of product lines, such as coffee (Sanchez 2019). In essence, it seems that Coca-Cola has learned to adjust to evolving consumer interests and tastes around the world.

Conclusion

Perhaps more than ever, the fear of losing their footing and prosperity in wealthy nations has generated ongoing incentives to take advantage of new opportunities in emerging economies. Junk food industries have been keen to take advantage of a rising middle-income class, lower socioeconomic groups with greater access to money and credit due to generous anti-poverty programs, and nascent public awareness about good nutrition and healthy lifestyles. When combined with the ongoing prosperity of soda, ultraprocessed foods, and fast food restaurants, these industries have been unwaveringly committed to not only investing in emerging economies but also targeting those communities where their sales and influence can prosper—such as with children and the poor.

As we will see in the following chapters, however, fear and opportunity have generated incentives for these industries to engage in a host of political, bureaucratic, and social initiatives, with the goal to bolster their political influence and legitimacy. Today, these industries realize that in order to survive and thrive in a global context that is becoming increasingly aware of the importance of avoiding sugary and ultraprocessed foods, good health, and nutrition, they must combine their marketing skills with new political and social skill sets, establishing initiatives that can safeguard their investment strategies and sustain profits in the long run.

3

Mexico

The consumption of sugar, sodas, and snacks has a long tradition in Mexico. And yet, with the introduction of free market reforms during the 1990s, increased international trade, and globalization, the consumption of these foods has burgeoned. In fact, today Mexico is recognized as having the highest level of per capita consumption of sodas in the world (Watson and Treanor 2016). In tandem with this surge in junk food consumption has been a rise in noncommunicable diseases, such as obesity, type 2 diabetes, high blood pressure, and cancer. Particularly concerning has been the ongoing rise of these ailments among Mexico's most vulnerable populations, such as children and the poor. To its credit, in recent years the government has recognized this problem and has implemented a host of prevention programs, ranging from public awareness campaigns, to state-sponsored exercise programs, and even to an impressive soda tax. However, to this day, the government has never sought to increase the regulation of junk food industry marketing and sales, not through the creation of more stringent policies or the successful implementation of existing regulations (e.g., monitoring policy and imposing penalties and fines for noncompliance). In this context, companies such as Coca-Cola, PepsiCo, and Nestlé have been able to increase their sales and profits, while NCDs continue to increase. But why has this occurred after nearly a decade of government commitment to implementing several innovative prevention programs?

As this chapter explains, this outcome is mainly attributed to the fact that these junk food companies have become increasingly influential within government and society. In line with IPCI, within government, these companies have partnered with secretary of health officials to create innovative public health programs, with the goal of garnering political support as companies genuinely concerned with the health and well-being of Mexico's most vulnerable populations, and thus generating few incentives for politicians to increase regulation. At the same time, companies have consistently engaged in aggressive "insider" lobbying tactics by incessantly pressuring and persuading government officials not to impose stricter regulations, while offering lucrative largesse—mainly by way of campaign contributions—to those in support. These companies have also shaped civil societal interests in their favor, both by supporting academic researchers and NGOs while contributing to their communities, and in some instances by integrating into local religious cultures; nevertheless, these endeavors have generated conflicting interests and opposition between civil societal members, primarily among NGOs, and have hampered civic mobilization in opposition to companies' various political and social strategies. Despite these challenges, in recent years, a new wave of civil societal activism and mobilization has emerged to gradually overcome these industrial tactics and question the government's ongoing relationship with these corporate powers.

In accordance with the IPCI analytical framework, however, company's political and social strategies are insufficient for explaining its ability to influence regulatory policy. Complementary institutions also matter. More specifically, in recent years, for both personal and political reasons, Mexican presidents, who wield considerable agenda-setting powers, have supported these companies mainly because they view these companies' success as vital for achieving presidents' alternative social welfare policies, and thus political objectives. Indeed, companies' political and social strategies have been deeply facilitated by these continuously supportive complementary institutions.

The Rise of Big Industry and NCDs

Since the 1990s, Mexico has seen the burgeoning growth and profitability of major soda and junk food industries. Industries producing and supplying junk food products began to emerge in response to the opening up of Mexico's economy and as a result of free trade and investment opportunities. A major contributor to this process was the 1995 North American Free Trade Agreement (NAFTA), which encouraged and facilitated US foreign direct investment into food production, importation, and the supply of junk foods from the United States and Canada (Giuntella et al. 2020; United States Department of Agriculture 2018). According to the United States Department of Agriculture (2021), "The U.S. direct investment in Mexico's food and beverage industries expanded greatly during the first decade of NAFTA, growing from a total of about $2.3 billion in 1993 to about $10.9 billion in 2012. The total declined to about $6.8 billion in 2013. Since then, the total has been in the neighborhood of $7–8 billion" (1). Through increased free market reform and competition, during this period Mexican investors began to establish several food production companies. Some of Mexico's largest food production and supply companies include Sigma Alimentos, Lala (for dairy), Bachoco (poultry), Bimbo (baked goods), and Grupo Maseca (flour and tortilla) (Castellanos 2019, 5). According to Castellanos, most of these companies have their own supply-chains and export to other countries.

Due in part to NAFTA and in part to ongoing free market reforms, US and Mexican investment into food distribution networks, such as chains of local and large retail stores selling junk food products, flourished by the late 1990s. According to GRAIN (2015), some experts, such as Professor Corinna Hawkes, stated that NAFTA led to explosive growth of these supermarket chains and convenience stores (GRAIN 2015). According to Hawkes, moreover, these stores increased in number from 3,850 in 1997 to 5,729 in 2004 (GRAIN 2015). Coca-Cola's local chain store OXXO, for example, tripled in number between 1999 and 2004, quickly surpassing other Mexican grocery chains, such as Soriana, in sales (GRAIN 2015). According to recent estimates, OXXO remains the leading chain store in Mexico. In 2017, OXXO had 16,000 stores and, according to market analysts, this was "eight times more than closest competitor 7-Eleven" (Seale and Associates 2018, 2). Walmart also went from owning one store in Mexico in 1991 to 2,114 stores by 2015 (McMillan 2015). By opening these stores and expanding, companies could ensure the ongoing distribution and sale of their products, while strategically placing them in key locations.

Recent estimates suggest that total junk food industry sales for restaurant chains, fast food franchises, convenience stores, retail chains, and vendors increased from $179.4 billion (Mexican currency) to $203.3 billion in 2017, with a projected increase to $221.4 billion in 2020 (Seale and Associates 2018, 2). Sales for imported and local packaged food, which includes items such as snacks, meats, ice creams, ready-made meals, sweet biscuits, and snack bars also increased to US$52.6 billion in 2019 (Food Export Association 2019, 1). This, in turn, makes Mexico the eleventh largest market in the world for these products (Food Export Association 2019).

Sales of processed foods in Mexico also totaled $124 billion in 2012 (GRAIN 2015). Moreover, according to the same article, processed food corporations made $28.3 billion in profits that same year. Following NAFTA, sales for foreign-owned processed foods grew by approximately "5 to 10 percent per year from 1995 to 2003" (Kilpatrick 2015, 1). Of all the food products imported into Mexico, it was the sale of junk foods that saw the steepest rise in total imported sales—even surpassing sodas (GRAIN 2015).

The rise and development of soda companies also benefited greatly from NAFTA and free market reforms (Lopez and Jacobs 2018). Today, this market is dominated in sales and production by only a handful of companies. Two in particular stand out: Coca-Cola, which owns approximately 70 percent of the soda market, and PepsiCo, which owns approximately 15 percent (Carriedo-Lutzenkirchen 2018, 89); other smaller though competitive brands include Ajemex, Socieadad Cooperativa Trabajadores de Pascual, Jarochito, and Mister Q (Cortes 2009). Coca-Cola FEMSA is by far the largest producer and distributor of sodas (Carriedo-Lutzenkirchen 2018). Moreover, total sales are consistently dominated by Coca-Cola and PepsiCo, as foreign brands, as well as Peñafiel, followed thereafter by Ajemex and Sociedad Cooperativa Trabajadores de Pascual (Cortes 2009; Gómez 2019a).

The profitability of Mexico's soda industry lends credence to claims that Mexico leads the world in the consumption of soda products. According to Kilpatrick (2015), "Mexico has become the No. 1 per capita consumer of soda, with the average person drinking more than 46 gallons per year—86 percent more than the average American" (1).

When taken together, Mexico's soda and junk food companies have become a formidable economic and political force. These industries have become two of the fastest growing economic sectors in the nation, providing thousands of jobs while ensuring a consistent stream of government revenue through taxes as well as the 2014 soda and junk food tax. In 2017, for example, it was estimated that revenues from this soda tax equated to approximately MXN$100 billion (US$5.5 billion) four years after the law was passed (News Desk 2018). Moreover, with unfettered access to the media as well as aggressive marketing campaigns, the products that these industries produce have contributed to the rise of what others have commonly referred to as "industrial epidemics" (Hastings 2012)—namely, obesity, type 2 diabetes, heart disease, and cancer. But how serious is this situation in Mexico, and which populations have been affected the most?

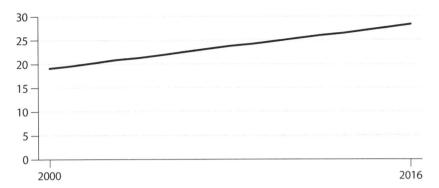

Mexico: prevalence (%) of obesity among adults. *Source*: WHO, 2021. https://www.who.int/data/gho/data/indicators/indicator-details/GHO/prevalence-of-obesity-among-adults-bmi-=-30-(crude-estimate)-(-)

Vulnerable Populations

While several socioeconomic, environmental, cultural, and genetic factors have contributed to the rise of NCDs in Mexico, the consumption of foods high in calories and low in nutrients have played a significant role in contributing to these ailments (Beaubien 2017). In Mexico, NCDs that are closely associated with the consumption of these foods include type 2 diabetes, obesity, high blood pressure, heart disease, and cancer (Nieto et al. 2019; Soares 2016). According to the University of Washington's Institute for Health Metrics and Evaluation (2019a), in 2019 diabetes was second only to ischemic heart disease in cause of death. Moreover, according to the WHO, diabetes is a leading cause of death in Mexico, claiming nearly eighty thousand lives each year (Beaubien 2017; PAHO 2012). All together, NCDs in Mexico account for 75 percent of all deaths, with the biggest risk factors for mortality being obesity and unhealthy diets; furthermore, obesity-related comorbidity contributes to the deaths of approximately 28 percent of the population each year (Aceves-Martins et al. 2016, 2).

Obesity and type 2 diabetes have now emerged as epidemics in Mexico. At the global level, Mexico also ranks in the top ten, second only to the United States, for having the highest percentage of obese individuals (BBC 2018) and among the top twenty—ranking in sixth place—in the world for type 2 diabetics (H. T. 2013). In Mexico, the number of obese individuals increased from 23.3 percent in 2005 to 28.9 percent in 2016. Additionally, Mexico trails behind only the United States in having the most obesity cases

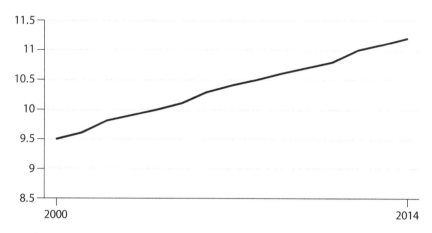

Mexico: prevalence (%) of adult diabetes. *Source*: WHO, 2021. https://www.who
.int/data/gho/data/indicators/indicator-details/GHO/raised-fasting-blood
-glucose-(-=7-0-mmol-l-or-on-medication)(age-standardized-estimate)

among adults in the Americas (WHO, Global Health Observatory 2020). The
total number of diabetics, measured by a raised blood glucose level above 7,
also increased from 10.1 percent in 2005 to 11.2 percent in 2014 (WHO 2020).

While these diseases are certainly present among all socioeconomic groups
in Mexico (Astudillo 2013), recent studies suggest that they have increased
at a significantly higher rate in two populations: children and the poor. According to Mexico's secretary of health, in recent years Mexico has led the
world in having the highest level of childhood overweight and obesity cases
(Aceves-Martins et al. 2016; Kilpatrick 2015; Secretary of Health, IMSS 2015).
Based on survey results obtained from 37,147 children through the 2012 National Health and Nutrition Examination Survey, Hernández-Cordero and
her colleagues found that "in 2012, 33.5% of children < 5 years of age (both
sexes) were at risk of overweight or were overweight (OW); 32% and 36.9%
of girls and boys 5–11 years of age were OW+OB, respectively, and 35.8% and
34.1% of female and male adolescents were OW+OB, respectively" (2017, 1).
According to the same study, high-income communities in urban areas had
the most cases of childhood overweight and obesity.

Perhaps even more concerning was the statistical trend that Hernández-
Cordero and colleagues (2017) discovered during their analysis. While children from higher-income groups in urban areas had the highest percentage
of overweight and obesity, when examining the *rate of increase* in these ail-

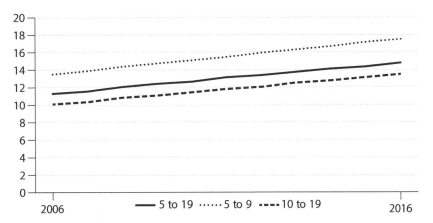

Mexico: prevalence (%) of childhood obesity (ages 5–19). *Source*: WHO, 2021. https://www.who.int/data/gho/data/indicators/indicator-details/GHO/preva lence-of-obesity-among-children-and-adolescents-bmi-2-standard-deviations -above-the-median-(crude-estimate)-(-)

ments, children from lower-income groups saw the highest increase. This finding confirms other studies suggesting that Mexico's poorest children have struggled the most with respect to overweight and obesity due to the excessive consumption of unhealthy junk foods (Arredondo 2007; Rodriguez et al. 2018). In fact, according to findings by Agren (2020), research conducted by El Poder del Consumidor, an NGO in Mexico, showed that approximately 70 percent of schoolchildren in the poor areas of Guerrero state consume soda for breakfast. The work of Rodriguez and colleagues (2018) also cites a study claiming that "SSBs comprehended 17.5% of the total daily caloric intake among Mexican children aged 1 to 19 years old" (3). Furthermore, according to Aceves-Martins and others (2016), "Between 1999 and 2006, an increase of 226% in consumption of carbonated drinks and sweetened beverages was documented among Mexican children and adolescents" (3).

Across all income groups, the poor, on average, have also seen a disproportionately higher incidence of overweight and obesity. According to Barquera and colleagues (2013), a major characteristic of Mexico's obesity epidemic has been the fact that obesity is increasing at a more alarming rate among the poor, as well as among children. National Health Survey research conducted by Fernald and colleagues (2004) for the years 2000 and 2003 comports with the 2013 findings of Barquera and colleagues. Arredondo (2007) further finds that poor migrants moving from Mexico's rural areas to large urban centers, such as Mexico City, have seen a disproportionately higher incidence of obesity due to their increase in income and subsequent purchases of unhealthy foods; moreover, the author also finds that this pattern is consistent with what is found in the United States, such that this is a context where individuals from lower socioeconomic status suffer more than any other income group from obesity and other related ailments. Others have argued that comparatively lower levels of income between the rich and poor has led the latter to establish a homogenous pattern of consuming less nutritious foods, due to differences in access and prices, whereas the former has had the income needed to purchase, diversify, and improve the quality of food consumed (Torres and Rojas 2018). These differences in income level and consumption patterns may account for disproportionate effects of overweight and obesity on the poor.

Type 2 diabetes has also been mainly prevalent among lower income groups, especially adults. Since the early 1990s, according to the 1993 National Survey of Chronic Diseases, low-income adults had the highest prevalence of type 2 diabetes when compared to other income groups (Rull et al. 2005). In fact, Rull and colleagues found that this was the only income strata with a prevalence above 10 percent (2005, 192). Though not as prevalent as in adults, incidence of type 2 diabetes among children has also increased (Rull et al. 2005). Nationwide surveys indicated that this form of diabetes has increased by 25 percent over a seven-year period since 1995 (OMICS International 2019). Other studies confirm these trends, underscoring a continued rise in type 2 diabetes among children, though with the prevalence of type 1 being higher (Evia-Viscarra et al. 2016).

Several factors account for these troubling statistical trends. First, an increase in access to cheaper high-calorie foods, when combined with busier family work schedules and less time for home-cooked meals, has motivated poor families to purchase junk foods to the detriment of their and their children's health. Other studies claim that the lower the socioeconomic level in Mexico, the more likely families are to purchase and consume foods with the highest calories at the cheapest price (Schaffer 2017). This problem is further compounded by poor families receiving conditional grant transfers through popular anti-poverty cash transfer programs, such as Prospera (previously known as Oportunidades), the effectiveness of which some have argued requires reevaluation (Rivera et al. 2016). Where and what kinds of foods families can purchase with this cash-transfer money is unregulated, thus incentivizing families to purchase these products. Finally, broader social factors—that is, the "social determinants of health"—are also to blame. One in particular has been a steady decline in physical activity due to limited access to close and safe parks, increased media viewing (e.g., TV, social media, gaming), in the case of children, as well as inadequate parental understanding of sound nutrition and the absence of regular physical activity programs in schools (Rodriguez et al. 2018). Finally, a major contributor has been the junk food and soda industries' unrelenting marketing targeting children (Astudillo 2013), as well as the absence of effective federal regulations limiting these activities.

Government Policy Response

Government attention to the linkages between junk food products, NCDs, and their disproportionate influence on children and the poor was considerably delayed. This lack of attentiveness in large part stemmed from the government's unrelenting efforts during this period to promote industrial growth and economic development. During the 1980s and up through the early 1990s, the government was focused on liberalizing the economy through privatization, deregulation, free trade, and foreign direct investment (Villarreal 2010). This period also saw strong government support for nurturing and developing domestic and foreign-owned food enterprises, especially those that were linked to agricultural farming and sugarcane production. At the same time the government was committed to reducing the role of the state in agriculture (Smith 1992). For decades, the agricultural sugarcane sector was heavily backed by the government, seen as an industry that served to simultaneously develop the food processing and agricultural sector while solidifying the government's corporatist political relationship with labor and business—the cornerstone to Mexican corporatist political stability (Centeno 1997). In response to the sugarcane industry's decline in profitability and near bankruptcy, in 2001, then president Vicente Fox led efforts to pass the Sugarcane Law in 2005, in the process guaranteeing consistently fair pricing for sugarcane producers (Buzzanell 2010). In fact, the largest demand for sugarcane came from major food processing and soda companies, as well as chemical, cosmetic, and pharmaceutical companies (Aguilar-Rivera et al. 2012). Therefore, for the government, nurturing and developing the junk food industry was not only vital for its goal of achieving economic development and growth but also for securing farmer and agricultural political support.

Nevertheless, during the 1980s health officials began to acknowledge a steady increase in overweight and obesity. The government also began to realize during this period that all income levels were suffering from these ailments and that women were the most affected (Astudillo 2013). However, the government's efforts to establish a firm linkage between the rise of these NCDs and the consumption of junk foods did not begin in earnest until the mid-2000s. Indeed, it appears that it was only after researchers at the prestigious National Institute of Public Health (INSP) in Cuernavaca, Mexico, began to analyze and report several national income expenditure surveys that the Ministry of Health started to develop an interest in creating federal programs to control overweight and obesity patterns (Barquera et al. 2013). In 2002, these INSP researchers found that households were spending less money on traditional foods (e.g., fruits, vegetables, dairy, meats) and instead were increasing their spending on refined carbohydrates and sugar-sweetened beverages (SSBs). Mexico was undergoing a massive nutrition transition, with obesity, type 2 diabetes, and other NCDs emerging in tandem with the consumption of unhealthy foods. It was in this context, according to Barquera and colleagues (2013), that "researchers from the MOH identified the urgent need to develop and implement programmes to control the increase in the prevalence of OW+O [overweight and obesity]" (14).

By 2006, Barquera and colleagues (2013) claimed that the government was committed to introducing several obesity prevention programs as well as programs focused on nutrition-related diseases. By this point, the government had also become increasingly aware that junk food industries were one of the main contributors to this nutrition transition (NCDs) and that these industries' activities needed to be addressed. Several new prevention policies were introduced, some of which began to tackle the junk food industry head-on through the regulation of their sales and marketing activities.

Prevention First, Regulation Second

Amid the backdrop of a government that was for years dedicated to safeguarding and nurturing junk food industries, the government's first policy priority was not to aggressively take on these industries through aggressive regulation, such as restricting the marketing and sales of their products, but instead to emphasize NCD prevention by providing information to consumers. In 2005, for example, Mexico's largest public health insurance provider covering formal sector workers in the social security system, IMSS (Instituto Mexicano del Seguro Social), began issuing public warning messages about the rise of overweight and obesity. Titled PrevenIMSS, this program used TV advertisements and other media outlets to broadcast its obesity prevention messages (Barquera et al. 2013). The INSP also organized a conference with the United States Institute of Medicine on the issue of addressing rising rates of obesity among youth and children with Mexican origins residing alongside the US-Mexican border (14). During this conference, multifaceted prevention policy approaches were suggested with a focus on children. In 2008, the Secretariat of Health furthered its prevention awareness campaign by introducing a report and guide titled *Recomendaciones sobre el consumo de bebidas para la población Mexicana* (Recommendations for the Consumption of Beverages for the Mexican Population), which emerged from an expert committee organized by the Secretariat of Health (Rivera et al. 2008). Based on survey results obtained from INSP researchers showing a heightened increase in the consumption of sugary drinks, the Secretariat of Health published a "healthy beverage picture" showing the government's recommended breakdown of daily beverage intake; the report from which this recommendation was based suggested that "less than 10% of an individual's energy intake should come from beverages and that SSBs should be avoided or consumed sparingly" (Barquera et al. 2013, 72). This "healthy beverage picture" was widely distributed over social media and the press.

It was not until 2010 that the government began to directly regulate the activities of junk food industries—though at a very modest level. That year, based on recommendations from civil societal activists, NGOs, industry leaders, and academics, the National Agreement for Healthy Nutrition (ANSA) was established. In large part guided by the WHO's 2004 *Global Strategy on Diet, Physical Activity and Health*, ANSA proposed a phalanx of prevention and regulatory measures aimed at not only reducing NCDs but also restricting the sale of certain foods (Barquera et at. 2013). ANSA was focused on four goals: first, providing individuals with access to reliable information based on scientific evidence and health education, with the goal of improving consumer decisions as well as promoting a healthy lifestyle; second, policies focused on physical education and public spaces for physical exercise, as well as the regulation of industry marketing activities; third, monitoring and evaluating the efficacy of these and related policies; and finally, research in exploring other potential interventions, such as a soda tax and improved health literacy (Latnovic and Cabrera 2013). According to Latnovic and Cabrera (2013), the overall goal of ANSA was to "position obesity and over-weight as one of the major barriers to national sustainable development, and to issue a call for action of the public and private sectors as well as society, to sum up the actions for obesity and non-communicable chronic diseases prevention" (S14). The food industry was willing to sign off on this agreement based on its guiding governance principles, such as establishing a common goal with government, "shared responsibility, transparency, accountability, gradual implementation, and solidarity" (S13). Through ANSA, there was also an increase in inter-secretariat coordination, that is, between education, health, and other related federal agencies, as well as NGOs, to work together to not only implement these polices but also introduce efforts to regulate industry marketing and sales.

Worried about the ongoing rise in childhood obesity rates, according to Barquera and colleagues (2013), a direct result of ANSA was the creation of the *Guidelines on Nutrition Standards for Foods and Beverages*. Managed by the Secretary of Education and Health, these guidelines set national criteria for the production and distribution of foods sold in schools (Latnovic and Cabrera 2013). In addition, the guidelines recommend a reduction in the high caloric values of foods, such as snacks, sold in schools (Latnovic and Cabrera 2013), the provision of health foods, as well as a commitment to "ban sodas; limit the availability of other SSBs, whole milk, salty and sweet snacks, and desserts that comply with nutritional criteria developed by the expert group to a maximum of two days per week; and eliminate the products that do not comply with the nutritional criteria" (Barquera et al. 2013, 14; see also Ávila and Montañez 2011). Macari and others (2019) maintain that national school feeding guidelines were made more stringent in 2014, and that these guidelines were "mandatory and prohibited ultra-processed food products from being sold in schools from Monday to Thursday. On Fridays, only ultra-processed products that comply with certain nutrition criteria are permitted" (108).

Next, in 2014, Mexico impressed the world by becoming the first nation to pass legislation creating a national soda and snack tax. The product of endless haggling between industry and government, this tax proposal was passed by the congress during President Enrique Peña Nieto's administration as part of a broader national fiscal package. Indeed, it is important to emphasize that this tax was sold as part of a broader *economic*, and not *public health*, measure. On these grounds, despite vehement industry opposition, the tax was passed by the PRI political party and those political parties that were part of the government's national coalition alliance, namely the opposition PAN (Partido Acion Democratica) and PRD (Partido Revolucionario Democratica). The tax imposed a one-peso tax on every liter of sugary beverage. The endeavor was quickly hailed by the international community as a milestone achievement, a trendsetter, providing an example for other nations (PAHO 2016). President Peña Nieto assuaged taxpayers by claiming that the revenues obtained from this tax would be used to finance the provision of safe drinking water in schools and other related prevention measures.

In 2013, the Secretariat of Health stepped up its efforts to simultaneously address prevention and regulatory efforts through the introduction of the National Strategy for Prevention and Control of Overweight, Obesity, and Diabetes (henceforth, National Strategy). This was by far the most comprehensive national effort to start tackling these industries head-on through increased regulation while finding alternative ways to increase consumer awareness and eating habits. This program was introduced with an increased political concern and prioritization, as evident through President Peña Nieto's statement when introducing the National Strategy to the public that "what is at risk is literally the lives of millions of Mexicans" (quoted in Astudillo 2013, 1). In the National Strategy's report, it also stated that obesity and type 2 diabetes "have gradually become the main health problem in the country, not only for the health systems of the country but to the quality of life of all Mexicans" (quoted in Kilpatrick 2015, 1). The National Strategy entails three primary areas: improving public health, which means improving healthy lifestyles through the provision of government campaigns and assistance in promoting healthy lifestyles, monitoring NCDs, and implementing prevention policies; second, the early identification of individuals with NCD risk factors; and third, the introduction of fiscal policies for promoting public health, with the tax on soda and junk foods falling under this category (Astudillo 2013, 15–16).

With respect to industry regulation, the National Strategy for the first time created federal laws prohibiting the advertisement of junk food products during hours when children and adolescents regularly watch television; during the week (Monday to Friday), these hours included 2:30 p.m. to 7:30 p.m., and during the weekend (Saturday and Sunday), 7:30 a.m.–7:30 p.m.

(Hennessy 2014). These industries, according to Hennessy (2014), were also prohibited from advertising their products in national cinemas. The regulation was focused on kids between the ages of 4 and 12 (Vilar-Compte 2018). As Vilar-Compte (2018) points out, during the initial phase of this legislation, cookies, sodas, sugary drinks, and snacks were prohibited from being advertised, followed later by other products, such as fat, dairy products, sandwiches, soups, and cereals (12). This legislation was important, as prior efforts to regulate advertising were relegated to ineffective industry self-regulatory tactics, such as the 2009 *Code of Self-Regulation on Advertising Food and Non-alcoholic Beverages to Children* (Latnovic and Cabrera 2013; Vilar-Compte 2018). Through the National Strategy, the government finally moved from allowing this form of self-regulation to direct government regulation. Policy makers appeared to be confident that this regulatory endeavor would be successful and that penalties would be imposed on industries for non-compliance, reaching up to US$50,000 (Vilar-Compte 2018, 12). What's more, according to Vilar-Compte (2018), "policy makers estimated that the enactment of the policy would lead to a decrease in about 10,200 yearly advertisements during children's TV programming through the regulations" (12). Finally, as a component of the National Strategy, in 2014 the government required industries to provide front-of-package food labels, known as guideline daily amounts (Nieto et al. 2020). The GDA made this front-of-package labeling officially legal, requiring that food manufacturers provide nutritional content information that is easy to read and understandable.

Policy Challenges

Despite the creation of this impressive phalanx of prevention and treatment programs, it is important to emphasize that several attempts were made at an earlier stage to introduce similar policy measures, yet to no avail. For example, industry lobbyists vehemently resisted and altered policies on the sale of industry food and beverage products in schools (Taylor and Jacobson 2016). Efforts under the aforementioned National Strategy to introduce regulations on the advertising of unhealthy food products had also fallen short of achieving this goal, viewed by some as a violation of children's rights to information and health (*Proceso* 2017). What's more, the 2014 soda tax was an idea that had been introduced several years before in 2008, an idea that was put forth by nutrition activists (Gómez 2019a). However, due to opposing pressures from industry and labor representatives from the sugarcane industry—namely, the Cámara Nacional de las Industrias Azucarera y Alco-holera (CNIAA), which feared a decrease in sales and employment (Carriedo-Lutzenkirchen 2018)—the idea of a soda tax was eventually ignored (Gómez 2019a). Thus, junk food companies during the early 2000s were taking advantage of a government that was (1) not yet fully cognizant and concerned about the rising NCD epidemic, particularly among Mexico's most vulnerable populations, and (2) easily manipulated through industry pressures.

In addition to this delay in policy reform, because of ongoing industry pressures and political tactics (as we'll see later on), several studies reveal that these policies have not been effectively enforced. For example, when it came to prevention policies focusing on providing accurate nutritional information to consumers, shortly after the aforementioned 2008 *Recomendaciones de Bebidas* (Recommendation of Drinks) was created, researchers found that soda companies drew attention away from this recommendation, ensuring that they were not widely distributed among the population (Alianza por la Salud Alimentaria 2013).

Furthermore, with respect to policy regulations concerning childhood obesity, beginning with ANSA's efforts to coordinate dietary changes in schools, shortly after this policy was promulgated industry representatives were successful at delaying and essentially thwarting these regulations. It seems that a key strategy that these industries took was to use federal government regulatory institutions, such as the National Commission for the Improvement of Regulations (NCIR), which organizes public hearings and discussions on new proposals, to somehow convince government allies within the NCIR to reevaluate the adequacy and effectiveness of these regulations (see Barquera et al. 2013). Indeed, shortly after the initial public hearing about the ANSA regulations, the NCIR rejected its proposal and declared that the Secretariat of Health and Secretariat of Public Education needed to reevaluate their policies (Barquera et al. 2013). It is important to emphasize that this occurred despite overwhelming support for the regulation's passage during the NCIR's initial meeting, which received 842 comments, with nearly two-thirds, or 63 percent, in support and the remaining 37 percent opposed—with 99 percent of industry entirely opposed. A full 86 percent of academic and social actors were nevertheless in favor of the proposed regulations (74). With the Secretariat of Health and Secretariat of Public Education required to address the remaining questions raised by industry and engage in further negotiations, Barquera and colleagues (2013) found that major parts of this legislation were ultimately ignored, such as the elimination of energy density and alterations to the limits of sugar and fat in foods. This suggests that industries were capable of working with their allies within the NCIR and convincing them to reject the initial proposal and to proceed with ongoing negotiations. Ultimately, because of this process, while sodas were banned from schools, Barquera and colleagues (2013) found that "other SSBs, including juices and flavored waters with some amount of juice, and milk were allowed" (74).

To this day, policy evaluations reveal that ANSA school feeding guidelines have never been effectively enforced and are essentially ignored in schools across the country. In fact, in 2015, research conducted by Dr. Teresa Shamah of the National Institute of Public Health in Mexico revealed that up to that year, 51 percent of schools still sold junk foods (Agencia EFE 2019). Additional survey research of 645 students across 13 elementary schools by Pérez-Ferrer and others (2018) also concluded that "school compliance with the standards was in general very poor and very few children brought or purchased a healthy snack to consume during school hours" (6). Recently, the NGOs El Poder del Consumidor and the Network for the Rights of Children in Mexico, through their online My Healthy School platform, which relies on school community observations, also established that school feeding guidelines prohibiting the sale of ultraprocessed foods during most of the week in schools were not adequately implemented (Macari et al. 2019). Through this online platform, local school community members were allowed to upload their observations of their schools. Strikingly, through this online platform Macari and colleagues (2019) found the following:

> The platform has received around 8 000 individual reports of non-compliance over the past five years from teachers, parents and students at primary schools across the country. These reports suggest that non-compliance has been on the rise. There has been an increase in the proportion of reports indicating that sugary soft drinks and ultra-processed foods are being sold in schools, as well as an increase in reports complaining that fruit and vegetables are not sold and that potable water is not freely available. Furthermore, schools are supposed to have established a committee to monitor and oversee compliance with regulation, but these do not exist in the overwhelming majority of primary schools. (108–109)

ANSA's efforts to enact regulations on food advertising toward children has also been problematic. Part of the issue has been that, when compared to SSB taxes, there has been less of an effort to monitor and evaluate the advertising regulations' policy effectiveness (Vilar-Compte 2018). At the same time, Vilar-Compte (2018) maintains that "other studies show that food and beverages still advertised on Mexican TV do not meet more stringent nutritional quality, leaving Mexican children exposed to unhealthy food advertisements despite the enacted regulations" (15). Activists and academics in Mexico have also argued that there were several problems with the design of the legislation, such as limited TV viewing times, excluding other advertisement formats such as the internet and social media, and omitting the age group of 13–18 (Vilar-Compte 2018). It is also very important to note that civil society, including academics and even children, was never consulted during the formation of these regulations, which may certainly account for its limitations. Nevertheless, Vilar-Compte (2018) points out that "governmental documents state that the food industry provided inputs for the regulation (SSA 2014), but civil society organizations and academia were left out of such participatory policy-making processes" (13).

With respect to the 2014 soda tax, while recent findings suggest that this effort has led to a gradual reduction in sugar-sweetened beverage sales ("Diabetes Endocrinology," 2017), here again, there continued to be strong industry interference and efforts to undermine the tax. In 2016, industry representatives, led by the industry lobby group ANPRAC (Asociación Nacional de Productores de Refrescos y Aguas Carbonatadas), as well as Coca-Cola FEMSA, approached the governing PRI political party, which held the majority in congress, and argued for a lowering of the tax to 5 percent for sodas with 5 grams of sugar per 100 milliliters (Bonilla-Chacín et al. 2016). In addition to providing new evidence that the tax was only leading to a 1.9 percent reduction in soda sales, ANPRAC argued once again that the existing tax was harming industry, contributing to lost jobs due to escalating manufacturing costs, and negatively affecting the poor's purchasing power and income. It also did not help that during this period the Peña Neito administration decided to stop increasing federal taxes across the board. However, industry's request was eventually rejected by the Senate, in light of research findings suggesting that the tax was indeed working, specifically that it was leading to a decrease in soda consumption among low socioeconomic households (Bonilla-Chacín et al. 2016).

A good example of industry obstruction of existing federal regulations has also been in the area of front-of-package labeling. Despite the 2014 National Strategy's success in requiring that all soda and food companies provide clearly written and visible GDAs on their products, these industries also succeeded in hampering efforts to improve the quality and effectiveness of these labels. In 2019, several nutrition activists from organizations such as Poder del Consumidor, ContraPeso, and La Alianza por la Salud Alimentaria claimed that the existing GDAs were difficult to read, and that they failed to distinguish between natural and artificial sugars (*Arestegui Noticias* 2019). Activists went as far as to claim the GDA labels were not understandable (Olvera 2019), and put pressure on soda and food companies to clarify these labels. Mexico's Supreme Court eventually heard the case. In May 2019, the court ruled 30–2 that the GDAs required no further clarification, that they were understandable and in compliance with the WHO's recommendations (Aristegui 2019). This ruling supported the junk food industry's views and convinced leading activists, such as Alejandro Calvillo, director of the NGO El Poder del Consumidor, to state that the Supreme Court's decision reflected industry's claims, and that the decisions were based on "lies" (quoted in Olvera 2019).

Furthermore, in June 2019, a congressional hearing was organized to reevaluate the effectiveness of GDA labeling as well as a proposed annex of food and beverage labeling regulations, suggested by the opposition MORENA political party and the soda and food industry, which proposed new procedures for evaluating the GDA. Unfortunately, there were not enough congressional members present to establish the quorum needed for voting on these proposed regulations. Activists immediately claimed that this lack of quorum was due to industry pressures not to establish the quorum (Olvera 2019).

Obstructing Science

Junk food industries in Mexico have also expanded their policy influence by finding ways to alter scientific information and research informing NCD policy. Similar to what we saw in the United States during the 1960s, when the sugar industry paid off Harvard researchers to downplay the linkages between sugar and heart disease (O'Connor 2016), one of the main strategies that these industries have used is to fund supportive scientific research questioning the linkages between not only the consumption of their products and obesity, diabetes, and heart disease but also the effectiveness of a taxation on junk foods. Perhaps the most vivid example of this in Mexico has been the soda industry's efforts to work closely with nonprofit foundations to fund supportive scientific studies. For example, shortly after the 2014 soda tax was adopted, the private foundation ConMéxico (which receives support from Coca-Cola and other companies) financed the work of economists at prestigious universities, such as ITAM, El Colegio de México, and Universidade de Monterrey (Gómez 2019a). Economic researchers from these institutions subsequently published in-depth policy reports, with sophisticated econometric analysis, suggesting that the soda tax did not have a strong effect on the reduced consumption of soda products (Gómez 2019a). One good example of this was a study that ConMéxico commissioned from ITAM economists titled "Taxing Calories in Mexico" (Aguilar et al. 2015). This study provided statistical data questioning the effects that the soda tax had on consumption. Other reports indicated that the tax was regressive—that is, disproportionately affecting the poor's income (News Desk 2018).

These industries have also influenced reports published by prestigious think tanks. One in particular is Funsalud. Funsalud is arguably Mexico's most influential, independent public health think tank, well known for its constant ability to influence public health legislation (Rosenberg 2015; Gómez 2019a). For several years, Nestlé and Coca-Cola had strong connections with Funsalud (Rosenberg 2015). During this period, Funsalud supported these companies' position, questioning the reduction of consuming products high in calories, claiming instead that individuals needed to exercise more in order to burn calories and avoid weight gain (Rosenberg 2015). Furthermore, the former director of Funsalud, Mercedes Juan López, was known for her questioning of the effectiveness of the soda tax, emphasizing instead the importance of health education (Rosenberg 2015). López went on to become the secretary of health under President Enrique Peña Nieto. Funsalud worked with Coca-Cola Export Corporation and the soda and mineral water producer Peñafiel on a childhood obesity project (Cecil 2017). Coca-Cola has also worked with researchers and sponsored conferences that downplay the relationship between the consumption of their products and NCDs, as well as the effectiveness of the government's NCD policies (Gómez 2019a).

Given these companies' success in obstructing NCD policies, how did they achieve this process? What were some of the strategies they engaged in? And what was the political context facilitating their influence?

Political Action

As IPCI emphasizes, one of the key strategies behind the junk food industry's political influence is its efforts to become close partners with government officials in creating NCD prevention programs. Fearing a decline in sales and the imposition of stiffer regulations, these companies have worked hard to show that they are a major solution to Mexico's NCD problem and a genuine government partner in defeating Mexico's childhood obesity and type 2 diabetes epidemic.

One way that these companies have achieved this is by working with government officials to propose new NCD programs. During the Peña Nieto administration, for example, several companies worked closely with Mercedes Juan López, the secretary of health, to explore new prevention initiatives. As previously mentioned, Lopéz had worked closely with these companies when she served as director of the board for Funsalud (Cecil 2017), a position that she had before going into public office (Lira 2018). Taking advantage of this connection, company representatives subsequently maintained close ties with her (Gómez 2019a), and her views that children's obesity prevention programs should focus on increasing physical activity in schools and neighborhoods aligned with the soda industry's position. Coca-Cola had also worked with Secretariat of Health to create the Ponte 100 program, which provided funding for schools to increase daily physical activity (Gómez 2019a). In yet another example, in 2007, PepsiCo worked with the Secretary of Public Education, Josefina Vazquez Mota, to create the Vida Saludable Esquela (Healthy School Lifestyle) program (*Proceso* 2008). This program emphasized that schools increase daily physical activities to help prevent childhood obesity (*Proceso* 2008). In what appeared to be a sign of support for PepsiCo's partnership with the Secretariat of Health, Julio Frenk, the former secretary of health (2000–2006), inaugurated one of PepsiCo's new plants. Frenk also confirmed that there is no such thing as bad ingredients, just informed and uninformed diets (*Proceso* 2008).

Other strategies have entailed working with federal agencies to promote scientific discoveries in the area of nutrition. Mexico's Consejo Nacional de Ciencia y Tecnología (CONACYT), the government's primary agency for supporting scientific research, has worked closely with Coca-Cola on several initiatives (Sánchez 2015). In response to industry requests for innovative ideas, Coca-Cola works in partnership with CONACYT to provide technical assistance to industries in need of assistance. Furthermore, Coca-Cola has financed an annual CONACYT award, Premio de Investigación en Biomedicine Dr. Rubén Lisker, awarding two million Mexican pesos to any individual (with more than ten years of research experience) for the most innovative project addressing one of Mexico's major public health problems (Sánchez 2015).

In addition to working closely with politicians, policy makers, and federal agencies, several companies have also strategically worked within national committees organized by the government to help shape NCD legislation. In 2013, for example, as part of the aforementioned National Strategy, the Observatorio Mexícano de Enfermedades no Transmisibles (OMENT, Mexican Observatory for NCDs) was created as a monitoring and advisory committee within the Secretariat of Health to provide policy recommendations. Comprised of government officials, NGOs, think tanks, and the private sector, since this committee was formed, companies have succeeded at ensuring their overrepresentation and policy influence (Gómez 2019a). This has been achieved by appointing NGOs and think tanks that are funded by these companies, such as the Queremos Mexicanos Activos (QUEMA) and Movimiento por una Vida Saludable (MOVISA), in addition to companies' presence within the OMENT. The number of company and company-supported NGOs/think tanks has consistently exceeded those NGOs and advocacy groups representing civil society's interests within the OMENT (Gómez 2019a). Furthermore, White and Barquera (2020) maintain that the OMENT "includes a significant and powerful industry presence, while national health institutes and many civil society organizations are excluded" (e1752063-4). By establishing a strong presence within the OMENT (see also Carriedo-Lutzenkirchen 2018), these companies have been able to solidify their partnership with government and proactively work with health officials to help monitor and design NCD policies. White and Barquera also found that food companies are disproportionately present within several other government-appointed federal regulatory committees, "since, by design, they include mandatory participation of industry and commerce" (e1752063-4).

These companies have also engaged in various lobbying strategies. During the 1990s and early 2000s, several companies established allies within the Congress by donating to campaigns and providing largesse (Gómez 2019a). At the same time, they frequently lobbied the Congress in opposition to policies, benefiting from the presence of their supporters (Gómez 2019a; Rosenberg 2015). Intensive industry opposition stalled several attempts to introduce NCD obesity and diabetes programs (Alianza por la Salud Alimentaria 2017; Gómez 2019a).

For example, soda company lobbyists and labor unions succeeded in thwarting earlier efforts under President Vicente Fox to introduce a soda tax (Gómez 2019a). Other companies were also successful at interfering with health polices, such as those falling under the National Strategy for the Prevention and Control of Overweight, Obesity, and Diabetes (Calvillo and Peterander 2018). Later during debates sounding the 2013 tax proposal, the CNIAA, the primary interest group representing the sugar industry, opposed this policy on the grounds that the tax would lead to a reduction in industrial demand for sugarcane, opting instead for cheaper high-fructose corn syrup—easily accessible, as mentioned earlier, because of NAFTA (Carreido-Lutzenkirchen 2018). This process would nevertheless entail a sharp reduction in sugarcane profits and employability, argued the CNIAA (Carriedo-Lutzenkirchen 2018).

Yet, in 2011 a congressional ruling was passed, making it illegal for businesses to directly lobby and interfere with policy without first registering with the congress. The ruling also imposed restrictions on the number of lobbyists permitted to work with particular congressional committees (Christian 2014). Industry contributions to campaigns were also limited (O'Neil 2013), while the receipt of gifts of any kind to congressional representatives was henceforth prohibited (Christian 2014). Even with the passage of these rules, incessant pressure from activists, and periodic media coverage, these lobbying activities persist; it is as if these rules never existed, leading to several successful clandestine efforts to continue to influence policy. In fact, in recent years, analysts have viewed the Congress as "home turf" for these industries, expecting that they are always there, safeguarding their interests, influencing policy (Rosenberg 2015). One senator from the PAN political party commented: "When we want help with a campaign, they [industry] are here to help" (quoted in Rosenberg 2015, 1). Such comments smack of industries' ongoing lobbying interference despite the 2011 congressional ruling. As noted earlier, industry lobbying is a process that continues to interfere not only with the creation of NCD policy but also periodic congressional evaluation of existing prevention programs and ways to improve them—as seen with the recent GDA food labeling hearings mentioned earlier.

Transnational Partnerships

In a context of heightened globalization, where more than ever, powerful international organizations and donors influence domestic policy, junk food companies have also turned to the international community to establish policy-making partnerships. Taking advantage of the WHO's funding crisis, especially for programs focused on NCDs, in recent years these companies have proactively established partnerships with regional WHO offices with considerable domestic policy-making influence.

A good example is the food industry's work with the Pan American Health Organization (PAHO), the WHO's regional office for Latin America. In 2010, due to insufficient revenues obtained from the WHO to help combat obesity in the Americas, PAHO agreed to a strategic "partnership" with companies such as Coca-Cola, Nestlé, and Unilever, companies that donated US$50,000, US$150,000, and US$150,000 to PAHO, respectively, in 2012 (Wilson and Kerlin 2012). Coca-Cola, in a context where the WHO was in need of support, placed one of its representatives on the steering board for the WHO's Pan American Forum for Action on Non-communicable Diseases. This Pan-American steering group helps to design and influence obesity policies in Mexico. Through this international steering group, Coca-Cola has been able to work with other committee members and propose policy ideas, all in the name of helping solve Mexico's ongoing obesity problem. Furthermore, it is interesting to note that while this Pan-American forum claims to maintain complete autonomy in decision making, its very own website harbors membership benefits that reflect Coca-Cola and other companies' interests—that is, helping participating businesses "avoid regulation" and "influence regulatory environments" (1).

Restructuring Society

In addition to these domestic and international political strategies, junk food companies have also gradually restructured civil society in their favor by building supportive allies who agree with companies' policy views. As IPCI emphasizes, to this end, companies pursue several strategies, such as supporting academic researchers, NGOs, and think tanks sharing similar normative beliefs in individual liberty and responsibility, as well as targeting poor communities and providing them with employment opportunities.

All of these efforts have been used to engender networks of social support that serve to not only increase these companies' legitimacy but also their popularity in society.

As mentioned earlier, these companies have been successful at establishing allies and support networks within academic institutions and think tanks. One way this has been achieved is by providing research funding through private foundations. For example, the ConMéxico foundation, which was funded by Coca-Cola and other major companies, provided support for university researchers investigating the effectiveness of a soda tax (Gómez 2019a). Coca-Cola has also provided funding to the NGO Instituto de Bebidas para la Salud y el Bienestar, to fund researchers focused on topics such as improved hydration, food ingredients, and diets, as well as healthy and physical lifestyles (ExpokNews 2012). Furthermore, in 1992, Nestlé provided the prestigious think tank Funsalud with a grant to conduct nutrition research and support training in medical schools (Mexican Health Foundation 2019). Through this support, Funsalud also created the Nestlé Nutrition Fund, which conducts research and provides funding to improve the nutritional status of Mexican people through scientific innovation, the creation of professional networks, medical school training, and the diffusion of nutrition-related knowledge (Mexican Health Foundation 2019).

Other strategies have included supporting academic careers by providing venues at which to share research. For instance, Coca-Cola has worked with Mexico's Federacíon Mexicana de Diabetes (National Diabetes Federation) to invite famous keynote speakers, who are often acclaimed medical or nutrition scientists, to share research findings that support the company's views—such as the importance of individual responsibility and exercise (Asociación Mexicans de Diabetes 2019; Gómez 2019a).

Junk food companies have also partnered with NGOs and think tanks that share similar policy views and ideological beliefs. Several NGOs, such as Quiero Saber Salud, QUEMA, and MOVISA, advocate for the importance of liberty, individual responsibility, and freedom in food consumption and exercise. With respect to policy, these NGOs agree with companies' views that it is not the prohibition of foods or taxes that helps avoid childhood obesity and type 2 diabetes but, rather, the quality of nutritional information and assistance in changing daily lifestyles, such as daily exercise (Servín 2017). For example, Coca-Cola FEMSA has partnered with MOVISA to implement its 2016 Latin American Commitment to a Healthy Future, in a multisectoral collaboration with Healthy Weight Commitment Foundation and other companies, "with the goal of promoting the execution of national initiatives that empower school-aged children and their families to make adequate decisions concerning their eating habits and physical activity to generate healthy habits through different educational tools" (Coca-Cola FEMSA 2016, 36). According to Coca-Cola FEMSA, moreover, "the partnership with Movimiento por una Vida Saludable (MOVISA) played a key role in launching this commitment in Mexico" (36). These NGOs have also published several advertisements equating these libertarian views with enjoying food and exercise.

These companies nevertheless realize that to sustain their popularity and support in society, they also need to work closely with local communities. Nestlé, for example, has achieved this by providing career opportunities. Through the company's Mi Dulce Negocio (My Sweet Business) program, Nestlé planned to train fifteen thousand women to provide sweet but nutritious desserts that contained Nestlé products (GRAIN 2015). While selling these products, these women were to provide Nestlé kits and also train potential women—approximately ten each—who might also join the company by way of this employment program (GRAIN 2015). Pundits claim that "a 'small army' of 15,000 Mexican women will be mobilized in 'priority zones' across the country to promote the Nestlé way of nourishing children, with the financial support of Mexico's Ministry of Social Development" (GRAIN 2015, 1). Nestlé also offers programs to help young people find employment and develop career skills through its funding of the Alliance for YOUth (Nestlé 2018b). The alliance has pledged to create thirty thousand work opportunities for youth aged 15–24 in Mexico, as well as in Chile, Colombia, and Peru (Nestlé 2018b). Nestlé claims that this program has been implemented to help achieve the UN Sustainable Development Goal of sustainably reducing the number of unemployed youth. Nestlé Mexico has also provided several infrastructural and educational opportunities in poor communities.

Nestlé has also gone so far as to build local infrastructure to help people get to and from work while working with local schools to provide sporting activities for kids (Nestlé 2015b). In a recent YouTube documentary published by Nestlé, local community members claim that the company has always been there to support them (Nestlé 2015b). Nestlé's Nespresso AAA program has also worked with local coffee farmers to not only help their businesses develop in an environmentally sustainable way but also to help build a sense of community (Nespresso, n.d.). Finally, in partnership with the secretary of health, in an effort to stem the rising tide of obesity rates in children, Nestlé has also worked with local communities to increase awareness of the importance of staying hydrated. Through the creation of a National Healthy Hydration day, media tours, and local activities, the company has been able to reach thousands of families (Nestlé 2019b), and the company is working in close partnership with the Secretariat of Health on this issue (Secretaría de Salud 2016). These activities have been critical for building social acceptability and support for Nestlé and its products.

Creating Divisions in Society

As IPCI also explains, in the process of creating their own allies and support base in society, these companies have also contributed to the emergence of a divided society, hampering the latter's capacity to mobilize in response to companies' ongoing policy influence. In Mexico, this challenge emerged due to these companies' ongoing focus on building supportive allies among NGOs and think tanks that, in turn, decreased the number of activists and researchers that could potentially work with those organizations unaffiliated with these companies and representing the interests of the general public.

Indeed, as the work of Gómez (2019a) explains, major junk food companies have worked closely with influential foundations such as ConMéxico, NGOs such as the Mexican Diabetes Association, and influential university academics in order to fund research and campaign initiatives. Interestingly, the Mexican Diabetes Association has funded conferences that align with the soda industry's message emphasizing the importance of individual responsibility and exercise (Gómez 2019a). However, university academics and think tanks have often not been willing to work with other NGOs advocating for the need to strengthen NCD programs, such as El Poder del Consumidor, ContraPESO, and Fundación Midete (Gómez 2019a). Gómez (2019a) also writes that those university academics and think tanks aligned with industry foundations also have far more financial resources than those NGOs working for the public's health (see also Barquera et al. 2013). In this context, and as Gómez (2019a) explains, there has been a lack of unity in society and an ability to collectively monitor and push back against the ongoing influence of junk food companies.

Complementary Institutions

In addition to engaging in strategic political and social tactics, Mexico's political structure has also facilitated these companies' ability to influence NCD policy. Indeed, one must understand the broader institutional context within which these companies operate, as well as the incentives that politicians have to facilitate their economic expansion and policy influence. As IPCI explains, this process is captured by focusing on the presence of complementary institutions. These institutions arise when influential presidents have a preexisting connection with companies and are supportive of their cause, and seek to establish strong partnerships with companies in order to achieve alternative policy and, thus, political objectives while also potentially creating institutions within government that solidify this partnership. Either way, complementary institutions serve to indirectly reinforce companies' political activities and policy influence.

In Mexico, the office of the presidency has played a key role in this process. But why is this the case? Historically, presidents in Mexico have wielded considerable policy influence because they have simultaneously been presidents of the governing political party, which in the case of Mexico has been a party that historically dominated the government since the revolution—the PRI (Partido Revolucionario Institucional) (Centeno 1996). In recent years, however, the major opposition parties, such as the PAN, have won the presidency, beginning with Vicente Fox in 2000, and the governorship in several key states. Since then, with the rise of these parties, the president has had to establish a party coalition in the congress and senate. Nevertheless, when it comes to policy making, the office of the presidency continues to display a considerable amount of influence in setting the policy agenda, mainly by way of handpicking agency secretaries (Edmonds-Poli and Shirt 2016). This agenda-setting power persists regardless of which political party the president is from and the governing coalition present (Edmonds-Poli and Shirt 2016).

During the 1990s and early 2000s, when junk food companies in Mexico began to flourish, presidents played a critical role in nurturing and facilitating these companies' policy influence. Nowhere was this more apparent than under the Vicente Fox administration. Fox was unique in that prior to his arrival into office, he was chief executive of Coca-Cola's Latin America regional operations, leading the company's expansion into Mexico and throughout Latin America. During his presidential campaign, he benefited greatly from the support of friends at Coca-Cola and other supportive corporate partners (Cruz and Durán 2017; Gómez 2019a). As president, Fox returned the favor by not only ensuring Coca-Cola's and other companies' prosperity but also avoiding—as mentioned earlier—the first attempt to impose a tax on soda products containing sugarcane in 2003 (Gómez 2019a; Juárez and Rio 2017). Fox also appointed some of his former Coca-Cola associates as personal advisors within his administration (Cruz and Durán 2017; Gómez 2019a). During the Fox administration, Coca-Cola had a considerable amount of influence over health policy (Gómez 2019a; Rosenberg 2015). What's more, the political connections that were established under Fox were maintained by Coca-Cola, in turn facilitating its ability to have policy influence under future presidential administrations (Gómez 2019a). Moreover, under the subsequent Felipe Calderón and Enrique Peña Nieto administrations, the power of the president to appoint secretaries of health also facilitated this process. For instance, essentially all secretaries of health since the Fox administration (e.g., Secretaries Julio Frenk and Mercedes Juan López) supported soda companies either by recognizing their expansion (under Frenk) or by supporting their public health messages (under López).

Subsequent presidents also supported these companies. The Felipe Calderón administration (PAN, 2006–2012) was particularly supportive of PepsiCo (*Proceso* 2008). In fact, Calderón allowed PepsiCo to work closely with the secretary of public education to establish several exercise programs in schools (*Proceso* 2008). Additionally, at the World Economic Forum held in Davos, Switzerland, in January 2010, Calderón met with Nestlé CEO Paul Bulcke to announce that his administration was committed to furthering Nestlé's investments in Mexico by about US$400 million for the next three years while making a similar agreement with Coca-Cola and PepsiCo for US$5 million and US$6.5 million, respectively (La Información 2010). Calderón was never shy about attending public ceremonies for the opening of new manufacturing sites for companies, such as the Italian multinational Ferrero, the makers of Nutella and Kinder products. In fact, at a press conference Calderon announced Ferrero would open its first Mexican production plant in the state of Guanajuato in February 2012 (Nieburg 2012). While Calderon viewed these companies as contributing to his goal of increased economic development and employment opportunities, he was not as committed to reducing poverty (Wilkinson 2011) and, furthermore, using these companies to meet this alternative social policy objective. Calderon made fighting poverty the focus of his last three years in office. His first few years were focused on fighting drug cartels (MYSA News 2009).

This contrasted with the following Enrique Peña Nieto administration (PRI, 2012–2018). Peña Nieto also supported PepsiCo and Nestlé, viewing these companies as contributing to Mexican growth and opportunity. Unlike his predecessor, however, Peña Nieto viewed these companies as helping strengthen his campaign against hunger, primarily through his Cruzada Nacional Contra el Hambre (National Crusade against Hunger) federal program. Through this program, he worked closely with Nestlé to provide nutritious cookies and snacks for the poor (Gómez 2019a). But for many, this partnership violated international agreements put forth by the United Nations regarding the avoidance of conflict of interest in public health policy, as well as supporting companies, such as Nestlé, that provided breastfeeding substitute formulas (Baby Milk Action 2013). Activists also critiqued Peña Nieto for partnering with an industry that was simultaneously contributing to malnutrition through its products (Baby Milk Action 2013; see also Lakhani, 2013). Despite these accusations, Peña Nieto remained supportive of Nestlé's operations. In fact, in October 2016, he attended the inauguration ceremony of a Nestlé plant, which claimed to focus on producing healthy children's food, in the state of Jalisco (Agencia EFE 2016). In the process, he publicly reaffirmed his support for the Swedish company. At the same time, Peña Nieto hired PepsiCo to provide milk products for his Cruzada Nacional Contra el Hambre program (Gómez 2019a), and during the World Economic Forum meeting held in Davos, Switzerland, in January 2014, Peña Nieto met with then PepsiCo CEO, Indra Nooyi, to welcome her company's new investment of US$5 million into local Mexican communities, commenting that this investment displayed the confidence that companies have in Mexico's economy (Olson 2014). Finally, in a move that surprised many, to further reinforce his support for big soda, one day Peña Nieto publicly stated his support for Coca-Cola by claiming that he drinks Coca-Cola Light every day (Tourliere 2016).

Andrés Manuel López (aka Amlo) (MORENA, 2018–present) entered office with a mandate to improve Mexico's public health situation. To date, however, he has remained rather silent on polices to combat childhood obesity and type 2 diabetes. And surprisingly, this has occurred despite lobbyists from major junk food companies such as Coca-Cola FEMSA, PepsiCo,

Lana, Bimbo, Danone, Nestlé, and Sigma recently calling a meeting with Amlo to discuss the economic and employment costs of front-of-package (GDA) labeling and the soda tax (Maldonado 2019). While Amlo has voiced his commitment to working closely with activists and NGOs to address the issue, something that prior administrations were never committed to, he has yet to organize the OMENT and ensure that non-industry-affiliated NGOs and activists are fairly represented within it. Moreover, he has yet to propose any legislation suggesting a change in the government's approach to working with junk food companies.

But why were presidents before Amlo so insistent in working closely with junk food companies? This is rather puzzling when one considers the government's gradual increase in attention and commitment to tackling NCDs, particularly obesity and type 2 diabetes, among their most vulnerable populations. Several reasons emerge. First, these presidents were firmly committed to safeguarding and strengthening the government's historic commitment to protecting politically important agricultural sectors, such as sugarcane. Mexico indeed has a long history of state-run partnerships in the area of sugarcane production (Aguilar-Rivera et al. 2012). And, as mentioned earlier, politically, these presidents were dependent on agriculture continuing to thrive and prosper, viewing the latter's partnership with junk food companies as helping ensure this process (Gómez 2019a). Presidents therefore had an incentive to support these companies. Second, these companies were also important for ensuring that presidents could meet alternative social policy objectives. With a growing presence in the countryside and a sophisticated process of locating and advertising to the poor, ambitious presidents such as Enrique Peña Nieto depended on these companies to work with the government to effectively distribute food to combat hunger (Gómez 2019a).

The Rise and Influence of Civic Activism

The rise and influence of the activist community in response to NCDs was slow to develop in Mexico. In large part, this happened for two primary reasons. First, the long history of centralized political rule and the limited opportunities that civil society had to get involved in the health policy–making process (Gonzalez-Rossetti 2001). This, in turn, engendered a historic expectation on the part of the government that activists, as well as individuals in other sectors, such as labor unions, would not be included or even consulted during the health policy–making process. Second, with the exception, perhaps, of the scientific community, public awareness and concern about overweight and obesity issues, particularly as they relate to the consumption of junk food, was minimal for many years. Nevertheless, as the public became increasingly aware of these issues, seeing obesity and type 2 diabetes touching the lives of Mexico's most vulnerable populations (especially children), families, activists, and the broader public became increasingly concerned and began to demand policy change. This helped to kindle the emergence of several leading activist groups and NGOs who have been instrumental in addressing policy needs in recent years.

Some of the key NGOs leading these processes have included organizations such as El Poder del Consumidor and Contra Peso. Organized by passionate activists and researchers, these organizations have led the charge in increasing public awareness of myriad nutrition issues, releasing countless reports and news testimonies, and hosting conferences. These organizations have also been highly proactive in pressuring the government to create policies that address these nutritional issues, ranging from the soda tax to food labeling. Indeed, one can argue that the introduction of the new front-of-package warning labels, which features excess warning signs on the high level of sugar, salt, and fat (saturated and trans fats) within a black octagon, is attributed to these organizations, as well as other university researchers' and activists' unrelenting pressures for improvements to these labels. Effective October 1, 2020, these labels have replaced the previously mentioned GDA labels (White and Barquera 2020). A shift in political context may have also helped to make this regulation possible. Indeed, some claim that the transition to Amlo's leftist government and his anti-corruption electoral campaign, when combined with strong, internationally supported activist networks and NGOs that held politicians accountable and emphasized transparency in conflicts of interests between government and industry while also using aggressive social media and public awareness campaigns, provided a propitious context for the emergence of these new warning labels (White and Barquera 2020).

The recent success of these NGOs has certainly contributed to a broader belief in Mexico that civil society can have a positive impact on NCD regulatory policy. Success has led to inspiration, further movement, and commitment to working with other activists, the scientific community, and even select government officials in striving to introduce more regulatory policy measures, helping place Mexico on the path to success.

Conclusion

A product of its face-paced economic growth, Mexico has seen in recent years the burgeoning of foreign direct investment and the thriving of junk food companies. Within the past two to three decades, Mexico experienced a rapid nutrition transition, where traditional food staples have been replaced with easily accessible, high-calorie foods. In this context, obesity and type 2 diabetes cases have burgeoned. And unfortunately, Mexico's most vulnerable populations, such as children and the poor, have borne the brunt of these ailments.

The federal government was slow to respond. National prevention programs emphasizing communication and awareness about good diet, nutrition, and exercise were first introduced through the aforementioned PrevemIMSS program. Impressively, a soda and snack food tax was created in 2014, making Mexico the first in the developing world to achieve this. And yet, introducing effective regulatory policies focusing on the marketing and sale of junk foods still has not been attained. Furthermore, efforts to limit the sale of such foods in schools and to improve access to nutritious meals have been undermined. And for many years, food labels were also highly inadequate.

Why did this happen? Why, in a context where the government has been vocal about its commitment to preventing NCDs; why, in a context of being a global trendsetter in soda and junk food taxation; and why, in this impressively laudable prevention policy context has the government been unwilling to be equally as committed and successful in effectively regulating junk food companies?

As the IPCI analytical framework explains, in a context of "fear and opportunity," a puzzling challenge has emerged due to junk food companies' political, institutional, and civil societal engagement. In addition to engaging in strategic policy partnerships with the Ministry of Health to help address obesity (especially among children), lobbying and largesse, companies have also strategically infiltrated national bureaucratic committees to ensure that their policy views are secured within government. At the same time, these companies have engaged in various corporate social responsibility initiatives, providing several programs that add to their social credibility and influence. All of these endeavors smack of companies that, in essence, have become highly political, strategic, and influential.

And yet, as the IPCI analytical framework emphasizes, companies are not the only ones responsible. Government is also a major culprit. Mexico's recent presidents have reached out to companies, using them to achieve these politicians' alternative policy and political objectives. IPCI's emphasis on the presence of complementary institutions highlights this dynamic nicely. As seen in recent years, Mexico's powerful and charismatic presidents have strategically viewed these companies as partners that can help them achieve their alternative economic and even social welfare objectives. These presidential endeavors have in the process indirectly supported companies' political tactics, in turn facilitating their efforts to undermine NCD policies to the detriment of the health of children and the poor.

APPENDIX
Mexico: Summary of Chapter Findings

Political Action	Restructuring Society	Complementary Institutions	Regulatory Policy Failure and Absence
Policy partnership Coca-Cola and Secretary of Education (SoE) Ponte al 100 program to increase exercise in schools, reduce obesity PepsiCo and SoE Vida Saludable Esquela program to increase exercise in schools, reduce obesity	*Corporate social responsibility* Nestlé–Mi Dulce Negocio program (community employment) to help families and empower women	President Vicente Fox's preexisting relationship with Coca-Cola indirectly facilitated company's ongoing policy influence President Felipe Calderón's partnership with PepsiCo and Nestlé provides recognition and influence to industry President Enrique Peña Nieto's partnership with PepsiCo and Nestlé to help eradicate hunger provides legitimacy and industry influence	Obstruction of national recommendations for drink consumption Absence of effective National Agreement for Healthy Nutrition (ANSA) enforcement of dietary guidelines at the school level Delayed improvement to front-of-package labeling (GDA)

(*continued*)

Political Action	Restructuring Society	Complementary Institutions	Regulatory Policy Failure and Absence
Lobbying and largesse	*Partnering with society*		
Industry donations to political campaigns	Industry support for foundations that provide research support (e.g., ConMéxico)		
Soda industry and interest group lobbying (e.g., CNIAA, or Cámara Nacional de las Industrias Azucarera y Alcoholera) to influence soda tax policy	Industry (e.g., Coca-Cola) partnership with NGOs (e.g., MOVISA) to promote healthy lifestyles		
Institutional infiltration	*Dividing society*		
Industry presence within OMENT (Mexican observatory for NCDs) policy monitoring and advising committee	Industry collaboration with NGOs and allied NGOs' unwillingness to partner with other NGOs defending public health interests (e.g., El Poder del Consumidor, ContraPeso)		
	Lack of unity in civil society and absence of strong collective pressures for policy reform		

4

Brazil

Similar to what we saw in Mexico, Brazil, home to the largest democracy and free market in the Americas, has in recent years seen a burgeoning growth of noncommunicable diseases due to free market reforms and an increase in international trade. NCDs closely associated with the consumption of junk foods, such as type 2 diabetes, obesity, and cancer, have not only increased in general but even more so among Brazil's most vulnerable populations: children and the poor. As an aspiring middle-income country and member of the BRICS (Brazil, Russia, India, China, and South Africa) emerging powers group, for several years Brazil's leaders had strong geopolitical and domestic incentives to aggressively tackle these NCDs, revealing not only their capacity to do so but also their unwavering commitment to human rights in health (Gómez 2018). At the same time, the Ministry of Health's (MoH) ongoing excellence in providing timely epidemiological evidence generated further interest within government. Since the early 1990s, impressively, this context led to a host of innovative public health programs, with a focus on the prevention, early detection, and treatment of these ailments. When it came to children, when compared to other countries Brazil was perhaps the earliest responder to obesity, building on a rich tradition of ensuring children's health through the availability of nutritious foods. All of these prevention programs have revealed the government's steadfast dedication to combating these NCDs.

However, when it came to regulating those junk food industries that are, in large part, responsible for the rise of NCDs, the government's track record has not been as impressive, to say the least. While efforts have been made to restrict the marketing and sale of industry products, no concrete legislation has ever been adopted. Moreover, those limited policies that do exist are never enforced, either by monitoring policy implementation or through the imposition of penalties and fines. Instead, the government has stepped back and allowed these industries to engage in self-regulatory practices. Furthermore, fiscal policies aimed at discouraging the consumption of their products, such as a soda tax, have yet to emerge. In short, and like what we saw in Mexico (though arguably to a worse extent), the government still has not been committed to aggressively regulating these industries and getting to the root of the problem. That is, limiting these industries' ability to market and sell their products to Brazil's most vulnerable populations. What is puzzling, however, is that for a government that was at the forefront of obesity and type 2 diabetes prevention, introducing innovative federal programs and receiving international acclaim (Gómez 2015), why has the government been unwilling to engage in effective regulatory practices?

Like we saw in Mexico, junk food industries have worked hard to establish strong alliances within government and society, notwithstanding their pernicious policy and social consequences. As IPCI emphasizes, within government, companies such as Nestlé and PepsiCo have worked closely with government officials to create innovative prevention programs targeting children and the poor, in turn giving the impression that these companies are a critical solution to Brazil's NCD problem, especially among children. These efforts have dovetailed with very aggressive and successful industry lobbying activities, as well as the provision of largesse, mainly via campaign contributions. At the same time, however, these industries have established a strong support base within society, both by working closely with academic researchers and supportive NGOs, and also by providing lucrative employment opportunities for the poor. However, and as seen in Mexico, these industries' social alliance–building strategies has generated divisions within society, ultimately undermining society's ability to successfully mobilize and pressure the government to regulate these industries. More recently, however, activists and NGOs have become increasingly influential at highlighting these problems, mobilizing and pressuring the government, notwithstanding their ongoing lack of access to key policy makers and an increasingly apathetic government.

And yet, political context and institutions have also mattered. Indeed, IPCI underscores that industry political and social strategies, on their own, are insufficient for explaining Brazil's lackluster regulatory outcomes. The support of influential presidents and institutions also matters—or what IPCI refers to as complementary institutions. Complementary institutions have led to two dynamics. First, as seen in Mexico, Brazil's industries have benefited from influential presidents who saw these industries as not only contributing to economic growth and employment but, more importantly, helping presidents implement popular anti-poverty and hunger programs. And second, presidents have also built institutions to ensure that this policy partnership continues and strengthens. More recently, a radical change in government has led to the election of more conservative presidents who are not as concerned about anti-poverty and welfare programs; instead, they are worried about safeguarding companies' contributions to rejuvenating employment and economic growth.

The Rise of Brazil's Junk Food Industry

The emergence of Brazil's thriving junk food industry was in large part the product of economic structural changes that began in the early 1990s, in tandem with the transition back to democracy in 1986. As the new conservative-leaning, democratic governments took office, efforts were made to gradually liberalize the market, which entailed the privatization of industries and increased international trade and foreign direct investment. Nevertheless, a high level of corruption and political instability, particularly under the Fernando Collor administration (1990–1992), discouraged further foreign direct investment and international bank lending. Eventually, economic stability, an increased domestic demand for food products, access to cheap food inputs (e.g., sugarcane), fiscal incentives, and low labor costs further incentivized foreign direct investment in this sector (Farina and Viegas 2003). Through direct investments and mergers and acquisitions, with the food and beverage sector seeing the largest of these mergers and acquisitions (Farina and Viegas 2003), these investments also reflected an increase in foreign investor confidence, as the Real program succeeded in stabilizing inflation, decreasing public sector spending, and all the while providing more investment opportunities. Furthermore, during this period there was the development of a thriving middle-income class with higher salaries, increased access to credit, and an insatiable demand for new consumer products (including foods). This further incentivized foreign and domestic investments into the food and beverage industry (Farina and Viegas 2003). Despite market reforms during this time, the government also main-

tained its historic role of supporting agricultural and food production industries, mainly by providing subsidies and tax benefits.

On January 1, 1995, the Mercosur free trade agreement, signed between
Brazil, Argentina, Paraguay, and Uruguay, substantially reduced tariffs on
the import of foods, in turn facilitating food production while further entic-
ing investment into these industries. These industries also viewed Brazil as
a strategic area in the southern Western Hemisphere to situate their company headquarters (Farina and Viegas 2003). By 2000, Farina and Viegas
further claim that by 2000 eight out of ten of Brazil's largest food companies were international multinational corporations; this number increased
from just five companies in 1994. Moreover, in 1996 and 1997, approximately
80 percent of multinationals that engaged in domestic acquisitions were
foreign-owned, hailing mainly from the United States, Argentina, and Italy
(2003, 6).

During the 1990s, a substantial rise in income and spending among the
poor created a context favorable for ongoing investment in the food and
beverage sector. Due to increased economic growth and stabilization, the
poor's disposable income increased by the mid-1990s. Monthly incomes for
the poor, the poorest 20 percent, nearly doubled during this period, and because of this the poor benefited from lower food prices (Farina 2001). Farina
asserts that, "for an average 30% increase in real incomes, frozen food, yo-
gurt, dairy desserts, and *petit suisse* cheese demand grew more than 80%;
processed meats, juices, and vegetables grew more than 30%" (2001, 324).
Later, under the Luiz Inácio "Lula" da Silva presidential administration
(2002–2010), the poor's disposable income further increased through Lula's
provision of the Bolsa Familia anti-poverty cash transfer program. Some
researchers believe that the increased consumption of processed and ultraprocessed foods among the poor may be related to the poor's rise in monthly
income from cash transfer programs (Sperandio et al. 2017). This context
certainly appears to provide even further opportunity and incentive for junk
food industries to invest in Brazil.

Because of Brazil's thriving economic performance during the first few
years of the twenty-first century, low cost for food production, government
financial support, and increased consumer demand, the country began to
receive international notoriety for its investment prospects. By 2011, the
World Investment Prospects Survey 2009–2011 revealed that "Brazil was
ranked the fourth most attractive destination country for FDI [foreign di-

rect investment], after China, the US and India" (Doctor 2010, 6). According to Doctor (2010), Brazil went from having 165 transnational corporations in 2005 to 226 by 2008, some of which were food industries, such as the meat processors JBS and Sadia-Perdigão, as well as Ambev (Americas' Beverage Company). There were approximately 49,000 food processing industries in Brazil in 2017, and they had approximately US$198 billion in total sales that year (Fonseca 2018). The food sector alone accounted for "81 percent and beverages 19 percent of total sales" (2). What's more, the food sector comprised "10 percent of the country's GDP and employ[ed] 1.6 million workers" (2). In 2016, the largest food producers were JBS (producers of meat), AmBev (soft drinks and beer), Bunge Alimentos (soybean), and BRF (meat) (Fonseca and Nascimento 2018).

During this period, foreign and domestic investment into the distribution of junk foods also increased. In response to heightened consumer demand (each day, approximately one in ten Brazilians eat in fast food establishments [Arjun 2013]), both large supermarkets and smaller local supermarkets have emerged (Farina 2001). Despite the more recent economic recession, because cheaper junk food products are more affordable, investing in the distribution of these foods has been an ongoing business attraction. According to the Brazilian millionaire Carlos Wizard Martins, who owns a host of fast food franchises such as KFC and Pizza Hut, "even in times of recession, the fast food industry grows at a rate of ten percent a year" (quoted in Alves 2018, 1). Junk food is a sure investment. Freitas Jr. quotes Leticia Menegon, a professor of business at the Superior School of Advertising and Marketing, who in 2019 claimed that throughout Brazil's economic crisis, "fast-food chains were the only ones that didn't suffer." With fast food chains comprising only 10 percent of the restaurant market in Brazil, there is certainly more room for growth—compare this to 60 percent in the United States (Freitas Jr. 2019, 1). According to Phillips (2016), between 2008 and 2013, the market value for Brazil's fast food market increased by 82 percent; moreover, he claims that the number of fast food restaurants increased by 11 percent, despite the presence of an economic recession in 2015.

In recent years, despite a slight decrease in 2019 due to the economic recession (Euromonitor International 2020a), the number of convenience stores and supermarkets has increased, reflecting consumer desires to find quicker, more affordable meals, often due to busier work schedules. The number of "self-service" stores has increased from an estimated 37,500 in

1994 to 84,500 in 2015 (FGV Projectos 2016). The French-owned company Carrefour, for example, has one of the most popular convenience store chains, Carrefour Express, and plans to further expand throughout the nation (Slattery and Mello 2018). In contrast to what we saw in Mexico with OXXO, however, there is no dominant local convenience store in Brazil. Brazilians instead shop at a myriad of small convenience stores peppered throughout their city, often selecting privately owned stores and bakeries. Analysts indeed claim that on average, 34 percent of Brazilians shop at bakeries (Euphrasio 2017), and many frequent privately owned corner cafés, such as the popular Sabor da Roça in Rio's favelas.

Similar patterns can be seen at commercial fast food restaurants. Bob's, a popular Brazilian franchise that primarily sells hamburgers, continues to thrive and has even started investing in other countries (Violent Capitalist 2010). Other, smaller independent burger restaurants comprise approximately 386,000 stores (Kharpal 2013). These alternatives burger establishments have challenged popular foreign multinational companies such as McDonald's, which has 1,308 stores in the country (Kharpal 2013). The number of Burger King chains has also increased (mainly in urban centers), further constraining McDonald's growth (Freitas Jr. 2019). KFC and its special "carnival box"—comprised of chicken with "extra chili mayonnaise and barbecue dip"—is an ongoing delight (BBC 2014, 1). Other fast food chains, such as the American franchise Subway, which on the surface appears to offer relatively healthier meals (though most meals contain processed meat and are high in calories), have also grown. In fact, Subway has the most stores of its kind in Brazil, with approximately 1,871 stores as of 2014 (Picasso 2015). Subway sells popular items such as the "Barato do Dia," which roughly translates to "sub of the day," as well as its "super cheap" "Baratissimo" sandwiches (1). Finally, major retail stores, such as Walmart, flourished during Brazil's economic boom (notwithstanding US corporate ownership's recent decrease in its share of Walmart Brazil stocks, down to 20 percent due to a stagnant economy [Bose and Bautzer 2018]).

With respect to the soft drink industry, the market is dominated by a handful of companies. As is the case in Mexico, Coca-Cola is the largest producer and distributor of soft drinks (producing Coke, Fanta, Sprite, and Kuat) in Brazil, with approximately 62 percent of the market value share. AmBev, which produces Pepsi, Guaraná Antarctica, H2Oh!, and Soda Limonada, has a market value share of 21 percent, followed by Brasil Kirin, which produces

Itubaína and Guaraná and has a market value share of 4 percent (Utsumi 2014, 1). There are also a host of smaller soda companies, lower in price, that mainly target the poor, such as Dolly, Convenção, Refrix, Xamego, and Cotuba (1). The sale of energy drinks has also blossomed. Red Bull owns the lion's share of the market at 50 percent, followed by Coca-Cola, which produces the drinks Gladiator and Burn (Geromel 2012). Other companies include Monster and TNT (Geromel 2012).

The production and sale of junk foods is also mainly owned by select major companies. Multinational corporations such as Nestlé, General Mills, Kellogg's, and Mondelez International are some of the largest snack and processed food companies in Brazil and are exhibiting ongoing growth (Alpert 2017; Heneghan 2016; MarketResearch.com 2022; Nestlé 2021). Other, smaller Brazilian-owned companies, such as Dori Alimentos, are also key players and have grown over the years, extending to more than sixty countries (Schroeder 2016). The Brazilian companies Grano, Bernas, Peccin, Ebare, Marilan, Emex, Garoto, and Jazam also plan to expand to other countries (Confectionery Production 2019, 1).

When taken together, considering the junk food industry's ongoing success and expansion, even in a context of economic recession, these industries have emerged as powerful economic, and thus political, forces. As we will soon see, this industry's growing importance has facilitated its ability to reshape politics and civil society in its favor.

NCD Growth and Vulnerable Populations

Within the past three to four decades, Brazil's epidemics of obesity and type 2 diabetes arose in tandem with the thriving junk food industry. While the consumption of these foods is one of many potential factors contributing to these ailments (others include sedentary lifestyles, stress, lack of exercise, and challenging socioeconomic environments), recent studies in Brazil nevertheless suggest a strong correlation between these NCDs and the consumption of junk foods (Monteiro and da Costa Louzada, n.d.). Research by Monteiro and da Costa Louzada discusses studies claiming that in recent years the consumption of raw, minimally processed foods, such as fruits, vegetables, *moquecas* with onions, tomatoes, and chicken (Gomes 2015), has declined while the consumption of ultraprocessed foods and sweetened beverages has increased, in turn contributing to rising overweight cases (see also Block et al. 2017). Recent studies have found that in the Amer-

Brazil: prevalence (%) of obesity among adults. *Source*: WHO, 2021. https://www
.who.int/data/gho/data/indicators/indicator-details/GHO/prevalence-of
-obesity-among-adults-bmi-=-30-(crude-estimate)-(-)

icas, Brazil is second only to the United States with respect to the per capita
consumption of sugar (600 kcal/day) (Block et al. 2017, 281). Globally, recent
WHO estimates put Brazil fourth overall in the global consumption of sugar,
estimated at twelve million tons per year and lagging behind the European
Union, China, and India (Bassette 2019, 1). What's more, Brazilians are grav-
itating toward eating more foods outside of the home. According to findings
from national surveys conducted in Brazil, from 2002 to 2008, the average
calories consumed outside the home increased from 24 to 31 percent, with
most of this food including fast foods, sodas, and sweet and fried foods
(Andrade et al. 2018, 2).

Obesity and type 2 diabetes are now major—indeed, worsening—public
health epidemics in Brazil. The total prevalence of overweight individuals
(measured using an age-standardized estimate percentage) increased from
31.1 percent in 1980 to 56.5 percent in 2016, while the number of obese increased from 6.6 percent in 1980 to 22.1 percent in 2016 (WHO 2021). According to Block and colleagues, from 1974 to 2009, the percentage of the
incidence of overweight increased from 18.5 percent to 50.1 percent for men
and from 28.7 percent to 48 percent for women (2017, 275). By 2014, Brazil,
along with Mexico, the United States, China, Germany, and several other
countries, comprised more than half of the world's obese population (BBC
2018). Additionally, medical scientists in Brazil had claimed that by 2020,
Brazil will join the United States and Mexico in having the highest preva-

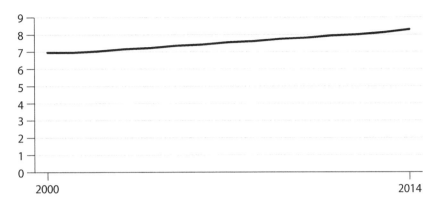

Brazil: prevalence (%) of adult diabetes. *Source*: WHO, 2021. https://www.who
.int/data/gho/data/indicators/indicator-details/GHO/raised-fasting-blood
-glucose-(-=7-0-mmol-l-or-on-medication)(age-standardized-estimate)

lence of obesity in the Americas—with roughly 35 percent of its population
being overweight (Allison 2018, 1). The number of type 2 diabetics has also
surged. According to Duncan and others, from 1990 to 2015, the number of
diabetic cases increased from 3.6 percent to 6.1 percent throughout the country (2017, 1).

Obesity, type 2 diabetes, and their related health ailments have also contributed greatly to the overall burden of disease. According to the Institute
for Health Metrics and Evaluation, those NCDs contributing most to deaths
in 2019 included ischemic heart disease (ranked first), followed by stroke,
lower respiratory infections, and diabetes ranked in sixth place. Moreover,
the greatest risk factors for death and disability in 2019 were high body mass
index (BMI) (first), followed by high blood pressure and then tobacco consumption (Institute for Health Metrics and Evaluation 2020). In 2016, for
women, the top four contributors to DALY (disability-adjusted life year) risk
factors included high BMI, high blood pressure, dietary risks, and high fasting plasma glucose; for men, alcohol and drug use posed the biggest risk
factors, followed by high systolic blood pressure, dietary risk, high BMI, tobacco use, and high fasting plasma glucose (Marinho et al. 2018). From 1990
to 2015, DALYs related specifically to type 2 diabetes increased by 118.6 percent (Duncan et al. 2017, 1). According to the WHO, in 2014, the number of
deaths from ailments associated with obesity was strikingly high. In fact,
that year, the largest contributor to death was cardiovascular disease (esti-

mated to be 46.2 per 100,000), followed by acute myocardial infarction (39.7 per 100,000), pneumonia (31.8 per 100,000), and diabetes (26.7 per 100,000) (WHO 2016).

While obesity and type 2 diabetes has affected all socioeconomic groups, they have become increasing prevalent among Brazil's most vulnerable populations. As Fradkin and colleagues (2018) note, several recent national and regional surveys reveal that overweight and obesity rates are increasing among children and adolescents across all socioeconomic levels, with the highest overweight and obesity levels among children in the high socioeconomic status bracket in the south of Brazil. "According to the Instituto Brasileiro de Geografia e Estatística (IBGE) . . . obesity among Brazilian adolescents has increased by fourteen times for males and almost six times for females" within the past four decades (1). Still others claim that childhood obesity has "increased by 600% over the past forty years" (Fradkin and Yunes 2014, 117). In Brazil, obesity rates among children and adolescents have increased over time, with the highest rate found among 5-to-9-year-olds (WHO 2020). As a product of increased consumption of ultraprocessed foods, sugary beverages, lack of adequate exercise, and poor parental understanding of obesity risk factors, most childhood obesity cases have been located in urban areas and in the more affluent southern region (Fradkin et al. 2018; Leme et al. 2019; Sentalin et al. 2019). Recent surveys have also shown that the consumption of soft drinks and sweet foods, while increasing among all ages, has nevertheless been higher for younger age groups: 18-to-24-year-olds regularly consumed 35.5 percent soft drinks and artificial juice, versus 28.2 percent for those aged 25 to 39 years, and 19.2 percent for those aged 40–59 (Claro et al. 2015, 4). And with respect to the consumption of sweets, those between the ages of 18 and 24 saw 32 percent consumption, versus 22.5 percent for 25-to-39-year-olds and 18.5 percent for 40-to-59-year-olds (4). Other studies suggest that schools that sell ultraprocessed foods, as opposed to schools participating in the PNAE (National School Feeding Program), which provides nutritious meals for free, have seen a higher probability that these products are consumed (Noll et al. 2019). Furthermore, a recent study of 124 municipalities across Brazil revealed "that there are food outlets or cafeterias inside or near schools in 58.6 percent and 47.7 percent of public and private schools, respectively" (3).

Nutrition scientists and epidemiologists in Brazil have also recently claimed that obesity and type 2 diabetes has surged among the poor (Block

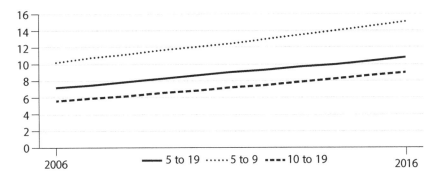

Brazil: prevalence (%) of childhood obesity (ages 5–19). *Source*: WHO, 2021.
https://www.who.int/data/gho/data/indicators/indicator-details/GHO/preva
lence-of-obesity-among-children-and-adolescents-bmi-2-standard-deviations
-above-the-median-(crude-estimate)-(-)

et al. 2017; Malta et al. 2011; Phillips 2016). In Brazil, the incidence of these
NCDs among the poor has been prominent within congested urban centers,
where poor neighborhoods often lack access to grocery stores and shops
selling healthier, unprocessed foods, fruits, and vegetables—commonly referred to as "food desserts" (Borges et al. 2018). For example, surveys conducted within cities in Brazil in 2010, such as in the municipality of Pau da
Lima (located in the state of Salvador) in the northeast, revealed that poor
slum (favela) neighborhoods had a higher prevalence of overweight/obesity
(46.5 percent) and type 2 diabetes (10.1 percent) versus 5.2 percent for diabetics and 40.6 percent for overweight/obese in Salvador's general public
(Snyder et al. 2017, 1). In general, these ailments have increasingly affected
poor families. These families have also seen an increase in disposable income
through anti-poverty programs, such as Bolsa Familia, and have purchased
high-calorie processed foods with the majority of their monthly allowances
from this program (Freitas et al. 2014). With additional income, the poor
appear to have had more of an interest in consuming foods that were previously inaccessible to them, such as fast food (e.g., Bob's). Indeed, according to Veronica Cabral, a low-income resident from Rio struggling with her
weight who was interviewed by Dom Phillips of the *Washington Post* in 2016:
"Everything we could not do in childhood we did as adults. . . . Eat what you
want. You go to the mall, you go to McDonald's, you go to Bob's" (quoted in
Phillips 2016, 1).

Policy Response

However, and like what we saw in Mexico, Brazil's government was initially delayed in recognizing the linkages between junk food consumption and NCDs, as well as their effects on children and the poor. In large part, this stemmed from the government's focus during the military dictatorship (1964–1986) and the preceding conservative democratic presidential administrations of Fernando Collor de Mello (1990–1992) and Itamar Franco (1992–1994) on economic growth via industrial development, foreign direct investment, and international trade. Moreover, public health policies, in general, received scant government attention, mainly reflecting government efforts to reduce public sector spending and stabilize the economy (Almeida et al. 2000). Building on a long tradition of state-led industrialization through the provision of subsidies and tax benefits for select industries, the goal during this period was to nurture agricultural, food, and other major industries such as automobiles and airlines, with an eye toward accelerated economic growth. In addition, Ray and Schaffer (2013) discuss a study claiming that the government invested approximately US$2.5 billion in yearly direct and indirect financial support in development of Brazil's sugar industry, which is also a large source of export revenue and a major international supplier of sugar (1). In addition to providing a strong political support base, sugarcane not only provided a lucrative form of revenue through export, but over time it provided an invaluable source of energy through the production of ethanol. Ethanol, which was required by federal law to be blended with petroleum as an alternative fuel source, was pursued by the government because of fears of being overly dependent on international sources of fuel throughout the 1970s (Chatenay 2013). With the automobile industry thriving, and with most car producers designing engines that could run on ethanol or gas, farmers, the general public, and the government appeared to benefit from the burgeoning sugarcane and ethanol industry. For industrial and economic development purposes, then, Brazil's government had, for many years, a good reason to overlook the public health consequences of its thriving junk food industries.

At the same time, when it came to public health, much of the government's focus during the latter part of the twentieth century was on how to reduce poverty and malnutrition. Since the 1970s, through national conferences cosponsored with nutrition scientists and activists, the MoH was focused on how to ensure food security, decrease malnutrition (especially among children), and guarantee access to nutritious food as a human right (Aranha et al. 2009). Consequently, responding to obesity and type 2 diabetes during the 1980s and 1990s was not a government priority; these diseases were perceived more as "diseases of luxury" and therefore relegated to the more affluent socioeconomic classes (Gómez 2018).

The Office of the President, Congress, and much of the MoH did not begin to address the rising obesity and type 2 diabetes situation until the first few years of the twenty-first century. While the MoH had for several years been reporting to the government the rise of these and other related NCDs, in order to increase government commitment to addressing obesity and improvements to nutritional diets it took the reporting of national surveys to raise attention, while, in a context of resistant politicians, Rocha and colleagues (2016) claimed that "government institutions and other stakeholders used their funding, influence, and coalition allies to pursue new policy objectives related to preventing obesity and promoting healthful diets" (1). As Gómez (2018) explains, an important motivational force during this period was Brazil's concern for its international reputation as a government neglecting these diseases, joining the United States in having the embarrassing reputation of being an unfit, obese nation (keep in mind that during this period Brazil was also in the process of hosting the Olympic Games). In the face of international criticism, the government sought to maintain its international reputation for being a nation committed to eradicating disease, a reputation first established through the government's successful fight against HIV/AIDS and grounded in the principles of universal access to health care as a human right and establishing a healthy, thriving society (Gómez 2018).

Prevention First, Regulation Second

When the government finally decided to respond to obesity and type 2 diabetes, the primary focus was on implementing prevention programs, mainly by increasing awareness, monitoring cases, and educating families. The first major federal program to emerge along these lines was the Política Nacional de Alimentação (PNAN, National Policy of Nutrition). Created in 1999, PNAN was a prevention program focused on increasing awareness about obesity, diabetes, and other NCDs. In general, the program emphasized the "protection and support of eating practices and lifestyles conducive to optimum nutritional and health status for all" (Monteiro et al. 2002, 111). In addition to other policies on the mandatory provision of effective processed food labeling and the regulation of nutritional health claims in products, PNAN also emphasized the provision of healthier foods in schools, such as having minimally processed and fresh foods available to students through the government's national school feeding program (Monteiro et al. 2002). PNAN also provided funding for training primary care workers within Brazil's SUS universal health care system to work with patients on avoiding NCDs (Brazil, Ministry of Health 2008).

In 2001, the MoH's first, and successful, attempt was made in requiring food labels on all processed food packages and cans. Approved on March 21, 2001, this MoH resolution mandated that all labels include information such as "calories, protein, carbohydrates, total fats, saturated fats, cholesterol, calcium, iron, sodium and dietary fibre in standardized, consumer-friendly tables" (Coitinho et al. 2002, 264; see also Block et al. 2017). Also, this label contained information on "serving sizes and percentage of recommended daily quintiles (Coitinho et al. 2002, 264). Moreover, Coitinho and colleagues note that Brazil became the first nation in the world to include on these labels "nutritionally adequate serving sizes." Subsequent success in 2003 was made in mandating, by July 2006 and extended to January 2007 at the request of industry, the reporting of trans fats on food labels (Block et al. 2017, 278). Moreover, according to Block and colleagues, this regulation required "'trans' fatty acids be listed as '"trans" fat' on a separate line under the listing of saturated fat in the nutrition label" (278). Finally, according to Figueiredo and others (2017), several other MoH and Anvisa (Brazilian Health Regulatory Agency) rules were added during this period, such as penalties and fines for failing to adjust industry products in accordance with the government's nutritional policy requirements, that industries meet the costs of ensuring these requirements (e.g., paying for the inclusion of additional nutrient ingredients to ensure compliance), and that industries maintain a commitment to "display detailed nutritional information" (2358).

In 2006, yet another attempt at regulating the junk food industry's activities came when the MoH, in partnership with the Ministry of Education, created the Inter-ministerial Ordinance 1010/2006. According to Silva and colleagues (2013), this ordinance "instituted guidelines to promote healthy eating in schools and whose priorities include: dietary and nutritional education; encouragement of the creation of school gardens; promotion of the establishment of good food handling practices at schools; the provision of food services in the school environment; restriction of the sale and advertising of foods and preparations with high levels of saturated fat, trans fat, white sugar and salt in the school environment; incentivizing fruit and vegetable consumption; and Food and Nutrition Surveillance in Schools" (S10).

In the area of childhood obesity prevention, in 2007, President Lula also issued presidential decree no. 6.286, mandating that the MoH work in partnership with the Ministry of Education to create the Programa Saúde nas Escolas (PSE, School Health Program). The PSE was focused on improving children's overall health and nutrition in schools. It accomplished this by monitoring and evaluating children's health, as well as increasing student awareness in classrooms and through media about improved nutrition and health (Brazil, Ministry of Health 2012). In addition to engaging in monitoring and evaluation of existing school nutrition programs, the PSE also ensured adequate human resource support for implementing the program in schools (Gómez 2018).

To further ensure that children were eating well in schools and avoiding obesity, in 2009, the MoH expanded on the PNAE by creating the School Feeding Law 11.947 (Peixinho 2013). Previously restricted to children in primary schools, this law expanded the provision of free school meals to all children enrolled in basic education above the age of six months (Sidaner et al. 2012). In addition, through the PNAE, the MoH provided funding to schools, which was managed by the Fundo Nacional de Desenvolvimento da Educação (FNDE, National Development Fund for Schools), to ensure that the nutritional needs of students were being met (Reis et al. 2011). Through the School Feeding Law 11.947, schools are required to use 30 percent of their funding received from the FNDE to purchase agricultural products from local farmers for school meals (Reis et al. 2011). This program reinforced the 2003 Food Acquisition Program, which promoted the purchasing of agricultural products from local farmers for schools (Sidaner et al. 2012).

Perhaps the most aggressive federal campaign to tackle obesity came in 2010 with the Plano de Ações Estratégicas para o Enfrentamento das Doenças Crônicas não Transmissíves (DCNT). The DCNT provided ten-year federal guidelines and procedures for striving to reduce premature mortality by focusing on the control of several risk factors, such as smoking, drinking, inadequate exercising, and poor diet (Block et al. 2017, 277). The DCNT's focus was therefore on preventing the rise of obesity (and other NCDs) across all socioeconomic groups. This program also entailed a substantial rise in MoH funding for obesity awareness campaigns and prevention activities (Gómez 2018).

Efforts to prevent childhood obesity were further strengthened the following year, in 2011, when the MoH created the Academia da Saúde (Academy of Health). This program provided more funding to construct physical activity areas, which are also referred to as *polos* (i.e., public areas where physical activity classes can take place), and also train local health care personnel to provide these services—which also includes counseling on healthy lifestyles. Implemented throughout four thousand cities, this program benefits both children and adults, especially in poor areas (Parra et al. 2013). In December 2011, additional funding was provided from the MoH in the amount of 108 million reais for 2,271 municipal governments that joined the PSE program in 2010 (Rosa, n.d., 1). According to Rosa, those schools receiving funds were also expected to implement the PSE's initiatives. SUS Family Health Program teams were required to monitor these activities and report them back to the MoH, which, in turn, helped to increase accountability and implementation (Gómez 2018).

In 2014, President Dilma Rousseff (2011–2016) also launched a myriad of federal programs aimed at increasing nutritional awareness and improving eating habits. Once again, the focus was on prevention via the provision of educational information and encouragement. To that end, in 2014 the MoH launched the *Guia Alimentaria para a População Brasileira* (Feeding Guide for the Brazilian Population) (Gómez 2018). The *Guia* provides a series of guidelines and recommendations to families on what types of nutritious foods to eat, such as fruits and vegetables, and the importance of home-cooked meals and how to enjoy them while encouraging healthy eating (Gómez 2018). The *Guia* also sought to communicate with the public the importance of reviving Brazil's long-lost food culture, including understanding the value of good food and viewing "eating as a sociopolitical and cultural act" (Gómez 2015, 2). What's more, in 2015, the MoH, through PNAN, created the prevention campaign Da Saúde se Cuida Todos os Dias (Healthcare Is Every Day) (Gómez 2018). This campaign helps people make smart and healthy behavioral changes while recognizing how their social context shapes this process, and that it is not entirely based on individual willpower (Brazil, Ministry of Health 2015). The following year, in 2016, Dilma took the extra step of creating the Pacto Nacional para Alimentação Saudável (National Pact for Healthy Food), which once again encouraged families to eat more healthily by focusing on the consumption of organic foods (Gómez 2018). In partnership with the junk food industries and NGOs, in 2016 the MoH also created the prevention campaign Campanha Brasil Saudável e Sustentável (Brazil Healthy and Sustainable Campaign), which sponsored a plethora of information on eating more nutritiously, focusing on individual self-reflection of eating habits, and informing individuals of their health risks (Gómez 2018). As Gómez (2018) explains, under the Lula and Dilma administrations, the Congress was fully committed to increasing funding for these programs.

Even under the more politically conservative government of Jair Bolsonaro, the MoH has focused on creating innovative obesity prevention programs, with a focus on children. In 2019, for example, the MoH, under the leadership of Minister Luiz Henrique Mandetta, launched the campanha 1,2,3 e já! (campaign 1,2,3 and now!) (Nitahara 2019). The focus of this MoH campaign is to prevent and reduce childhood obesity by encouraging children to follow three simple steps: (1) have a more active lifestyle; (2) eat more nutritious meals; and (3) refrain from spending too much time watching TV, playing video games, and operating cell phones (Nitahara 2019).

Thus, in sum, the government's primary focus has been on creating innovative obesity and type 2 diabetes prevention programs, targeting both children and the general population. In recognition of these efforts, in 2010, Brazil joined the United Kingdom in being recognized by a panel of international experts for their outstanding accomplishments in the area of obesity prevention (Gómez 2015).

Policy Challenges: The Daunting Effort to Regulate

These impressive accomplishments notwithstanding, there continues to be ongoing policy challenges, both with respect to prevention and especially the regulation of industry marketing and sales. With respect to prevention, several studies reveal the lack of effective MoH programs and the oversight of the state health department in ensuring that the aforementioned federal prevention programs targeting schools are providing nutritious foods (Andrade et al. 2018). While the PSE has incentivized state health departments to demonstrate the purchasing of fresh foods from local farmers to receive grant assistance (Gómez 2015), this has not necessarily led to the provision of healthier meals in schools. What's more, research by Sidaner and colleagues (2012) notes that federal FNDE guidelines (as the agency responsible for implementing the PNAE) for establishing new menus with healthier foods in schools still "falls short of the recommendations," despite some general improvements in the quality of menus provided (992).

Additionally, key areas of public health prevention have yet to be addressed. Despite joining Mexico and Chile as one of the three out of five countries in Latin America with the largest daily per capita sales of sugar-sweetened beverages (Popkin and Reardon 2018, 1034), no effort has been made to introduce a tax on sodas to date (Studdert et al. 2015). While a tax was recently introduced on beer, energy drinks, and fruit juices (Studdert et al. 2015), Brazil's much larger, and thriving, soda industry has been spared from this taxation effort (Baker et al. 2018; Studdert et al. 2015).

But perhaps the biggest challenge has been the lack of federal government regulatory oversight and efforts to tackle the junk food industry head-on through the imposition of effective sales and marketing regulations. While efforts to introduce food labels have been introduced, they are inadequate as well as insufficient, on their own, in squarely addressing the industry's activities and consumption patterns. Despite the government having a long tradition of overseeing and regulating food quality (e.g., exposure to hazardous chemicals, a tradition that in fact dates back to the First Republic [1889–1930]), interestingly, the government has repeatedly refrained from aggressively regulating the food industry in the area of nutritional ingredients and advertising (Figueiredo et al. 2017).

While the government did a commendable job of introducing food labeling regulations early on (in 2001), several ongoing challenges nevertheless reveal the lack of sufficient government attention and support for ensuring that these labels are effective. Indeed, in recent years nutrition scientists claim that current labels are still insufficient in providing sufficient, easy-to-understand information (Martins 2015). Surveys have revealed that consumers have difficulty understanding what they are reading on these labels, while there is often conflicting or missing information on them (Câmara et al. 2008; Martins 2015). Block and colleagues (2017) mention a study conducted by Câmara and others in 2008 that revealed that between 1997 and 2004, a total of forty-nine academic studies were published in Brazil concluding that "there were many inadequacies in food labels, mainly to nutritional information, indicating lack of enforcement over regulations" (284). Furthermore, cheap, readily accessible foods packaged in containers smaller than 100 centimeters, as well as packaged foods prepared at commercial establishments and restaurants do not require nutritional labeling (282, 284).

Efforts to improve the quality and effectiveness of food labels continues. However, it appears that the Jair Bolsonaro presidential administration (2019–present) is not committed to improving the quality of these labels. Improving food labels could be accomplished, for example, by providing more detailed information regarding nutritional food content, as well as adopting official "warning labels," which have proven to be effective in neighboring countries, such as Chile (Dillman Carpentier et al. 2020). Alternatively, Bolsonaro's minister of health at the time, Luiz Henrique Mandetta, considered adopting Italy's food labeling model, which provides "basic guideline daily amounts" (Vital Strategies 2019b, 1). Yet, recent national opinion polls and focus group interviews conducted by the Brazilian organization IDEC (Instituto Brasileiro de Defesa do Consumidor, Brazilian Institute of Consumer Protection) and the University of São Paulo reveals that this type of food labeling is "not as effective" (1).

There certainly exists sales regulations focusing on children, such as the government's school meal program, as well as the National Fund for the Development of Education (FNDE) Resolution no. 38/2009, which forbids the purchase of soft drinks with FNDE funds (Sidaner et al. 2012; Silva et al. 2013). And with respect to restrictions on the sale of unhealthy foods, Andrade and colleagues (2018) found that "the lack of a national law forbidding these foods, results in an unhealthy food environment in many Brazilian schools" (9). What this suggests is that the government's school meal program is not an "enforceable" federal law with a penalty for noncompliance. In fact, when considered from this perspective, there still is a lot of work to be done in establishing regulations that protect the public from the harmful consumption of soda products (Johns and Bortoletto 2016).

Furthermore, there have not been any serious attempts at restricting the sale of sodas near schools in private commercial establishments. In fact, research by Andrade and colleagues (2018) finds that "the sale of unhealthy foods and sugary beverages is common in commercial spaces inside or around schools, such as snack bars. These sales are associated with an increase in ultra-processed food consumption, suggesting the need for implementing laws to regulate commerce in these locations" (8). As I explain in more detail shortly, soda companies have instead engaged in a process of self-regulation—

that is, taking it upon themselves to be responsible for restricting the sale of their products in schools. And yet, Johns and Bortoletto (2016) recently found that industries often get around this dilemma when schools purchase their products through third-party vendors.

With respect to regulating the advertising and sale of junk foods to children, limited, though questionable, progress has been made. In 2006, the government created the Regulation for the Marketing of Food to Infants and Young Children (Silva et al. 2013). This effort seeks to restrict advertising and marketing toward infants and young children; this regulation includes the marketing of "baby bottles, nipples and pacifiers, in order to avoid aggressive and unethical approaches, which promote the acquisition of these products" (S10). Despite these kinds of efforts, however, activists claim that the government has not reduced the marketing of sugary, fatty, and salty foods to children (Rocha et al. 2016).

With respect to children older than 18, or adolescents, essentially no federal regulations exist to effectively control the advertisement of these products (Figueiredo et al. 2017; Kassahara and Sarti 2018). Based on an extensive literature review conducted by Kassahara and Sarti (2018), there is a need for the government to impose stern penalties for those industries that do not comply with their self-regulatory promises and that engage in unethical marketing behavior toward children and adolescents. And this has occurred in a context where, in 2010, a survey in the state of São Paulo conducted by the Alana Institute revealed that approximately 85 percent of parents claimed that this advertising influenced their children's demands for food products (Fraser 2013).

Despite the creation of the 2006 Regulation for Marketing of Foods to Infants and Young Children, the ongoing challenge is policy enforcement and industry compliance. Indeed, according to policy advocates I interviewed, regulatory policies have never been effectively enforced, mainly because of the absence of government institutions that monitor and enforce these policy regulations. What's more, in this cultural institutional context, industries use this as an excuse not to comply with the regulations. In this situation, it is far easier for industries to ignore these regulations and obtain a fine, rather than to comply (interview with Pedro Hartung, September 23, 2020).

In 2014, yet another attempt was made to restrict advertising to minors through the *Norma 163 do CONANDA* (Conselho Nacional do Director Humanos da Criança e do Adolescente), which was published in the congressional bulletin *Diário Oficial da União* (National Union Diary) (Tokarnia 2014). *Norma 163* was focused on highlighting industry's usage of children's musical soundtracks, children's characters, or gifts with junk food products (e.g., toys accompanying packaged foods), viewing these actions as abusive in their intention to persuade children into consuming certain products (Tokarnia 2014). It is important to emphasize that the *Norma 163* does not explicitly prohibit advertising to children but rather underscores the abusive action toward children and interprets this as illegal activity as determined through the interpretation of federal constitutional rules defending the rights of children, which are found in Article 227 (Henriques and Hartung 2014). Nevertheless, analysts from the Economist Intelligence Unit claim that the *Norma 163* resolution "is not properly enforced. Despite the illegality of child-targeted advertising in Brazil, children are still exposed to commercials and advertising that are aimed at them" and that "the repercussions of failing to comply with the CONANDA Resolution, however, are insufficient to dissuade companies from engaging in child-directed advertising" (Economist Intelligence Unit 2017, 4, 14).

With respect to advertising and marketing products to the general public, essentially no progress has been made. Efforts to introduce federal regulations took on a series of gradual consensus-building steps that, ultimately, amounted to nothing. First, in 2006 Anvisa took the first step in proposing the creation of advertising regulations for food products high in sugar, trans fat, saturated fat, and sodium through its publication of a formal proposal for public consultation on the issue (Jaime et al. 2013). To achieve this, shortly after the 2006 promulgation, a series of "Working Group" meetings were held to provide input into what the regulations should look like. These discussions eventually led to the creation of a final document, provided to the general public for review, and entailed approximately 254 regulations (93; Block et al. 2017). According to Jaime and colleagues (2013), in August 2009 a public hearing was held to present the new document, "with strong participation of civil society groups, members of the academic community and representatives of the food retailers, manufacturers and media marketing groups involved, and the final text was published on 15 June 2012" (93).

These efforts eventually led to the official adoption and publication of Anvisa's Resolution of the Executive Board, RDC 24/2010 (Kassahara and Sarti 2018). This resolution sought to regulate several activities, such as "the supply, advertising, marketing, information and other related practices in the commercial distribution and promotion of foods with high sugar, satu-rated fat, trans fat, and sodium content and drinks of low nutritional value" (Jaime et al. 2013, 93). The resolution also focused on ensuring adequate information in order to avoid poor and unhealthy eating habits, especially among children (Jaime et al. 2013). Moreover, this regulation sought to pub-lish consumer alerts that were highly visible through several media outlets, such as TV, internet, and printed materials. But this endeavor was suspended, mainly due to incessant pressures and strategies used by powerful industry lobbyists, as well as tactics used to enlist the federal court's support—as discussed in more detail shortly (Silva et al. 2013).

In the absence of federal regulations restricting the marketing and sale of their products to the general public, industries have instead opted to en-gage in self-regulatory practices, which are monitored by CONAR (Conselho de Autoregulamentação Publicitá, National Council of Self-Regulatory Pol-icy) (Gossett 2011; Kassahara and Sarti 2018). Created in 1980, CONAR is responsible for managing a code of ethics on food marketing strategies while closely monitoring industry compliance with this code (Gossett 2011; Kassahara and Sarti 2018). This code of ethics is focused on protecting the consumer by forbidding any false and misleading advertising (Gossett 2011). Several major food industries, such as "AmBev, Batavo, Bimbo, Danone, Mc-Donald's, Nestle, and Pepsico [sic]," have agreed to restrict the marketing and sale of their products, especially towards children, in compliance with CONAR's Code (130). While some studies reveal that CONAR has been suc-cessful in working with industries to limit advertising, without specific en-forcement mechanisms, such as penalties, in place, industry noncompliance to CONAR's code has been an ongoing problem (Kassahara and Sarti 2018).

Indeed, studies find that these industries have not followed through with their voluntary self-regulatory agreements (Gómez et al. 2011). Gonçalves (2012) discusses a study by the Child and Consumer project in 2010, stating that of the 24 companies that agreed to adopt these self-regulations, such as Ambev, Bob's, Burger King, Cadbury, Coca-Cola Brasil, Danone, Kraft, Gen-eral Mills Brasil, and Nestlé (among many others), "only 12 published their individual pledges on their websites, and only eight of them presented the nutritional criteria description used to lead marketing communication pol-icies directed to children" (5).

Nevertheless, industries insist on pursuing self-regulation when it comes to advertising their products. In 2016, eleven companies—Coca-Cola Brasil, Ferraro, Kellogg's, McDonald's, Nestlé, Unilever, PepsiCo, Mondeléz International, Mars, General Mills, and Grupo Bimbo—formed an agreement to restrict the marketing of products deemed high in fat and sugar, such as sodas and chocolates, to minors below the age of 12 (Alves 2016). These eleven companies also agreed that products should have a minimum nutritional criteria before they are eligible to be advertised to children (Alves 2016). In 2016, moreover, ABIR (Associação Brasileira das Indústrias de Refrigerantes e de Bebidas não Alcoólicas; Brazilian Association of Soft Drink Industries) announced its commitment to reduce the advertisement of its nonalcoholic products to children up to the age of 12, an endeavor that was announced and celebrated by nutrition activists from the Alana Institute (Revista ABIR 2019).

Recent analysts note that the MoH, through the aforementioned Plano de Ações Estratégicas para o Enfrentamento das Doenças Crônicas não Transmissíves, proposed a "partnership with the food industry and suggest[ed] that industry voluntarily refrain from advertising unhealthy foods" (Dias et al. 2017, 5). Instead of effectively regulating the junk food industry's ability to market and sell their products, the MoH decided to engage in what Figueiredo and colleagues (2014) refer to as "agreements and terms of commitment" with industries. Essentially, agreements and terms of commitment equates to industry "self-regulation"—that is, industries negotiating with the MoH and agreeing to improve the nutritional content of industries' food products, for example, by lowering levels of free sugars, fat, and sodium. By creating formal agreements, this appears to help establish a sense of trust, cooperation, and accountability between industry and government. This level of trust and accountability is further reinforced with these industries' willingness to be monitored by CONAR, as mentioned earlier, which holds these industries to a code of ethics in marketing activities. In 2007 and 2010, major junk food industries established formal agreements with the MoH to improve the nutritional content in their processed foods, such as reducing trans fats, iodine [salt], and sugar (Block et al. 2017), rather than Anvisa imposing federal regulatory restrictions and penalties for noncompliance. According to activist organizations in Brazil, by late 2018, the MoH entered into yet another voluntary agreement with the food industry, with the goal of reducing, by 2022, 144,000 tons of sugar in processed food products (ACT

Promoção da Saúde 2019). And yet there was concern by activists that this agreement did not include popular food products, including those that are well-liked by children.

And yet, several problems have emerged with these agreements and terms of commitment self-regulatory practices. First, in a sense, these practices have revealed the MoH's unwillingness to effectively regulate these industries while "undermining the authority of the state in its interventions to limit private sector in ways that ensure that the public interest prevails" (Figueiredo et al. 2017, 2361). Second, Figueiredo and colleagues (2017) emphasize that these agreements "create precedents for avoiding or delaying regulation and the disciplining of the reduction in the levels of key nutrients" (2362) while at the same time neglecting to include civil societal actors in these negotiated agreements with industry in the hopes of avoiding further tensions and conflict with industry's interests. And third, these negotiation processes can lead to positive externalities in industry's favor. That is, repeated negotiations open opportunities for a tit-for-tat informal bargaining process that ultimately benefits industry. By periodically providing cooperation and support for particular policies, such as food labeling, industries are then trusted as government allies in the plight against NCDs and are consequently allowed to engage in "self-regulation"—kind of an informal "You scratch my back, I'll scratch yours" kind of process.

What is puzzling about the government's repeated unwillingness to engage in aggressive regulation is that it has, for many years, proffered an ideational (normative) commitment to do so. Starting as far back as the decrees implemented during the First Republic, and more recently after the transition to democracy in 1986 and the Organic Law on Health, No. 8080/90, which regulates SUS's work on health surveillance, the government has extended its commitment to federal intervention in the name of "prevention," safeguarding the public from a variety of health and environmental threats (Figueiredo et al. 2017). In this endeavor, the government has combined its technical scientific knowledge with the law, engendering legitimacy and authority in regulatory intervention (Figueiredo et al. 2017). There is, therefore, a well-established legal precedent that the government can, and more importantly *should*, interfere in any health, economic, or physical activities that pose a serious threat to public health. And yet, despite this principle, when it comes to Brazil's thriving junk food industry, it has repeatedly failed to do so. Why?

Political Action

It is all about politics. As stipulated in IPCI, an ongoing reason for why more aggressive regulatory policies have not emerged in Brazil has to do with the strategies that junk food industries take to establish enduring political allies and support within government. An important tactic that industries pursue is partnering with government to create innovative NCD policies. In so doing, not only do these industries garner more support within government, but it also discourages health officials from pursuing more aggressive regulatory policies. On top of this, they also succeed in increasing their public image as being a solution to Brazil's ongoing obesity and type 2 diabetes problem.

For example, several industries worked closely with the MoH to create the aforementioned 2001 food labels. After the MoH drafted a regulation concerning its proposed inclusion of appropriate serving sizes on labels through periodic workshops organized by the MoH, industry representatives, with recommendations from nutrition scientists and activists, worked closely with these health officials to provide information on serving sizes for each of their products available on the market (Coitinho et al. 2002). As Coitinho and colleagues (2002) describe the situation: "It was one of the most participatory and co-operative processes involving government and the private sector ever accomplished regarding food and nutrition" (264). Through a series of workshops the food industry was able to reach a consensus about these labeling serving sizes with government, and through this participatory process the food industry "became the best [ally] in the fight against nutritionally inadequate serving sizes" (264).

Partnering with government to reformulate food products in order to improve their nutritional content has also been an important partnership strategy. In 2007, through an official technical cooperation agreement, the Brazilian Food Industry Association (ABIA, Associação Brasileira das Indústrias da Alimentação) and the MoH agreed that food industries would reduce the amount of sugar, sodium, and fat in their products (Nilson 2015). Furthermore, and as Nilson (2015) maintains, in 2008, ABIA and the MoH set a goal for reducing the amount of trans fatty acids in foods, in accordance with the Pan American Health Organization's Regional Targets; subsequent studies in 2010 revealed "that almost 95% of the food products in the Brazilian market achieved the targets, representing the exclusion of 230 tons of trans fats from foods per year" (245). The food industry, the MoH, and other stakeholders continued to work together through annual MoH seminars to explore ways to reduce and monitor the amount of sodium in foods commonly consumed (Nilson 2015). Research conducted in 2013 revealed that several industries had indeed succeeded in reducing sodium in their products (Nilson 2015). More recently, several industries have agreed to work with the MoH through a formal term of agreement to reduce 144 million tons of sugar in chocolate, cake mix, sugary drinks, cookies, and products that contain dairy by the year 2022 (Bassette 2019). However, Monteiro and Cannon (2012) suggest that these partnerships with government based on food reformulation have in the end benefited food industries more so than consumers, as they claim "the reformulation strategy of transnational corporations may have the effect of heading off legislation designed, for example, to sharply limit or prohibit the advertising and marketing of ultra-processed products to children" (3).

Junk food industries have also proactively worked with the MoH to devise new policy ideas in the areas of good nutrition, healthy eating, and an active lifestyle. In fact, in November 2007, at the first Healthy Eating Forum (Fórum da Alimentação Saudável) held in Rio de Janeiro, once again, it was agreed that a "technical cooperation agreement" be established between the MoH, Anvisa, and ABIA "to elaborate a national plan of healthy life, covering aspects of healthy eating, physical activity and nutritional education, and the gradual reduction of 'trans' and saturated fats in processed food as well as sugar and sodium" (Block et al. 2017, 278).

Large multinational industries have also worked with nonprofits and local municipal preschools to prevent obesity. In March 2017, for example, the Monsanto Fund, the philanthropic arm of the Monsanto Corporation, a major agricultural producer whose products have been used by the ultra-processed food industry, partnered with the nonprofit INMED Partnerships for Children / INMED Brasil to "improve nutrition and access to healthful food for mothers and young children in Brazil" (Monsanto Fund 2017, 1). With US$3 million in support from the Monsanto Fund over a three-year period, INMED Brasil's Crescer Saudável (Health Growing), established in 2016, planned to provide vegetable gardens for 125 preschools to increase access to healthy foods (Monsanto Fund 2017, 1). In an effort to encourage and develop permanent healthy eating habits in schools and at home, moreover, this funding will also be used to provide educational resources for pre-school teachers, mothers, and local health officials (Monsanto Fund 2017).

In yet another instance, Mondeléz International, which, as mentioned earlier, is one of the largest producers of snack foods, through its Mondeléz International Foundation entered into a public-private partnership with nonprofit organizations, as well as cooperative agreements with the Ministry of Health, Education, Agricultural, and local mayors, via the Health in Action (HIA) program (Pérez-Escamilla 2018). HIA works in partnership with the Institute of Sport and Education, as well as the nonprofit INMED Partnerships for Children and INMED Brazil, and the Mondeléz International Foundation in order to promote increased physical activities in schools; deliver school staff training on physical activity and nutrition; offer semi-annual eight-hour training sessions on health, hygiene, nutrition, gardening, healthy lifestyles, and sanitation; and provide training to community health care agents working with families. This program also provides vegetable gardens (Pérez-Escamilla 2018). Furthermore, the HIA program's governance process "includes regular meetings between INMED project coordinators in all towns and representatives from the education departments and other local government bodies to provide program updates and to plan training and other activities" (S8). The HIA program currently operates in the states of Pernambuco, São Paulo, and Paraná, "where many vulnerable children live," and has engaged with approximately one thousand schools thus far (S8).

In the end, these kinds of policy partnerships have helped to increase the political legitimacy and influence of junk food industries (interview with Pedro Hartung, September 23, 2020). According to activists I interviewed, these partnerships have helped to increase the acceptability of these industries by politicians, who engage in important partnerships and other corporate social responsibility endeavors (interview with Pedro Hartung, September 23, 2020). But these partnership activities have also increased the broader social acceptability of these industries as well, in turn helping to ignore the harmful effects of their products on the population (interview with Pedro Hartung, September 23, 2020).

Lobbying and Largesse

Yet another strategy that Brazil's junk food industries have used to manipulate policy in their favor is the traditional staple of industry political influence: lobbying. Since the government's increased commitment to tackling obesity and type 2 diabetes at the turn of the twentieth century, several industries have incessantly pressured congressional members to refrain from passing any legislation threatening their interests (Gómez 2021). Activists note that industry representatives are essentially at all major public hearings about legislation, incessantly working hard to change proposed bills in their favor (interview with Pedro Hartung, September 23, 2020). Furthermore, policy makers work with industries to develop interpersonal relationships with them (interview with Pedro Hartung, September 23, 2020). This reflects the industry's effort throughout Latin America to come together, such as through the Latin American Food and Beverage Alliance, to oppose the introduction of taxes and marketing regulations (Huber 2016). Huber (2016) instead notes that industries have been advocating for a more voluntary approach to regulation. The Grocery Manufacturers Association, now known as the Consumer Brands Association, based in the United States, has also joined the alliance (Huber 2016).

Perhaps the most powerful lobbying group influencing NCD prevention and regulatory policy is ABIA. Indeed, industries work with ABIA to influence the policy-making process (interview with Pedro Hartung, September 23, 2020). As the representative of hundreds of soft drink, alcohol, and processed food companies, ABIA, in coordination with CONAR (Conselho Nacional de Autorregulamentação Publicitária), initially lobbied the government (though at times not successful); nevertheless, with the business community it eventually pressured several areas of government into altering legislation going against industry interests, such as in the area of advertising toward children (Baird 2015). Other major soft drink industry representatives, such as ABIR, testified on behalf of the industries they represent, claiming that the consumption of their products is not the biggest risk factor contributing to obesity and diabetes. Instead, they emphasize that there are many factors contributing to obesity, such as poor diet and sedentary lifestyles, while downplaying the efficacy of a soda tax (TV Câmara, Câmara Dos Deputatos 2017).

In the area of regulatory policy, one of ABIA's most earnest lobbying efforts came when, as mentioned earlier, Anvisa first proposed new regulations restricting the industry's marketing and advertising of its products to the general public. During the drafting of proposed advertising regulations for public consultation prior to the eventual publication of Resolution (RDC)

n. 24, the business community claimed that based on Article 22 of the constitution, only the federal union had the constitutional right to draft laws on regulation (Baird 2015). Thus, based on this claim, it was the Congress, not Anvisa, that was the appropriate and constitutionally legitimate institution for drafting advertising regulations (Baird 2015). Furthermore, industry representatives referred to Article 220 of the federal constitution, which specified the items legally subject to regulation, such as alcoholic drinks, tobacco, medicine, and therapies; other products (such as food) were not on this list (Baird 2015). At the very beginning of Anvisa's discussions about its proposed regulations in 2005, ABIA and other industry delegates were represented in Anvisa's Working Group, which was a consultation forum comprised of several organizations and ministry departments used to generate a proposal for regulations. In addition, according to Baird (2015), the business community was well represented and proactive when submitting their criticisms and suggestions through Anvisa's public consultations about its proposed regulations, as were other represented members, emblematic of a truly participatory—though contentious—process. Furthermore, the food industry complained that restricting advertising through the proposed regulations was an act of government censorship, words that carried a lot of weight in a society that had experienced, until 1985, two decades of military dictatorship (Jacobs and Richtel 2017).

By the time Anvisa's Resolution RDC n. 24 was published, industry representatives, such as the Brazilian Association of Advertising Agencies, the Brazilian Association of Radio and Television Broadcasters, and CONAR, had substantial influence within the Congress and the federal courts (Baird 2015). Initiated by a process that was led by the Brazilian Association of Advertising Agencies and Brazilian Association of Radio and Television Broadcasters, congressman Milton Monti, congressional representative from the state of São Paulo (Partido da República political party), eventually submitted a draft legislative decree Projecto de Decreto Legislativo No. 2.830 (Baird 2015). This proposal sought to permanently suspend the Resolution RDC n. 24. With seemingly little resistance, this proposed decree was achieved, in turn confirming the business community's influence within Brazil's congressional walls (Baird 2015).

Furthermore, it did not help that after the adoption of Resolution RDC n. 24 a total of eleven lawsuits were levied against Anvisa from these industries, which "included the national association of biscuit manufacturers, the corn growers lobby and an alliance of chocolate, cocoa and candy companies" (Jacobs and Richtel 2017, 1). Baird (2015) further claims that the advertising community, particularly CONAR, was successful in its ability to obtain the support of the Office of the Attorney General, at the time led by president-appointed Attorney General Luís Inácio Adams (see also Jacobs and Richtel 2017). Mr. Adams supported the industry's views (Jacobs and Richtel 2017). This context eventually led to the Sixteenth Federal Court's decision to rule in favor of an injunction against Anvisa's proposed marketing restrictions until the merits of the case could be further analyzed and concluded (Baird 2015). While the Anvisa advertising ruling still exists today, it has not been used; it is essentially inactive, awaiting further analysis and consensus.

The intensive Working Group and public consultations leading up to Resolution RDC n. 24 generated a lack of trust between junk food industries and Anvisa. On the eve of a presidential election in 2010, industry representatives approached then presidential candidate Dilma Rousseff of the Partido Trabalor political campaign with a few "grievances" (Jacobs and Richtel 2017). According to the political scientist Marcello Fragano Baird, who was interviewed by Jacobs and Richtel (2017) in an article for the *New York Times*, Rousseff promised these executives that she would "clean house" within Anvisa after being elected to office (see also Baird 2015). Shortly after becoming president, Rousseff replaced Anvisa's previous director, Dirceu Raposo de Mello, with Jaime César de Moura Oliveira (Jacobs and Richtel 2017). Oliveira was "a longtime political ally and former lawyer for the Brazilian subsidiary of the food giant Unilever" (1).

The events that transpired between 2006 and 2013 revealed to the government that the food and beverage industry was indeed politically powerful and that achieving concrete regulatory measures would be extremely difficult in this context. Others note that the policy influence of industry, facilitated by its economic power and lobbyists' access to government institutions, was quite visible during the formulation of RDC n. 24, with dire consequences: "As a result, in its final draft, elements related to advertising aimed at children that had been included in the initial proposal were excluded, making it less restrictive" (Mariath and Martins 2020, 6).

In addition, regarding NCD prevention, food industries have lobbied against any proposal to introduce a tax on their sugar-sweetened beverages (Santarelli et al. 2018). In October 2017, for example, a representative of the Sociedade Brasileira de Alimentação e Nutrição (SBAN) gave a presentation at a public hearing in the Congress questioning if a soda tax was effective in achieving reductions in the sale of soda, referring to a study about Mexico (TVCâmara, Câmara Dos Deputatos 2017). One must keep in mind that SBAN is an influential NGO that has received conference sponsorship support from the ultraprocessed food and soda industries (Peres 2018a). In addition, at this congressional meeting in October 2017, a representative from ABIR also displayed data obtained from VIGETEL, showing a decline in overall soda consumption in Brazil amidst an increase in obesity, while questioning why the government is only focusing on soda consumption and not the multiple contributors to obesity (TVCâmara, Câmara Dos Deputatos 2017).

Industries have reinforced their bargaining power within government by providing largesse to congressional members. Indeed, over the years, the food industry's ability to build a strong support base within congress was facilitated by the provision of campaign contributions. In 2014, Jacobs and Richtel (2017) found that these industries donated an estimated US$158 million to several congressional members, marking "a threefold increase over 2010, according to Transparência Brasil" (1). Furthermore, a study conducted by *Transparencia* in 2016 found that "more than half of Brazil's current federal legislators had been elected with donations from the food industry— before the Supreme Court banned corporate contributions in 2015" (1). When compared to each other, the largest campaign contributor has been the meat company JBS (Jacobs and Richtel 2017). JBS provided candidates with an estimated US$112 million in 2014; the next largest contribution was from Coca-Cola, US$6.5 million, followed by McDonald's at US$561,000 (1). A study conducted by an activist for ACT, Marília Albiero, also found that JBS was the largest campaign contributor in 2014, providing approximately R$376 million reais in campaign funding (Brasíl de Fato, 2017, 1). Albiero further found that 36 percent of the congressional caucus received JBS campaign support (1). And in 2014, surveys conducted by Albiero found that the food and beverage industry had donated contributions to approximately 57 percent of congressional deputies and 48 percent of senators (1). Industries such as Coca-Cola. Schweppes, and the Mitsubishi group continue to have connections with congressional members, with the latter benefiting from this relationship (Lara 2018).

In response to vehement protest against these activities, in 2015 the Supreme Court banned future corporate donations to electoral candidates. This landmark decision arose amidst several corruption scandals, mainly having to deal with campaign contributions and the well-known Lava Jato, "Operation Car Wash," scandal in 2014 (Douglas 2016). And yet, some fear that that it will be difficult to impose this restriction, mainly due to the presence of *caixa dois* (off-the-books) bank accounts set up by political parties, as well as funneling contributions through individual donations, which are still legal (Douglas 2016).

And finally, yet another strategy complementing the junk food industries 'insider' lobbying tactics is its strategic placement of academic researchers within Anvisa that can consistently manipulate policy decisions in industry's favor; this is an instance of what IPCI refers to as institutional infiltration. This infiltration process emerges when industries clandestinely infiltrate government institutions (either directly or indirectly) to ensure that industry's policy ideas, views, and interests are represented and secured. And this is precisely what occurred through the industry and its representative interest groups' strategic usage of the Anvisa regulatory agency.

Indeed, since Anvisa's inception in 1999, and as mentioned earlier, Anvisa has created working groups to discuss any proposed regulations. Some of the academics participating in working groups are from the International Life Sciences Institute, which was founded by Coca-Cola in 1978 (Peres 2018b). In addition to having their own representation within these working groups, Peres (2018b) found that food industries have also ensured that working groups are made up of like-minded researchers (Peres 2018b). It seems that this tactic has helped give industries the majority view in certain areas within Anvisa (Peres 2018b). That is, while civil societal representatives from working groups oppose industry, and industry opposes proposed regulations, academics were often perceived as potentially tipping the scale in a particular direction (Peres 2018b). Therefore, academics within the working groups were in a position to potentially "unbalance the game," especially if an academic who is appointed shares similar views (1). In addition, after reviewing in excess of one hundred minutes of working group meetings, documents, and interviews, Peres (2018b) found that International Life Sciences Institute representatives' views have never diverged from industry's views and interests. Moreover, for each meeting, Peres's (2018b) interview with retired Professor Marcia Vitolo of the Federal University of Health Sciences of Porto Alegre showed that representatives from different groups in society are present in working groups, while industry is consistently present, and this, in turn, aligns with industry's interests.

Restructuring Society

According to IPCI, yet another strategy that Brazil's junk food industries have pursued is reshaping civil society in its favor; this process contributes to industry national policy legitimacy and social acceptability while complicating civil society's ability to effectively mobilize in opposition to industry policy influence. Per IPCI, building industry legitimacy and social acceptability is achieved through several initiatives, such as establishing allies in academia to fund research that is supportive of industry's policy views; providing employment opportunities in local communities; and providing progressive human rights campaigns. Nevertheless, IPCI posits that these processes eventually divide society, challenging its ability to mobilize in opposition to industry's ongoing policy influence.

Finding allies in academia, while also building its political and social credibility and influence, has been an ongoing strategy. In Brazil, this has mainly been achieved by industries providing research grants to prestigious nutrition scientists as well as funding academic conferences (Jack 2011; Peres 2018a). As Peres (2018a) highlights, researchers from prestigious universities in Brazil, such as the University of São Paulo, have also had to look for funding from the private sector due to limited resources.

Financing prominent academic conferences has also helped to increase industry's policy credibility and influence. In 2011, for example, several prominent food and beverage companies provided funding to SBAN to help sponsor a biannual national congress on the issue of "evidence-based nutrition," with a goal to "expose how scientific evidence should be determined" (Canella et al. 2015, 340). Moreover, the "diamond sponsor" of this conference (i.e., the highest categorical level for financial contributions) was a prominent nonalcoholic beverage concentrate and syrup manufacturer (Canella et al. 2015). The other "gold sponsors" were three major beverage and food companies, as well as two pharmaceutical companies (340). Canella and colleagues further claim that several of these food and beverage industries organized satellite symposiums at this congress during lunch hours or events in the evenings, complete with tasty lunch boxes, dinners, even happy hours, and were focused on issues such as the "strategy for the adoption of healthy lifestyles" (340), one of several seminar topics. This comports with industries' position that physical exercise and individual responsibility are important for improving nutrition and health outcomes, such as obesity. Canella and others further note that "partnerships with entities in the health sector provide legitimacy to practices and products of food and beverage industries. With these partnerships, it is possible to buy credibility, create bonds between brands and positive emotions attributed to the partner organization, and gain loyalty from health professionals who act as opinion leaders" (340).

In yet another instance, Coca-Cola has worked with universities to sponsor activities. Recently, the President of the University of Brasília agreed to partner with the Instituto de Bebidas para a Saúde e o Bem-Estar, which is a Coca-Cola initiative, to create the first Seminário Sobre Actividade Física e Esporte na Saúde (Peres 2018a). This seminar was the opening ceremonial event for the "University Week" activities. According to Peres (2018a), through these activities, pundits in Brazil, such as the Academic Nutrition Center, claimed that industries sought to increase their image among policy makers, legitimize industry views, assigning blame to individuals, while underscoring industry's minimal role in addressing the global obesity situation.

In recent years, companies such as Nestlé, Danone, Unilever, Piracanjuba, Herbalife, and Coca-Cola sponsored an academic conference focused on nutrition in Brazil (Peres 2018a). In 2015, for example, these industries helped sponsor the Thirteenth Congresso da Sociedade Brasileira de Alimentação e Nutrição, which is organized by SBAN. Peres's (2018a) research also notes that these industries are continuously seeking out the academic nutrition community to promote their brands. Furthermore, in 2014, Conbran (the Brazilian Nutritional Congress) was criticized for allowing industries to sponsor its congressional event. According to Peres (2018a), critics such as Professor Elisabetta Recine of the University of Brasília and at the time president of CONSEA (Conselho Nacional de Segurança Alimentar e Nutricional, National Council of Nutritional Security and Health) claimed that industry's foods at Conbran's conferences were displayed in the same area where discussions were being held about risk factors for chronic disease. Professor Recine claimed that this was a contradiction (Peres 2018a).

In yet another instance, in 2014, Coca-Cola sponsored the Fifth International Congress on Physical Activity and Public Health on April 8–11, 2014, which was held in Rio de Janeiro (Hérick de Sá 2014). This was the first time that an academic conference on physical activity received financial sponsorship from Coca-Cola, which, according to Hérick de Sá (2014), was "an organisation whose policies, practices, or products conflict with those of public health" (1). As Hérick de Sá (2014) further maintains, in addition to funding this conference, Coca-Cola representatives infiltrated every other aspect of the scientific meeting, such as attending side meetings and giving away products.

In light of the junk food industry's ongoing efforts to partner with academics, and to strategically use them in their favor, the nutrition community recently proposed initiatives that would define appropriate relationships between industry and scientific researchers. In 2018, for example, the Conselho Federal de Nutricionistas (Federal Council of Nutritionists) proposed a Code of Ethics about the type of professional relationship that nutrition scientists should have with industry, as well as limiting the industry's sponsorship of research and events with the academic community (Peres 2018a). This Code of Ethics explicitly prohibits nutritionists from promoting in any way industry products and an association with a company's image. This document was scheduled to be presented at the Congresso Brasileiro de Nutrição (Conbran, Brazilian Nutrition Congress) in April 2018. According to Peres's (2018a) interview with Maria Adelaide Wanderley Rego, a contributor to the Code's draft, the idea is to protect nutrition scientists' professional autonomy as well as civil society. What's more, Conbran's new managerial structure had agreed to establish a more rigorous relationship with the private sector (Peres 2018a).

In its efforts to embed itself within local communities, by gaining social acceptability, trust and support through several endeavors, the junk food industry has also made substantial headway. Building on its historic mission of integrating itself and having a positive, enduring impact in local communities, Nestlé, for example, has pursued several activities to achieve these outcomes.

For example, in 2008, through its Nestlé Torce por Você (Nestlé Cheers for You) program, the Nestlé Brazil Foundation provided funding for NGOs throughout Brazil focused on promoting the importance of good nutrition and sports, supporting community initiatives such as education on healthy eating, building vegetable gardens, providing cooking workshops, and creating soccer schools (Nutrição em Pauta 2008). The Nestlé Torce por Você program received more than 260 applications; 10 NGOs were selected and allocated R$70,000 in funding (1).

In 2006, Nestlé furthered its community endeavors by creating the Nestlé até Você (Nestlé Comes to You) program. This is an employment program that trains and hires women to sell Nestlé products in their communities, many of which are in peripheral, hard-to-reach areas (Campos 2009). As Campos's (2009) interview with one of Nestlé's directors for this program, Alexandre Costa, points out, this program is present in areas where supermarkets are scarce and where people must travel long distances carrying products. In what appears to be the same program, Jacobs and Richtel (2017) also discuss Nestlé's door-to-door vending employment program for women in Brazil. Some of Nestlé's door-to-door vendors have been reported to have been paid US$185 a month, providing a nice complement to their family income and purchasing power (Jacobs and Richtel 2017). It also helps that Nestlé's door-to-door vendors know when the monthly Bolsa Família checks will arrive. And, unlike most companies, through this program Nestlé provides consumers with up to one month to pay for their products. Nestlé's door-to-door program has served approximately "700,000 'low-income consumers each month'" (Jacobs and Richtel 2017).

In a context of ongoing unemployment and recession, Nestlé's Até Você program has provided decent salaries as well as a sense of independence and responsibility for women. Nestlé's program also trains vendors on how to provide health and nutritional information to their clients (Campos 2009). In addition to this program, President Lula praised Nestlé for its ongoing investments in Brazil, opening new production plants in the poorer northeast region of the country and therefore increasing access to their foods. Indeed, at one point Lula commented: "Nestlé's initiative is a concrete example of how to generate jobs and income to make this country a fairer place, a place where people have the right to work, study and buy affordable products" (quoted in Nestlé 2007, 1).

Nestlé then took its products to the far reaches of the Amazon. In 2010, to reach remote communities, the company created large blue Nestlé boats, referred to by critics as the "junk-food barge," which traveled up and down the Amazon River to find new clients (Huber 2016, 1). Nestlé halted these boats in July 2017 (Jacobs and Richtel, 2017). Nevertheless, once again, the goal was to extend Nestlé's reach to the rural poor.

Finally, Nestlé's door-to-door vendor program is "creating shared values" with community members, said Mr. Sean Westcott, head of Nestlé's food research and development, by allowing them to start up their own micro businesses (Jacobs and Richtel 2017, 1). Furthermore, Nestlé can help communities by "sending positive messages around nutrition," argued Wescott (quoted in Jacobs and Richtel 2017, 1). It seems that these activities have, in turn, helped to build a sense of cohesion and trust between poor communities and Nestlé, as well as support for the company's products and image. Indeed, by combining these shared values and community outreach activities with the sale of their products, it seems that Nestlé has been able to transform society's perceptions of their products, seeing them as symbols of good health and nutrition.

Nestlé has ongoing plans to further expand its reach and help increase employment in Brazil. One of the ways it plans to do this is through its Nestlé student transition to employment program in cooperation with institutions in Brazil (Nestlé 2020). Titled Nestlé's Nurturing Young People's Dreams, this program works with other educational institutions in Brazil, such as the National Service for Industrial Learning and the Business School Integration Center, to help train the country's youth, who are enrolled in the Brazilian Ministry of Labor's Young Apprentice program, for future employment opportunities (Nestlé 2020). This program is a component of Nestlé's preexisting international program titled the Nestlé Global Youth Initiative.

Finally, yet another tactic that junk food companies have pursued is investing in other social welfare campaigns. For example, Coca-Cola has, in recent years, supported of gay rights, women's empowerment, and anti-violence NGOs, as well as those working to improve the environment. Through the Negras Potências program (in partnership with Benfeitoria and the Baobá Fund), Coca-Cola Brazil has provided match funding for sixteen projects empowering black women in three key areas: economic empowerment, anti-violence, as well as education, culture, and sharing information (*Nos, Ação Social das Empresas* 2018; Nunes 2018). Funding for these initiatives will be doubled through matching funds totaling R$500,000 from Coca-Cola Brazil's Movimento Coletivo fund (*Nos, Ação Social das Empresas* 2018). Coca-Cola, along with Nestlé, Mars, Johnson & Johnson, Microsoft, Avon, Bradesco, Alpargatas, Grupo Boticário, Magazine Luiza, Natura, Telefonica Vivo, and MasterCard, has also participated in public events endorsing the UN Women's global program Alliance without Stereotype, which focuses on breaking down gender stereotypes of women in advertising activities (ONU Mulheres, Brasil 2019). Interestingly, this United Nation's initiative was hosted by Unilever at its headquarters in São Paulo in February 2019 (ONU Mulheres, Brasil 2019).

"Esse Coca é Fanta" (That Coke Is a Fanta) is a homophobic expression used in Brazil to indicate that someone is a gay man (Villarreal 2018). In response, and in a sign of support for the gay community, in 2018, Coca-Cola used the phrase to create an empowering campaign. It produced a special Coca-Cola can with the slogan "'Essa Coca-Cola É Fanta, E Daí?' (This Coca-Cola Is a Fanta, So What?)" (Villarreal 2018). Launched on International LGBT Pride Day, the Coke can had Fanta inside of it (Walsh, n.d.). The gay community shared the beverage on social media, while popular drag queen stars, such as Pabllo Vittar, published a video with the special Coke product in hand (Villarreal 2018). Through these efforts, Coca-Cola succeeded in helping change a derogatory homophobic expression into a positive and empowering message for all (Villarreal 2018; Walsh, n.d.). "We can be Cokes, we can be Fantas, we can be whatever we want!" claimed a proud gay partygoer in a recent campaign film discussed by Walsh (n.d.).

Dividing Society

All of the activities, mentioned earlier, aimed at transforming civil society in industries' favor have ultimately created divisions in society, to industry's benefit. As IPCI explains, this process emerges when industry strategies to build allies and support from influential scientists, NGOs, and poor communities reduces the number of potential allies that other activists and NGOs striving to mobilize and thwart industry interests can work with—in a sense, reducing potential "civic resources" for the activist community. Furthermore, by industry creating their own civic network of support, this can lead to a considerable amount of conflict and disagreement between those civil societal actors supporting industry views and those that do not, in turn generating disagreements over the true representation of civil society's public health needs and interests. When combined, this process challenges civil society's ability to effectively mobilize and resist industry's ability to influence policy.

Activists I interviewed confirm that this challenge is occurring in Brazil. Because industries partner most often with NGOs, this process has led to conflicts with those NGOs working on nutrition issues within civil society (interview with Pedro Hartung, September 23, 2020). Others maintain that in this situation, there is a high level of polarization between NGOs in society, causing tension between them (interview with Flavia Mori Sarti, August 31, 2020). This has constrained leftist NGOs' ability to mobilize, due to the fact that NGOs working on nutrition cannot reach a middle ground on policy issues with other NGOs working with industry (interview with Flavia Mori Sarti, August 31, 2020).

Complementary Institutions

The political context facilitating the junk food industry's ongoing policy influence has not been established of its own accord, however. Junk food politics is a two-way street, with government leaders also contributing to industry's ongoing policy influence. As IPCI explains, presidents, their alternative policy interests, and electoral incentives have often led to a supportive political environment that comports with—and indeed emboldens—industries' various political tactics. But some of Brazil's most popular and influential presidents have been a bit more proactive in nurturing and developing junk food industries in order to achieve their alternative policy agendas, endeavors that sustain their electoral popularity and position within government.

The presidency of Luiz Inácio "Lula" da Silva (2003–2010) provides an excellent example. Building on his long history of fighting for the rights of workers, eradicating poverty and inequality, during his presidential campaign, Lula was focused on proposing policies that would address these issues head-on. Moreover, in response to worsening hunger and malnutrition indicators, due to a lack of regular access to food, itself a product of worsening poverty levels, Lula was focused on devising programs that completely eradicated hunger by guaranteeing access to food for all in need. Eradicating hunger became a priority for his government, guiding the government's vision (Graziano da Silva et al. 2019). After winning the presidency in 2003, Lula realized that his ongoing political popularity and support, particularly among the poor, as well as his more leftist liberal constituency base, would depend on the successful implementation of policies addressing hunger, malnutrition, and poverty.

To achieve this, Lula introduced a holistic government policy strategy and vision during his first term in office (2003–2007): Fome Zero. Launched several days after his election in 2003, Fome Zero is a comprehensive, national, intergovernmental effort that entails the creation of several policies focused on eradicating hunger and broader structural transformations, such as increased job opportunities and a decent minimum wage (DelGrossi et al. 2019). Fome Zero was also guided by the normative principles of access to food as a human right, which aligned with international human rights principles of access to food as a fundamental right, enshrined through Article 25 of the Universal Declaration of Human Rights (Elver 2019). A key program falling under Fome Zero's purview was Bolsa Família, created in 2004, which supplied a monthly stipend for qualifying families to purchase food, under the proviso that their children attend school and receive regular health checkups and immunizations.

Lula saw Brazil's thriving industries as key partners in helping address the country's social problems. In 2004, at a public event honoring Brazil's "Most Admired Companies," which selected Nestlé, Natura, and Petrobras that year, Lula stated that the government, on its own, could not rescue the country from its social debt, inviting industries to participate while stating that they were accomplices in exploring ways to improve Brazilian life (*Correio do Brasil* 2004). Lula made it clear that being recognized as Brazil's most admired companies during this event also reflected these companies' good development initiatives and their willingness to partner with the federal, state, and even city governments on social policies, as well as their own endeavors in this area (*Correio do Brasil* 2004).

To facilitate the government's partnership with these industries, the office of the presidency went as far as to create a special advisory office, the specific coordinator of business mobilization, within the Special Social Mobilization Advisor to the President office (Assessoria Especial de Mobilização Social da Presidência da República), located within the presidential palace (Tomazini and Leite 2015). Oded Grajew, who was appointed as specific coordinator of business mobilization, was tasked with encouraging major industries to partner with the Fome Zero program (Tomazini and Leite 2015). Several major companies, such as Coca-Cola, Nestlé Brasil, Sugar Loaf, Pfizer, Bayer, Carrefour, Editora Global, Unilever, Shell Brasil, and Volkswagen, contributed to the Fome Zero program (Tomazini and Leite 2015).

During his term in office, Lula also acknowledged Nestlé's contribution to his Fome Zero program and their work together (Bruce 2003). Indeed, Lula once commented in an interview with the BBC: "I would like to remind you that a Swiss company, Nestlé, has been actively participating in our programme to eradicate hunger, Fome Zero. . . . Companies can help by participating in Fome Zero" (quoted in Bruce 2003, 1). In an effort to engage in a strong partnership with Nestlé, Lula publicly supported the company. Within a year of being elected into office, Lula attended the opening ceremony of a new Nestlé coffee factory in his home state of São Paulo, giving a speech that acknowledged the company for its willingness to partner with him in eradicating hunger and provide employment programs (Discurso do Presidente da República 2004). But Lula went further than just offering praise; he also publicly supported Nestlé's expansion. In 2007, for example, he acknowledged Nestlé's expansion by attending, along with Switzerland's economic affairs minister, Doris Leuthard, the opening of a Nestlé factory in the state of Bahia (Nestlé 2007). At the same time, Lula worked with Nestlé to help eradicate hunger and provide job opportunities (Bruce 2003). After meeting with Lula, Nestlé's CEO, Peter Brubeck-Letmathe, provided US$23 million in support of the president's Fome Zero program, which funded not only employment programs but also advertising for Fome Zero (Penteado 2003). Lula's public spokesman, André Singer, stated that Lula considered Nestlé's participation as very important for Fome Zero (Agéncia Estado 2003). With the support of Lula, Nestlé would continue to supply families with food such as Negresco biscuits, Bono, Ideal (a powdered milk containing vitamins, iron, and calcium), and Nescafé Dolca (Nestlé 2007). Nestlé also provided nutritious cooking training for local schools (Bühler et al. 2010). In recognition of Nestlé's assistance, the government awarded the company with the government's first Zero Hunger Program Partnership Certificate (Bühler et al. 2010).

Lula's successor, former President Dilma Rousseff, sustained Lula's commitment to working on anti-poverty and hunger issues. Mentored by Lula during her rise to prominence as Brazil's first woman president, as a presidential candidate, according to Alessandro Teixeira, Rousseff's policy advisor at the time, Rousseff also shared a concern about eradicating hunger and, if elected, would improve Lula's policies, such as Bolsa Familia (Teixeira interviewed by Gasnier 2010). Indeed, since the beginning of her administration, she appeared committed to supporting the government's ongoing work in the area of poverty alleviation and anti-hunger, with plans to continue Lula's federal programs (Dangl 2010).

Following Rousseff's impeachment in 2016, a more conservative interim president, Michel Temer of the PMDB party, emerged. A conservative, pro-market politician seeking to hastily stabilize the economy, Temer sought to reduce government spending, overcoming a large public sector deficit from the prior administration (Laporta 2016). Nevertheless, as someone committed to free markets, Temer was committed to the business sector and sought to facilitate its further expansion. For instance, through the annual Encontro Nacional de Industria (National Industry Meetings), organized by the National Confederation of Industry, in July 2018 Temer met with industry leaders to show his support for their contribution to Brazil's future (Presidência da República Planalto 2018). While Temer may not have been interested in partnering with Nestlé and other industries in support of Fome Zero, he was still committed to ensuring industry's ongoing prosperity as a goal for economic growth and development.

Indeed, the historic tenants of state-led industrialization, which, as mentioned earlier, fostered and deepened the junk food industry's historic rise to prominence in Brazil, in a sense returned with the more conservative governments of Michel Temer and Jair Bolsonaro. These presidents have been unwaveringly committed to rekindling Brazil's industrial prowess, economic competitiveness, and growth. In this context, junk food and other major industries have once again appear to have been sheltered by the government due to their perceived contribution to meeting these presidents' economic policy objectives and securing the electoral support base while rejuvenating economic growth and foreign investment.

In recent years, yet another sign of government shelter and support of junk food industries has been its continued unwillingness to aggressively tackle tax scandals committed by major soda industries. This recently surfaced with respect to a tax scandal that was discovered in the state of Amazonas. In 2018, investigative journalists discovered a major discrepancy in the IPI tax filed by soda bottling companies purchasing syrup formula from local companies owned by Coca-Cola and other conglomerates (Peres and Neto 2018). For example, Coca-Cola Brazil's syrup-concentrate producing company, Recofarma, as well as factories owned by AmBev and Brasil Kirin, were artificially inflating the price of its syrup to bottlers (many of which are also owned by Coca-Cola as franchises), between approximately R$40 to R$200, while being exported to other countries at a price of approximately R$70 (Peres and Neto 2018, 1). Because the IPI tax was set at 20 percent, with escalated prices for syrup, tax refunds from the government provided for those bottling companies purchasing syrup outside of the Amazon region gave a nice subsidy (Peres and Neto 2018). This is because in the Amazon's "Free Zone" area, by state law industries are free from paying an IPI tax. Thus, for those bottlers residing in another part of the country, the IPI tax paid is credited back to bottling industries. Since 2017, researchers believe that this subsidy has cost the average taxpayer approximately R$35 due to taxes lost via subsidy (Peres and Neto 2018).

Qui bono? (Who benefits?) Well, it appears that it is some of the senators who stand to benefit from this situation. Individuals such as Senator Tasso Jereissati, from the state of Ceará, who owns the bottling manufacturing company Solar (estimated to be one of the largest), is part of this system (Peres and Neto 2018). In return, other senators connected to the soda industry created a parliamentary coalition to block government efforts to decrease the IPI tax from 20 percent to 4 percent (1).

Under pressure from other senators and activists, President Temer agreed to address this issue by lowering the IPI from 20 percent to 4 percent (Desidério 2018). Coca-Cola immediately opposed the measure and threatened to move the production of their syrups to other countries (Desidério 2018). ABIR representatives claimed that the IPI tax should be increased to 15 percent, and that at 4 percent this tax and credit for industries would severely impact businesses, leading to increased unemployment in the Amazonian region, such as in the state of Manaus (Desidério 2018). In response, in July 2019, through executive decree No. 9.897, Bolsonaro increased the tax from 8 percent to 10 percent, effective from October 1 to December 31, 2019 (Cucolo 2019). This appears to have signaled to Coca-Cola and other industries that his administration is doing what it can to ensure industry profitability and growth, even if it means a loss of tax revenue for the state.

According to Desidério (2018), small soda manufacturers nevertheless continue to complain that Coca-Cola and others continue to inflate prices and that this is a market distortion. What's more, still no effort has been made by the government to address the IPI taxation and high syrup pricing issue. This is an issue under investigation by Brazil's federal taxation authorities.

However, shifts in presidential policy ambitions can also dismantle national participatory institutions, which are vital for securing strong state-civil societal discussions and the creation of NCD prevention and regulatory policy. However, presidential dismantlement of these participatory institutions can indirectly support the junk food industry's efforts to avoid building political and civil societal support in favor of more aggressive regulatory measures.

In the area of national nutrition policy, perhaps the most important participatory institution, bringing together civil society, the president, congressional legislators, and the private sector, has been CONSEA. Strategically housed within the Office of the President, CONSEA periodically met in order to ensure that civil society's nutritional needs were being addressed, discussing a broad range of nutrition policies and initiatives (Gómez 2018). Initially created in 1993, CONSEA was given little consideration during the transition period from the Itamar Franco (1992–1995) administration to the Fernando H. Cardoso (1995–2003) administration amid an economic recession, then briefly shut down during the Cardoso administration and was replaced with other programs (Gómez 2021; Vasconceles 2005). CONSEA was later reinstated under the Lula administration, given his focus on eradicating hunger, malnutrition, and poverty (Gómez 2018). As Gómez (2018) notes, it was during this period that civil societal activists and concerned health officials made the most progress in addressing obesity and type 2 diabetes.

Swift changes in presidential policy priorities in favor of fiscal stabilization and industrial growth have once again led to CONSEA's suspension under the Bolsonaro administration (Mazui 2019). Under the Michel Temer administration and then the current Jair Bolsonaro administration, the focus has been on rejuvenating Brazil's thriving industrial sector. Moreover, we must remember that Temer's and Bolsonaro's administrations were focused on dismantling the economic effects that Lula's and Rousseff's more progressive social welfare programs had on the economy. CONSEA's closure under Bolsonaro greatly facilitated the junk food industry's political efforts to avoid any further discussion about regulating their activities. This served as a great advantage for these industries because, since CONSEA was strategically located within the Office of the President, and because presidents have traditionally had strong agenda-setting powers within the Congress, they would no longer have to fear further progress being made on those regulatory policies going against industry's interests.

Civil Societal Activism: A Never-Ending Struggle

Nevertheless, civil society's efforts to mobilize and fight against the interests of major junk food industries persists. More so than ever, with escalating obesity and type 2 diabetes cases burgeoning, especially among Brazil's most vulnerable populations, activists continue to raise awareness, counteract industry's activities, and find ways to inform policy discussions.

It is important to emphasize, however, that these social health movements are nothing new. Efforts to increase the general public's awareness about the importance of sound nutrition, particularly for children, emerged during the 1970s. Led mainly by a coalition of concerned mothers, prior to the transition to democracy in 1988, they worked closely with nutrition activists and MoH officials to increase awareness and design public health programs focused on improved access to nutritious foods; these policy recommendations were grounded on the tenants of access to nutritious foods as a human right, rising in tandem with, and indeed benefiting from, other social health movements, such as the Sanitarista movement, which was a pro-democracy movement that fought for universal access to health care along such lines (Gómez 2018).

Despite the constraining industrial and institutional limitations they face, Brazil's activists have had success in questioning industry's policies, guided by its narrative views, while NGOs have also raised attention to ongoing policy needs. For example, in Brazil in 2013, Coca-Cola vowed not to advertise their products to children under the age of 12 (Octoboni 2013). In general, the Alana Institute applauded Coca-Cola's efforts to reduce their advertising to children, providing an example for other companies to follow (Octoboni 2013). And yet, according to Alves (2018), with respect to several industries' attempts to reduce food advertising to children, Alana has also questioned if there is any safe and tolerable form of industry advertising toward children. Furthermore, Alana and IDEC have claimed that industry's approach is insufficient—that there has been no attempt to limit the provision of gifts with foods and the usage of visual aids in advertisements (Dias et al. 2012). These NGOs have therefore called on Brazil's regulatory agency, Anvisa, to address these issues through concrete regulations (Dias et al. 2012). In recent years, other NGOs have also emerged, such as the Advocacy Hub, bringing attention to the need to address children's rights in the area of nutrition. In general, all of these NGOs have been unwaveringly committed to raising awareness and creating effective policies in response to NCDs, increasing understanding of the harmful effects of junk food products, and addressing consumer rights.

With the closure of CONSEA and a general political atmosphere that, in recent years, has been reluctant to work closely with them, NGOs have also started to unify, bringing together what resources, ideas, and interests they can muster to magnify their voice and influence. In 2016, several NGOs, individuals, social movements, associations, and professional organizations formed the Aliança pela Alimentação Adequada e Saudável, which was created during the XXIV Congresso Brasileiro de Nutrição in the city of Porto Alegre (Aliança pela Alimentação Adequada e Saudável 2020). The Aliança is focused on achieving adequate nutrition as a human right through several collective initiatives (Aliança pela Alimentação Adequada e Saudável 2020). Moreover, the Aliança is focused on ten strategy themes, which include initiatives such as circumscribing the marketing of ultraprocessed foods, improving nutritional information of food labels, recommending fiscal measures to promote improved health and adequate nutrition, ensuring adequate nutrition within schools; providing access to water as a human right, and monitoring and revealing policies and industrial practices that encourage unhealthy eating behaviors (Aliança pela Alimentação Adequada e Saudável 2020). The Aliança has also held politicians accountable by publicly inviting them to sign declarations about their commitment to improving the health of the public, particularly in the areas of food and nutrition education, before key elections (Zocchio 2018). Additionally, the Aliança creates public media campaigns focusing on key prevention and regulatory matters that still need to be adequately addressed.

In 2017, for example, the Aliança created the campaign Você tem o Director de Saber o que Come (You Have the Right to Know What You Eat) (Instituto Nacional de Câncer 2017). This awareness campaign was focused on several issues, such as the importance of improved food labels with greater transparency in information and the danger of food advertisements, which can encourage unhealthy eating habits, particularly among children (Instituto Nacional de Câncer 2017), but the campaign was also keen on increasing public awareness about the connection between the consumption of these foods and obesity, as well as obesity's relationship to several different types of cancers. Through these and several other public awareness campaigns, the Aliança has done a commendable job of informing families and individuals about how to eat nutritiously and to be careful with misguided, false advertising. In December 2017, the Instituto Nacional de Câncer (INCA, National Cancer Institute), an agency under the MoH, notified the public about this campaign, claiming that it has received INCA's support (Instituto Nacional de Câncer 2017).

Conclusion

Since the late 1990s, Brazil has joined several other emerging economies in seeing the rapid rise of NCDs such as obesity and type 2 diabetes. This was the result, in part, of the heightened consumption of junk food products. To the national government's benefit, it created several impressive national NCD prevention programs that focused on issues such as the importance of improved nutrition and exercise while working with schools and local communities to implement these programs. In 2010, Brazil was even recognized by the international community, along with the United Kingdom, for its policy success in the area of obesity prevention.

Nevertheless, when it came to the creation of regulatory policies targeting the marketing and sale of industry products, the story has been very different. While regulations that prohibit the marketing of products to children (though not adolescents) have been enacted, these regulations are rarely, if ever, enforced, underscoring the absence of institutions ensuring that policies are implemented. On the other hand, other regulations, such as food labels, continue to be limited in their effectiveness. There also continues to be an absence of enforceable federal laws (with stringent penalties for noncompliance) prohibiting the sale of sodas and junk foods in schools. At the same time, the government has repeatedly neglected to introduce marketing regulations toward the general public. And despite being one of the largest consumers of soda per capita in the Americas, no soda tax exists. When taken together, either regulations are not enforced, they are limited, or they are not pursued. It is clear, then, that despite the government's international acclaimed commitment to obesity prevention, the government has been repeatedly unwilling to cross the line of directly tackling the interests and activities of powerful junk food industries operating in Brazil, focusing instead on broader prevention campaigns—which are good but nevertheless wholly insufficient on their own for confronting the nation's ongoing NCD crisis and safeguarding its most vulnerable populations.

But why has this occurred? As IPCI has helped to explain, in Brazil, industries have become deeply political and influential in their endeavors. By engaging in policy partnerships with government, they have become influential and supportive within government, generating little interest, it seems, in pursuing effective regulations. At the same time industries have engaged in lobbying activities and provided campaign contributions to secure their policy positions. Brazil's largest industries have also worked with their representative interest groups to infiltrate national regulatory agencies in order to ensure that the former's policy views are sustained and that potential regulations are avoided. Add to this the various innovative corporate social responsibility activities that they are engaged in—from nutrition to employment programs for the poor—and you have industries that have succeeded in building social and, in turn, political legitimacy. For junk food industries, this makes influencing NCD regulatory policy easier and more effective.

But again, as IPCI emphasizes, industry activities are partly to blame. Governments are also at fault. In particular, complementary institutions also matter. In Brazil, presidents have repeatedly viewed junk food industries as key partners in helping achieve their alternative policy and, hence, political agendas. As complementary institutions emphasize, presidents have also gone so far as to create federal offices that ensure industry representation within government as key policy allies. Through these and other supportive fiscal policies, it has become rather clear in Brazil that these complementary institutions have helped to supplement these industries' other political strategies and regulatory policy influence. With the aid of these complementary institutions, it seems, industries have become successful political machines in Brazil, influencing NCD policies in their favor—and yet at the expense of the health of children and the poor.

APPENDIX
Brazil: Summary of Chapter Findings

Political Action	Restructuring Society	Complementary Institutions	Regulatory Policy Failure and Absence
Policy partnership Food industry–MOH partnerships to reformulate nutritional food content and information on food labels (e.g., serving sizes)	*Corporate social responsibility* Food industry (e.g., Nestlé) support for NGOs focused on improved nutrition and sports Nestlé empowering women through employment programs Coca-Cola empowering minority communities and supporting gay rights	President Lula's support and usage of Nestlé to achieve popular anti-hunger campaigns (e.g., Fome Zero) President Lula's creation of an office within the president's administration to facilitate partnership with industry to implement Fome Zero	Inadequate and ineffective food nutrition labels Absence of federal enforceable laws (with penalties) on the sale of sodas and junk foods in schools Absence of enforced and effective government regulations for the advertisement of junk food products to children

Political Action	Restructuring Society	Complementary Institutions	Regulatory Policy Failure and Absence
Lobbying and largesse	*Partnering with society*		Absence of soda and junk food tax
Industry attendance at public policy hearings; develop interpersonal relationships with policy makers	Food and beverage industry sponsorship of nutrition science conferences		
Electoral campaign contributions from companies such as Coca-Cola, McDonald's, and JBS	Food industry (e.g., Nestlé) support for NGOs focused on improved nutrition and sports		
Institutional infiltration	*Dividing society*		
Industry infiltration of ANVISA regulatory bureaucracy through industry-supported NGOs (e.g., the International Life Sciences Institute [ILSI])	Industry-supported NGOs having conflicting views with NGOs and other members of civil society, hampering consensus and mobilization		

5

India

Similar to what we saw in the other emerging economies discussed in this book, by the early 1990s, the obesity and type 2 diabetes epidemics emerged rather suddenly in India. The product of globalization, neoliberal polices, such as free trade and market reform, have led to a nutrition transition where individuals have gradually replaced traditional food staples with sugary beverages, carbonated drinks, and fast foods. Initially a concern among the more affluent urban classes, this nutrition transition and its associated NCDs of obesity and type 2 diabetes have now emerged among India's most vulnerable populations: children and the poor. And this has occurred in a context where there continues to be ongoing poverty and malnutrition in these vulnerable populations.

Nevertheless, the national government was slow to respond to this situation. Eventually, the Ministry of Health and Family Welfare created several prevention programs, which focused on disease surveillance, improved nutrition, and public awareness. However, efforts to address the regulation of junk food marketing and sales were delayed and riddled with problems. Food labeling has been deemed repeatedly insufficient and unclear, while policies on advertising have relied on industry self-regulation. While a "sin tax" on sugary drinks eventually emerged, it was slow to be implemented. To this day, there exists no federal or state regulations limiting the advertising of junk foods and no regulation on the sale of these products (especially in schools), despite the escalating childhood obesity and adolescent type 2 diabetes epidemics. These outcomes, in turn, reveal that the government is not fully committed to regulating the junk food industry. In this context, NCDs have flourished and, sadly, affected India's most vulnerable populations.

But why has this occurred? In accordance with the Industry Politics and Complementary Institutions analytical framework, the political and social activities of junk food industries are to blame, as well as the complementary role of institutions. Striving to increase their legitimacy and influence within government, industries have engaged in several partnerships with federal and, especially, state governments to create prevention programs, such as health and educational programs for children and the poor. Furthermore, industries and their representative institutions, such as the All India Food Processors' Association, have engaged in several successful lobbying tactics, going so far as to infiltrate committees within the highest echelons of the federal bureaucracy. At the same time, and as IPCI further emphasizes, industries have successfully restructured civil society in their favor: that is, they have engaged in several corporate social responsibility activities to build legitimacy and support within local communities and, in the process, the national government. And by allying with supportive NGOs and scientists, this appears to have led to the creation of a divided society, where civil society has not been able to effectively mobilize in opposition to industry's political activities and policy influence due to differences of opinion and interests among civil societal actors.

At the same time, however, complementary institutions have also mattered and, once again, facilitated industry's political and social activities. In recent years, Prime Minister Narendra Modi (2014–present) has viewed major industries as vital partners in helping to achieve his objective of strengthening India's economy and social welfare programs. In so doing, however, this partnership has further legitimized industry and enhanced its ability to influence NCD policy in its favor.

But why and how did the junk food industry emerge so powerfully in India? Let's take a deeper look into the birth and consolidation of these industries, the sectors that have thrived, and the health consequences of junk food consumption.

Rise and Influence of India's Junk Food Industry

The rise and influence of the junk food industry in India took a long time to develop, influenced by challenging political, economic, and cultural contexts. Nationalist governments committed to socialist economic development, punctuated by brief political crises, essentially thwarted the industry's swift and early arrival, emerging only after a major economic crisis, international pressures to liberalize the economy, and government interest in nurturing markets and industry.

Following India's independence from British rule in 1947, the socialist government accorded limited space for private industry to thrive and develop on its own, with considerable government regulation (Mukherji 2009). While Prime Minister Jawaharlal Nehru and the Congress (I) parliamentary government continued to support business (even allowing Coca-Cola to emerge in 1949), the government's focus at the time was on socialist development. Coinciding with a growing sense of nationalism, this led to a gradual decline in private sector growth and development. Between 1969 and 1974, the government emphasized state-led development, nationalized major industries and banks, and reduced foreign ownership while increasing private industry regulation. In 1974, amid a political crisis, Prime Minister Indira Gandhi of the Congress (I) party introduced the Foreign Exchange Regulation Act of 1974 (Mukherji 2009). This act substantially reduced foreign multinational equity ownership from 51 percent to 40 percent (87). Coca-Cola, for example, was also required to share "its top-secret syrup recipe" (Obermeier 2019). Under these conditions, Coca-Cola decided to leave India, as well as other major multinational industries like IBM and Kodak (Obermeier 2019). During this time, moreover, George Fernandes, who would be the future minister of industry, claimed that Coca-Cola's products were entering villages. According to Fernandes, "When I chucked out Coca-Cola in 1977, I made the point that 90 percent of India's villages did not have safe drinking water, whereas Coke had reached every village . . . Do we really need Coke? Do we need Pepsi?" (quoted in a 1992 New York Times article cited by Obermeier 2019). Fernandes's call to action suggested that the government was genuinely concerned about the health and well-being of India's poor, safeguarding them from the ill effects of soda.

But was the government truly committed? Interestingly, only two years later, in 1977, following Indira Gandhi's removal from office in response to her 1975 National Emergency, which threatened to install an authoritarian government due to growing political unrest and economic instability, with the arrival of the new Janata political party in 1977 and a return to democratic normalcy, the government asked the Central Food Technological Research Institute to create the formula for India's own Double Seven soft drink (Dabas 2017). This arose because multinationals were asked by George Fernandes, who was the Minister of Industries at the time, to partner with a local Swadeshi enterprise. However, for Coca-Cola, such a partnership would also entail sharing its "secret recipe" with local enterprises, which the company refused to do (Dabas 2017). Double Seven also had political connotations associated with it: it signaled the end of the national emergency and the arrival of the Janata Party, and was presented as a gift by this party to the masses, who were "terrified by [the] emergency and atrocities of Indira government" (Dabas 2017). The government had taken the historic step of creating its own delicious soda, in a sense celebrating its nationalist pride and production capacity while providing a sign of better days to come. And yet it seems that Minister Fernandes's and the government's concern for the health and well-being of the poor had dissipated. While Double Seven lost its position in the market two years later, following the Janata Party's leave from office, locally owned soda companies such as Thums Up and RimZim, owned by the Parle Group, emerged to fill the large void left in the market (Obermeier 2019). By the 1980s, Thums Up snagged approximately 80 percent of the soda market (Hughes 2013).

Despite the government's turn against multinational industries, yet another factor delaying their entry was India's food culture. Unlike Brazil and Mexico throughout the 1990s, most Indian consumers were accustomed to cooking and eating at home (Anitharaj 2018; Kannan 2014). Religious beliefs in food purity, dovetailing with the predominant Hindu religion and culture, generated few incentives to consume foods (especially meat products) outside of the home. At the same time, most of the poor, particularly in rural areas, were not yet exposed to these alternative, mainly Western-based foods, many of which were overpriced.

Throughout the 1980s, the government gradually began to liberalize the market once again, allowing for the reemergence of private industry and international trade, but mainly in key sectors, such as electronics (Mukherji 2009). By 1991, however, the domestic context dramatically changed, paving the way for the reentry of major domestic and multinational soda and ultra-processed food industries. Not only was the legacy of the Foreign Exchange Regulation Act of 1974 essentially overturned after 1991 (Mukherji 2009), but the government also implemented a host of structural adjustment measures; these measures facilitated the growth of free markets, international trade, and ultraprocessed food products by removing tariffs on the import of food products, facilitating multinational corporation investment, and reducing industry regulations (Anitharaj 2018; Mukherji 2009). This turn to neoliberalism was mainly driven by India's worsening balance of payments situation, economic recession, international pressures, and the success of neighboring countries, such as Malaysia, introducing similar reforms (Mukherji 2009). During this period, multinational soda industries, such as PepsiCo, could reenter the market—under the proviso that Pepsi "'Indianize' its name," which it did, briefly renaming its soda *Lehar* Pepsi (which translates to "wave" in Hindi) (Obermeier 2019). Coca-Cola arrived shortly after PepsiCo's reentry into the market in 1990 (Hughes 2013). Other foreign and domestic ultraprocessed foods also began to appear, such as PepsiCo, Nestlé, and Mondeléz International. Throughout the 1990s, in response to changes in consumer awareness, constraints on time for home cooking, women entering the labor force, and demand for ready-made ultraprocessed foods and carbonated drinks, investments—both foreign and domestic—began to burgeon in the junk food sector. Within the next two decades, major junk food companies such as Coca-Cola, Dunkin' Donuts, PepsiCo, Pizza Hut, KFC, and Subway began to take advantage of this shifting context and sought to aggressively invest in India (Balch 2012).

Taking advantage of India's vast agricultural sector and food production (second only to China), the government has also shown strong support for ultraprocessed food and beverage processing (Rais et al. 2013). The vast availability of sugarcane, fruits, pulse, wheat, rice, and other key ingredients for those foods, when combined with the government's increased invitation for domestic and foreign investment and favorable state government taxation policies, has led to a substantial rise in ultraprocessed food production and multinational corporation investment (on these investments, see Rais et al. 2013 and Rastogi 2017). According to some analysts, "Foreign Direct Investment (FDI) is permissible for all the processed food products under 100% automatic route (except for items reserved for Micro, Small & Medium Enterprises, where FDI is permissible under automatic route up to 24%), subject to applicable laws/regulations/securities and other conditions" (Adukia, n.d., 31). Foreign direct investment in this sector has increased by "USD 1.7 Billion during April 2014 to December 2016 and USD 263.71 million from April [to] June 2017" (Government of India, n.d.), and has great future potential (Kasotia 2008). For the fiscal year 2017–2018, US$263 million was invested in the food production sector (EY 2017).

Multinational companies taking advantage of this favorable context include Kellogg's, Ferrero, and BSA International (Government of India, n.d.).

The largest ultraprocessed food production industries operating in India currently include PepsiCo, GlaxoSmithKline (GSK), Mapro Foods, Dabur, Parle, Nestlé, Frito-Lay, Haldiram's, Atul, Godrej, Coca-Cola, Britannia, ITC, Cadbury India, Hindustan Lever, and MTR (ONICRA 2007). Recent estimates reveal that the highest-grossing ultraprocessed food sectors include savory snacks, produced by companies such as by PepsiCo, ITC, Haldiram's, Parle, and Bikanervala, with a 25.28 percent growth rate; followed by natural healthy beverages, produced by companies such as PepsiCo, Dabur, and Tata Global Beverages (22 percent); breakfast cereals, produced by companies such as Kellogg's, Bagrry's, GlaxoSmithKline, and PepsiCo (21.8 percent); confectionary (e.g., chocolates), produced by companies such as Mars International, Mondeléz, Parle, and Ferrero (17.22 percent); and ready-made meals, produced by companies like MTR, ITC, Nestlé, Gits Food, and Bambino (14.80 percent) (EY 2017). The food processing sector was valued at US$135 billion, estimated to reach a value of US$200 billion by 2015 (Adukia n.d., 14), and was the fifth largest industry with respect to export, production, and local consumption (Rastogi 2017). In addition, the agro food processing industry "employs around 18% of the country's industrial work force" (Singh et al. 2012, 82).

During this time, the distribution of junk food products by local convenience stores, fast food restaurants, and grocery stores also increased. Processed foods have sold through these outlets since 1999 (Baker and Friel 2016). Furthermore, beginning mainly in Delhi and Bombay, major fast food restaurant chains such as McDonald's (arriving in 1996), Pizza Hut, Dominos, and KFC have invested in India (LA Times Archives, 1996; Malhotra, n.d.). "Pizza Hut has 143 stores across 34 cities in India" (Malhotra, n.d.). The fast food industry is growing at an estimated 19 percent annually, which analysts claim is higher than China's annual 15 percent (AIMS Institutes 2020, 1). By 2020, analysts predict that the fast food restaurant industry will see an annual growth rate of approximately 18 percent, worth approximately US$27.57 billion (Anitharaj 2018). Add to this the increased growth of shopping centers and food courts, which India's National Restaurant Association claims has seen strong growth (AIMS Institutes 2020).

Despite the expanse of these formal food distribution networks, they are mainly concentrated within India's urban centers (Gauba 2015). In addition, approximately 70 percent of the food service industry is unregistered, comprising approximately RS 1,72,685 crore in value; this includes roadside restaurants, *dhabas*, and vendors (AIMS Institutes 2020). One must also keep in mind that of India's population of 1.2 billion, there are only "2,700 chain fast food outlets, leaving most people unreached, according to Euromonitor International" (Gauba 2015). When combined with an expanding, young workforce, this context provides ample space for the expected expanse of India's fast food sector and more diverse menus (see Gauba 2015).

In recent years, major soda companies have emerged to garner the majority of sales and profitability. India's beverage market is mainly dominated by Coca-Cola, which sells its traditional products (Coke, Fanta, and Sprite), as well as Thums Up through its ownership of the Pearl conglomerate (see Raj 2020 and Knowledge@Wharton 2017). Together, Coca-Cola and PepsiCo dominate the market, owning approximately 95 percent of the soda market share (Bundhun 2017). Coca-Cola's "sales across its 1.5m outlets nationwide have increased every quarter for the past six years" (Balch 2012). As it did during the 1970s, when it was initially criticized by George Fernandes, Coca-Cola has also been very successful at targeting poor rural areas, such as villages, increasing its presence from 9 percent of villages in 2000 to 28 percent in 2004 (Coca-Cola India 2004, 68).

Other Indian-owned companies produce soda, such as the Pure corporation's Campa Cola and Campa Orange and McDowell & Company's Sprint and Rush Orange (Dubashi 1984). Furthermore, recent local market entrants, comprising "at least two-dozen regional aerated drinks makers, including Gujarat's Hajoori & Sons, Alwar-based Jayanti Beverages, Delhi's City Cola, Boss Beverages from Bareilly and Shri Brahm Shakti Prince Beverages of Delhi," have also emerged in recent years to challenge Coca-Cola and PepsiCo; similar to Coca-Cola's penetration of rural markets, analysts note that, together, these smaller competitors snagged roughly 10 percent of the aerated drinks market (Bhushan 2015). In response, Coca-Cola and PepsiCo have had to lower their prices for its 200-milliliter glass bottles from Rs 12 to Rs 10 in some local markets (Bhushan 2015). In somewhat of a backlash to Coca-Cola and PepsiCo's ongoing dominance, other companies have started to offer healthier bottled fruit juices, such as Paper Boat, Milke Mantra, and RAW Pressery, emphasizing healthier options with "authentic Indian ingredients" (see Ramadurai 2017)—thus appealing to conservative nationalist impulses. Some products, like Paper Boat, have "a smart ethnic story" (Knowledge@ Wharton 2017).

In sum, while the emergence of India's junk food industry faced considerable political, economic, and cultural obstacles, ongoing demand for these products, when combined with increased ultraprocessed food production, sales, and employment, this industry has emerged as an integral aspect of India's thriving economy and, by extension, politics. As these industries— particularly the largest ones, Coca-Cola, PepsiCo, and Nestlé—continue to expand and become a vital part of the economy, they will continue to influence politics and policy-making processes—as we'll see shortly.

Nevertheless, there have been several nutritional and health consequences associated with the increased consumption of these foods. As I explain in the next section, these consequences appear to be disproportionately affecting India's highest at-risk groups: children and the poor.

NCDs and Vulnerable Populations

In addition to several other genetic and behavioral risk factors, such as tobacco use, alcohol use, and sedentary lifestyles, the consumption of junk food has contributed to a substantial rise in NCDs such as type 2 diabetes, heart disease, and cancer in India (Durairaj 2018; Sharma 2018). Recent studies have noted, for example, that an increase in fat, oil, cholesterol, sodium, and sugar intakes (natural and artificial), as well as the consumption of sugar-sweetened beverages and fast foods, are major behavioral risk factors contributing to NCDs (Arokiasamy 2018; Banerjee 2019; Gulati and Miura 2014). Moreover, another major risk factor, often attributed to the consumption of these foods, is weight gain and obesity. In India, the NCDs most commonly associated with overweight and obesity include, for example, type 2 diabetes, hypertension, and cardiovascular disease (Khandelwal and Reddy 2013).

NCDs are also the biggest contributor to the overall burden of disease in India. According to the University of Washington's Institute for Health Metrics and Evaluation (2019c), the greatest causes of death in 2017 was, in ranking order, ischemic heart disease, COPD (chronic obstructive pulmonary disease), stroke, diarrhea, lower respiratory infection, tuberculosis, neonatal disorders, asthma, diabetes, and chronic kidney disease. Disability-adjusted life years (DALY) indicators, which measure the number of life years affected by health disabilities, revealed the following greatest burdens in rank order: neonatal disorders, ischemic heart disease, COPD, diarrhea, lower respiratory infection, stroke, tuberculosis, dietary iron deficiency, diabetes, and, lastly, road injuries (Institute for Health Metrics and Evaluation 2019c). In

2017, the risk factors driving the most deaths in India included, in ranking order, malnutrition, dietary risks, air pollution, high blood pressure, tobacco, high fasting plasma glucose, WASH (water, sanitation, and hygiene), alcohol use, high body mass index (overweight and obesity), and high LDL (cholesterol); what is more alarming is that in 2007, dietary risk factors was ranked fourth, climbing to second place in 2017 (Institute for Health Metrics and Evaluation 2019c). Moreover, according to Chakravorty (2019), a recent study conducted by *The Lancet* revealed that India is second only to China with respect to diet-related death rates, reaching 1,573,595 deaths in India versus China's 3,128,516 deaths caused by poor diet. Thus, those NCDs attributed to the consumption of junk foods, such as diabetes, stroke, and ischemic heart disease, rank within the top ten of the overall burden of disease in India. These findings confirm other studies underscoring the fact that among India's most burdensome NCDs, cardiovascular disease (ischemic heart disease and stroke) is the most prevalent cause of death and disability in India, with hypertension (high blood pressure, often attributed to increased salt intake and cholesterol) quickly becoming the highest risk factor (Gupta and Xavier 2018).

In recent years, due to a host of factors including the consumption of ultraprocessed foods (high in fat and sugar), increased sedimentary lifestyles, migration from rural to urban centers, and environmental factors, rates of obesity and type 2 diabetes have burgeoned (Gulati and Miura 2014; Unnikrishnan et al. 2016). And yet, cultural factors have also mattered. To this day, mothers still consider their children to be healthy if they are overweight (Ghosh 2013; Gómez 2018). In large part, this has to do with the long history of malnourishment and stunting throughout the country. Gómez (2018) notes that studies have shown a gradual increase in children's demand for soda and fast foods as a fashionable item, leading to peer pressure and pressure on parents to obtain these foods for them. According to recent estimates from the WHO, the overall rate of obesity among adults (18 years of age and older), when measured with respect to a body mass index greater than 30, increased from 0.8 percent of the population in 1990 to 3.8 percent in 2016 (WHO 2019). And with respect to type 2 diabetes, according to WHO estimates, when measured with respect to raised fasting blood glucose levels greater than 7 mmol/L or on medication, increased from 4.4 percent of the population in 1990 to 7.8 percent in 2014 (WHO 2019).

In India, rates of overweight and obesity first began to appear within

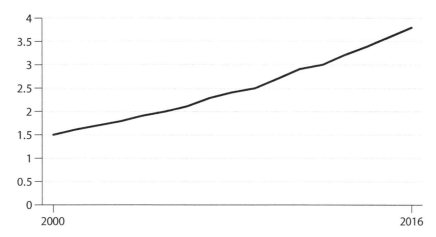

India: prevalence (%) of obesity among adults. *Source*: WHO, 2021. https://www
.who.int/data/gho/data/indicators/indicator-details/GHO/prevalence-of
-obesity-among-adults-bmi-=-30-(crude-estimate)-(-)

major urban centers, gradually spreading out to rural areas. Studies of several select regions in India revealed that urban areas in general have higher rates of overweight, BMI, as well as generalized, abdominal, and combined (generalized and abdominal) obesity levels (Pradeepa et al. 2015). Survey research conducted in 2011 revealed that obesity rates in India's urban population reached approximately 58 percent (Gaiha, Jha, and Kilkarni 2011, 17). Examining National Family Health Surveys (NFHS) released by the government between 1999 and 2016, Luhar and colleagues (2018) found that among urban men, overweight and obesity increased from 0.167 to 0.276 from 2005 to 2016, while an increase among women was seen from 0.236 in 1999 to 0.385 in 2016. Overweight and obesity rates, as well as associated NCDs, such as diabetes, are also starting to emerge in rural and less affluent areas (Khandelwal and Reddy 2013; Little et al. 2017; Luhar et al. 2018; Patil et al. 2016; Undavalli et al. 2018). In fact, recent overweight and obesity estimates for men in rural areas "almost tripled from 0.059 to 0.148 between 2005 and 2016, and among women, the prevalence increased from 0.059 to 0.182 between 1998 and 2016" (Luhar et al. 2018, 3–4).

India's Vulnerable Populations

However, it is important to emphasize that obesity is no longer considered a disease of affluence: that is, relegated only to higher socioeconomic

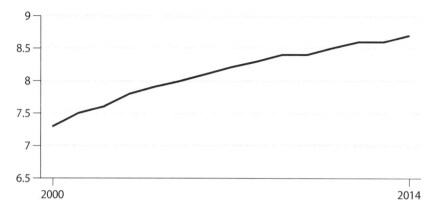

India: prevalence (%) of adult diabetes. *Source*: WHO, 2021. https://www.who
.int/data/gho/data/indicators/indicator-details/GHO/raised-fasting-blood
-glucose-(-=7-0-mmol-l-or-on-medication)(age-standardized-estimate)

classes (Luhar et al. 2018; Undavalli et al. 2018). Obesity has now developed
among the rich *and* the poor (Luhar et al. 2018). In fact, recent evidence
suggests that obesity is increasing more among the urban and rural poor
when compared to the more affluent socioeconomic classes (Luhar et al.
2018). Indeed, when measured with respect to percentage change in those
overweight and obesity rates, Luhar and colleagues' (2018) most recent analysis of the NFHS in 1999, 2006, and 2016 revealed that the greatest percentage increase in those overweight and obese was found among the lowest
socioeconomic groups as well as those with no education. Research by Shannawaz and Arokiasamy (2018) also finds that among men, "illiterate men and
men educated up to primary level of education observed a higher increase in
overweight/obesity level compared to men educated up to higher level"; the
same trend was observed among women (2). Still other studies have mentioned that India's urban poor and those residing in slums are at a higher
risk of being overweight when compared to the rural poor (Varadharajan et
al. 2013).

    But what accounts for the poor's increased obesity rates? Several factors
come into play. First, due to childhood fears of lacking sufficient food, many
of India's urban poor have tried to consume as much as possible and have
taken advantage of the readily available ultraprocessed foods and cheap
prices of soda (Le Ker, n.d.). Indeed, other studies have emphasized how

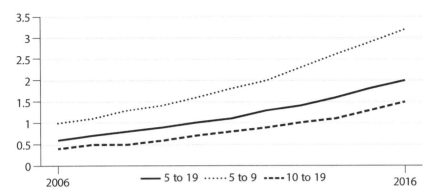

India: prevalence (%) of childhood obesity (ages 5–19). *Source*: WHO, 2021.
https://www.who.int/data/gho/data/indicators/indicator-details/GHO/preva
lence-of-obesity-among-children-and-adolescents-bmi-2-standard-deviations
-above-the-median-(crude-estimate)-(-)

it is often cheaper for the poor to consume processed foods outside of the
home, even in India's rural areas, especially among children (Pingali et al.
2019). Pingali and colleagues (2019) further note that "based upon a household survey of slums in Delhi, Sing, Gupta, Ghosh, Lock, and Ghosh-Jerath
(2015) find that on average households spend around 11% of their monthly
food expenditure on snacks, while 15% of the working member reported eating lunch outside" (84). Finally, others claim that the poor view eating junk
food and eating out at fast food chains as increasing their upward mobility
and social status (Balch 2012).

Like we saw in Mexico and Brazil, rates of childhood and adolescent obesity are also increasing in India. According to data from the WHO (2019),
obesity among children and adolescents (between the ages of 5 and 19) has
increased from 0.1 percent of the population in 1990 to 2 percent in 2016. By
2016, the number of obese teens (between the ages of 13 and 18) nearly doubled, from 16 percent in 2010 to 29 percent in 2015 (George 2016). Dey (2016)
found that childhood obesity had "around [a] 22% prevalence rate over the
last 5 years in children and adolescents aged between 5–19 years." Moreover,
some of the earliest studies to report on the development of childhood obesity in India noted a sharp increase in obesity among schoolchildren in the
southern, more affluent part of the country, from 4.94 percent of students
in 2003 to 6.57 percent in 2005 (Kar and Kar 2015). Surprisingly, in 2017,

India trailed behind only China in having the highest number of childhood obesity cases in the world, with 14.4 million cases to 15.3 million, respectively (Bhat 2017).

Several state- and regional-level studies, mainly utilizing survey research in select urban and rural areas, reveal that childhood obesity is primarily concentrated in urban areas and among higher socioeconomic groups. This urban concentration is attributed to a host of factors, including an increased reliance on cars and buses for transportation to school, a lack of exercise due to increased heat and bad air quality, poor food habits, as well as greater exposure to junk food advertisements and fast food outlets, with working mothers also being a contributing factor (Basu 2017; Dey 2016; Mehandra et al. 2017). Due in part to these environmental factors, survey research in select cities in India, such as Rajasthan, suggests that children in private schools have tended to be more overweight and obese when compared to their rural counterparts (Mehandra et al. 2017). Some studies, however, claim that obesity rates among schoolchildren in rural areas, such as in Salem District, Tamil Nadu, were higher than in their urban counterparts (Kowsalya and Parimalavalli 2014). As Ranjani and colleagues (2014) maintain, reflecting on studies showing the presence of overweight among children in government schools (with underweight nevertheless still being higher), they claim that "slowly, but steadily, the epidemic of childhood obesity is now spreading to the lower socio-economic groups as well" (S19). Interestingly, this urban concentration of childhood obesity is different from the aforementioned adult population, where obesity is increasing among adults in urban *and* rural areas. Furthermore, with respect to socioeconomic conditions, several studies report a high correlation between childhood and adolescent obesity and high family income and families with working parents (Chaturvedi 2019; Deshpande et al. 2015; Jain et al. 2016; Patil et al. 2016).

Research across several states has revealed various factors contributing to this spike in children's obesity rates. Some have attributed this situation to an increase in consumption of junk food and sugar-sweetened beverages (Basu 2017; Jain et al. 2016; Ranjani et al. 2014). Due in large part to aggressive advertising and exposure to different (predominantly Western) food cultures, more than ever, children are demanding greater access to junk food; when combined with children's pressure on parents to provide them, the consumption of these products has burgeoned. In fact, Basu (2017) writes that according to the Obesity Foundation of India, "Children's consumption of sugary sodas has increased by 300% in the last two decades" (Basu 2017). Others emphasize the increased consumption of chocolates, chips, and other foods high in carbohydrates and calories; easier access to fast food restaurants and eating out; and aggressive industry marketing toward children (Basu 2017; Chaturvedi 2019; Deshpande et al. 2015; Devulapalli 2019; Jain et al. 2016; Menon 2013; Rajan et al. 2018; Ranjani et al. 2014). Other findings reveal that those children eating outside of the home were statistically more likely to be overweight or obese (Jain et al. 2016; Ranjani et al. 2014), reflecting a growing trend of families eating out (George 2016). Still other studies underscore a lack of physical exercise and increased sedentary lifestyles (e.g., in the form of TV viewing and gaming) coupled with parental pressure for children to stay at home, study, and perform well in school (Arora et al. 2017; Basu 2017; Chaturvedi 2019; Deshpande et al. 2015; Jain et al. 2016; Menon 2013).

A confluence of factors has contributed to India's ongoing childhood obesity problem. Food consumption, particularly the consumption of junk food, is an increasingly major factor contributing to this challenge (Devulapalli 2019; Jain et al. 2016; Menon 2013). Nutrition experts in India, "like Seema Gulati, chief project officer (nutrition) at the Diabetes Foundation of India, say excessive consumption of food high in salt, sugar and fat is the main culprit for obesity and NCDs among children" (quoted in Taneja and Khurana 2017).

Even more startling is the fact that, in this context, worried parents are now demanding gastrointestinal surgeries for their children (Basu 2017; Pandit 2016). Basu (2017) found that some of these patients were only 13 years of age (Basu 2017). Doctors prefer to conduct this procedure only as a last resort, as it is too much of a health risk (Pandit 2016).

Obesity is not the only health ailment associated with the consumption of junk food. Type 2 diabetes has also proliferated alongside obesity, so much so that a new medical term has emerged referencing the presence, projected to be highly prevalent in India, of obesity along with an increase in diabetes: *diabesity* (Debroy 2014). While China may outrank India when it comes to obesity, India certainly takes the cake in having the highest number of type 2 diabetics in the world. In fact, according to Sanghera (2018), it is estimated that approximately 49 percent of the world diabetic population is found in India, and in 2017, India had an approximately 72 million cases. Sanghera (2018) further notes that this "figure [is] expected to almost double to 134 million by 2025." As Pradeepa and Mohan (2017) maintain, the number of diabetics increased from 32.7 million in 2000 to 69.2 million in 2015 (817). According to Singh and colleagues (2017), it is important to emphasize, however, that the International Diabetes Federation (IDF) states that approximately 52.1 percent of diabetics in India are not aware of their disease, while less than a third of those diagnosed have their condition under "good control" (1364).

Influenced by the consumption of junk food and possibly genetics (see Durairaj 2018), type 2 diabetes has surfaced among all socioeconomic groups, and has spread from urban to rural areas (Pradeepa and Mohan 2017). Most cases of diabetes for those over the age of 20 are currently concentrated in major urban cities, such as Mumbai, Delhi, Calcutta, Chennai, Bangalore, and Hyderabad, where disease prevalence has averaged between 8 percent and 18 percent; in rural areas, the prevalence of this disease is 3 percent to 9 percent and increasing (Singh et al. 2017, 1366). According to Little and colleagues (2017), "A review of studies in rural India conducted by Misra and colleagues (2011) found that prevalence increased from 1.9% in 1994 to upwards of 12% in 2009" (Little et al. 2017, 1). Moreover, some believe that the number of type 2 diabetics is even more prevalent in rural areas, where most of the population is undiagnosed (Singh et al. 2017). A qualitative interview conducted by Little and colleagues (2013) of a resident in one of India's largest villages revealed the arrival of new foods (i.e., sodas, sweets, and ultra-processed foods), while other interviewees blamed these foods for the rise of diabetes.

Type 2 diabetes has now become increasingly prevalent among the urban poor (Sanghera 2018). As mentioned earlier, one of the highest behavioral risk factors for acquiring type 2 diabetes is the consumption of junk food, and it is the urban poor who, like everyone else in recent years, have taken advantage of the increased accessibility of these products and altered their diets for the worse (Durairaj 2018; Sanghera 2018). Furthermore, while the greatest risk factor for type 2 diabetes has been overweight and obesity, it is now increasing among individuals with normal weight patterns (for their age and height), as well as in the younger population (Mukherjee 2019).

Indeed, much like what we have seen in the United States and Mexico, type 2 diabetes has now appeared in children and adolescents in India (Khurana and Dhangar 2014; Ramachandran et al., n.d.). In India today, studies have revealed a relationship between high BMI and type 2 diabetes among children (Khurana and Dhangar 2014; Praveen and Tandon 2016). Today, it is no longer rare to see young adults with type 2 diabetes, where the disease is high and increasing in this population (George 2017; Karla and Dhingra 2018; Sharma 2017). While data on children's diabetes in India is difficult to find (George 2017; Praveen and Tandon 2016), according to Sharma (2017), approximately "one in every four (25.3%) people under 25 with diabetes in India has adult-onset type-2 diabetes." According to Praveen and Tandon (2016), "adolescents aged 14–19 years reported that 64% of the obese adolescents in India had fasting hyperinsulinemia, a surrogate marker of insulin resistance" (18–19). Praveen and Tandon further found that insulin resistance for children between the ages of 10 and 17, for both sexes, increased from those exhibiting a normal weight to obese children. Furthermore, Sharma, quoting Professor Nikhil Tandon from the All India Institute of Medical Sciences, found that "the risk of complications for younger persons with type-2 diabetes is twofold to threefold higher than type-1 diabetes" (quoted in Sharma 2017).

Policy Response

When compared to Brazil and Mexico, the Indian government's response to obesity and type 2 diabetes was somewhat delayed. Through the early 2000s, parliament and the Ministry of Health and Family Welfare were primarily focused on eradicating malnutrition and poverty (Gómez 2018; Irwin 2010). In fact, by 2010, "a third of the over 180 million chronically malnourished children in the world live[d] in India and 55 percent of preschool children [were] underweight" (*Economic Times* 2010). Further complicating matters was the prime minister's proclamation during this period that malnutrition was a shameful situation for the country (Gómez 2018; Khandelwal and Reddy 2013). In this context, the state governments were also left to respond to NCDs such as type 2 diabetes, challenging, in some locations, hospitals' ability to manage the heath complications associated with diabetes (BBC 2001). Gómez (2018) maintains that after international pressures for a stronger policy response, the MHFW began to pursue several public health programs addressing obesity, type 2 diabetes, and other NCDs.

Similar to what we saw in Brazil, the Indian government's priority was creating national prevention programs, with less of an emphasis on regulating the marketing and sale of junk food products. The MHFW's first attempt to tackle NCDs came, it seems, with a national MHFW report in 2006, which declared the government's commitment to creating a comprehensive national strategy with an emphasis on monitoring at-risk groups and creating prevention campaigns (Gómez 2018; India, Government 2006). The following year, in 2007, the MHFW established national pilot programs titled the WHO Indian Council of Medical Research NCD risk factor surveillance study and the Integrated Disease Surveillance project (2007–2008) (Gómez 2018). The focus of these two projects was to conduct surveys and disclose the levels of obesity, diabetes, and hypertension present in urban and rural areas (Gómez 2018; Khandelwal and Reddy 2013). In 2008, the MHFW also reformulated its BMI overweight and obesity cutoff points, decreasing them from the WHO's recommended BMI of greater than 30 for obesity and greater than 25–30 for overweight to a BMI of greater than 25 for obesity and between 23 and 25 for overweight (Gómez 2018; Mudur 2008); this was done because of India's unique situation, where the health ailments associated with the WHO's cutoff for obesity were consistently seen at a lower BMI level for the Indian population (Gómez 2018; *Lancet* 2004).

The government's first concrete national program to address NCDs came with the Ministry of Women and Child Development (MWCD) in 2008. That year, the MWCD created new federal nutritional guidelines focused on improved diet and exercise, and guidelines were provided to schools for improved diets (Gómez 2018; Parth 2008). The MWCD continued to raise awareness about children's obesity and diabetes as well as propose new policy measures. These proposals included the MWCD's suggestion, in 2015, to remove all junk food vendors within a two-hundred-meter radius of schools while prohibiting shops from selling these foods to easily identifiable schoolchildren in uniforms (Dwyer 2015). In 2008, that same year, in a move that seemingly precipitated the national government's movement on the issue, the MHFW engaged in a partnership with the Diabetics Foundation India and several other health organizations to formulate their "first India-specific guidelines for prevention and management of obesity and metabolic syndrome" (*Times of India* 2008). In 2011, the government's National Institute of Nutrition also created new nutrition guidelines emphasizing the importance of a balanced diet, limiting the consumption of sugar and processed foods, a return to traditional home cooking, and a new food pyramid (Khurana and Dhangar 2014). This food pyramid included the consumption of junk food (e.g., chocolates, ice cream, burgers, pizza, and fries) but with the recommendation to "eat [these foods] sparingly," as indicated at the top of the food pyramid (7). What is also important to note is that the National Institute of Nutrition guidelines underscored the effects that the marketing of junk foods had on consumer perceptions of food (Khurana and Dhangar 2014).

The MHFW's first-ever national NCD prevention program occurred in 2008: the National Programme for Prevention and Control of Cancer, Diabetes, Cardiovascular Diseases, and Stroke (NPCDCS) (Gómez 2018; Khandelwal and Reddy 2013). The NPCDCS program provided technical and financial assistance to preexisting state and local community programs while also complementing other national programs, such as the National Rural Health Mission, National Tobacco Control Programme, and the National Programme for Health Care of the Elderly (Bloom et al. 2014; Gómez 2018). This program was focused on several action points: early diagnosis and management of NCDs; NCD prevention and control through recommended behavioral and lifestyle changes; capacity building in the areas of prevention, treatment, and diagnosis; creating palliative and rehabilitative care capacity; human resource training, and increased detection of those at risk of having NCDs (Bloom et al. 2014; Gómez 2018). The NPCDCS operated at the state level, and was implemented, during its pilot phase, in approximately twenty thousand health subcenters and seven hundred community health centers across twenty one states (Bloom et al. 2014; Gómez 2018). In addition, in 2013, the government created the National Action Plan and Monitoring Framework for Prevention and Control of NCDs to be implemented from 2013 to 2020; this program had an explicit focus on government intervention through a variety of monitoring and prevention programs with specific targets for a variety of prevention and control outcomes (India, Ministry of Health and Family Welfare, Government of India, n.d.). Further adding to this increased government commitment to stemming the rising tide of obesity was Prime Minister Modi's recent "Fit India" movement, established in September 2019, which promoted the importance of regular exercise and healthy eating with the goal of establishing a "culture of fitness" throughout the nation (Kaul 2019). On the one-year anniversary of Modi's Fit India movement, on September 24, 2020, the prime minister also planned to organize online sessions, in conversation with citizens and some of India's leading fitness experts, to emphasize "raising awareness about the importance of fitness and health, especially during a global pandemic" (*Hindustan Times* 2020, 1). As the *Hindustan Times* (2020) emphasized: "This movement is an initiative by the Prime Minister himself, who envisioned it as a movement meant for the people. It seeks to involve the people of the nation into a dialogue about the importance of fitness, and to draw out a plan for making India a Fit Nation." In September 2019, the Ministry of Health and Family Welfare introduced the Poshan Maah nutrition campaign (to be recognized yearly in the month of September), which focuses on promoting healthier, more balanced eating habits while reducing malnutrition in rural areas through the assistance of well-trained frontline health care workers (Kaul 2018).

On July 10, 2018, India's Food Safety and Standards Authority of India (FSSAI) also created the Eat Right India campaign (Mathew 2019). This public awareness campaign is focused, it seems, on increasing awareness about eating right by, for example, reducing the intake of sugar, salt, and fat, while companies agreed to reduce the amount of sugar and salt in their products (Mathew 2019). Through its Swasth Bharat Yatra, introduced on October 16, 2018, the FSSAI also organized a cyclothon across several locations in India "to spread the message of [the] 'Eat Right Movement' across the country" (1). An Indian restaurant chain voluntarily agreed to reduce the salt content of one of their products, which prompted complaints from consumers about the new taste, though the restaurant ended up providing additional salt packets to unhappy customers (Mathew 2019).

In the area of regulation, the government has also established food labeling laws. Historically, the food labeling process was managed by the Prevention of Food Adulteration Act of 1954 (Khandelwal and Reddy 2013). More recently, however, in the area of food packaging and labeling, an amendment (part VII of the Prevention of Food Adulteration Rules of 1955) was introduced. This amendment stated that all packaged products must include labels outlining nutritional claims and health information (Khandelwal and Reddy 2013). For example, according to Khandelwal and Reddy (2013), the "FSSSAI suggests that nutritional information or nutritional facts per 100 g, 100 mL or servings of the product should be given on the label and should contain (i) energy value in kcal; (ii) the amounts of proteins, carbohydrates (specify quantity of sugar) and fats in g or mL; and (iii) the amount of any other nutrient for which a nutrition or health claim is made" (120). Furthermore, part VII of the Prevention of Food Adulteration Rules of 1955 required that labels "provide detailed information on macronutrients, namely, carbohydrates, proteins and fats, along with total calorie content, sugars, trans fats and saturated fats per serving of the product" (120). Furthermore, in April 2018 the FSSAI released the "draft 'Food and Safety Standards (Labeling and Display) Regulation'" (Srivastava 2019). This draft resolution (still in progress) includes a recommended color-coded visual aid on labels, with red used to indicate that the product is high in fat, sugar, or salt (Srivastava 2019).

Finally, with respect to the marketing and advertisement of junk food products, the government has limited regulatory policies on this issue. For instance, clause 53 in section 56 of the Food Safety and Standards Act of 2006 has established regulations on the quality of advertising, stating "that any person who publishes or is a party to the publication of an advertisement which a) falsely describes any food or b) is likely to mislead as to the nature or substance or quality of any food or gives false guarantee, shall be liable to a penalty which may extend to ten lakh rupees. Authorities entrusted for food safety will be responsible for enforcing the law" (Bhatnagar et al. 2014, 1190). This is further reinforced by the 1994 Cable Television Networks Rules, which stipulates, for example, that any advertisements endangering children, displaying them in an undignified manner, or leading them to engage in unhealthy practices are forbidden, and states that children's programs should not include indecent language and violence. Nevertheless, Bhatanagar and colleagues (2014) claim that "no clear reference to marketing of unhealthy food to children or exact time regulations were made in this act" (1190).

Policy Challenges

Still, there have been several ongoing policy challenges, with respect to prevention and especially regulation policy. Concerning prevention, there was a considerably long delay in creating a tax on sodas and junk food. In 2015, a working group chaired by the government's chief economic advisor, Arvind Subramanian, proposed the idea of introducing a "40% 'sin tax' on aerated drinks" (Whitehead 2015b). Another proposal put forth by the Modi administration, in 2014, was to ban the sale of junk food in schools (Prasad 2014). Moreover, Prasad (2014) claims that "this was followed up with an increase in the prices of soft drinks in the recent budget." Major companies were also affected by the Modi administration's proposed "fat tax" on junk food products, claiming that it was protectionist in nature because smaller restaurants, for example, did not see a tax while larger ones, such as McDonald's and Domino's, had to pay it (All That's Interesting 2017). Similar to what we saw in Mexico, this sin tax was "part of a broader fiscal overhaul" (Wilkes 2015). The Modi administration was also considering a "fat tax" on all junk food (Kalra 2017).These efforts were mere proposals that did not lead to immediate legislation due to lack of political will (Basu et al. 2017; Gómez 2018). In this context, the states implemented these types of taxes on their own. In 2016, for example, the state of Kerala imposed a 14.5 percent tax on all junk food products in order to improve the overall health and dietary consciousness of food consumption, while nevertheless claiming that the tax was focused on the "elite section of the society" (Menon 2016, 1).

In 2017, however, the Modi administration eventually succeeded in creating its proposed "sin tax" (India Resource Center 2017a). More specifically, sweetened carbonated drinks, which also include sweetened waters, have been lumped together with harmful products such as tobacco and were imposed a 28 percent tax through the 2017 Goods and Services Tax policy (India Resource Center 2017a). An additional 12 percent tax, dubbed a "'compensation cess,' or sin tax, a category reserved primarily for harmful products such as tobacco," was imposed (quoted in India Resource Center 2017a). And according to Sunita Narain, who is the director general of India's Centre for Science and Environment, "The 40 per cent 'sin' tax in India would add Rs 15.60 on one litre of colas. This is much higher than the tax in Mexico and hence will hopefully count" (Narain 2017).

With regard to food labeling, pundits claim that they still provide insufficient, unclear information on nutritional content (Taneja and Khurana 2017), as well as misleading statements (Khurana and Dhangar 2014). Others note that they need to include a statement about the moderate consumption of food, the addictive quality of some foods (especially for children), and statements about how such products should not replace balanced meals (Misra and Pathania 2016). Labels not only need to include this information but also need to be written in a clear, easy-to-understand manner, such as front-of-package labels highlighting critical ingredients, such as the levels of sugar, fat, and salt (Taneja and Khurana 2017). Additionally, according to Khurana and Dhangar (2014), researchers at the Centre for Science and Environment (CSE) found that existing labels on junk food products provide "misleading claims on the amount of trans fats present, lack of standardised serving sizes and information on contribution to RDA" (Khurana and Dhangar 2014, 24; see also Balch 2012 on this issue). Establishments serving burgers and pizzas were also found to only advertise information about the nutritional content of their foods on their company websites, rather than at point of sale (Khurana and Dhangar 2014). Restaurants are not required by law to provide food labels listing the nutritional content of their products (Balch 2012).

With respect to regulations safeguarding children's health, to date, no federal law—or even bureaucratic resolution—exists prohibiting the sale of junk foods within and/or near schools. The first attempt in this direction came in 2010. That year, a concerned parent, Mr. Rahul Verma, "filed [a] public interest lawsuit in the Delhi High Court . . . seeking a ban on the sale of junk food and soft drinks in and around schools across India" (Anand 2017). According to Anand (2017), Mr. Verma based "his case on the constitutional authority of courts to intervene to protect citizens' right to life." The Delhi High Court subsequently issued a "decree" ordering that these foods be "restricted in schools and [within] a fifty meter radius around schools" (Thekaekara 2015). The FSSAI was required to ensure the implementation of this ruling, and the Delhi High Court also ordered the FSSAI to develop new cafeteria (canteen) policies in order to ensure the provision of healthy foods in schools (Thekaekara 2015; see also Centre for Science and Environment 2015). As Taneja and Khurana (2017) explain, the High Court's overall mandate delegated to the FSSAI included the following: (1) the restriction of junk food sales within schools and at least fifty meters away from school; (2) a school canteen policy based on a color-coded scheme of red, yellow, and green (as mentioned previously), indicating the prohibition of foods high in sugar and fat (red), moderate sale of specific foods in small quantities, "eaten sparingly" (yellow), and that nutritious foods comprise 80 percent of the food items sold (green) (see also the Centre for Science and Environment 2015). The High Court's guidelines also call on the creation of healthy menu options, such as fruit salads and vegetables (Centre for Science and Environment 2015), and the regulation of junk food advertising toward children "to be regulated through a framework that includes all types of media, celebrity endorsements and promotional activities" (Centre for Science and Environment 2015). Through these guidelines the High Court also suggested that schools increase their commitment to providing nutritional information to students by way of a specified educational curriculum (Centre for Science and Environment 2015).

Considering this a matter of national urgency, the High Court ordered the FSSAI to, within a period of only three months, convert these guidelines into official federal regulations, in accordance with the 2006 Food Safety and Standards Act (Centre for Science and Environment 2015). The director general of the Centre for Science and Environment, Sunita Narain, commented on the issue: "The Court has emphasised on time-bound enforcement across the country and has put immense faith in the FSSAI." Moreover, in an effort to expedite the process, the court asked the Delhi school administrator to work with schools to implement the guidelines, via the imposition of "Rule 43 of the Delhi School Education Rules, 1973." For those schools outside of Delhi, and falling under the management of the Central Board of Secondary Education (CBSE), the court requested the CBSE to consider these guidelines and to induce school compliance by making CBSE membership conditional on their adoption of the court's school guidelines (Centre for Science and Environment 2015). Additionally, the Ministry of Health and Family Welfare also requested that chief ministers (state governors) and health officials "prohibit the sale of junk food on school premises" (Khandelwal and Reddy 2013, 119). And in 2015, according to Dwyer (2015), the Ministry of Women and Child Development further "recommended that vendors be banned from selling junk food to children within a 200-meter radius of school—a distance roughly the equivalent of two football fields back-to-back."

However, to this day, to my knowledge, no federal policies or mandates have been imposed on schools prohibiting the sale of junk food. Indeed, this is still a policy measure that has been recommended by policy analysts (see Chaturvedi 2019). Worse still, according to Chibber (2012), "The Indian government in a written response to the Delhi High Court said that while it cannot and would not ban junk food in and around schools, it would however prescribe strict health standards for ingredients in such foods." Interestingly, the government has decided in the past to ban the sale of these products within parliament's cafeterias due to reported pesticide residue contamination of Coke and Pepsi products (Kaye 2004). Furthermore, according to Amit Srivastava of the India Resource Center, "The Indian Parliament has banned the sale of Coke and Pepsi products in its cafeteria . . . the parliamentarians should take the next logical step, and ban the sale of Coke and Pepsi products in the entire country" (quoted in Killer Coke.org, n.d.).

In addition, not only has the FSSAI failed to transform the court's guidelines into effective regulations (i.e., entailing stringent penalties for noncompliance), but it has also been reluctant to earnestly pursue the enforcement of the court's guidelines to prohibit the sale of these foods in schools (*The Pioneer* 2016; Taneja and Khurana 2017), instead providing only meagre "suggestions" to do so (Bhushan 2018). In addition to ongoing delays in creating enforceable regulations, due in large part to intergovernmental negotiations and disagreements, officials appear to be hesitant at implementing them. Indeed, as FSSAI director Pawan Kumar Agarwal recently commented: "About three years ago, the High Court asked us to come out with regulation on healthy diets for school children. We have been struggling to put that regulation together. Because if you have to make a law, it has to be implemented" (quoted in Press Trust of India 2019a). Instead, Mr. Kumar's FSSAI offered a mere draft resolution, specifically, "a draft regulation on availability of safe, wholesome and nutritious food in schools" (Press Trust of India 2019a), which was submitted for comments to the general public (Bhushan 2018).

Other studies find that children continue to purchase junk food at schools and local vendors or bring them to school in their lunchbox (Taneja and Khurana 2017). Despite the government's sensitivity to international criticism in the area of public health (Gómez 2018), this has not motivated the government to impose sales restrictions in schools. In 2011, for example, a policy recommendation from the WHO prohibited the sale of sodas and snack foods in schools (Khandelwal and Reddy 2013). India's government failed to follow up with a federal policy mandate along these lines, with only the cities of Delhi and Uttar Pradesh providing guidelines to do so (Khandelwal and Reddy 2013). Only a handful of other state governments, such as Punjab, Nagaland, and Maharasthra, have adopted the High Court's guidelines on banning junk food in schools (Taneja and Khurana 2017).

In the absence of stern and enforceable FSSAI regulations, all that government officials can do is provide policy guidelines and recommendations to schools. BB Chavan, India's deputy director of education for Mumbai, stated: "We cannot stop a school from serving junk food, as there is no official ban in place. We can at best advise them to opt for healthier choices" (quoted in Dutt and Pednekar 2017). In this context, it appears as if schools have been free to create their own food policies, in turn leading to considerable variation in the extent to which they are willing to prohibit the sale of junk food. As Rathi and colleagues (2017) report in an in-depth study of private schools in the state of Kolkata, a limited number of schools have food policies in place. After ten in-depth interviews with school principals in this state, only four had written policies and agreed to it, while others only had verbal agreements (345). Moreover, Rathi and others (2017) found that due to incessant pressure from children, school principals often give in and supply sodas and junk foods. Rathi and colleagues concluded that "no school food policies, i.e., written and verbal have been defined by any Indian government protocol" (347).

Even fewer government attempts have been made to create federal regulations prohibiting the advertisement of junk food (Balch 2012; Khandelwal and Reddy 2013). In 2016, DLA Piper noted that there were no federal or state laws prohibiting the advertisement of foods high in sugar, salt, and fat toward children (DLA Piper 2016). There is only passing mention of protecting children in the 1994 India Cable Television Networks (Regulation) Act, and in 2006 a committee was formed by the Ministry of Information and Broadcasting to revise the Network (Regulation) Act's codes and to explore how to enforce these revised codes (Hawkes 2007). Nevertheless, these kinds of enforcement policy suggestions, such as monitoring TV advertisements, by bureaucratic agencies were still never pursued (Miryala 2011). Additionally, Keshari and Mishra (2016) found that the Cable Television Network Act of 1994 needs to "be strictly enforced" (1360); they further emphasize that the Ministry of Information and Broadcasting needs to create firmer controls on advertising.

Similar to what we saw in Brazil, in India there primarily exists industry self-regulatory practices in the area of food advertising, with nongovernmental voluntary private entities, such as the Advertising Agencies Association of India (AAAI) and the Advertising Standards Council of India (ASCI), governing this process and focused on ensuring that all food advertisements are not misguided in their nutritional information while imposing only "moral pressure on advertisers and companies to withdraw objectionable advertisements" (Miryala 2011, 47). It seems that the government has provided support throughout this process. In fact, the FSSAI went so far as to create an official guideline titled "Guidelines: Code of Self Regulation in Food Advertisement" (see Khandelwal and Reddy 2013, 120).

Several major soda and ultraprocessed food industries have engaged in self-regulatory practices. This process has mainly been monitored and managed by the ASCI (Taneja and Khurana 2017). The ASCI serves to monitor and ethically enforce these industries' voluntary self-regulations, holding them accountable for their actions. However, the ASCI does not impose any penalty for noncompliance, for, as Taneja and Khurana (2017) claim, the ASCI "does not have any punitive power on its own." By working closely with the ASCI and other voluntary regulatory agencies and allowing them to hold industries accountable, this appears to increase the credibility and trust of these industries in the eyes of the government.

In addition, the ASCI has been proactive in encouraging the public to report industry violations of misleading advertising; concerned citizens are encouraged to report these violations on ASCI's website (Bhatnagar et al. 2014). In 2013, the ASCI instituted new measures to facilitate and expedite the reporting of these complaints. This was achieved mainly through the "FTCC (Fast Track Intra Industry Complaint) and SPI (Suspension Pending Investigation)" (1189). What's more, the ASCI also created the National Advertising Monitoring Service (IDEOS 2018) in order to further aid in the monitoring and reporting of violations (Bhatnagar et al. 2014). The National Advertising Monitoring Service monitors approximately 1,500 advertisements from these industries each month (1189).

In 2016, in cooperation with major junk food industries, the Food and Beverage Alliance of India (FBAI) published its India's Policy on Marketing Communications to Children (Bhattacharya 2016). Through this effort, several industries, such as Coca-Cola, Mondelez India, PepsiCo, Kellogg, and Nestlé, have agreed to engage in self-regulatory practices, explicitly prohibiting themselves from selling their products to children under the age of 12. The FBAI agreed to periodically publish reports revealing the progress industries are making to adhere to these self-regulatory policies, either with respect to children falling under the FBAI nutrition criteria, which would have entailed industry compliance with WHO nutrition reporting protocols, or to all children under the age of 12 regardless (Bhattacharya 2016).

Coca-Cola and PepsiCo have also signed up for the International Food and Beverage Alliance's India Pledge (Balch 2012). This pledge allows for the marketing of their products to children under the age of 12 "only when the promoted products meet 'strict science-based nutrition criteria'" (Balch 2012).

And in 2019, as an endorser of the government's aforementioned Eat Right public awareness campaign and pledge, Nestlé has committed to reducing the amount of sugar, salt, and fat in their products (Mabiyan 2019). Indeed, in an interview with reporter Rashmi Mabiyan of ET HealthWorld, Sanjay Khajuria, director of Nestlé India's Corporate Affairs division, stated that his company pledged to reduce, on average, "6% added sugar, 10% salt, and 2.5% total fat" in their relevant products by 2020 (quoted in Mabiyan 2019).

In February 2018, the government also publicly acknowledged that it had no plans to pursue any formal regulatory restrictions on junk food advertisements on television (*The Statesman* 2018). That day, during a parliamentary hearing, Rajyavardhan Singh Rathore, Minister of State for Information and Broadcasting, announced that the FBAI had already decided to restrict their food advertisements to children (*The Statesman* 2018). Rathore's ministry publicly acknowledged these efforts, in essence, seemingly using them as a scapegoat for not pursuing stern government regulations. It was actually the government that initially suggested the idea of prohibiting the advertising of unhealthy products through a FSSAI working group (*The Statesman* 2018). Indeed, during FSSAI expert working group meetings in which foods high in sugar, salt, and fat were discussed, FSSAI officials recommended that there be no advertising of these products on children's channels during shows designed for kids (*The Statesman* 2018). According to Smriti Irani, information and broadcasting minister, "On this recommendation, the remarks of the FSSAI were that the food businesses could be asked to voluntarily desist from advertising high fat, sugar and salt foods on children's channels" (quoted in *The Statesman* 2018). In general, however, pundits believe that these types of self-regulatory codes, often used by advertising agencies, are vaguely stated, voluntary, and lacking in adequate enforcement (Bhatnagar et al. 2014).

Even more troubling is that despite these industries' self-regulatory commitments, they appear to continue to advertise their products to children. Recent research by Gupta and others (2017) finds that "various food product manufacturing companies continue to advertise unhealthy food products to this vulnerable group [children] despite their own pledges and commitments" (45). Bhatnagar and colleagues (2014) mention a study claiming "that exposure of children to HFSS [high in fat, sugar, or salt] food advertising, as a proportion of all advertising seen, did not change despite adherence to advertising restrictions" (1190). Bhatnagar and others further claim that ongoing competition between these industries has weakened industries' ethical behaviors and self-regulatory codes.

Thus, in India, no federal regulations—or even attempts—exist to limit the advertisement of junk foods (see also Khandelwal and Reddy 2013). Keshari and Mishra (2016) claim that the aforementioned Cable Television Network Act of 1994 needs to enforce preexisting media regulations. Research by Misra and Pathania further emphasizes that India's "regulating bodies are found to be neither adequate nor effective. Rigorous enforcement of advertising regulations is necessary to ensure compliance and improve the effectiveness of regulatory bodies. Government should play an active role to make and implement rules and regulations against manufacturing promotion and sale of junk food" (2016, xi).

Thus, similar to what we saw in Mexico and Brazil, the government's priority has been on the creation of federal NCD awareness and prevention programs, rather than on effective regulatory legislation addressing the heart of the problem: junk food marketing and sales. But why has this occurred? This is particularly puzzling in a context where the national government has repeatedly emphasized its ongoing commitment to stemming the tide of NCDs and protecting the health and safety of its children and the poor. As I explain in the next section, this challenge primarily has to do with the political and social strategies that industries take to persuade the government not to pursue more aggressive regulations.

Political Action

Consistent with IPCI, a key factor leading to the aforementioned policy shortcomings has to do with the various political tactics that industries use to shape policy discussions in their favor. One important tactic has been building policy partnerships within government.

In recent years, for example, Coca-Cola India has partnered with government officials to provide education and health care services in several cities (Faheem 2009). Furthermore, as part of their corporate social responsibility campaign (more on these activities soon), Coca-Cola India also set up several education projects for children, such as their Jagriti Learning Centers, situated near their production factories in the state of Pune, in partnership with local NGOs (Faheem 2009). In the area of health care, Coca-Cola India has entered into a partnership with the Delhi government and the Indian Red Cross to establish health education camps in poor communities with a focus on raising awareness about issues such as sanitation, HIV/AIDS, hygiene, immunization, communicable disease, and children's health (Faheem 2009). In recognition of Coca-Cola India's efforts, in 2008, the Delhi government provided the company with the "'Bhagidari Award' for its water conservation and community development initiatives" (25); several other recognitions have been provided from local communities and governments.

Furthermore, in 2011, Coca-Cola partnered with New Delhi TV, the government, and UN-Habitat to improve the health and well-being of schoolchildren (Marks 2019). Specifically, through its Support My School project and partnership with these entities, Coca-Cola aimed to "improve access to water, sanitation, and facilities in Indian schools" (Marks 2019, 96). According to Marks (2019), by 2017, the New Delhi TV (NDTV) station reported that one thousand schools had benefited from this project. Nevertheless, Marks (2019) underscores that if this project partnership had led to an increase in the consumption of Coca-Cola products, then this could have undermined the integrity of UN-Habitat and trust in the organization as one committed to sustainability.

But Coca-Cola is not alone in establishing these policy partnerships with government. Beginning in 2009, Nestlé also partnered with six regional universities in India, as well as Magic Bus India, an NGO, through Nestlé's Healthy Kids Program (ETBrandEquity 2019). Academic deans from public universities affiliated with this program have been proud to be a part of the initiative. For example, The dean of Punjab Agricultural University, Dr. Sandeep Bains, once commented: "Our partnership with Nestlé India spans a decade and we are proud to be associated with them for positively impacting young lives. We are extremely glad to have been a partner in this journey of bringing about healthier smiles on the faces of beneficiaries" (quoted in ETBrandEquity 2019). Nestlé's program drew praise from state officials, such as Bharat Bhushan Ashu, the state of Punjab's minister of food and civil supplies and consumer affairs, who stated: "Nestlé Healthy Kids Programme is a very thoughtful initiative which focuses on increasing awareness among beneficiaries about nutrition, health and wellness and I hope more such initiatives are introduced in the years to come for making a significant impact" (quoted in ETBrandEquity 2019).

In yet another instance, Coca-Cola has partnered with the FSSAI to improve the distribution of healthy and safe food. According to Mitra (2017): "T. Krishnakumar, president (India and south-west Asia), Coca-Cola, said life is easier when companies and the sector regulator work in a 'collaborative manner.'" In 2017, Coca-Cola entered into a memorandum of understanding (MOU) with the FSSAI to train street vendors to ensure the provision of safe foods, as well as to improve hygiene and waste management (*DT Next* 2017; Mitra 2017). According to *DT Next* (2017), Venkatesh Kini, former president of Coca-Cola India and Southwest Asia, reportedly stated that "Coca-Cola India is enthusiastic about partnering with FSSAI to make a significant contribution to improving the lives of the vendors and also enhancing the eating out experience for consumers." Through the FSSAI's Project Clean Street Food and this MOU, Coca-Cola agreed to train approximately fifty thousand street vendors over a three-year period with the goal of improving waste management and sanitation, and ensuring safe food preparation (*DT Next* 2017; Mitra 2017). Through Project Clean Street Food, the FSSAI has also worked with other government agencies and NGOs (*DT Next* 2017). Through this MOU, moreover, Coca-Cola "will be responsible for the program execution through its network of trainers and available infrastructure, [and] FSSAI will ensure the relevance of the training content and shall oversee the overall delivery" (*DT Next* 2017). FSSAI's CEO, Pawan Agarwal, also commented that he was "confident that this partnership will help in accelerating Hon'ble Prime Minister's vision for Skilled and Healthy India" (quoted in *DT Next* 2017).

In recent years, the FSSAI has considered food safety a shared responsibility across several sectors, public and private. Indeed, as FSSAI CEO Pawan Agarwal once commented: "I am delighted to see that corporates are taking up the responsibility to ensure safe and nutritious food across the country under FSSAI's 'Safe and Nutritious Food—A Shared Responsibility'" (quoted in *DT Next* 2017). In its work with industry, the FSSAI has taken steps to engage in partnerships with several other industries, such as Nestlé and CHIFFS (CII-HUL Initiative on Food Safety Sciences) (Nagarajan 2019). Agarwal also once commented that "besides Nestle and Coca-Cola, we are also working with companies like ITC Ltd, Mondelez India, TetraPak, Jubilant FoodWorks, Yum Brands, among others, for different projects related to nutrition and food safety" (quoted in LiveMint 2017). In yet another instance, ITC Limited pursued a partnership with the FSSAI to work with ten thousand schools to provide nutritious school meals (LiveMint 2017). What's more, according to the *Economic Times* (2017), "Agarwal said FSSAI will focus on spreading awareness about nutrition and safe food through its partnership with Mondelez and is also working with Dominos to train food vendors across the country."

Concerns quickly emerged about the FSSAI's partnership with food and soda industries: namely, that the endeavor represents a clear conflict of interest (India Resource Center, 2017b; Nagarajan 2019), and the hypocrisy of the FSSAI being created in response to a Joint Parliamentary Committee investigation that found high amounts of pesticides in Coca-Cola (and other) beverages, in turn disclosing the poor state of government regulation of food products (India Resource Center 2017b). The latter confirms what others have argued is an unethical contradiction, where the FSSAI should be regulating industry rather than "cosying up to" it, and, in the process, forgetting its original purpose of being "a legally mandated regulator" (Sharma 2019). In addition, others have argued that these types of partnerships should not be allowed. As Amit Srivastava of the India Resource Center maintains, "For Coca-Cola, a partnership with India's top food safety organization is a no brainier because it allows the company to use the Indian government's brand and logo to wash its hands of all the violations and the public health harm its products create. Even more troubling is that Coca-Cola will promote its unhealthy products using the Indian government brand. This is absolutely unacceptable" (quoted in India Resource Center 2017b). The FSSAI's CEO, Pawan Kumar Agarwal, nevertheless commented in the *Times of India*: "We are extremely careful in partnerships as far as conflict of interest is concerned" (quoted in Nagarajan 2019). But will this statement be enough to fend off criticism and ensure an effective, unbiased regulatory policy response?

Nestlé has also worked with the FSSAI. Nestlé's Food Safety Institute (NFSI), based in the state of Haryana Manesar, has worked with the FSSAI to provide training on how to improve that latter's food safety regulatory capacity (Vishwanath 2017). Agarwal, the FSSAI's CEO, not only inaugurated the NFSI in 2017, but according to Vishwanath (2017), he also "welcomed the partnership with Nestle as a 'well-thought strategy.'" Mitra (2017) claims that "the idea for the partnership, which Agarwal termed a 'well-thought strategy,' came in February, when top officials of Nestle India visited Agarwal's office. The meeting ended with an agreement on the imitative that would help the company mend fences with India's food regulator, a tribute to Agarwal's open mind as he sought ways to engage with food multinationals, even while aiming to ensure marketed food was safe for every Indian." When questioned by a newspaper, *ThePrint*, about NFSI's relationship with the FSSAI and this initiative, however, the FSSAI claimed that this was not an official partnership between them (Vishwanath 2017). Nevertheless, Vishwanath (2017) does describe an email in which the FSSAI alternatively claims that NFSI does have "the encouragement that needs to be viewed in the backdrop of the FSSAI's efforts to foster a collaborative and participatory approach, which is the need of the hour if we wish to ensure safe and nutritious food to 125 crore Indian citizens." Thus, this appears to be an unofficial collaborative agreement between the NFSI and FSSAI. Even more surprising is the fact that the FSSAI had previously taken Nestlé to court over the disputed poor quality of its Maggi noodles, a charge that the Supreme Court still has not settled (Vishwanath 2017). Critics therefore viewed these efforts as part of Nestlé's strategy to mend its relationship with the FSSAI (Mitra 2017).

Industry's efforts to establish policy partnerships with government have been facilitated by the government's belief in the advantages of engaging in these types of partnerships with the junk food industry. In fact, according to Agarwal, "If you want to ensure food safety, you have to work with them (companies), . . . you can't fight them. We can engage with them not only to improve their own practices, but to improve the entire ecosystem. . . . A healthy, trustworthy relationship is required between the regulator and the companies and other stakeholders. . . . Partnerships with private parties on food safety and standards are imperative for FSSAI. This is our effort to implement a first world regulatory ecosystem in India" (Mitra 2017).

According to several scholars and activists I interviewed, all of these policy partnerships have helped to increase the legitimacy and policy influence of the junk food industry (interview with Vandana Prasad, Public Health Resource Network, September 8, 2020; interview with Dipa Sinha, Ambedkar University, September 15, 2020). By partnering with government, these industries reveal that they are part of the solution to India's ongoing obesity and type 2 diabetes problem, especially among children and the poor, and that these industries can be trusted. What's more, some are of the view that these partnerships also help to boost industry's legitimacy within communities, tying a good human face to their products (interview with Vandana Prasad, September 8, 2020). Consequently, this appears to have made it difficult for the FSSAI, the Ministry of Health and Family Welfare, and parliament to pursue any further regulation affecting industry's market profitability.

Lobbying and Largesse

In addition to engaging in policy partnerships with government, India's junk food industry has also been involved in several lobbying and largesse tactics. As IPCI emphasizes, and as the political science interest group and corporate political activity literature attests, this is a well-established tactic that companies have relied on to influence policy in their favor.

Industries in India have engaged in several "insider" lobbying tactics, similar to what we saw in Brazil and Mexico. While interest groups and lobbyists have not been publicly visible in the past, referred to as "shadow warriors," clandestinely engaging in what Pepper Culpepper (2011) once referred to as quiet, back-door politics, this has changed considerably in recent years (Nayar et al. 2010). Interest groups and lobbyists have become increasingly professional in the tactics and strategies they use, are often seen in public, and "have become public figures, freely mixing with the powers-that-be" (Nayar et al. 2010). When making their case, lobbyists representing big business have used PowerPoint presentations, money, deals, and sneaky tricks, apparently "running the show" in some of India's biggest cities, such as Mumbai and Delhi (Nayar et al. 2010). "It's a complicated system, almost like a parallel government with its own rules, structures. People are fixed, punished, rewarded, . . . but that's how it is," stated an anonymous lobbyist interviewed by Nayar and colleagues (2010). The absence of any federal legal statue regulating lobbying appears to have induced this strategic and complex behavior; in this context, without any possibility of punishment for violating the law, it seems that lobbying firms are free to engage in whatever strategy they like. In response, experts from India note that the government needs to do a better job of regulating, monitoring, and increasing transparency in lobbying activity—similar to what is seen in the United States, United Kingdom, Germany, and Canada—while imposing penalties for violating lobbying procedures (see Agarwal 2010).

When it came to fending off regulations on the sale of junk food to children, well-organized interest groups were hard at work and very successful. The All India Food Processors' Association (AIFPA), one of the largest interest groups representing big soda and ultraprocessed foods, engaged in lobbying efforts when it came to the High Court's ruling in 2012 that junk food be banned from schools. On the eve of the High Court judges making their final decision on the matter, an attorney for the AIFPA met with a bench of judges headed by Acting Chief Justice A. K. Sikri to claim that a petition seeking to remove junk food from schools was unclear as to what precisely constitutes junk food (*Economic Times* 2011). A lawyer for the AIFPA claimed that the Prevention of Food Adulteration Act does not specify what precisely is junk food or even fast food (*Economic Times* 2011). Moreover, the Uday Foundation's petition was vaguely worded on what precisely constituted as the junk foods to be banned near schools, and because the current laws do not specify what constitutes such foods, there was no legal basis for banning them, claimed the AIFPA (Chibber 2012).

Shortly after the High Court made its ruling in September 2012, a committee of experts was formed by the MHFW to assess and respond to the court's ruling (Singh 2013). However, this committee was avoided and heavily criticized by the AIFPA and the National Restaurants of India. These groups went to the High Court to complain, questioning the need and legitimacy of the committee, which was comprised of scientists, medical doctors, government health officials, and industry and civil societal representatives. An attorney representing the food industry claimed that the special committee organized by the MHFW was not in accordance with rules specified under the Food Safety and Standards Act of 2005. According to section 13 of this act, the FSSAI, not the MHFW, is the only government entity allowed to form committees that are focused on food and beverages. However, Singh (2013) claims that health activists saw industry's accusations as a tactic used to "scuttle the process of ensuring healthy foods in schools." Industry wanted to ensure that only the FSSAI would be handling these matters. And yet, as I address in more detail later, the FSSAI is dominated by industry's interests. By seeking to discredit the MHFW's committee, then, and by restricting policy decisions to the FSSAI, this helped to guarantee that no concrete policy regulations would emerge on the prohibition of junk food sales in schools.

Furthermore, according to Chibber (2012), the central government eventually made a decision that complemented industry's wishes: that there would be no formal legal ban on the sale of junk food products within and near schools. Nevertheless, the government would commit to recommending improved standards for enhancing the ingredients of foods provided in school cafeterias. The MHFW stated that "junk foods" did not fall under the Food Safety Act. According to this act, such foods were titled "proprietary and novel" and not dangerous on their own. However, the act does state that these foods, such as sodas, burgers, candy, and the like, must fall within certain safety parameters. Chibber (2012) claims that the MHFW's position on this matter "vindicated the stand of the All India Processors Association (AIFPA), which in November had asked to be made party to the PIL, which it said was flawed as it failed to clarify the kinds of foods to be banned in the vicinity of schools."

When it came to food labeling, interest groups were also aggressive in publicly questioning and thwarting proposed regulatory legislation. The AIFPA has relied on the usage of narrative discourse and messaging that questions the appropriateness and cultural implications of proposed policies, such as the government's draft regulation on introducing color-coded food labels. For instance, shortly after this draft regulation was announced in 2019, a spokesman for the AIFPA, Subodh Jindal, claimed that adopting this legislation was concerning, as "once it is implemented, 90 per cent of Indian products will have red labels. All your heritage drinks and rasgullas will be framed as bad products. They [the FSSAI] want all Indian ethnic and traditional foods to be stopped" (quoted in Mathew 2019). Jacobs (2019a) notes that industries were eventually successful in delaying the government's creation of new food labels in 2018. Discussions within the FSSAI are still ongoing with no clear resolution in sight.

In an effort to assuage the concerns of critics troubled by the delay in adopting new food regulations, Jacobs (2019a) notes that the government devised an expert panel to review these policies. However, the person chosen to head this panel, Dr. Boindala Sesikeran, is a former director of the government's National Institute of Nutrition; a former advisor to Nestlé, Italian chocolate maker Ferrero, and Japan's Ajinomoto food company; and last but not least, a trustee of the International Life Sciences Institute (see Jacobs 2019a). The International Life Sciences Institute was founded by a former Coca-Cola executive and, as Jacobs (2019a) notes, "has been quietly infiltrating government health and nutrition bodies around the world."

Efforts to introduce a soda tax were also derailed for many years due to aggressive "insider" lobbying tactics. Since 2015, the government was engaged in discussions about taxes, as well as labeling regulations, which the Modi administration started to look into in 2017 (FirstPost 2017). At that time, the government was "also considering a nationwide 'fat tax' for so-called 'junk foods.'" In response, in February 2017, "executives from companies including PepsiCo, Nestlé, and Indian consumer firm ITC met trade groups in New Delhi to coordinate efforts and urge the government to resist pressure from health advocates, according to an industry source aware of the meeting. The attendees, who felt their efforts to push back had been too piecemeal, talked about forming a core group to unify their message when engaging the government, the source said" (FirstPost 2017; see also White-head 2017 on this issue). According to Whitehead (2017), based on a newswire that was released, members of the All India Food Processors' Association attended a couple of meetings in February 2017 and "some of these members *'planned to send a joint representation to the government and approach health and food officials to express concerns about stringent regulations.'* " While, as mentioned earlier, the parliament did eventually succeed in introducing a 40 percent sin tax on these and other harmful products, it appears that in-dustry groups were successful in substantially delaying its adoption.

Institutional Infiltration

Perhaps the most effective "insider" strategy that the AIFPA and other interest groups have used is engaging in a process of strategic infil-tration. As IPCI emphasizes, bureaucratic infiltration in lobbying processes occurs when industries strategically place like-minded interest groups, NGOs, and researchers within bureaucratic committees voting on regulatory pol-icy. This process, in turn, helps to ensure that industry's ideas and views are consistently represented and that they can influence decisions in their favor.

And this is precisely what occurred during the Delhi High Court's initial response to the Uday Foundation's petition in 2010 to ban the sale of junk food within and near schools. As Sunita Narain of the Centre for Science and Environment mentions in Khurana and Dhangar (2014), in 2013, after the foundation submitted its report, the Delhi High Court ordered the forma-tion of a committee of experts to discuss the creation of junk food guide-lines. Among other stakeholders, this committee included representatives from the AIFPA and the National Restaurant Association of India (NRAI). There were no direct representatives from industry; rather, they worked in-directly through the AIFPA and the NRAI (Khurana and Dhangar 2014). As Sunita Narain observed: "As discussions got under way, it became clear that the big junk food industry was present in the meeting" (quoted in Khurana and Dhangar 2014, 5). Narain and her colleagues eventually found out that the NRAI representative on the committee was a high-level Coca-Cola exec-utive. Furthermore, Nestlé was represented through the AIFPA (Khurana and Dhangar 2014). Thus, through interest groups, major industries had in-filtrated a key government meeting discussing what junk food is and explor-ing regulatory ideas. It was a tactic that would help industries, through their representatives, question and possibly derail policy.

But it has been within the FSSAI that industry has engaged in bureau-cratic infiltration processes. FSSAI scientific committees are made up of chairpersons from all major scientific panels in the FSSAI as well as six independent experts (Government of India, n.d.). However, according to Gandhi (2017), in the past the FSSAI has often included industry representatives on its scientific committees. Within the FSSAI, AIFPA representatives have also had connections with major beverage industries, and these industry representatives have been nominated by the government itself (Alliance against Conflict of Interest 2014). In 2013, this situation motivated individuals such as Santosh Kumar Mishra of the Lok Jagriti to file a lawsuit against the government, through the High Court, for "the 'mis-governance and mismanagement' in the FSSAI" (2). Thus, it appears as if industries have been working through their industry representatives within the FSSAI. Furthermore, others find that the FSSAI has consistently failed to include committee representatives from consumer or business groups, in turn motivating some to consider the FSSAI as autocratic in its approach, with industries opposed to this practice, and one industry representative "going as far as to call the regulator a *den of corruption*'" (Whitehead 2015c). It is important to emphasize that the industry's infiltration of the FSSAI has occurred despite the Delhi High Court's 2011 decision requiring the FSSAI to have a mechanism in place to ensure that no such conflicts of interest are present within its scientific panels (Alliance against Conflict of Interest 2014).

Restructuring Society

When working with civil society, India's junk food industries have also been focused on participating in several corporate social responsibility activities. In accordance with IPCI, these industries have engaged in a plethora of CSR activities focused on rural areas—the very hot spot that these industries have been targeting. According to IPCI, the objective has been to increase industry's social legitimacy and acceptability, which, in turn, supplements national political tactics targeted at bolstering the industry's policy influence within government.

In the case of India, however, it is also important to emphasize that other factors have motivated industries to engage in CSR activities. Many of these initial efforts were instigated by allegations that industries were harming consumers and the environment. In 2003, for example, analysts note allegations that Coca-Cola's products contained an unhealthy amount of pesticide residue and contributed to water contamination, and that this situation prompted the company to engage in environmental CSR activities in order to rejuvenate its reputation (Kaur and Aggarwal 2012). In addition, others claimed that Coca-Cola India's production plants were using an exorbitant amount of local water reserves, leaving little for rural farmers in the process, as seen in the state of Kerala (Holzendorff 2013). A wave of protests emerged in response, with protestors demanding the shutting down of Coca-Cola India's bottling plants (Holzendorff 2013).

Partnering with Academia and NGOs

What are some of the CSR activities that have been pursued by industry? As IPCI underscores, one has been industry efforts to partner with academia. However, in the case of India, to my knowledge junk food industries have not attempted to establish partnerships with research scientists and NGOs in order to increase their social and, by extension, political legitimacy. This reflects two characteristics about industry partnership strategies: first, that they are targeting individuals within government; and second, that they prefer to rely on quiet, "insider" strategies that do not draw a lot of media attention. The latter may be due to the excessive amount of criticism that industries such as Coca-Cola have received due to accusations that the company's bottling production plants have negatively affected farming and water quality in certain areas of India (Mathiason 2006) and that pesticides were present in Coca-Cola as well as PepsiCo's products—thirty and thirty-six times the level of allowable pesticide residue in products set forth by European Union regulators, respectively (Ramesh 2004). In this context, industries appear to be more focused on engaging in various CSR tactics in order to restore their social reputation, as mentioned earlier (Kaur and Aggarwal 2012).

While these industries may not have a strong alliance with research think tanks and academics, they have financed NGOs that are working with the government. For example, the MHFW recently created the Reproductive, Maternal, Newborn, and Child Health Coalition. Through this endeavor, health officials work with NGOs, activists, researchers, the media, and UN agency representatives to discuss several nutritional issues focused on maternal and children's health (Gómez 2018). However, the NGO that has been appointed to lead the Reproductive, Maternal, Newborn, and Child Health Coalition is Save the Children India, though under the government's auspices (Partnership for Maternal, Newborn and Child Health 2013). Save the Children is an NGO headquartered in the United States that has received ample funding from Coca-Cola and PepsiCo in the past (Neuman 2010). Coca-Cola India has also partnered with Save the Children to provide relief assistance to cyclone victims in West Bengal (Coca-Colaindia.com 2020).

While junk food industries may not have been colluding with academia, they were certainly involved in other CSR activities. In the area of health care, for example, several industries have introduced initiatives to help regain society's trust and support, and maintain their reputation.

For instance, in 1993, Nestlé introduced its global Heathier Kids program. In 2010, at a government school in the Indian village of Pattikalyana, Samalkha, Nestlé's Healthy Kids Programme was launched with the objective "to create and raise awareness regarding good nutritional practices, cooking methods to enhance the nutritional content of foods and physical fitness among students in village schools" (Nestlé, "Nestlé Healthy Kids Programme," 1). This program operates in communities near Nestlé factories to provide two hours of instruction, spread out over six weeks (Nestlé, "Nestlé Healthy Kids Programme"). This initiative was developed in collaboration with six regional universities (Kamal 2019; Nestlé, "Nestlé Healthy Kids Programme") and the Magic Bus India Foundation (Kamal 2019). Nestlé claims that "since 2009, over 46500 students have successfully participated in the Programme" (Nestlé, "Nestlé Healthy Kids Programme," 1). Sanjay Khajuria, the company's senior vice president for corporate affairs for Nestlé India, commented a few years ago that "the programme has benefited as many as over 150,000 adolescents across 18 states of India" (quoted in India CSR Network, n.d.). In 2019, Khajuria noted that in the past ten years, approximately three hundred thousand kids benefited from this program across twenty-two states (Mabiyan 2019). That same year, Khajuria claimed that between 2015 and 2018 "the program has contributed towards [a] 29% increase in school attendance, [an] 18% increase in hand washing practices, [a] 37% increase in consumption of green vegetables and [an] 18% increase in consumption of fruits at least thrice a week" (quoted in Mabiyan 2019).

To further extend its reach and influence, the Nestlé Healthy Kids Programme also partnered with the Magic Bus India Foundation to provide greater understanding of the importance of nutrition and physical activity among adolescents (CSR Network, n.d.). Magic Bus India provides an invaluable resource for Nestlé's program. According to Matthew Spacie, Magic

Bus's founder: "We equip around 400000 beneficiaries with the skills and knowledge they need to grow up and move out of poverty through our network of more than 9,000 youth mentors across 22 States and 58 districts in the country" (quoted in India CSR Network, n.d.). According to Nestlé, "Since 2014, 50,000 students have been covered in 5 metros—Delhi, Bangalore, Mumbai, Hyderabad and Chennai through government schools" (Nestlé, "Nestlé Healthy Kids Programme," 1).

Nestlé's Healthier Kids program was quickly praised by parliament. According to K. V. Thomas, a parliamentary member: "I wish both the partners all the best and would encourage this program to steer adolescents in marginalised communities towards a healthy lifestyle with better nutritional awareness" (India CSR Network, n.d.). The program received media attention. Soon thereafter, the *Economic Times* published an interview story with Sanjay Khajuria, Nestlé India's director of corporate affairs, about the program's impact (Mabiyan 2019).

A few years ago, Nestlé also introduced its School Sanitation Project in India (Nestlé, *Nestlé's Commitments to Every Women Every Child*). The primary goal of this project is to improve the health of girls by installing sanitation and hygiene facilities such as toilets in schools in rural villages while encouraging girls to attend school. This program also provided several posters and educational materials for children that emphasized the importance of establishing good hygiene and sanitation. By December 2010, Nestlé's sanitation program had reached eighteen government schools in the Moga region, for a total of 2,362 girls in the 13–17 age group. The company aims to construct twenty-five new sanitation facilities each year and to expand to urban areas.

Nestlé has introduced other public health programs, such as Project Jagriti. The goal of this program is to enhance public health services by providing community support services to improve the nutrition and health of adolescents, as well as caregivers and young families (Halder 2019). In 2019, Nestlé India furthered its work in the area of public health by creating Project Vriddhi, in partnership with the S M Sehgal Foundation (ACN Correspondent 2019). Focusing on the rural village of Rohira, in the Nuh district of Haryana, the objective of this program is to improve the overall livelihood of community members (ACN Correspondent 2019). The program takes an "integrated approach" and emphasizes several aspects of community well-being in rural areas, such as health, education, sanitation, and water conservation, while improving the public health service provision in these areas (1). This project will operate for three years in this area and will serve fourteen hundred Rohira community members (ACN Correspondent 2019). Interestingly, it seems that Nestlé's goal was to ensure that this project dovetailed with the national government's commitment to improving rural health. In fact, according to Suresh Narayanan, chairman and managing director of Nestlé India: "We focus on programmes which are relevant nationally and resonate with our global objective" (quoted in ACN Correspondent 2019, 1). This smacks of an effort to strategically use this program to further Nestlé's political legitimacy and influence at the national level.

Other major industries have played their part in striving to improve the health and well-being of India's children and poor. Through its PepsiCo Foundation, PepsiCo allocated approximately US$11 million to fund several projects for the 2008–2010 period (Kumari and Sharma 2014, 2). Through its Get Active program and the Good Nutrition and Active Lifestyle Program for Children, PepsiCo India has partnered with local NGOs and the Indian Medical Association and implemented programs in schools (Kumari and Sharma 2014). The Get Active program provides educational programs for schoolchildren that are focused on the importance of good and well-balanced nutrition and physical activity (Kumari and Sharma 2014). Kumari and Sharma go on to say that PepsiCo's program "Get Active covered 300,000 children across 10 cities and 350 schools in 2009" (4). And PepsiCo India, in partnership with the Akshaya Patra Foundation, has worked to establish a hunger-free school environment. The Akshaya Patra Foundation has been committed to supporting the government's "Mid-Day Meal Programme." PepsiCo provides assistance, for example, by financing the construction of school kitchens "near Kapashera, Delhi with a capacity to feed 75,000 children through the mid-day meal program" (5). Through its Health Alliance Project, PepsiCo has also provided approximately $1.13 million between 2007 and 2010 to fund projects in the state of Kerala to help reduce chronic diseases, and does this through the promotion of nutritional diets and increased physical exercise (2). Through its Save the Children project, the PepsiCo Foundation has used community-based health care interventions, primarily through community health care educators who work with families, to improve the health and nutritional status of children under the age of 5, as well as young, pregnant mothers and lactating women, by sharing information on nutrition, health, hygiene, water, and sanitation. A total of $4.4 million has been allocated for this initiative (3). Finally, PepsiCo has created its own Pepsi-Corp (Torkornoo and Dzigbede 2017). Through this initiative, which is not only found in India but also Brazil, Ghana, South Africa, China, and the Philippines, PepsiCorp "organizes small groups of employees to engage with local communities and complete projects that enhance access to safe water, enrich food sources, and promote eco-tourism" (Torkornoo and Dzigbede 2017, 24).

Lastly, Coca-Cola has provided its share of CSR initiatives in the area of health care. For example, through its Support My School campaign, Coca-Cola, in partnership with NDTV and the government as well as in association with UN-Habitat (see also Marks 2019), has focused on improving schools throughout India, strengthening the school environment, and providing sound sanitation, access to water, and sports facilitates in schools, with the end goal of increasing and maintaining student enrollment—especially for girls (Krishnakumar, n.d., 1). This program reached approximately "1100+ schools and 100+ communities" (Coca-Cola-Company, n.d., 22). Through this program, Coca-Cola claims to have shown its contribution to not only the Swachh Bharat Swachh Vidyalaya (Clean India: Clean Schools) national campaign but also the prime minister's Swachh Bharat (Clean India Mission) country vision (Coca-Cola Company 2017). Furthermore, Coca-Cola partnered with NDTV to provide "a mass media campaign" and "to bring further focus on this issue including finding solutions to the issues and impact of healthy and active schools, which have sanitation and access to water as its primary focus across India" (Coca-Cola Company 2017). Through its own NGO, the Coca-Cola India Foundation, Coca-Cola has also introduced community programs focused on several initiatives, such as emphasizing renewable sources of energy, promoting water sustainability, and advocating for "active and healthy lifestyles" (1).

Similar to what we saw in Mexico and Brazil, India's junk food industries have also focused on addressing critical gender issues, such as women's empowerment. In 2013, for example, Coca-Cola created its 5by20 global initiative. Through this program, Coca-Cola was committed to creating five million independent women-owned businesses by the year 2020 and, in the process, breaking down barriers to starting up businesses, facilitated by the delivery of business skills, peer mentoring, and financial resources (Coca-

Cola Company 2016). One of 5by20's key programs is its eKOcool Solar Cooler program (Coca-Cola Company 2013). This program is focused on assisting and empowering women in rural areas to start their own business in areas where electricity is scarce (Coca-Cola Company 2013). The "Solar Cooler" provided by Coca-Cola "comes with value-added features and has an inbuilt mobile charger and a port to charge the solar lantern." The mobile charger helps the user stay connected and can be provided for her family members and customers (Coca-Cola Company 2013). In Coca-Cola's 2013/2014 global sustainability report, the company claimed that "through 2013, more than 1,000 eKOCool units have been installed in women-run outlets across five states in India" (Coca-Cola Company 2014a, 5). Coca-Cola has also introduced a "splash bar" in India (Bhushan 2016). Splash bars are independent kiosks where women sell small portions—"tiny 'shots'"—of Coca-Cola for Rs.3 (Journey Staff 2017). This kind of opportunity has not only helped women to become entrepreneurs, but it has also helped them become leaders while contributing to the development of their community, even building community centers (My Digital Media 2016). By 2016, more than thirty thousand splash bars had been established throughout several villages and towns (My Digital Media 2016). According to Bhushan (2016), Coca-Cola's CEO, James Quincey, summed up the situation nicely, stating that India has "certainly been growing and there's a lot of the focus on affordability. . . . You can see some of the splash bars, which is the cheapest, most accessible Coke you can probably buy in the world."

Furthermore, through the Pragati (progress) program, which is managed by the Bottling Investments Group, Coca-Cola helps to build the retail capabilities of independent woman entrepreneurs in remote rural areas by providing training, information about products, and business start-up assistance (Coca-Cola Company 2014b). Led by Coca-Cola University, this effort is further complemented by the company's Parivartan (positive change) initiative, which provides similar training in hard-to-reach areas through its mobile classroom buses (Coca-Cola Company 2014). In August 2017, Bandaru Dattatreya, Union Minister of State for Labour and Employment, recognized Hindustan Coca-Cola Beverages for its contributions to women's economic empowerment (BW Online Bureau 2017). In a room full of dignitaries at the Le Méridien, New Delhi, Minister Dattatreya provided Hindustan Coca-Cola Beverages with the "Bureaucracy Today CSR Excellence Award 2017 under the category of Women Empowerment. The award recognizes

HCCB's efforts in training 50,000 women to help them become economically independent" (BW Online Bureau 2017).

And finally, the PepsiCo Foundation, in partnership with CARE, has allocated US$18.2 million to CARE's She Feeds the World program (PepsiCo 2019). The program helps women farmers increase their farm crop yield and income by providing training, land rights, financial resources, seeds, and the skills needed to develop sustainable farms while increasing access to their nutritious foods in new markets (PepsiCo 2019). The goal of this program has been not only to empower women but also to reduce gender inequality in agricultural production (PepsiCo 2019). Nestlé has also empowered women dairy farmers by providing training through its Village Women Dairy Development Programme (Nestlé, "Village Women Dairy Development Programme"). This program provides training by a team of all women on a host of topics, such as economic independence, good dairy practices, animal care, water conservation, hygiene, personal health, and developing sustainable agricultural practices. This program also helps women improve their productivity as well as the overall quality of their dairy products (Nestlé, "Village Women Dairy Development Programme").

Consistent with IPCI, all of the CSR endeavors used by several industries appears to have accomplished two objectives: first, to bolster industry's social legitimacy and acceptability, and second, to supplement these industries' national political tactics and strategies to further augment their political legitimacy and regulatory policy influence. Indeed, as mentioned earlier, national government officials have recognized these industries' CSR activities, going as far as to suggest that other industries follow their lead in positively contributing to society. Nevertheless, these CSR activities have negatively influenced civil society's ability to collectively mobilize and limit industry's policy influence.

Creating Divisions in Society

Consistent with IPCI, industry's work in society can also have pernicious effects on the latter's ability to mobilize in opposition to industry's regulatory policy influence. A key challenge has been reducing the number of potential allies that NGOs and activists working on behalf of children and the poor can work with. That is, by these industries partnering with influential NGOs and research scientists, other NGOs and activists that are fighting for these vulnerable populations have not been able to further develop their collective movement and influence by partnering with those NGOs and researchers working with industry. This situation may also generate conflicting interests and opinions among these groups in society.

Indeed, in India, industry's partnerships with NGOs generated these social consequences. For several years, junk food industries have been providing funding to specific NGOs in order to help fund conferences and seminars (interview with anonymous source, 2020). Nevertheless, according to individuals I interviewed, industries working with particular NGOs focused on nutrition campaigns has engendered a division between activists and NGOs striving to raise awareness about vital health issues, such as the right to wholesome food, versus those that are receiving funding and are aligned with industry (interview with Dipa Sinha, September 15, 2020). While NGOs striving to defend the health of the general population still have their own space to operate and flourish, this tension nevertheless exists. In this context, interviewees suggest that the collective movement in response to industry activities would be much stronger in the absence of industry-NGO partnership (interview with Dipa Sinha, September 15, 2020). On the other hand, others believe that this degree of conflict in society has not been as problematic. Some activists believe that those NGOs that are working with industry are not interested in getting politically involved and mobilizing (interview with Vandana Prasad, September 8, 2020).

Complementary Institutions

Junk food industry efforts to manipulate national NCD regulatory policy has not only been facilitated by creating divisions within civil society; national political institutions have also mattered, further augmenting industry's policy influence. More specifically, and as I explain in IPCI, it is the complementary role of presidential institutions that indirectly contributes to industry political legitimacy and policy influence. According to IPCI, one key aspect of complementary institutions arises when presidents strategically partner with and use junk food industries to achieve alternative economic development and social welfare policy objectives. Here, presidents seek out and use these partnerships to implement and provide social welfare benefits such as anti-hunger and anti-poverty measures in order to ensure political popularity and ongoing electoral support.

Shortly upon entering office as prime minister in 2014, Narendra Modi's policy focus was twofold: to modernize India's economy, mainly by way of strengthening industry and domestic production as well as encouraging FDI, while introducing several social welfare programs. Similar to the East Asian development model, Modi believed that investing in social welfare, in the areas of education, poverty alleviation, and the environment, was critical to ensuring India's prosperous development. Modi's development approach was perceived as a welfare economic model similar to East Asia's (Samanta 2019). This approach may appear puzzling, however, considering the BJP and its center-right coalition's criticism of the previous Congress Party's obsessive focus on social welfare entitlements, none of which, the BJP claimed, were successful, according to Modi: "The Left kept telling us about social problems. . . . They kept talking but did nothing" (quoted in Samanta 2019). Instead, it appeared as if Modi sought to correct this situation through the creation of several innovative social welfare programs, using the Congress's social policy shortcomings as an opportunity to make the BJP shine.

With respect to the economy, Modi viewed junk food industries as a key partner in achieving his broader economic objectives. With respect to increasing FDI, his administration has been very proactive in meeting with CEOs of major industries, informing them of the Modi government's commitment to ease of doing business reforms and encouraging them to invest in India's thriving sectors (PTI 2017). In 2017, at a World Food event in New Delhi, Modi met with executives from Hershey, Amazon, Walmart, Nestlé, Coca-Cola, PepsiCo, Mondelez, and GlaxoSmithKline and asked these companies' executives "to have at least one global board meeting in India in 2018 so they get a sense of what the country is all about and the changes that are taking place" (Bhushan 2017a). During this meeting, Modi commented that not much had been done at the national level in the area of food processing, that wealth needed to be created from food waste (an ongoing challenge, as mentioned earlier), and that there were opportunities for these industries. Modi further noted that "the impact of consumerism is most with the middle class, [and] there is huge opportunity with the middle class" (Bhushan 2017a). In September 2019, at the Bloomberg Global Business Forum in New York City, Modi gave a keynote address and met with global CEOs at a roundtable titled "Harnessing Investment Opportunities in India and Boosting Commercial Linkages between India and the USA" (*Business Today* 2019). Modi wanted the executives from these companies, such as Coca-Cola, Bank of America, Shell, IBM, and Lockheed Martin, to invest in India and to "become part of its growth story" (*Business Today* 2019). Modi also assured these executives that his government would act as "a bridge to fill any gap." Modi commented at this event: "Your prudent method and our pragmatic minds can write new stories in management, and your rational ways and our human values can show the path, which the world is looking for" (quoted in *Business Today* 2019). At what appeared to be the same event, LiveMint (2019) claimed that Modi emphasized that these CEOs should "leverage the 'Startup India' innovation platforms to formulate solutions for the entire world on challenging issues like nutrition and waste management" (LiveMint 2019). This comment dovetails nicely with some of these industries' CSR activities, as mentioned earlier.

And yet, it is also important to emphasize Modi's appeal to India's broader stable political and policy environment during this event (LiveMint 2019). Indeed, during this roundtable meeting, Ben van Beurden, Shell's CEO, commented that "Modi had a very 'strong and impassionate 'Come to India' speech' and his four D's of democracy, demography, demand and decisiveness are very powerful arguments to invest in India" (LiveMint 2019).

During the Bloomberg Global Business Forum in New York, Modi posted on his Twitter account the following statement about Mr. James Quincey of Coca-Cola, in turn revealing to the world his relationship with the company: "Really excited to be in the Prime Minister's investment summit, says James Quincey, Chairman and CEO of @CocaColaCo" (*Business Today* 2019). In 2016, Modi again went out of his way to meet with executives of several companies in Switzerland, such as Nestlé, ABB, Lafarge, and Novartis, to not only encourage their investment in India but also to, according to IANS (2016), mention his country's need to "create an economy of the order of 'two or three Switzerlands,' which provides a massive opportunity for partnerships." In fact, when speaking to these companies, Modi stated: "Within my country I need to create 2 or 3 Switzerlands. So scope for partnership [with industry] is immense" (quoted in IANS 2016).

Yet another economic objective for Modi has been investing in strengthening Indian manufacturing and production. In September 2014, for example, Modi created the Make in India campaign. This campaign is focused on transforming India into a manufacturing hub and world leader by increasing investment and development of several sectors while providing jobs (see PTI 2014a), with food processing being an important part of this process (Make in India, n.d.). Make in India not only feeds into Modi's overall economic development objective but also his nationalist political efforts, generating a sense of economic independence and pride, and solidifying India's geopolitical prominence as an emerging power. In this process, a key aspect of developing India's food sector has been avoiding food waste as well as increasing employment and demand for agricultural products made at the local level (see Mani and Anthony 2017). During this period, Modi also requested major soda producers, such as PepsiCo, to make sure that they include more fresh fruits from India in their soda formulas in order to "help distressed farmers find a new market for their produce" (PTI 2014b). Moreover, according to PTI (2014b), writing for *The Economic Times*, Modi commented: "We drink Pepsi, Coca-Cola and I do not know how many similar beverages are available in the market. The trade runs into billions of rupees. I have asked the companies if they can blend 5 per cent natural fruit juice in the beverages they make. . . . I am not asking for much. If 5 per cent of juice from fruits produced by our farmers is added, the farmer will not be forced to search for a market to sell" (quoted in PTI 2014b, 1). In 2017, PepsiCo's former CEO, Indra Nooyi, completely agreed, stating: "As I shared with Prime Minister Modi, PepsiCo is well-positioned to help the government deliver on the national development goals he has outlined for farmers and supporting their livelihoods. The Prime Minister and I had an engaging dialogue on how PepsiCo is making investments to grow, process and use more Indian-grown fruit juice in our sparkling beverages" (quoted in *Hindu Business Line* 2017). Thus, partnering with industry not only helped to avoid food waste, but it also helped to secure additional work for farmers, one of Modi's key objectives. It is important to note that Coca-Cola India started using local fruits in their products in a strategic move to appeal to local consumers' interests in customization and "looking for ethnicity" in products (quoted in Bhushan 2017b).

To further solidify his partnership with these industries, Modi's government periodically hosted major events to celebrate his Make in India initiative and invited industry allies to participate. For example, Modi inaugurated the "Make in India Week 2016" event in Mumbai, organized by the central government, the Department of Industrial Policy and Promotion, and the Maharashtra state government (Nestlé 2016). Perhaps the largest business expo event ever organized by the government, one of the intentions behind this event was also to acknowledge India as a hospitable place for investment (Nestlé 2016). In a news media article published by Nestlé India, the company stated that this event provided an "opportunity to show-case our contribution to India's growth and development for over a century and to remain a committed partner living by the ideals of 'Make in India'" (Nestlé 2016).

Thus, it appears that Modi views these industries as helping him achieve his economic development objectives while at the same time securing polit-ical support from the rural agricultural community. And, as mentioned ear-lier, with PepsiCo's involvement, industry has been happy to help.

Since his arrival in office in 2014, Modi has also been committed to im-proving social welfare (Sen 2019). In addition to continuing several of the previous Indian National Congress government's United Progressive Alli-ance social welfare benefit programs, such as providing rural employment schemes, Modi introduced additional populist welfare programs (Sen 2019). These programs range from direct cash transfer subsidies into bank accounts for the poor, Modi's Jan Dhan Yojana program of financial inclusion, social security benefits to those participating in this program, and cleaning up streets and improving sanitation through his Swachh Bharat Abhiyan (Clean India) program (see Finnigan 2019; Jayaswal 2020; Tripathi 2019). Modi's interests in Swachh Bharat Abhiyan stemmed from his personal experience: at one point, Modi claimed that "Swachh Bharat is the culmination of all the experience I had before I became the PM. It is not a scheme thought over-night, but my dream since my RSS Pracharak days" (quoted in Finnigan 2019). This view stemmed from his experiences in 1979, at the age of 29, when a town that he had lived in, Morbi, within the state of Gujarat, experienced the collapse of a damn due to a monsoon storm, in turn leading to massive flooding and thousands of deaths, and prompting him to help with the cleanup, as well as his experience during the public scare of bubonic and pneumonic plague that emerged in the city of Surat in 1994—though it turned out to be a false scare (Finnigan 2019). Analysts claim that providing social welfare services such as the provision of cooking gas to poor house-holds was a successful aspect of Modi's first term in office, with evidence also showing that it provided considerable electoral benefits for the BJP during the 2019 election (Sen 2019). Sen (2019) claims that during Modi's electoral victory speech in 2019, "he said that in 21st-century India, there would be only two castes: those who are poor and those who work for the upliftment of the poor."

A vital aspect of Modi's political platform has been to make great strides in advancing public health and nutrition. To achieve this, Modi viewed junk food industries as partners in accomplishing this health policy objective. For example, in recent years, Modi's government viewed PepsiCo as an important partner in helping the government achieve its objective of improving the diet and nutrition of India's children (Campbell 2014; see also *digital-LEARNING Network News* 2014). According to Campbell (2014), one must recall that, according to the United Nations, approximately 47 percent of India's children under the age of three were underweight. To help improve children's nutritional status, in 2014, Harsimrat Kaur Badal, Modi's minister of state for food processing industries, met with PepsiCo's CEO, Indra Nooyi, "to discuss the possibility of developing nutritious processed foods for use in school lunches across the country," which is information that Campbell (2014) obtained from a Bloomberg report. Campbell (2014) further notes that this effort was part of Modi's goal to improve the diet of his citizens and especially children. Minister Badal went on to comment: "I suggested [that PepsiCo develop] products which will be healthy and will also contain proteins. . . . As people are becoming busy, the children will be immensely benefited if such products are launched" (quoted in Campbell 2014). In another meeting, Minister Badal urged PepsiCo's CEO to, as Kazmin explains, "focus on healthier, more nutritious foods that could be used in India's vast school lunch programmes, especially for rural children suffering from anaemia" (Kazmin 2014a). To my knowledge, this was the first time that India's government partnered with PepsiCo—or any major US-based soda company—to provide food to malnourished children. Minister Badal also approached PepsiCo with the idea to invest more in India for research and development in processed foods, which could be provided for by the government's Mid-Day Meal Scheme in rural areas, with a focus on possibly providing healthy school lunches while addressing the ongoing challenges of iron deficiency among children in these areas (digitalLEARNING Network News 2014). Nooyi was glad to help, stating: "PepsiCo has already invested substantially in India's food processing sector and we wish to double this investment in the coming years" (quoted in *digitalLEARNING Network News* 2014). In recent years, Campbell (2014) notes that nutrition activists have questioned if it is appropriate to provide processed foods from these industries (i.e., industries that are known to provide unhealthy foods, such as sodas and potato chips) in response to malnutrition.

Alarmed by the deteriorating environmental health conditions in India since the beginning of his administration, Modi has also been committed to improving India's overall sanitary conditions, such as discouraging open-space defecation while encouraging the use of, and increased access to, toilets (Bicchieri 2019). According to Bicchieri (2019), "Up until 2014, over 500 million Indians had been engaging in open defecation, accounting for the world's majority of open defecators." Bicchieri goes on to say that India has shared "60% of the global burden of open defecation until 2014." Realizing this, in 2014, Modi introduced his Swachh Bharat Abhiyan (Clean India) program. This national program underscored the importance of cleaning India's streets, achieving an attitudinal shift toward cleanliness in society (ET Bureau 2014), striving for universal access to sanitation services (Raman and Muralidharan 2019), and eliminating open defecation mainly through the construction of public and household toilets (BQ Desk 2019). The program sought to improve sanitary conditions in schools, such as "the need for separate boys' and girls' facilities in schools" (Finnigan 2019).

Once again, the Modi administration partnered with companies to help improve sanitary conditions in schools and to fulfil his Swachh Bharat Abhiyan campaign. As mentioned earlier, through its Support My School program, Coca-Cola India has worked with NDTV and UN-Habitat, to provide toilets in schools (Coca-Cola Company, n.d.). Through these endeavors it seems that Coca-Cola was supporting Modi's Swachh Bharat Abhiyan campaign. Indeed, a press release published by Coca-Cola India in 2015 states that "Support my School—has completed a significant milestone. The programme that adds to the Prime Minister's efforts under Swachh Bharat, Swachh Vidyalaya has completed the revitalization of 500 schools" (Coca-Cola India 2015). According to Coca-Cola India, Modi also appointed Sourav Ganguly as one of the ambassadors of the Swachh Bharat campaign and was tasked with the endeavor of "guid[ing] and support[ing] the Support My School campaign in reaching 1000 schools by 2017. He will actively contribute towards spreading awareness about the campaign and taking it to a larger number of students across the country" (Coca-Cola India 2015). Speaking at an event in New Delhi in 2015, in signaling his support for Modi's campaign, Venkatesh Kini, Coca-Cola president for India and SWA, stated: "After the Hon'ble Prime Minister's Swachh Bharat, Swachh Vidyalaya announcement last year, we have committed to scaling up our target to 1,000 schools by

2017. . . . I thank Swachh Bharat Ambassador Sourav Ganguly for lending his hand to the campaign and Farhan Akhtar for steering this concept as the Coca-Cola brand Ambassador. We are on an ambitious journey of trying to keep our children, where they belong, but it is a journey that we are traversing together" (quoted in Coca-Cola India 2015).

Nestlé joined the cause through its school sanitation and clean water projects. The company worked to ensure that toilets were provided for schools in rural villages to improve sanitary conditions and to help reduce the schoolgirl dropout rate, and raised awareness about the importance of access to clean water while encouraging students, through the formation of "water committees," to maintain water storage tanks in schools (Nestlé 2015a). The Confederation of Indian Industry (CII) also stated that it would contribute to Modi's Swachh Bharat Mission by providing school sanitation facilitates, and that it would provide ten thousand toilets between 2015 and 2016 (ET Bureau 2014). According to Sumit Mazumder, CII's president-designate at the time: "CII will work with industry and the government to make Swachh Bharat a reality" (quoted in ET Bureau 2014). While, to my knowledge, PepsiCo has not provided toilets for schools or participated in any other sanitation projects, its CEO has publicly emphasized the importance of establishing a cleaner environment in India (see ET Bureau 2014). For this to be achieved, though, according to D. Shivakumar, PepsiCo India chairman and CEO at the time, "we need an attitudinal shift to change deep rooted habits and cleanliness practices" (quoted in ET Bureau 2014).

Proud of his program and the other social welfare programs that his government has implemented, offering them as examples of hope for a better world in the future, Modi addressed the 74th session of the UN General Assembly in 2019, saying: "When a developing country is able to successfully implement the world's biggest sanitation campaign within the 'Clean India Mission,' building over 110 million toilets in just five years for its countrymen, all its achievements and outcomes are an inspirational message for the entire world" (quoted in Press Trust of India 2019b). In 2019, Bill Gates also awarded Modi with the Global Goalkeeper Award for his Swachh Bharat Abhiyan program (Press Trust of India 2019b). Modi acknowledged that his public welfare programs were the result of India's collective efforts and a sense of duty, and that they exhibited dreams that the entire world has (Press Trust of India 2019b).

When taken together, Modi's complementary efforts appear to have helped increase the political legitimacy and influence of junk food industries. By engaging in partnerships with several prominent companies, not only has this helped Modi to achieve his economic and social policy objectives, but this partnership also appears to have convinced government officials that industry is a key solution to India's NCD challenges. At the same time, Modi's complementary institutional efforts appear to be supplementing these industries' political, bureaucratic, and civil societal tactics, further solidifying their influence on NCD regulatory policy.

Resurgence of Civil Society?

In this challenging context, where industry appears to have ongoing political, social, and policy influence, civil society is nevertheless rising to draw greater attention to the need to highlight industry's activities and to tackle NCDs. In recent years, several NGOs, such as the Public Health Resource Network and the Centre for Science and Environment, and university researchers have been calling attention to the need to improve the nation's health, tackle NCDs, and introduce policies that reduce disease burden.

Nevertheless, and similar to what we have seen in the other emerging economies discussed in this book, the social movement in response to obesity and type 2 diabetes is very new and not as well organized when compared to other NGO sectors. According to some, these ailments still have not garnered the attention of broader segments of society (interview with Dipa Sinha, September 15, 2020). For many, the focus instead has been on food security and farmers' rights, and it has been difficult to get these groups interested in obesity and type 2 diabetes (interview with Dipa Sinha, September 15, 2020). At the same time, according to some activists that I have interviewed, many in society, especially those from the affluent classes, prefer to work with industry and allow them to engage in the aforementioned self-regulatory practices (interview with Vandana Prasad, September 8, 2020). Thus, while civil society's response to NCDs and policy reform is emerging, the movement is still new and being developed.

Further complicating matters is the national government's limited commitment to seeking out and working closely with NGOs and community activists. Indeed, some activists are of the view that the current government has not paid attention to their work—in essence, keeping them out in the cold (interview with Vandana Prasad, September 8, 2020). Others further contend that, under the current government, the space for civil societal activism, particularly in the form of rights-based NGOs, has been reduced considerably (interview with Dipa Sinha, Ambedkar University, September 15, 2020). Worse still, some even felt that there was more space accorded for international philanthropies, such as the Bill and Melinda Gates Foundation (interview with Dipa Sinha, September 15, 2020). Activists interviewed claim that international entities are more influential because they do not have political agendas and have their own funding (interview with Dipa Sinha, September 15, 2020).

Further complicating matters is civil society's inability to obtain the attention and support of government officials in the area of nutrition policy (Khandelwal and Reddy 2013). This reflects not only the elitist nature of health administration and policy making, but also a general lack of trust in NGOs, who were often seen as corrupt (see Gómez 2018). It certainly did not help that in 2013, a Delhi High Court bench, led by Justice Pradeep Nandrajog, stated that "99% of the existing NGOs are fraud and simply moneymaking devices. Only one out of every hundred NGOs serve the purpose they are set up for" (quoted in Nair 2013). Because of this, the court called for more stringent norms for the licensing of NGOs (Nair 2013).

Despite these challenges, civil society is gradually emerging to highlight the junk food industry's activities, the need for more aggressive policies, and, above all, the need to safeguard the health and prosperity of all, especially India's most vulnerable populations. With more time, NGOs and activists will become more important in the public fight against NCDs and for a healthy Indian population in general.

Conclusion

In recent years, India has joined her counterparts in other emerging economies in seeing a rise in obesity and type 2 diabetes cases, the product of economic reform, modernization, and shifting consumer preferences. In addition to spreading throughout the general population, sadly, obesity and type 2 diabetes has also emerged among India's most vulnerable populations. While the government has introduced several public health prevention programs, it still has not generated the political will and commitment needed to create effective regulations that limit these food industries' ability to market and sell their products. Children are still exposed to and lured by these foods, even within safe school environments. And, more than ever, the poor have had greater access to these products, without any regulatory efforts to limit this access and avoid disease.

By applying IPCI, I have shown how and why junk food industries continue to have so much political, policy, and social influence. These industries are increasingly striving to shape parliamentary and bureaucratic discussions in their favor, garnering political legitimacy and support through joint policy partnerships while structuring civil society to fit their needs. But at the same time, and as IPCI emphasizes, political leaders are also to blame. Prime Minister Modi's efforts to establish industry partnerships that support his alternative political, economic, and social welfare agendas appear to have further bolstered industry's policy influence while also supplementing industry's other political tactics.

APPENDIX

India: Summary of Chapter Findings

Political Action	Restructuring Society	Complementary Institutions	Regulatory Policy Failure and Absence
Policy partnership Coca-Cola partnership with New Delhi TV, government, and UN-Habitat for improved school sanitation Coca-Cola and FSSAI partnership to train street vendors to provide safe food products	*Corporate social responsibility* Nestlé's Healthy Kids Program on raising awareness and improving nutrition and health in schools PepsiCo Get Active and the Good Nutrition and Active Lifestyle programs work with NGOs to educate schools about good nutrition and physical fitness Coca-Cola's Support My School campaign to improve school environment, sanitation, and student retention	Prime Minister Modi seeks partnerships with major industries to increase investment and develop the economy Modi's government has partnered with PepsiCo to work toward Modi's objective of improving children's nutrition	Food labels have insufficient/unclear information on nutritional content, misleading statements Absence of federal/state laws prohibiting sale of junk foods in or near schools No enforcement of existing federal court guidelines on sale of junk foods in schools Absence of federal regulations on junk food advertising

Political Action	Restructuring Society	Complementary Institutions	Regulatory Policy Failure and Absence
Lobbying and largesse	*Partnering with society*		
All India Food Processors' Association (AIFPA) meeting with courts to question definition of junk foods and sales in/near schools	In India, junk food industries have not emphasized establishing partnerships with university researchers and think tanks		
AIFPA arguments against color-coded food labeling			
Institutional infiltration	*Dividing society*		
Major industries working through interest group associations within the FSSAI and other court-ordered expert committees	Industry working with NGOs generates conflicts with other NGOs/ activists working for improved nutrition and health; however, the latter still has the space and autonomy needed to achieve their objectives		

6

Indonesia

Indonesia has now joined Mexico, Brazil, and India in becoming a prosperous emerging economy with a host of noncommunicable disease challenges. In a historical context of poverty, inequality, and malnutrition (e.g., stunting), due to the recent nutrition transition, obesity and type 2 diabetes have emerged as major public health threats among the country's most vulnerable populations: children and the poor. This double burden has posed a significant challenge for politicians, who have been historically accustomed to focusing on challenges such as stunting and undernutrition. Junk food industries have viewed this as a chance to invest in and expand their operations throughout Indonesia's vast islands. While the rise and influence of these industries was not as swift and smooth as seen in other countries in this book, Indonesia continues to be viewed as a golden investment opportunity.

To its credit, Indonesia's national government in recent years has recognized the rise of obesity and type 2 diabetes among children and the poor, respectively. Similar to what we have seen in Mexico, Brazil, and India, while innovative NCD prevention programs have been introduced in Indonesia (though considerably delayed when compared to these other nations), the government still has not introduced effective regulations on the marketing and sale of junk food products. Important prevention strategies, such as a soda tax, were once introduced but then quickly discarded due to vehement protests from well-organized industry lobbyists. As we saw in Mexico, Brazil, and India, once again, junk food industries have been able to derail the government's commitment to these NCD regulatory policies.

In accordance with the Industry Politics and Complementary Institutions analytical framework, these outcomes have occurred due to the industry's usage of political tactics such as strategic lobbying, generous corporate social responsibility initiatives, and industry's ability to reshape and divide societies through their partnership with particular civil societal actors. In accordance with IPCI, however, these tactics have been reinforced through the presence of presidential complementary institutions: that is, presidents eager to strategically partner with industries to achieve alternative policy and political objectives. All of these industry political tactics and complementary institutions have engendered a context where industry's political legitimacy and influence over NCD policies have increased. In turn, this facilitates industries' ability to hamper both the enforcement of existing regulations and the introduction of new ones.

Nevertheless, civil societal actors have done a commendable job of raising awareness and gradually building a consensus within society and government; this consensus focuses on the importance of addressing the junk food industry's ongoing policy influence within government and the need for more effective NCD regulatory policies. With the current president, Joko Widodo, also known as "Jokowi," seemingly committed to working with civil society in achieving these policy objectives, the government's ability to take on big industry and improve the health of the country's children and poor may eventually increase.

But how did junk food industries in Indonesia become so prosperous and influential in the first place? As I explain in the next section, their road to success was anything but smooth.

The Rise and Development of Junk Food Industries

Similar to what we have seen in other emerging economies, the arrival of junk food industries in Indonesia was shaped by the prevailing political context and gradual economic liberalization process. After attaining political independence from the Dutch in 1949, by 1956, Indonesia's "Guided Democracy," led by its first postindependence political leader, Sukarno, emphasized greater domestic investment and ownership, with limited opportunities for foreign investment. Coca-Cola entered Indonesia's market as early as 1927 (Guterres 2018). By 1932, Coca-Cola began trading in Indonesia's capital city, Jakarta, under the name De Nederlands Indische Minerals Water Fabrick, and according to Guterres (2018) was managed by a gentleman by the name of Bernie Vonings, a citizen of the Netherlands. Since Sukarno's government was quasi-socialist, closely aligned with communist principles, and unrelentingly committed to economic nationalism, foreign ownership of soda and ultraprocessed food industries, particularly bottling plants, were nevertheless limited to approximately 45 percent of the market (Wie and Yoshihara 1987, 332).

Domestic and foreign investment gradually increased with further political and economic developments. Amid waning economic conditions and the possibility of a communist coup, in 1967 Indonesia's military intervened and took over the government (Rossotti 2019; Wie and Yoshihara 1987). The military appointed General Suharto as its presidential leader a couple years later, introducing an authoritarian government that was committed to bringing about economic reform while establishing a "New Order" (Rossotti 2019). Unlike in previous governments, Suharto was committed to rejuvenating the economy through the introduction of market reforms, such as attracting foreign investment and ensuring financial stability, guided by the appointment and ideas of Western-trained economists, or what is known as the "Berkeley Mafia." In addition to encouraging pragmatic market reforms, currency devaluation, reduced subsidies, fiscal reforms, and restrictions on foreign direct investment (FDI) were significantly eased during Suharto's rule (Rossotti 2019). Nevertheless, during the first few years of his government, Suharto introduced an import substitution industrialization growth-led model that ensured high tariffs and state support for nascent industry while encouraging domestic and foreign investment in the production of local consumer products (Wie and Yoshihara 1987). By the late 1970s and early 1980s, the state turned to developing more "upstream" capital intensive and technologically advanced industries, such as the production of aircraft (Wie and Yoshihara 1987).

Despite its early presence in Indonesia, under Suharto, Coca-Cola appeared to lose its footing. Shortly after declaring independence from the Netherlands, Coca-Cola was managed by the public and renamed the Indonesian Beverages Limited (Guterres 2018). To ensure the survival of Indonesian Beverages Limited, the company worked with three Japanese companies: Mitsui Toatsu Chemical, Mitsui and Company, and Mikuni Coca-Cola Bottling Company (Guterres 2018, 6–7). According to Guterres (2018), these companies came together to form the PT Djaya Beverages Bottling Company (DBBC), which produced a host of beverages (including Coca-Cola, Fanta, and Sprite). The Coca-Cola Export Corporation later reentered the market in 1972 through its PT Coca-Cola Indonesia (Guterres 2018, 7). However, foreign-based soda and food industries did not thrive and overtake the Indonesian market during the 1970s and 1980s, though, according to Wie and Yoshihara (1987), they did share roughly the same amount of market ownership with domestic companies, who, different from their foreign competitors, often produced noncarbonated beverages at a lower price. One must keep in mind that during this period foreign companies (e.g., from Japan) were used for technical assistance in capital-intensive manufacturing (e.g., assembling foreign-brand automobiles), not industry ownership, which was domestic (Wie and Yoshihara 1987). Remaining industries were based domestically and primarily owned by ethnic Chinese and indigenous communities who were closely intertwined with the Suharto family and other politicians.

By 1993, the World Bank listed Indonesia as a rising "Asian Tiger" among several others throughout the region (Rossotti 2019). In addition to persistent economic growth, poverty rates continued to decrease, "from 28 percent in the mid-1980s to about 8 percent in the mid-1990s" (Balisacan et al. 2002, 1). Notwithstanding a minor setback with the Asian financial crisis in 1998, Indonesia weathered the storm, pursuing ongoing economic reforms (Rossotti 2019). It was during this period that the government introduced a *reformasi* (reform, reformation) of the political system—that is, moving from a military dictatorship to a representative form of parliamentary government with diffused political powers. Parliament and its political parties, as well as the judiciary, emerged as more independent (Rossotti 2019). Free parliamentary elections were held in 1999 and a decentralization of political and policy authority was pursued (Rossotti 2019; on the decentralization process, see Pisani 2014).

By the turn of the twenty-first century, ongoing market reforms provided even more opportunity for domestic and international investment in the junk food industry. The Indonesian Investment Law No. 25 of 2007 provided additional foreign investment opportunities, though it required foreign firms to register as limited liability companies (on the latter issue, see Yap and Tan 2019). By 2016, the previous "Negative List" restrictions on foreign ownership were revised, paving the way for "100% capital ownership in PT PMAs [limited liability companies] which operate restaurants, catering services, bars, and cafes" (Yap and Tan 2019). According to the Oxford Business Group (2018), "Foreign Direct Investment (FDI) in the food industry totalled $1.5 bn in 2015, according to the Indonesian Investment Coordinating

Board (BKPM), placing it third among manufacturers, behind metal, machinery and electronics investments ($3.1bn), and chemicals and pharmaceuticals ($1.96bn) and averaging $1.66bn growth each year between 2010 and 2015." However, due to the introduction of federal regulations in 2014, specifically over water rights usage, making it difficult for companies to access water, there were mild fluctuations in FDI performance in the food and beverage sector (declining somewhat in 2015, then increasing shortly thereafter) but with ample opportunity for growth and expectations for success (EU-Indonesia Business Network 2017; Oxford Business Group 2018).

In this context, and in contrast to what we saw in Mexico, Brazil, and India, the soda and food industries have mainly been owned by domestic investors, garnering approximately 60 percent of the market (Indonesia-Investments 2018a). At the conclusion of 2010, total investments in this sector reached "IDR 25 Trillion, in which IDR 9 Trillion of the investment came from foreign investment (FDI) and the remaining IDR 16 Trillion from domestic investment" (Dezan Shira and Associates 2011, 76). According to analysts for Indonesia-Investments (2018a), Adhi Lukman, chairman of the Indonesian Food and Beverage Association (GAPMMI), said: "There are actually many foreign investors interested to invest in Indonesia. However, they are often scared off by regulations that are regarded unconducive. Among the top concerns of foreign investors are the availability of quality human resources and the availability of raw materials" (1). Foreign junk food enterprises nevertheless appear to remain optimistic about Indonesia's market potential, especially as the size of the middle class grows.

The distribution and availability of junk food products has nevertheless increased in recent years. In the formal sector, a major source of distribution are convenience stores and supermarkets (see Development Solutions 2016). Some of the largest convenience stores in Indonesia are Indomaret, with 15,633 outlets, and Alfamart, with 13,991 outlets (see Retail News Asia 2018). Alfamart and Indomaret are mainly popular among Indonesia's youth and have thrived because of their ability to keep costs at a minimum while meeting consumer needs (Anbalagan 2018; Development Solutions 2016). Recent studies reveal that minimarkets have become the most popular place to purchase food and beverages, due to their accessibility and the diversity of cold beverages sold, among other factors (Haning et al. 2016). Larger supermarkets selling imported foods include Carrefour, with approximately 50 percent of the market, followed by Hypermart (25 percent) and Giant (20 percent), as well as Hero, Superindo, and Food Mart (Development Solutions 2016, 140). According to some estimates, by 2016, there were "around 29,600 convenience stores, 300 hypermarkets, and 1,400 supermarkets" (Swiss Global Enterprise 2019). These locally owned convenience and grocery stores have been preferred to other foreign franchises mainly due to a higher level of trust and belief that Indonesian stores provide products with a better value (especially when compared to foreign products) and that local stores have a better understanding of their local residents (Development Solutions 2016, 133). In addition, economic factors contributed to the downfall of foreign companies. For example, for several years, 7-Eleven, a popular US franchise, was open in Jakarta, but the chain ultimately proved too costly to operate, and prices were higher than those of their local competitors Alfamart and Indomarco (Hanan 2018). By 2017, 7-Eleven had to leave the Indonesian market (Hanan 2018; Phuong 2018). Alternatively, Warungs are smaller stores that sell food products at more affordable prices (see Development Solutions 2016).

In addition, the number of restaurants and fast food franchises has burgeoned, fueled by a heightened increase in out-of-home consumption, especially in busy urban areas (Przybylski 2018). Przybylski (2018) mentions that, according to *SWA Magazine*, "there were 380 million restaurant visits in Jakarta during 2013 and resultant revenues of IDR 22.23 trillion (approx. USD $1.15 billion)." The number of fast food franchises are also increasing. According to Przybylski (2018), the food franchises sector in Indonesia "currently employs in excess of 150,000 people, many of who are employed by internationally recognized brands having multiple outlets such as Pizza Hut, McDonald's and KFC."

With respect to ultraprocessed foods, Nestlé, having entered the market as early as 1971, dominates (EIBN 2014). By 2009, Nestlé Indonesia was the largest company in the food and beverage market, with sales of US$23,238 million (including sales from Papua New Guinea); followed by Indofood Sukses Akmur Terbuka, with US$4,493 million in sales; and Unilever Indonesia, with US$2,303 million (EIBN 2014, 20). Other foreign enterprises, such as Heinz ABC Indonesia and Kraft Foods Indonesia, are also major players in the market (Oxford Business Group 2018). Interestingly, when it comes to chocolates, however, the market is essentially dominated by local manufacturers (Swiss Business Hub Indonesia 2019). Petra Food and Mayora combined garner 80 percent of the market, followed by Mondeléz International,

Mars, Ferrero, Hershey, Lindt, and Nestlé. Petra's and Mayora's products are also sold at an affordable price compared to these foreign rivals and are easy to find in local markets (Swiss Business Hub Indonesia 2019).

The popularity and consumption of sodas and sugary beverages are somewhat different in Indonesia, when compared to the other emerging economies discussed in this book. Carbonated soda drinks appear not to be as popular as some isotonic drinks, which shows that consumers are becoming increasingly aware of the effects that soda consumption can have on their health (EIBN 2014). From 2006 to 2011, sales of isotonic drinks increased by approximately 16.3 percent (EIBN 2014, 17). However, with respect to carbonated soda drinks, by 2014 Coca-Cola appeared to be the most popular brand on the market (Nusaresearch Team 2014). But Coca-Cola certainly has its rivals. Big Cola, for example, is owned by the Peruvian company AJE and has been able to compete with Coca-Cola because of its ability to offer lower prices (Bland 2014). Due to the imposition of excessive government regulations, in October 2019, one of Coca-Cola's rivals, PepsiCo, decided to withdraw its operations from Indonesia (Gayanti and Arisa 2019).

Nevertheless, in 2014, Coca-Cola invested in solidifying its operations in Indonesia by purchasing "a 29.4 percent stake in the Indonesian business of Coca-Cola Amatil, Coca-Cola's only distributor in Indonesia" (Taylor and Jacobson 2016, 23). In 2013, the Atlanta company also planned to spend US$700 million in marketing and other activities (Silaen and Otto 2013), while between approximately 2012 and 2015, Coca-Cola Amatil Indonesia "commissioned 18 new production lines, deployed 150,000 coolers and built three mega distribution centres to increase capacity and build local capability with total investments exceeding $300 million" (*Atlanta Business Chronicle* 2015). "We have big plans for Indonesia. Indonesia is very important to our growth goals," claimed Ahmet Bozer, former president of Coca-Cola International (quoted in Otto 2013). And as Donald Keough, the former president of Coca-Cola, put it in 1991: "When I think of Indonesia—a country on the equator with 180 million people, a median age of 18, and a Muslim ban on alcohol—I feel I know what heaven looks like" (quoted in Taylor and Jacobson 2016, 23).

Soda industry sales have also increased over time. Throughout the early 2000s, soft drink sales burgeoned, by double-digit figures, attracting a host of foreign and domestic investors (Prijosoesilo and Sanusi 2018). According to Bourke and Veerman (2018), "In 2014, total sales of SSBs were 3.894 billion litres, of which carbonated soft drinks account for 944 million litres (24.2%), juice for 167 million litres (4.3%), ready-to-drink coffee 16 million litres (0.4%), ready-to-drink tea 2145 million litres (55.1%) and energy drinks 622 million litres (16%)" (2). Moreover, Bourke and Veerman (2018) note that "annual per capita sales of SSBs in Indonesia was around 16 litres in 2014, compared with over 70 litres in Singapore" (2). In 2017, however, there was a slight contraction in sales volume, by roughly 1 percent, which some believe may have been attributed to the "bleak purchasing power" of consumers, particularly among the middle- and lower-income classes, a view held by Triyono Prijosoesilo, chairman of the Association of Indonesian Soft Drink Producers (Indonesia Investments 2018a).

When taken together, the soda and ultraprocessed food industry has had a gradual though increasingly important impact on the economy. With a rising middle-income class, changes in lifestyles, and preferences for new diets and imported foreign processed foods (Rangkuti 2018), the beverage and food industry is expected to contribute more to the economy, with an estimated growth rate, for example, of 7.06 percent for the food service industry between 2018 and 2023 (Indonesia Investments 2018b). The food and beverage industry has also become an increasingly important sector for the government, contributing to its Industry Revolution 4.0 objective; other vital industries included in this initiative are the "petrochemical, automotive, electronic, [and] textile" sectors (Salama 2019). The food and beverage sector is also an important sector in the recent Masterplan for Acceleration and Expansion of Indonesian Economic Development (MP3EI) (Dezan Shira and Associates 2011). In addition to the food and beverage manufacturing sector's ongoing growth and contribution to the economy, the food manufacturing sector alone has been a major source of employment. In fact, Neilson and colleagues (2018) claim that employment in the food processing sector in Indonesia increased "from 2.93 million in 2010 to 4.26 million people in 2013; a remarkable rate of 15% annually" (3). According to some analysts, the food and beverage sector "absorbs the largest labor force among other manufacturing industries" (Dezan Shira and Associates 2011, 76). When compared to other subsectors, some claim that the food and beverage sector contributes the most to Indonesia's gross domestic product, as evident through its contribution "to the GDP of the non-oil and gas industry [of] about 34.95 percent in the third quarter of 2017" (Karawang New Industry City 2019). Big junk food and soda are significant economic and political players in emerging Indonesia.

The Rise and Impact of Noncommunicable Diseases

The success and influence of junk food companies in Indonesia appear to have gone hand in hand with an increase in health risk factors and noncommunicable diseases. Increased access to processed foods, a product of globalization and urbanization, has been associated with increased rates of overweight in Indonesia (see Oddo, Maehara, and Hyun-Rah 2019). Indeed, a product of globalization, economic prosperity, and growth, Indonesia has witnessed an accelerated nutrition transition. With respect to the factors accounting for overweight patterns, economic development, higher incomes, more working families, and the availability of unhealthy foods (primarily from the West) have been associated with a decline in consumption of more foods rich in grains, fruits, and vegetables, and seemingly replaced with the consumption of unhealthy processed foods high in fat and sugar (Green et al. 2019; Oddo, Maehara, and Hyun-Rah 2019; Wan 2018). Wan (2018) notes that according to data obtained in 2010 from Euromonitor International, local consumer spending for sugar and confectionary (i.e., chocolates), products that have become increasingly more accessible, has "increased from US$3.2b in 2007 to US$3.6b in 2009, and was projected to increase further to US$7.3b in 2014" (see also Tobin 2019 on this issue). Sugar consumption has seen an annual growth rate of 5.7 percent, which is apparently faster than the average growth throughout the region, recorded at 5.2 percent, and the global average of 2.2 percent (Otto and Rachman 2015). Tobin (2019) writes that, according to Euromonitor International, "the volume of confectionery products sold in Indonesia—such as processed snacks and biscuits—has increased 13 per cent in the past five years." According to some estimates, approximately 30 percent of budgets for food each month goes toward the purchase of processed foods (Food and Land Use Coalition 2019, 28). Indonesians are also increasingly eating food outside of their home. According to Vermeulen and others (2019), an online survey conducted in Indonesia in 2015 showed that approximately 11 percent of respondents tend to eat outside of their home once a day and that 44 percent purchased foods from local street vendors (26). Some believe that the consumption of unhealthy foods in Indonesia may be contributing to obesity (Wan 2018),

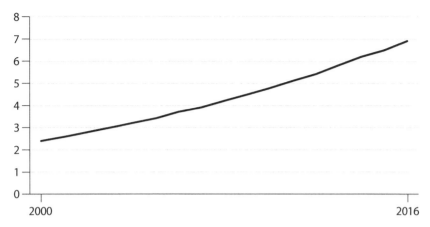

Indonesia: prevalence (%) of obesity among adults. *Source*: WHO, 2021. https://
www.who.int/data/gho/data/indicators/indicator-details/GHO/prevalence-of
-obesity-among-adults-bmi-=-30-(crude-estimate)-(-)

while others underscore an association with these foods and overweight and
obesity, even among youth, especially in urban areas (Nurwanti et al. 2019).

Like Mexico, Brazil, and India, Indonesia has also seen a surge in the
prevalence of obesity cases. In addition to an increase in the consumption
of junk foods, sedentary lifestyles, TV viewing, and exposure to advertisements have been associated with an increase in obesity (Maehara et al. 2019;
Oberlander 2018). The dearth of parks and sidewalks for regular physical
exercise may also be a contributing factor (Oddo et al. 2019a). There is also
an association between higher socioeconomic status and obesity (Harbuwono et al. 2018). Still, others highlight what appears to be the Health Ministry's lack of commitment to raising awareness about its dietary prevention
programs and the seriousness of obesity, in turn leading some nutrition experts, such as Johanes Chandrawinata, to claim that "maybe because they do
not consider it a national health threat despite around a quarter of the population suffering from obesity" (quoted in Dipa 2019). With data obtained
from the 1993–2014 Indonesian Family Life Survey, Oddo and colleagues
(2019a) claim that "between 1993 and 2014, the prevalence of overweight
among adults doubled from 17.1% to 33.0%" (1). According to data provided
by the World Health Organization (WHO) in 2020, the prevalence of obesity
increased from 1.2 percent nationwide in 1990 to 6.9 percent in 2016. Other
studies indicate that overweight and obesity among adults "have increased

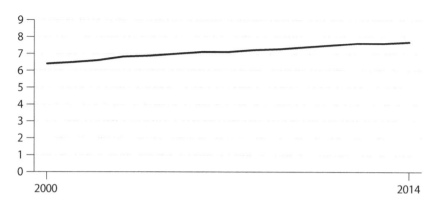

Indonesia: prevalence (%) of adult diabetes. *Source.* WHO, 2021. https://www
.who.int/data/gho/data/indicators/indicator-details/GHO/raised-fasting
-blood-glucose-(-=7-0-mmol-l-or-on-medication)(age-standardized-estimate)

from 8.6% and 10.5% in 2007 to 13.6% and 21.8% in 2018, respectively" (Nurwanti et al. 2019, 2).

While most overweight and obesity cases are found in urban centers
(Mihardja and Soetrisno 2012; Oddo, Maehara, and Hyun-Rah 2019), obesity
is also increasing in rural areas. Indeed, according to Oddo, Maehara, and
Hyun-Rah (2019), the increase in overweight has been higher in rural areas.
Research conducted by Rachmi and colleagues (2016) has also indicated that
the likelihood of concurrent stunting and overweight (among several other
risk factors) for young children was also found in rural areas, in turn highlighting the double burden of malnutrition (i.e., under- and overnutrition)
in these areas.

Indonesia also joins India in having one of the highest rates of type 2
diabetes. According to some estimates provided in 2013, Indonesia ranked
seventh highest in the world for its number of diabetics (Soewondo et al.
2013). A disease that is also strongly correlated with the consumption of
SSBs and ultraprocessed foods, when measured with respect to raised fasting blood glucose levels above 7.0mm (in crude estimates), rates of type 2
diabetes have increased from 5.7 percent in 2005 to 7 percent in 2014 (WHO
2020). According to Tobin (2019), the percentage of the Indonesian type 2
diabetic population "has doubled in the past 30 years," with approximately
16 million type 2 diabetics. In Jakarta, the nation's capital and Indonesia's
largest metropolitan city, the prevalence of diabetes "rose from 1.7% in 1982
to 5.7% in 1993, and then more than doubled to 12.8% in 2001" (Soewondo

et al. 2013, 4). And according to Vermeulen and others (2019), an estimated "10.3 million people aged 20–79, or 6.3 per cent of the adult population, diagnosed as at 2017" (15). While this disease is mainly present in major urban centers, it is now spreading to remote, rural areas, where some researchers claim the prevalence rate is "greater than 10%" (Oddo, Maehara, Izwardy, et al. 2019, 2). According to Tobin (2019), estimates provided by McKinsey revealed that diabetes in 2014 "cost the Indonesian health care system US$1.6 billion annually—consuming more than 40 per cent of government spending on non-communicable diseases." It is also estimated "that more than 14 million Indonesians will have diabetes by 2035" (Fountaine et al. 2016, 1). Diabetes is now considered to be "the third main cause of death after stroke and hypertension, ahead of cancer and chronic obstructive pulmonary disease" in Indonesia (Soewondo et al. 2013, 4).

NCDs among the Most Vulnerable Populations

While rates of obesity initially surged among wealthier individuals in urban areas, recent evidence suggests that the poor are also experiencing an increase in overweight and obesity. This is due to the increased consumption of sodas and ultraprocessed foods as well as aggressive marketing. In fact, and similar to that seen in Mexico, Brazil, and India, the growth rate in overweight and obesity in Indonesia has been higher among lower-income groups (Aizawa and Helble 2016). Indeed, as the investigators Toshiaki Aizawa and Matthias Helble (2016) point out when referring to a study by Aizawa and Helble (forthcoming): "Although the rates of overweight and obesity are higher among the wealthy, the growth in the rates of the less-advantaged group by far outnumbers that of the rich." Additionally, research by Mihardja and Soetrisno (2012), based on data obtained from Indonesia's National Basic Health Research dataset in 2007, further revealed that the burden of overweight and obesity is also high among lower-income classes, seemingly shifting toward the poor, although individuals with higher incomes were at greater risk. Other studies reveal that the number of overweight individuals has been evenly spread out among all income groups (Oddo, Maehara, and Hyun-Rah 2019), in turn showing that this health challenge is no longer associated with the more affluent classes (see also Aizawa and Helble 2016).

Nevertheless, based on the research of Cut Novianti Rachmi, a physician at the University of Sydney, Wirdana (2019) explains that despite a decline in general undernutrition among children in Indonesia over the past four-

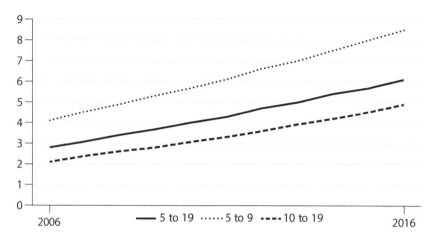

Indonesia: prevalence (%) of childhood obesity (ages 5–19). *Source*: WHO, 2021.
https://www.who.int/data/gho/data/indicators/indicator-details/GHO/preva
lence-of-obesity-among-children-and-adolescents-bmi-2-standard-deviations
-above-the-median-(crude-estimate)-(-)

teen years, overweight continues to increase. According to Oddo, Maehara, and Hyun-Rah (2019), for "children aged 6–12 years and 13–18 years, the prevalence of overweight increased from 5.1% to 15.6% and from 7.1% and 14.1% between 1993 and 2014, respectively" (1). Nurwanti and colleagues (2019) further explain that from 2013 to 2018, for children between the ages of 5 and 12, their prevalence of overweight remained stable at 10.8 percent (1). However, the prevalence of obese children in this age group during the same period increased from 8.8 percent to 9.2 percent (2). Others claim that for children under the age of 5, from 1993 to 2007, the prevalence of over-weight increased from 4.2 percent to 9.4 percent and that this prevalence rate leveled off thereafter from 2007 to 2014 (Oddo, Maehara, and Hyun-Rah 2019, 1). Moreover, studies indicate that Indonesia has "the highest preva-lence rate" of overweight and obesity for children under 5 years of age when compared to other nations in Southeast Asia (Rachmi et al. 2017, 21).

In Indonesia, overweight and obesity appear to be mainly prevalent among children and adolescents in urban areas (Green et al. 2019; Nurwanti et al. 2019). Rachmi and others (2017) note that in 2002, research conducted in the cities of Jakarta, Jogjakarta, and Kuta revealed that obesity was more prevalent among students between the ages of 13 and 15 and was found more often in students in urban areas, such as Jakarta. Other factors, such as coming from families with a higher income, attending private schools, and spending more time playing video games and using computers, also contributed. Rachmi and colleagues (2017) mention yet another study, conducted in 2011, that indicated that the pervasiveness of overweight and obesity for children between the ages of 0.5 and 12 throughout Indonesia "was more than double" in urban areas than in rural areas—"10.7% versus 5.1%, respectively" (25).

But why are Indonesia's children and adolescents gaining so much weight? Several studies reveal a plethora of potential risk factors associated with children's weight gain and obesity. These factors include increased availability and consumption of processed and commercial foods, parental efforts to keep children happy by providing them with these foods, and children coming from a family with a high household income (Green et al. 2018; Maehara et al. 2019; Oddo, Maehara, and Hyun-Rah 2019). Recent survey research across thirty-two cities revealed that children and adolescents had the highest consumption of sugar-sweetened beverages (SSBs), which "were consumed by 62% children, 72% adolescents and 61% of adults"; moreover, according to Laksmi and colleagues (2018), "24% of children, 41% of adolescents and 33% adults" were reported as consuming equal to or greater than one serving per day of SSBs (S89). Surveys conducted in East Jakarta found that the "convenience and price" of less healthy food was a factor in choosing to consume these foods, particularly within schools and especially among adolescents of poorer families (Maulida et al. 2016). Others allude to the challenges of increasingly sedentary lifestyles, often attributed to access to technology and the inability to engage in regular physical activity due to busy school schedules (Maehara et al. 2019; UNICEF 2019). Other studies found a strong association between household wealth (and living in a high socioeconomic status area) and adolescent overweight (Maehara et al. 2019). Some, nevertheless, claim that the concerns and efforts of educated mothers to safeguard their children from becoming underweight contributes to the risk of their child's weight gain (Syahrul et al. 2016). Finally, others blame the country's worsening obesogenic environment for children: that is, exposure to TV advertising (more on this soon; see Oberlander 2018), as well as "ease of access [of less healthy foods] in school canteens or from vendors outside the school for children" (Jember University with IIED 2019, 24).

With respect to type 2 diabetes, studies suggest that this disease is also surfacing among Indonesia's youth. While scant research and epidemiological evidence exists, recent interviews of diabetics conducted by Tobin (2019) suggest that due to genetic predisposition, poor lifestyle choices, and an increase in the consumption of unhealthy foods, this disease is now affecting Indonesia's youth. Pulungan and colleagues (2018) reference a study by Moelyo and others (2013) revealing that, according to the Indonesian National Registry (2009–2012), thirty-eight children and adolescents were reported to have type 2 diabetes (119); however, Pulungan and colleagues claim that the actual number of type 2 diabetics among Indonesian youth may be higher due to inadequate reporting and health care workers lacking awareness of the situation. It is expected that this disease will continue to rise within this population and pose extensive costs for Indonesia's health care system.

Policy Response

Indonesia's government, when compared to Mexico, Brazil, and India, has been relatively slow in its policy response to obesity and type 2 diabetes. In an article published in 2012 for the *Jakarta Post*, Elly Burhaini Faizal quotes Professor Hasbullah Thabrani from the University of Indonesia's School of Public Health as stating: "We should have made noncommunicable diseases a priority 10 years ago as the leading causes of death have shifted from infectious diseases to the noninfectious ones." To date, and in contrast with what we have seen in other countries, there are no national public health programs that specifically address these diseases. What has emerged instead are broader national development programs with public health components and, more recently, national programs that address NCDs at a very broad level, through interventions focused on healthy living and the social determinants of health.

The MoH's first attempt to prevent the rise of NCDs appeared to have emerged with the National Long-Term Development Plan of 2005–2025. The primary focus of this plan (in the area of nutrition and health) is to improve the overall quality of nutrition available for Indonesian households (Food and Land Use Coalition 2019). In addition, the government provided funding for several intervention programs focused on improving nutrition (Food and Land Use Coalition 2019). And through the Ministry of Villages, in order to help eradicate stunting, in 2018 a cash-for-work cash transfer program titled Padat Karya Tunai was provided for villages in order to fund children's nutrition programs, as well as help in other areas, such as public infrastructure (Food and Land Use Coalition 2019). The MoH also released the *Pedoman Gizi Sembang* (Balanced Nutritional Guidelines), which provided guidance for health professionals as well as messages to the general public on several nutritional issues (Vermeulen et al. 2019). According to Vermeulen and colleagues (2019), these messages included: "enjoy and be grateful for a variety of foods; eat lots of vegetables and enough fruits; include a wide variety of staple foods in your diet; make a habit of eating high protein side dishes; limit consumption of sweet, salty and fatty foods; enjoy breakfast; drink plenty of safe water; get used to reading labels on food packaging; wash hands with soap and running water; and do enough physical activity to maintain a normal weight" (23). The MoH also created the Posbindu PTM program to monitor and report dietary risk factors associated with NCDs (24). In 2010, the government once again emphasized the importance of national security through improved nutrition via the Medium-Term National Development Plan of 2010–2014 (Government of Indonesia 2010).

Federal programs were also created to enhance children's nutrition. For example, in collaboration with the SUN (Scaling UP Nutrition) Movement and other organizations, the government's program titled Generasi Sehat dan Cerdas (Healthy and Bright Generation) provided grants to "over 5,500 villages across 11 provinces to support the provision of iron supplements and antenatal care to pregnant women, together with nourishment and immunization programmes for children" (Vermeulen et al. 2019, 23).

In 2006, the MoH put forth the National Action Plan for Food and Nutrition (NAPFN, 2006–2010), a follow-up to the NAPFN (2001–2005). Through NAPFN (2006–2010), the MoH was committed to improving the health status of local communities with the objective of improving long-term health, intelligence, and individual productivity by enhancing "food and nutritional resilience" by the year 2010 (National Development Planning Board 2007, ii). The NAPFN (2006–2010) focused specifically on the following: (1) improving the knowledge, attitude, and healthy lifestyle of citizens; (2) increasing accessibility to affordable food; (3) enhancing accessibility to equitable and affordable health care and nutritional services; (4) increasing family access to health and nutritional information; (5) improving poverty alleviation by enhancing the provision of nutrition services for the poor; and, finally, (6) working with food producers to improve food safety as well as strengthen overall supervision of this process (ii). In sum, in addition to reducing overall malnutrition rates by 2010, the gist of the NAPFN was focused on four pillars: food accessibility, nutritional status, food security, and healthy life-styles (iii). Yet another National Action Plan for Food and Nutrition (2011–2015) was created in 2010, and provided guidelines for national, provincial, and municipal governments. This plan was focused on the following objectives: (1) improving community nutrition; (2) increasing food access; (3) improving food quality as well as safety; (4) establishing clean and healthy lifestyles; and (5) institutionalizing food and nutrition by giving subnational governments more policy authority in the area of nutrition and food as well as improved resource capacity (Government of Indonesia 2010, 5). Among other objectives, this program strove to improve the nutritional status of women and children, mainly through increased food availability and food safety, and to increase healthier lifestyles through improved nutrition awareness (Government of Indonesia 2010).

Furthermore, it is important to note that the government issued Presidential Instruction No. 3 to enact the National Action Plans for Food and Nutrition, as well as the Provincial Action Plans for Food and Nutrition, with the participation of subnational governments. This endeavor provides national "guidelines" on implementing food and nutrition programs at the national, provincial, and municipal government levels. Moreover, these guidelines are for government and community institutions as well as any other stakeholders working in the area of nutrition (Government of Indonesia 2010).

More recently, in an effort to stem the rising tide of obesity, type 2 diabetes, and other related NCDs, the MoH has been committed to pursuing broader health promotion activities. According to Endang Rahayu Sedyaningsih, Indonesia's former Minister of Health, in an effort to curb the death and health impediments associated with NCDs, health promotion has become a priority for the government. She claimed that "while continuing successful campaigns in the fight against infectious diseases, we will be paying more attention to noncommunicable diseases conducted through both health promotion and disease prevention" (quoted in Faizal 2012).

Perhaps the most comprehensive national program created to achieve this objective was the 2016 Gerakan Masyarakat Hidup Sehat (GERMAS, Community Movement for a Healthy Life) program. Created by Presidential Instruction No. 1/3027, GERMAS's mission was to improve the overall health of Indonesians by encouraging increased physical activity, consumption of healthy food, and regular health checkups (Moeloek 2017). GERMAS's objective is to increase multisectoral coordination by creating initiatives that motivate individuals to live a healthier lifestyle, reaching down to the lowest tiers of government. Interestingly, according to Moeloek (2017), this program is "coordinated" by the Ministry of National Development Planning (BAPPENAS), rather than the MoH. This, in turn, reflects the effort to make this a broader cross-sectoral, collective initiative while collaborating with preexisting primary care institutions, such as community Puskesmas health centers. Additionally, GERMAS focuses on the social determinants of diseases (e.g., the need to reduce poverty, address gender and environmental issues). To achieve this, program interventions are pursued at the community level to address disease risk factors, as well as determine groups that are at higher risk. Yet another strategy that GERMAS has adopted is community empowerment and improvements to primary care systems as a way of providing "promotive-preventive health services" in alignment with the government's preexisting commitment to achieving universal health care coverage (Moeloek 2017).

With respect to improving children's nutrition, the central government has historically been committed to providing a national school feeding program. Beginning in 1984 with the Usaha Kesehatan Sekolah (UKS) national school health program, which historically fell under the purview of BAPPENAS prior to decentralization, four ministries—namely, the Ministry of National Education, Ministry of Religious Affairs, Ministry of Health, and Ministry of Internal Affairs (now Home Affairs)—coordinated to provide funding and technical assistance to schools to improve children's nutrition through the creation of a healthier environment (Del Rosso and Arlianti 2009). Today, the UKS's overall goal is threefold: "health education, health services at schools and [a] healthy school environment" (5). Over time, the UKS program was decentralized to the provincial governments, with schools, since 2009, obtaining block grants from the central government to improve school canteens. According to Del Rosso and Arlianti (2009), "288 schools across 33 provinces and 36 districts—112 primary, 90 junior secondary, and 86 senior secondary—are receiving the equivalent of approximately $1,000 for one year" in federal block grant assistance (29). Furthermore, the Ministry of National Education provides technical assistance and training to schools to improve food canteen services, as well as food safety test kits and educational materials on healthy school canteens (29).

The government's overall approach to school feeding consists of the preparation of school meals in canteens with local sources funded by the central government (Del Rosso and Arlianti 2009). School feeding programs also provide biscuits and snacks. While the provincial governments are now primarily responsible for funding and administering school feeding programs, schools receive a great deal of managerial support from the World Food Programme. Indeed, according to Del Rosso and Arlianti (2009), the World Food Programme reaches "more than 200,000 children in more than 1000 schools in the provinces of NTB, NTT to East Java" (30).

In the area of NCD prevention, however, no stern effort has been made to create a tax on soda or junk food. The government did briefly introduce a tax on SSBs under the guise of a "luxury-goods tax" but quickly ended the endeavor in 2004 (Otto and Rachman 2015). Industry representatives such as the Beverages Industry Association argued that "the taxes crippled drink makers" (Otto and Rachman 2015). While tariffs on the import of beverages containing added sugar exist in the Ministry of Finance's Regulation 132 of 2015, no taxes have been imposed on domestic beverages (see Haning et al. 2016). In 2015, the government did propose the creation of a new tax on sugary beverages, but it did not establish a time frame for when this would occur (Diela 2015). In 2019, the government was still considering the creation of a tax on sugary drinks (Veerman et al. 2019). Nevertheless, ongoing resistance from major junk food industries have thwarted these efforts (more on this later).

To further prevent the rise of NCDs, the central government has also introduced several food labeling laws and regulations with impressive policy enforcement mechanisms (see Baker McKenzie 2018). Since 1996, according to Law No. 7, which is regulated by the National Agency of Drug and Food Control (BPOM), all food products in Indonesia are required to be registered and have food labels prior to being sold (Marketing Consultancy Division, n.d.). In 1999, Ministry of Health Regulation No. 69 (also known as GR 69), specifically articles 32 and 33, required the provision of food labels with the following information: "serving size, number of servings per product, energy per serving, macronutrient per serving, and the percentage of RDA" (Haning et al. 2016, 227; see also Baker McKenzie 2018 on this issue). GR 69 also requires labels to include the name of the product, a listing of the materials used in the product, either the net content or weight of the product, its date of expiration, and the name and location of the local manufacturer or importer (Baker McKenzie 2018, 26). All labels are also to be written in the Indonesian language (26). In 2013, Ministry of Health Regulation No. 30 was also created, mandating a description of all sugar, salt, and fat content on labels; moreover, these labels require "health messages" for any processed or fast food products (Haning et al. 2016, 224). What's more, the government through BPOM regulation No. 9/2016 also established an acceptable daily intake allowance on food labels (USDA 2011, 7).

In 2018, the BPOM created Regulation 31, which is focused on processed food labels. This regulation supersedes all previous related labels for processed foods and requires that businesses provide complete and accurate information on labels, specifying what should be on these labels and how the information on labels is to be written (Endahayu 2019, 1). Specifically, BPOM Reg. 31 requires the following information: "(a) the name of the product; (b) list of ingredients used; (c) net weight or net content; (d) name and address of the manufacturing and importing company; (e) halal logo (if applicable); (f) date and code of production; (g) expiration date; (h) marketing authorization number; (i) origins of certain food ingredient; [and] (j) nutrient and/or non-nutrient contents" (3). Furthermore, this regulation requires the following information on labels for all processed foods: "health message; intended users; method of serving; storage; allergen content; warning; organic processed food and 2D barcode" (4). BPOM Reg. 31's health messages on labels must be present for foods that contain sugar, salt, and fat in consumption amounts that can potentially lead to NCDs (4). Furthermore, BPOM Reg. 31 stipulates that businesses must comply with this new regulation within thirty months of its enactment. Any false, misleading, or offensive claims, for example, are also prohibited on food labels (Endahayu 2019). Finally, in 2019, the BPOM issued Regulation No. 20/2019, on food packaging, mandating that manufacturers use packaging materials that do not include materials that are hazardous to human health (Foreign Agricultural Service 2019).

Indonesia's government has also had a firm track record of attempting to regulate the marketing and advertising of junk food products. Beginning with its general 1999 Consumer Protection Law, Law No. 8/1999, this regulation required that all advertisements be truthful (Baker McKenzie 2018). According to the aforementioned GR 69 regulation of 1999, all advertisements should contain truthful statements and labels should provide all of the required information (Baker McKenzie 2018).

Stiff penalties also exist for producing poorly informed or false labels

(USDA 2011). According to Article 44 of the 1999 GR 69, all advertisements for food traded and sold must contain "true and illuminating information," with respect to audio messages, pictures, or any other form of communication (Indonesia Government 1999, 1); article 45 also prohibits any "untrue and/or misleading statements and/or information in advertisements" (Indonesia Government 1999, 1). According to the national Food Law, Article 144, the penalty for providing "misleading information or statements on food labels" is "imprisonment for three years or a maximum fine of IDR 6 billion" (Baker McKenzie 2018, 32). Article 145 of the Food Law, moreover, penalizes manufacturers for providing "misleading information or statements regarding food through advertising," resulting in "imprisonment for three years or a maximum fine of IDR 6 billion" for noncompliance (Baker McKenzie 2018, 32). With respect to the recent BPOM Reg. 31, failure to comply with this regulation could lead to the following sanctions: "(a) temporary suspension of activity, production and/or distribution; (b) forced product recall by the manufacturer; [or] (c) revocation of license (e.g., distribution license or trade license)" (Endahayu 2019, 1). The BPOM, Food and Drug Supervisory Agency, and the Directorate General of Standardization and Consumer Protection, Ministry of Trade (DJSPK), are the federal agencies responsible for enforcing all federal laws pertaining to food (Baker McKenzie 2018, 31).

Policy Problems

Despite these impressive policy initiatives, several policy shortcomings have arisen. First, with respect to the marketing and advertisement of junk food products, to this day, there is no federal legislation prohibiting the marketing and sale of these products to children and the poor. In this context, advertisements about unhealthy foods and beverages usually directed toward children and adolescents, mainly on TV and social media, are "increasing rapidly" (Food and Land Use Coalition 2019, 29). Indeed, according to the Food and Land Use Coalition (2019): "Many children and adolescents are highly exposed to food marketing of packaged foods, which contain high salt, sugar and fat, since they are the vulnerable population and easily influenced" (29).

And with respect to food labels, while the phalanx of laws and fines is noteworthy, recent research finds that several limitations exist concerning the effectiveness of these labels as well as contradictions between regulations. First, with respect to sugar content, while according to GR 69 all labels are required to list the amount of sugar present, there is no requirement that states that information on precise sugar content per serving needs to be included (Haning et al. 2016, 224). However, Haning and colleagues (2016) point out that Health Minister Regulation No. 30 does require information on sugar content, along with salt and fat on labels and health messages. This provides conflicting regulatory information that, according to Haning and others (2016), "can lead the government to become less assertive on this issue" (224). Thus, for Haning and colleagues, GR 69 "needs to be revised as the information on sugar content is very important to be known to the public" (224). There is no cap on the maximum amount of sugar that products, such as beverages with added sugar, can contain (223). According to a nutrition researcher I interviewed, the current president, Jokowi, and the government are trying to introduce these regulations, but it is difficult to achieve due to political obstacles (interview with Fransiska Rungkat-Zakaria, January 26, 2020).

Furthermore, there is a lack of legal enforcement in providing the nutritional food label information mandated by the government. For instance, as mentioned earlier, labels are required to display the amounts of protein, fat, sodium, and energy, but, according to the WHO, this has "not [been] implemented" (WHO 2018, 9). This, in turn, reflects the general problem discussed by Baker McKenzie (2018) that those agencies responsible for regulating food, including food quality, have "wide-ranging discretion in applying these laws and can change policy from time to time, often without public notice" (26). Researchers in Indonesia I interviewed confirm that the government is not committed to enforcing these regulations, that there is no habit of doing so, and that industry has complained that such regulations would be detrimental to the economy (interview with Rungkat-Zakaria, January 26, 2020). Others find that agencies have sought a gradual implementation of food labeling regulations (WHO 2018), which is ambiguous and smacks of a lack of government commitment to enforcement. In this context, a challenge emerges with respect to the incentives that industries have to implement these regulations (WHO 2018). Furthermore, with this in mind, why would industries take the aforementioned penalties and fines seriously?

But why have these policy challenges emerged in the first place? If the central and provincial governments are so committed to addressing NCDs and protecting Indonesia's most vulnerable populations, why are politicians

202 Junk Food Politics

and bureaucrats reluctant to not only create much-needed policies, such as a soda tax, but also increase product regulations and enforce existing laws? As we saw in the other emerging economies discussed in this book, there appears to exist a gray line that government is not willing to cross: that is, let us create NCD programs up to a certain point, regulate them up to a certain point, but refrain from creating regulations that directly threaten corporate interests. Why is the government not fully committed to crossing this line and taking on big business? As we will see in the next section, a combination of innovative industry political tactics and complementary institutions helps to explain why this is the case.

Political Action

In Indonesia, and in contrast to what we have seen in most of the countries discussed in this book thus far, there is no direct partnership between junk food industries and government in the areas of NCD policy making (interview with anonymous source, September 11, 2020). In fact, the MoH has refrained from such partnerships in order to avoid any potential conflict of interest (interview with anonymous source, September 11, 2020). In fact, in Indonesia, industry leaders have placed their focus on distracting the MoH's and politicians' attention away from the harmful health consequences, such as NCDs, of their food products, focusing instead on other malnutrition issues, such as stunting (interview with Rungkat-Zakaria, January 26, 2020). For example, industry representatives have provided policy makers with data illustrating the ongoing stunting problem so that they can advocate for an industry's nutritious food products reaching children and benefit economically from this (interview with Rungkat-Zakaria, January 26, 2020).

In addition to the fear that regulatory policies could have on their economic performance and the economy in general, industries have not been interested in partnering with MoH officials—or any government officials, for that matter—in order to create NCD regulatory or prevention programs. If anything, industry leaders consistently prefer to distract health officials from creating such policies for as long as possible. Industry's method is to flood officials with data on other major and ongoing public health challenges so that industries can sell their products through initiatives such as providing "emergency food" (e.g., providing fortified foods, imported flour and sugar), and thus benefit economically (interview with Rungkat-Zakaria, January 26, 2020).

Consequently, if there are any partnerships that exist with the government, it is in the area of stunting prevention. The upshot with these efforts, however, is that it has shifted attention away from focusing on NCD policies. Indeed, in this context, the government has been distracted from pursuing food regulations (interview with Rungkat-Zakaria, January 26, 2020). But, of course, this situation should not preclude the government from pursuing such policies. Furthermore, it appears that by partnering with government on stunting and malnutrition, industries are perceived as both contributing to Indonesia's nutritional problems and being an important government ally. Indeed, by partnering with government on stunting and malnutrition issues, this has bolstered these industries' political and policy legitimacy and influence on these nutritional issues (interview with Rungkat-Zakaria, January 26, 2020).

Lobbying and Largesse

In Indonesia, the junk food industry's policy influence through lobbying activities and the provision of electoral campaign contributions is not publicly well known. In sharp contrast to what we have seen in Mexico, Brazil, and India, these activities exist but are essentially invisible to the public (interview with Rungkat-Zakaria, January 26, 2020). Others have documented the excessive prevalence of corruption within government, as well as a general lack of any guidance or framework for lobbying activities (Christian 2011). One should keep in mind, though, that this very issue has also plagued Mexico, Brazil, and India, in turn providing countless opportunities for industry policy influence.

Nevertheless, perhaps because of the excessive amount of global media attention on the topic, there have been several documented attempts of industry's efforts to lobby against the creation of a soda or junk food tax. Industries in Indonesia have a history of fighting this effort—and with success. As mentioned earlier, in 2004, for example, the government succeeded in introducing a luxury goods tax, which included a tax on sugary beverages. However, this luxury tax was eventually eliminated due to pressure from industry (Whitehead 2016).

In 2015, the Ministry of Finance once again considered creating a tax on sugary drinks. Iskan Qolba Lubis, a parliamentary representative from the Prosperous Justice Party, stated that "this [tax] is to keep our people healthy" (quoted in Otto and Rachman 2015). According to nutrition researchers in Indonesia, however, this is the one area in which industry has been very influential with respect to their economic arguments against a tax, claiming that the endeavor would be harmful to the economy and would ultimately lead to the absence of a sugar tax (interview with Rungkat-Zakaria, January 26, 2020).

Industry representatives were certainly not on the same page. Once again, industry producers pressured the government and succeeded in convincing it to drop the 2015 tax effort (see Diela 2016). In so doing, industry representatives claimed that in a context of economic recession and stagnant growth, when considering new market entrants and competitors (particularly in the soda sector), this tax would impair the market (Chilkoti 2016) and lead to substantial job loss (Whitehead 2015c). Whitehead claims that Triyono Prijosoesilo, chairman of the Soft Drinks Industries Association, stated that, quoting Whitehead (2015c) here: "Up to 120,000 industry workers would stand to lose their jobs if a sugar tax were introduced, outweighing any health gains from the proposal" (1). Whitehead (2016) reports that according to a global research analyst, Howard Telford, a tax could be an impediment for Coca-Cola considering it invested US$500 million in October 2014 in the local Amatil bottling company. Furthermore, "[The] tax 'could be crippling for an industry that's just getting started,'" claimed Martin Gil, in charge of Coca-Cola Indonesia (quoted in Otto and Rachman 2015). Industry representatives further claimed that "sweetened beverages should not even be taxed as consumption remains very low. They only account for 6.5% of the total calories consumed by residents of big cities in Indonesia," argued Triyono Prijosoesilo (quoted in Whitehead 2015c, 1). Moreover, industry advocates explained that "there is no reason from health or fiscal perspectives [to introduce the tax]. . . . In the end, we'll only become a market. Indonesia will no longer be attractive as a production base," argued Adhi Lukman, who chaired the Indonesian Food and Beverage Association (quoted in Whitehead 2015c, 1). By 2016, the tax issue was shelved. Big industry won the debate.

But this did not stop the government from believing that some sort of tax was possible. As an alternative, the government proposed a tax on plastic bottles, at a rate "of between Rp 200 to Rp 500 for each plastic bottle used," to help replenish state coffers (Diela 2016). Nevertheless, industry representatives such as Edi Rivai, the Indonesian Olefin and Plastic Industry Association's (Inaplas) deputy chairman, argued that the tax idea was "misplaced" (quoted in Diela 2016). Rivai went on to claim that taxes should be used for discouraging the consumption of harmful products such as tobacco and alcohol (Diela 2016). Titie Sadarini, a Coca-Cola executive who also represented the corporate interest group GAPMMI at a public discussion, also stated: "We're not the only one[s] who will bear the burden from the tax. . . . Consumers will share the burden. Once the prices [of food and beverages] soar, their purchasing power drops, then the industry will get the blow as well. . . . Producers will charge the added costs to customers. When the customers stop buying, sales drop, [and] producers will take some efficiency measures which will cost jobs" (quoted in Diela 2016).

Nevertheless, efforts to introduce a tax continue. To this day, there appears to be an ongoing dialogue between the Ministry of Finance and industry leaders to introduce a tax. While President Joko Widodo is fully supportive of introducing a tax (interview with Rungkat-Zakaria, January 26, 2020), only time will tell if he is capable of finding the political support needed to overcome industry resistance and implement one.

One additional reason that Indonesia's junk food companies are so influential in their lobbying activities has to do with the country's ongoing revolving door problem, where individuals go back and forth from government to industry, leading to conflicts of interest. According to some analysts, "many business leaders moonlight as political party chairmen, [and] lobby groups have often thwarted government attempts to impose new taxes" (Diela 2016).

Restructuring Society

Similar to what we saw in the other emerging economies, in recent years industries in Indonesia have also engaged in CSR activities in order to increase their social and, eventually, political legitimacy and policy influence. Consistent with IPCI, industries in Indonesia, it seems, have used CSR activities to increase not only their social acceptability and support but their political legitimacy within Congress and the government. Efforts to engage in these activities are relatively new, beginning mainly throughout the 1990s in response to court cases about companies, such as Nike and Levi Strauss, violating worker and human rights (Phuong and Rachman 2017). Following efforts to decentralize greater policy responsibilities, civil societal actors also started to monitor industry activities, checking for irresponsible social behavior, while getting more involved in the decision-making process. In this context, public demands for greater industry social responsibility, such as contributing to education, health, the environment, and poverty reduction, also eventually increased. Industries paid attention and, as this section explains, engaged in a variety of voluntary CSR activities.

In the area of public health, industries have engaged in several CSR initiatives. In recent years, for example, Coca-Cola Amatil has provided "free medical services for . . . community members" throughout the country as well as infrastructural support for clean water facilities in cities such as Cibitung and Bali (Coca-Cola Amatil 2017, 66). In 2018, for example, Indonesia's Coca-Cola Foundation (established in 2000) "created a hygiene and sanitation program across four schools in Semarang Regency, Central Java" (Coca-Cola Amatil 2018, 66). This program worked to construct "two water tanks, 11 waste disposal facilities, [and] 18 hand washing areas and [renovated] toilets to improve its sanitation conditions." In 2018, the company claimed that this "program had a positive impact on the well-being of 1,244 students and 80 teachers" (66). These efforts are part of the Coca-Cola Foundation's broader commitment to contribute to the social welfare advancement of communities.

Nestlé has also established several health care programs. One of Nestlé's CSR activities has been strengthening the country's health care system at the local level. In 2012, for example, Nestlé Indonesia partnered with the PKK (family welfare movement) in order to train fifteen thousand volunteer health care workers in the Posyandu TAT located in Mataram, Indonesia (Afrida 2013). In 2013, Nestlé and the PKK had plans to expand this training program to six other provinces—namely, "Aceh, Jakarta, East Nusa Tenggara (NTT), NTB, Riau, and West Sulawesi." These training programs for volunteer primary health care workers focus on the provision of counseling services and strengthening the health of newborn babies and their mothers (Afrida 2013).

In 2012, Nestlé Indonesia delved deeper into health care matters by joining the Indonesia Nutrition Association (INA) to help improve the nutritional status of six-to-twelve-year-old students in elementary schools across seventeen areas, with the goal of implementing the Nestlé Healthy Kids program (NHK) (Rosdiana 2013). Through this endeavor, Nestlé provides administrative and financial support while the INA provides further technical assistance, mainly by training teachers, providing educational materials, and giving guidance in implementing Nestlé Indonesia's program in elementary schools throughout Indonesia (Rosdiana 2013). Subsequent technical evaluations (desk reviews) conducted by INA, based on a request from Nestlé, led to INA's recommendation that Nestlé help schools develop the capacity to create nutrition and health care programs on their own, in a sustainable way, with the goal of improving "students' knowledge and skills in selecting healthy food, but also support the students to maintain such changes in their behavior" (2). The INA recommended to Nestlé that it revise "the health, nutrition and physical activity guidelines for students and teachers, inviting medical personnel to provide education and counselling on nutrition, educating canteen vendors to serve nutritionally balanced food options for students, teachers/school staff, and giving examples of practices in consuming healthy foods" (2). There are two NHK subprograms: first, the School Health Initiatives program, which focuses on the sustainability of NHK's pilot programs; second, the SSN (NHK-sponsored schools) program, which strives to establish a network of collaborating elementary schools providing the NHK program (Rosdiana 2013). Schools received competitive grants (twenty-six approved) based on their commitment to improving nutrition, physical fitness activities, and personal cleanliness, and at the end of each year, those that received grants were required to provide a report detailing how they accomplished their proposed goals (3).

Through all of these efforts, the Swiss company maintained that teachers were able to provide instruction in nutrition and physical activities, with nutritional information provided in a more interesting and effective manner (e.g., by telling stories), while canteen cooks prepared healthier meals (Rosdiana 2013). Analysts claim that because of Nestle's efforts, by 2013, there were "28,500 students from 65 elementary schools [that were] informed about nutrition and physical activities, (b) 2,200 parents [that were] informed about child nutrition and health, and (c) 860 teachers, 65 principals and 72 community health centers [that] attended NHK training" (1). Finally, to help ensure program sustainability, Nestlé planned to get more parents and schools involved in managing these efforts in order to establish a greater "sense of ownership" and possible future support for these endeavors (4).

Other major food-processing companies, such as Unilever, have also played a part in addressing Indonesia's pressing health care issues. Beginning in 2004 with the support of the Unilever Indonesia Foundation and other partners, Unilever Indonesia launched its Indonesia Sehat campaign, which provided educational programs and knowledge while helping communities improve their hygienic behaviors (Unilever Indonesia 2020). Unilever Indonesia's objective through its Indonesia Sehat campaign has been "to inspire 100 million Indonesian people to take active participation [to improve] their health and well-being" (Unilever Indonesia 2020, 1). Furthermore, a generous donation of US$200,000 from Unilever Indonesia to UNICEF in 1999 allowed for the "re-opening of 900 health centres that had been closed during the crisis, when public funding was cut" (Clay 2005, 103). Unilever Indonesia provided family planning services in poor rural areas after the government abandoned the provision of these services following the financial crisis of the late 1990s, delivering funding "to keep more than 200 people engaged in this work" (103). At the same time, Unilever instructed its family planning staff to sell several of its products, with a sales commission in return, when providing services in rural areas (Clay 2005).

Unilever extended its work to schoolchildren. Unilever Indonesia's School Health Program, for example, was created to implement several educational activities in schools, with a focus on health, hygiene, and nutrition, in order to instill "good hygiene and health habits among primary and secondary school students" (Unilever Indonesia 2020). An innovative aspect of this program is the company's provision of health champions, also known as "little doctors" in primary schools and as "youth ambassadors" in secondary schools (1). These individuals serve as peer educators who lead by example and encourage students to learn and establish good health and hygiene practices. Not surprisingly, according to Unilever Indonesia (2020), the health messages that these health champions play "are strongly associated with and supported by" specific Unilever products (1). When promoting the importance of hand washing, for example, they introduce Unilever's soap, Lifebuoy; when encouraging daily tooth brushing, Pepsodent; when encouraging safe water consumption, Purelt; and when using the toilet correctly at home and school, its Domestos. Unilever Indonesia (2020) also claims that "approximately 1.6 million primary school students were reached through integrated health hygiene education in 2015" (1). Furthermore, the Unilever Indonesia Foundation has worked with international organizations, such as the World Food Programme, on school nutrition initiatives through the School Meal Programme. In a partnership with the World Food Programme, the Unilever Indonesia Foundation, through their Project Laser Beam initiative, provides home-cooked, nutritious meals made by cooking groups established by mothers, three days a week, to "more than 20,000 primary school students in 94 schools in the city of Kupang, district of Kupang and also Timor Tengah Selatan" (1). And in the Sumba Barat District of Nusa Tenggara Timor province, Unilever has supported Save the Children to help increase access to sanitation and water in schools, while Save the Children has trained school principals and teachers on how to provide instruction on good hygiene, in turn "benefiting a total of 4,600 students" (1).

Following Unilever's lead was Cargill, producer of confectionaries, ice cream ingredients, and other products. Beginning in 2017, the company partnered with the World Food Programme, the Ministry of Education and Culture, schools, local farmers, and NGOs to provide healthy school meals (Nutrition Connect 2019). The program was focused on strengthening the capacity of subnational governments and NGOs, including partners such as the Belu, Deli Serdang, Serang, and Pasuruan Districts, among several others, "to improve and expand school meals and purchases from local farmers, fisherman, shop owners, and communities, further strengthening economic capacity" (1). The focus was on helping the Ministry of Education "scale-up" the aforementioned PROGAS program (Program Gizi Anak Sekolah, the government's national school meals program), with the goal of diversifying diets and promoting good health and hygiene (1). Cargill worked with the World Food Programme to train government officials to scale up the program and with NGOs to cook for the program, while reviewing and improving the nutritional content of foods that are provided in "Cargill facility canteens" (1). Analysts claim that "the government scaled-up its national school meals programme from 4 to 11 districts and plans to add 39 more in 2019," while "about 100,000 students now have access to healthy school meals and four additional schools now benefit from PROGAS-like school meals" (1).

Unilever introduced other programs that focus on addressing mental health among youth in secondary schools. Through its Rexona (Remaja Berani Hidup Sehat) initiative, the company educates students about taking pride in their daily appearance and hygiene, in turn helping build self-esteem (Unilever Indonesia 2020). By 2015, Unilever claims to have reached "no less than 70,000 secondary school students in 20 cities in North Sumatra, Jakarta, East Java and Bali with support from four local partners, HeartIndo, YCAB, Spektra and Persada."

Unilever Indonesia also established several programs to improve community health throughout Indonesia. The company set the ambitious "target of inspiring 100 million Indonesian people in cities, towns and villages across the country to take steps to improve their health and well-being" by the year 2020 (Unilever Indonesia 2020, 1). Several programs, such as the Mothers Programme in Posyandu, have been created to achieve this. The Mothers Programme provides health hygiene education to children under the age of five and their mothers (Unilever Indonesia 2020). Unilever Indonesia's Healthy Village program also focuses on providing rural community members with the skills needed to respond to local hygiene, nutritional, and health care needs while also empowering these communities to promote good nutrition, hygiene, and health among themselves; moreover, community members involved in this program partner with their local community health center, Posyandu, to achieve their goals (Unilever Indonesia 2020). Finally, fostered by an idea of the governor of Jakarta's wife, Unilever Indonesia also "supported the development of child-friendly public spaces, locally known as Ruang Publik Terpadu Ramah Anak" (1). According to Clay (2005), he and his colleagues found that residents living near Unilever Indonesia's headquarters have also received benefits such as employment and increased local business.

In partnership with others, Coca-Cola Foundation Indonesia has also provided community educational initiatives, such as building libraries, in turn revealing that the foundation is unwaveringly committed to preparing youth for the future. In 2011, the Coca-Cola Foundation Indonesia announced the PerpuSeru project (Bill and Melinda Gates Foundation 2011). A nationwide library development program, PerpuSeru was focused on "providing access to Information Technology hardware and software, library staff training courses, and advocacy development at 40 district public libraries across Indonesia" (Bill and Melinda Gates Foundation 2011). The Bill and Melinda Gates Foundation also provided a grant of US$5 million for IT-based learning activities in libraries through its Global Libraries Initiative, while Coca-Cola Foundation Indonesia was the "implementing partner in providing support for the empowerment and sustainability of these participating libraries" (1). This support includes "regular monitoring, advocacy, and contribution of human resources." Titie Sadarini, the chief executive officer of Coca-Cola Foundation Indonesia, commented at the time: "We are very excited about our partnership with the Bill and Melinda Gates Foundation. This provides great opportunities to empower more Indonesian people to realize their full potential" (Bill and Melinda Gates Foundation 2011, 1). The Coca-Cola Foundation also provided grant support to the Yayasan Ancora (Ancora Foundation) initiative "to expand the Coca-Cola Vocational Scholarship Program to 52 deserving students from institutions throughout Java, Indonesia," with a generous award of $100,222 to support this endeavor (CSR News 2012). Finally, Coca-Cola Foundation Indonesia has also invested in improving access to water. Coca-Cola Foundation Indonesia partnered with USAID's IUWASH PLUS (Indonesia Urban Water, Sanitation and Hygiene Penyehatan Lingkungan untuk Semua) and the Surabaya provincial government in 2019 to install a water meter system throughout Surabaya (USAID 2016, 2019). This initiative provided "23 master meter systems for 900 house connections that benefit 4,500 people" (USAID 2019).

In other sectors, Unilever Indonesia also believes that its activities in the economy and public policy have benefited the organization. According to Clay (2005), Unilever Indonesia "believes that its track record and long-term commitment to Indonesia gives it credibility, influence, and responsibility throughout society." Moreover, Clay notes that Unilever Indonesia officials believe that "the government offers UI [Unilever Indonesia] as an example of a company which stayed in the country even when the overall investment climate was not optimal" (104).

Creating Divided Societies

And finally, an important strategy that industries have used to increase their political and policy influence and protect themselves from civil societal opposition is creating divisions in society. As IPCI emphasizes, these divisions emerge when industries strategically partner with academic researchers or NGOs in order to construct their own social allies; the goal is to generate dissenting views and a lack of cooperation within society, ultimately hampering the activist community's ability to mobilize in opposition to industry influence. In this situation, scientists and NGOs siding with industry's scientific views contributes to disagreements with activists and NGOs defending the public's health interests and, in the process, reduces the number of allies that the latter can work with. As we have seen in Mexico, Brazil, and India, this industry social tactic, even if it is not explicitly designed and written on paper, is highly influential in safeguarding industry from civic mobilization, opposition, and thus a decrease in national policy influence.

In Indonesia, this situation has also occurred and benefited industry. Industry representatives have provided research grants to university researchers focused on stunting (interview with Rungkat-Zakaria, January 26, 2020). However, according to nutrition policy experts I have interviewed, the problem is that these university researchers have forgotten to work with other academics and NGOs focused on addressing NCDs. This challenge has, in turn, decreased the latter's ability to build a larger civil societal coalition in opposition to industry's policy influence (interview with Rungkat-Zakaria, January 26, 2020). As will be discussed in more detail shortly, this division in society has come at a time when nutrition NGOs lack sufficient resources and influence, challenging their ability to effectively apply pressure against industry interference in NCD prevention and policy making.

Complementary Institutions

Consistent with IPCI, complementary institutions also play an important role in contributing to the political and policy influence of junk food industries. Seen as an intervening variable, an important aspect of complementary institutions arises when politicians, such as presidents, partner with and use these industries to pursue *alternative* policy and electoral objectives. In other words, presidents strategically use industries as a means to achieve their alternative policy and electoral interests. In this context, industries are proactively pursued by these politicians. In Indonesia, these presidential complementary institutions have been present for quite some time (as we will see in the following section).

Modernizing the Economy

It seems that Indonesia's complementary institutions first arose with the arrival of Suharto and his political and economic New Order. As mentioned earlier, one of Suharto's key objectives was to modernize Indonesia's economy while eschewing Communist rule (see Erlanger 1998). In addition to liberalizing the economy to trade, following the decline in world prices for oil and the corresponding fall in government revenues throughout the 1980s, Suharto focused on nurturing the private sector through deregulation measures (Wie 2006). While this system was in large part governed by corrupt relationships between political leaders and businesses as well as nepotism in Suharto's policy making (which involved family members benefiting from this process) (Wie 2006), Suharto also started a tradition of state partnerships with businesses to achieve the president's economic objectives. Following Suharto's resignation from power in 1998, due mainly to the economic aftermath of the Asian financial crisis, subsequent presidents followed his lead. While Presidents B. J. Habbie (1998–1999), Abdurrahman Wahid (1999–2001), Megawati Sukarnoputri (2001–2004), and Susilo Bambang Yudhoyono (2004–2014) (henceforth, SBY) would refrain from establishing corrupt ties with industry, the latter was seen as a partner in helping the government rejuvenate the economy.

This partnership was especially apparent under the SBY administration. Elected in 2004 with a mandate to rid the country of corruption and deepen political reformasi, one of SBY's priorities was to accelerate economic development. Tellingly, SBY choose Mr. Jusuf Kalla, a wealthy businessman from Eastern Indonesia, as his vice president (Indonesia Investments, "Susilo Bambang Yudhoyono Administration"). In 2004, SBY introduced his Medium-Term Development Plan (2004–2009), which was created with the goal of accelerating the country's investment climate (Wie 2006). During this period, the government also facilitated foreign and domestic investment by eliminating the need to obtain licenses for investments from the government's Capital Investment Coordinating Board. Instead of obtaining a license, a notary note informing the relevant agencies, such as the Department of Justice and other related agencies, that an investment was being made was required (Wie 2006). The SBY government was the first since Suharto's that "staked its reputation on improving the investment climate" (26). The SBY administration subsequently introduced the National Long-Term Development Plan 2005–2025, which sought to advance and expand economic development and create a "self-sufficient, advanced, just, and prosperous Indonesia" (Dezan Shira and Associates 2011, 15). Early on in his administration, SBY sought to work with industry to achieve his economic development objectives, viewing businesses as a key partner in this endeavor. In fact, SBY once commented: "In a gathering within the Kadin business community in Jakarta on 10 September 2009, I asked our country's business community to synergize and improve Indonesia's economy. In a simple and clear language

I expressed that our bigger mission within the next 5 years (2010–2015) was to exercise 'debottlenecking', acceleration and expansion of Indonesia's national development" (quoted in Dezan Shira and Associates 2011, 8).

Several years later, in 2011, building on the goals set forth by the National Long-Term Development Plan 2005–2025, the SBY administration introduced the Masterplan for Acceleration and Expansion of Indonesian Economic Development (Masterplan Parcepatan dan Perluasan Pembangunan Ekonomi Indonesia, aka MP3EI). MP3EI's priority was to accelerate and expand economic development in an equitable and sustainable manner by improving infrastructure, communications between regions, and human resource capacity; advancing technology; easing business through a reduction in regulations; and expanding the benefits of development to all community members (see Dezan Shira and Associates 2011). According to SBY, through the MP3EI Indonesia would also be able "to place itself [Indonesia] at the top ten advanced economies in the world by 2025 and the world's top six by the year 2050" (quoted in Dezan Shira and Associates 2011, 9). Analysts at the time also recommended that the government introduce a "new way of thinking," which was to partner with private industry and other stakeholders to achieve SBY's development objectives—a constructive public-private partnership (Indonesia Investments, "Masterplan for Acceleration and Expansion"). More specifically, analysts recommended that "the implementation of the new way of thinking regarding economic development, needs collaborative efforts among government, local governments, state-owned enterprises, private enterprises and the people" (Indonesia Investments, "Masterplan for Acceleration and Expansion," 1; see also Dezan Shira and Associates 2011), while other analysts note that "the private sector will be given a major and important role in economic development, particularly in investments to increase job opportunities" (Dezan Shira and Associates 2011, 10). President SBY was chair of the committee responsible for implementing MP3EI. What's more, the business sector, among other stakeholders such as state-owned enterprises, academic researchers, and government agencies, also participated in the original design of the MP3EI project (Dezan Shira and Associates 2011).

Analysts maintain that the food and beverage industry was a "significant contributor" to GDP, and that the industry, as mentioned earlier, "absorbs the largest labor force among other manufacturing industries" (Dezan Shira and Associates 2011, 76). To that end, the beverage and food sector was viewed as a critical partner in helping achieve SBY's MP3EI objectives, and addressing any roadblocks to the industry's development was critical. MP3EI therefore recommended improving regulations on these industries, such as lowering the costs of packaging materials, which has seen high import tariffs, in order to encourage investment in the food and beverage sector (Dezan Shira and Associates, 2011). Even more telling was that in a policy report, analysts note that to improve the situation, there needs to be "more effective marketing to capture domestic demand, which is growing rapidly" (77). This policy report included an introduction by SBY himself, thus seemingly endorsing the idea.

While the MP3EI name was not adopted under the Jokowi administration (2014–present), its general economic vision was nevertheless sustained (Indonesia Investments, "Masterplan for Acceleration and Expansion"). The focus was on infrastructural development, deregulation, and opening Indonesia up for business, with an eye toward increasing foreign investment in infrastructure (see Warburton 2016). Jokowi's alternative Nawa Cita plan essentially adopted MP3EI's objectives and introduced nine priority economic areas: (1) creating a safe environment; (2) ensuring a clean and effective democratic governance; (3) ensuring peripheral development; (4) reforming the law enforcement bureaucracy; (5) enhancing overall quality of life; (6) bolstering productivity and competitiveness in the economy; (7) facilitating economic independence through the development of strategic sectors; (8) reforming the nation's overall character; and (9) improving the social reform and establishing "unity in diversity" (UNDP 2015, 8–10).

Jokowi was particularly keen on reviving foreign investor confidence through a host of deregulatory and fiscal policy measures, stating that he was open to new ideas (Schonhardt 2016). He went so far as to attend international conferences to convey his views and claim that Indonesia was open for business. In 2014, for example, at the World Economic Forum conference held in Jakarta, Jokowi promised investors "incredible profits" (quoted in Connelly 2016, 12), going so far as to say that investors could call him if they ran into any problems (Connelly 2016). And at the Asia-Pacific Economic Cooperation CEO forum in October of that year, Jokowi also proclaimed that "we are waiting for you to come to Indonesia. We are waiting for you to invest in Indonesia" (quoted in Rowland 2016, 21).

In his second term in office, which some say was a result of Jokowi's ability to improve for the first time in two decades the country's overall investment grade rating (one of several economic accomplishments) (Parker 2019), Jokowi introduced his Making Indonesia 4.0 plan. This plan emphasized the importance of Indonesia's competitive export-led sectors, "centered on food and beverages, textiles and apparel, automotive products, electronics, and chemicals, and to boost net exports to a level representing a 10% contribution to GDP" (Fukuoka 2019, 1). In 2015 Jokowi also met with Paul Polman, the global CEO of Unilever at the time, in his State Palace. Polman discussed his company's growth in Indonesia and how it would benefit society (*Jakarta Post* 2015). Unilever's investments and expansions in Indonesia were, at the time, according to Polman, "in line with the Indonesian government's agenda of promoting economic growth outside of Java" (quoted in *Jakarta Post* 2015). Polman further expressed that he had a lot of hope for the Jokowi administration's inclusive economic agenda.

Another of Jokowi's economic objectives was to improve the nation's infrastructure, continue with deregulation, and improve labor productivity, with the latter being a hindrance to attracting FDI during his first term in office (Fukuoka 2019). Jokowi expressed considerable concern for strengthening Indonesia's human resource capacity, stating at the twenty-fourth World Economic Forum in 2015: "Today, we must change from consumption back to production, from consumption to investment in our infrastructure, investment in our industry, but most importantly, investment in our human capital, the most precious resource of the 21st century" (quoted in Rowland 2016, 21). Moreover, according to Parker (2019), Jokowi was "particularly keen on companies that can innovate and invest in Indonesia to develop more skilled jobs" (1).

Finally, achieving agricultural independence and food security have been primary national developmental goals for recent presidential administrations. Food security has been seen as a way to reduce malnutrition through greater accessibility to affordable nutritious foods for all in need, which has been limited in Indonesia (see Andoko and Doretha 2019). In Indonesia, it appears that this policy issue has been a political and policy priority for those politicians seeking to maintain their popularity and support in society, especially from rural farmers. The SBY administration claimed that attaining food security would be a priority for his administration (Salim 2010). And yet, the news agency Reuters noted that food self-sufficiency targets were not achieved in 2009 "due to red tape and corruption scandals over import quotas that caused shortages for food such as beef" (Reuters Staff 2014).

During his administration, Jokowi viewed collaboration with the private sector and other stakeholders as a way to accomplish his food security goals (Andoko and Doretha 2019). Indeed, according to Andoko and Doretha (2019), "The government has taken the form of cooperation with national scale organizations, banks, private sectors, and investors. For the sake of the success of the Food Security Agency programs, a legal collaboration was carried out with the agencies as follows: Gadjah Mada University, Sago Producing District Communication Forums throughout Indonesia (Kapassindro Focus) . . . the Indonesian Food and Beverage Entrepreneurs Association (GAPMMI), the Indonesian Women Entrepreneurs Association (IWAPI), . . . Bumiputera Nusantara Indonesian Entrepreneurs Association (ASPRINDO)," and a host of other universities, government agencies, and NGOs. In fact, according to Lumanauw and Hardum (2015), "Joko said he believed that with support from the government and the private sector, the productive farming practices in some regions could be upscaled to a national level." In 2011, at the World Economic Forum on East Asia meeting in Jakarta, the government also agreed to work with a consortium of private businesses and academic researchers focused on agricultural production and sustainability—namely, the PISAgro group—in order to ensure food security. This group was comprised of companies such as Nestlé Indonesia, Cargil Indonesia, and Brawijaya University, among others (Erwidodo 2017).

Poverty and Social Welfare

In a country riddled with socioeconomic inequality and poverty, taking these issues head-on through aggressive policy innovations has been the goal of essentially all presidential administrations since Suharto's New Order. Similar to what we have seen in the other emerging economies discussed in this book, presidents have viewed junk food industries as important partners in helping implement programs that bolster their political popularity and support.

Under the SBY administration, tackling poverty was a priority for the government—part of the Pelita five-year development plan—among other goals, such as reducing unemployment and increasing economic growth (see Royani 2009). In fact, poverty reduction—for example, in the form of anti-poverty cash transfer programs—was included as an important prerequisite for the successful implementation of SBY's MP3EI initiative (Dezan Shira and Associates 2011). To that end, it seems that the president once again viewed industries as partners in achieving this objective. On the issue of poverty alleviation, one policy report stated that "the role of society and businesses should be directed toward partnerships with local governments to solve the real problems of poverty specific to a certain region; businesses can help to reduce poverty by focusing on specific areas through the implementation of corporate social responsibility (CSR) programs" (Dezan Shira and Associates 2011, 31).

Jokowi focused on improving social welfare programs during his first term in office, although he also prioritized infrastructure and education (Parker 2019), which had been campaign priorities since the beginning of his administration (Wisnu and Supiarso 2015). According to Suryahadi and Izzati (2019), two initiatives were primarily pursued under the Jokowi administration: "Expanding the coverage of social assistance programmes and distributing Village Fund (Dana Desa) grants, which are put to purposes decided by villagers themselves" (1). These programs were nevertheless mainly initiatives that began under the SBY administration. On the campaign trail in 2019, Jokowi also promised to introduce three new social welfare card programs (Fitriyanti and Cindya 2019). First was a pre-employment card, which had been designed for unemployed workers and high school graduates to use for vocational training; second was the "Affordable Staple Foods Card that will allow women to buy staple foods at discounted prices, as we will be subsidizing some of them," Jokowi claimed (quoted in Fitriyanti and Cindya 2019; on this note, see also *Jakarta Post* 2019). Third was the Indonesia Smart Card (KIP) program (Fitriyanti and Cindya 2019), which Jokowi planned to expand educational benefits to university students, as this was previously restricted for students up through high school (*Jakarta Post* 2019). While these programs were geared toward poverty alleviation and improved social welfare, they also dovetailed nicely with Jokowi's goal of improving human capital. In fact, he claimed that "the draft of the 2020 state budget will prioritize human resources, focusing on education, health care and skills training to suit the needs of the market and industries" (quoted in Gorbiano 2019b).

Once again, industries were seen as critical partners in achieving Jokowi's objective of investing in people and thus building human capital. In 2015, at the twenty-fourth World Economic Forum on East Asia, Jokowi referred to investing in human capital as "the most precious resource of the 21st century" (quoted in Rowland 2016, 21). To that end, Jokowi's administration worked closely with the PISAgro group, which, as mentioned earlier, was a consortium of government, private sector, and academic allies dedicated to improving human capital in agricultural development. Major food industries, such as Nestlé, Mars, and Unilever, were members of the PISAgro group (PISAgro 2019). In November 2018, this group, together with Indonesia's Ministry of Agriculture, signed a memorandum of understanding with the Agency for Capacity Building and Development of Agricultural Human Resources (Baden Penyuluhan dan Pengembangan Sumber Daya Manusia Pertanian/BPPSDMP) and the Center for Agricultural Education (Pusat Pendidikan Pertanian/Pusdiktan) (PISAgro News 2019). Idha Widi Arsanti (also known as Ibu Santi), the head of the Center for Agricultural Education, believed that private industry could provide lessons, such as best practices, for educational curriculum within educational institutions under her control in order to improve farmers' skills (PISAgro News 2019). Moreover, according to one of PISAgro's monthly newsletters, it stated that "she is certain that collaborations with Indonesia Chamber of Commerce (KADIN) and PISAgro to facilitate discussion and communication between private sectors and education institution could speed up the process" (3). In the coffee sector, Nestlé, collaborating with GIZ, was involved in leading PISAgro's Coffee Working Group and was in fact "replicated at government's Agricultural Development Polytechnic (Politeknik Pembangunan Pertanian/Polbangtan) to prepare students with knowledge and skills to become agripreneurs" (5). Through a PISAgro working group, moreover, Nestlé, as well as Indolakto, also partnered with the Ministry of Agriculture and Agricultural Development Polytechnic to review the latter's training curriculum for dairy farming (PISAgro News 2019).

Interestingly, in other economic sectors, the government seemed to be committed to ensuring that industries help achieve the government's social welfare objectives by engaging in CSR activities. In fact, in 2007 the government went so far as to legally mandate that companies in the extractive and energy sectors disclose their CSR activities—and the first nation in the world to do so (Phuong and Rachman 2017). It is important to note, however, that there was no subsequent legislation ensuring the enforcement of this mandate and therefore "making it unenforceable" (1).

When combined, complementary institutions in the sphere of economic and social welfare policy provided a favorable context for junk food industries. By presidents strategically partnering and using major industries to advance their alternative policy objectives and electoral interests, this also appears to increase industries' political legitimacy and policy influence. Proactively sought after by presidents, these partnerships revealed that industries were willing to help the government solve the country's ongoing economic and social welfare challenges. In this context, it seems that government officials did not have any motivation to enact policies that threatened industry's interests. Moreover, agreeing with the president's views, in general, should allow junk food industries to continue to thrive in Indonesia while helping the nation solve its economic and social problems. As IPCI emphasizes, complementary institutions therefore acted as an important intervening variable that positively reinforced industry's aforementioned political and social activities.

In the context of these complementary institutions, CSR activities, which are highly encouraged by the government, also safeguarded industries and increased their influence. Indeed, for as Parker (2019) explains: "More generally, companies will continue to be encouraged and legally mandated to give back to the local communities where they work through corporate social responsibility programs. Companies that can link in to the president's policy goals will likely be looked on favorably by the government and therefore have more leverage when they face business challenges" (1). This context makes it particularly favorable for industries and could facilitate their ability to avoid regulations that threaten their interests.

Civil Society's Emergence and Policy Influence

Similar to what we have seen in Mexico, India, and, to a certain extent, Brazil, the presence of social movements and NGOs working on public health issues is a new phenomenon in Indonesia. Under Suharto's New Order authoritarian government, opportunities for civil societal advocacy and mobilization in opposition to the government was rather limited. The Suharto regime tolerated civil societal organizations as long as they were not involved in political matters (Antlöv et al. 2010). With the gradual transition to democracy via reformasi, however, more opportunities and incentives for civic mobilization and involvement increased. As Mietzner (2007) explains, the number of national and local NGOs exploded during this period. Reformasi entailed the military's withdrawal from politics, as well as decreasing the role and influence of the president through the emergence of a strong parliament, political parties, and decentralization (on the decentralization process, see Pisani 2014). With reformasi came the reform of the media and opportunities for civil society to share their opinions widely (especially via social media; see Tapsell 2012) and to pressure government officials on a wide range of social welfare issues, including health.

In this new climate, several NGOs emerged to focus on addressing nutrition and NCDs. NGOs such as Nutrition International, as well as academics at major research universities such as the Bogor Agricultural University, have done a commendable job of raising awareness about the importance of the double burden of malnutrition, obesity and type 2 diabetes, and the role of junk food industries in contributing to these problems. While this civic response is new, its participants are doing an admirable job of working together to inform the public and also to generate research and inform government of these health care challenges.

Nevertheless, several obstacles remain. First, it appears that NGOs still do not have strong representation and influence within the Ministry of Health. The government has certainly invoked a stronger interest and has been committed to incorporating NGOs and activists' (as well as other external stakeholders') participation in nutrition policy (Republic of Indonesia 2013; interview with anonymous source, September 11, 2020), while some academic researchers believe that they, at times, have an opportunity to discuss their policy views in meetings with health officials at the federal and district levels (interview with anonymous source, January 30, 2020). These kinds of meetings have also been confirmed by anonymous researchers I interviewed (interview with anonymous source, September 11, 2020). However, some researchers in Indonesia are still of the view that their academic research has not made an impact on the creation of national regulatory policies focused on soda and junk foods (interview with anonymous source, January 30, 2020). In addition, those NGOs that do work closely with the government on implementing programs tend to focus on stunting, which, as mentioned earlier, is the junk food industry's main focus. For example, IMA World Health, an NGO, through its National Nutrition Communications Campaign (NNCC), has done a commendable job of providing information to local district government decision makers about stunting, while urging them to prioritize the creation of stunting reduction programs (Esworthy 2018). Through this work it has been argued that district political leaders have now become advocates for reducing stunting, rather than the target of the NNCC's activist activities (Esworthy 2018)—in essence, so it seems, becoming partners with the NNCC on reducing stunting in their communities.

These challenges notwithstanding, NGOs are becoming a critical voice in society with the prospect of strengthening their relationship with government. The government has certainly expressed an interest in addressing NCDs and working with civil society to address obesity, diabetes, and the general double burden of malnutrition. As the NGO and activist community continues to increase the public's awareness, and as this community continues to approach and work with health officials in a context of gradual government opening toward partnering with civil society, a stronger partnership with the government can certainly emerge. Civil society's prospect as an influential partner in addressing the burgeoning growth of NCDs among Indonesia's most vulnerable populations should certainly increase with time.

Conclusion

While Indonesia's government has done a commendable job of introducing, in recent years, national government programs focused on NCD prevention and control, the government still has not crossed the line of being fully committed to creating effective regulatory policies limiting the junk food industry's marketing and sale of its products. Worse still, this has occurred in a context where obesity and type 2 diabetes continue to burgeon throughout the country, affecting the country's most vulnerable populations.

As IPCI helps to explain, industries in Indonesia have been successful because of their various political tactics, including aggressive industry lobbying (especially over a tax) and CSR activities, while restructuring and dividing society in industry's favor. And yet, at the same time, complementary institutions have also mattered. That is, industries' political activities have, in a sense, been indirectly supplemented through several presidents' efforts to strategically partner with and use industries to achieve various economic and social welfare policy objectives. Thus, through their efforts, along with the supplementary support of government, junk food industries have continued to thrive, prosper, and shape the policy context in their favor.

Indonesia: Summary of Chapter Findings

Political Action	Restructuring Society	Complementary Institutions	Regulatory Policy Failure and Absence
Policy partnership Nonexistent, focused on distracting government attention away from NCD prevention policy and focusing instead on malnutrition and stunting	*Corporate social responsibility* Coca-Cola Amatil provides free medical care services for communities and clean water infrastructure Nestlé Indonesia works with the Family Welfare Movement to provide health care training for volunteers; Nestlé, in partnership with Indonesian Nutrition Association, works to improve student nutrition in schools Unilever provides health, hygiene, and nutritional education activities in schools	President SBY works with industry to achieve his administration's long-term economic development plans President Jokowi works with industry to achieve his priority economic objectives (e.g., competitive export sectors, national food security goals, and building human capital)	Absence of federal regulations prohibiting the marketing and sale of junk food products to children and the poor Conflicting food label requirements between different regulations on sugar content in food labels Government failure to enforce food label regulations (e.g., information nutritional content) Absence of sugary beverage and soda tax
Lobbying and largesse Industry pressures to remove luxury goods tax and opposition against 2015 proposed soda tax	*Partnering with society* Nonexistent		

(continued)

Indonesia: Summary of Chapter Findings (*continued*)

Political Action	Restructuring Society	Complementary Institutions	Regulatory Policy Failure and Absence
Institutional infiltration	*Dividing society*		
Nonexistent	Industry support for university research on stunting hampers the mobilization of academic and NGOs' interests in broadening civic mobilization on NCD research and in opposition to industry policy interference		

7

China

As a by-product of China's fast-paced economic growth and globalization, easier access to junk foods and increased consumption have contributed to a surge in noncommunicable diseases. Obesity and type 2 diabetes have not only soared throughout the mainland but are now increasingly prevalent within China's most vulnerable populations: children and the poor. To the government's credit, since the early 2000s, a phalanx of national NCD prevention policy interventions and disease surveillance programs have been implemented. Despite these efforts, NCD policies have focused almost exclusively on general preventative measures, such as nutritional awareness, disease monitoring, and, especially, sharing the importance of physical exercise. While policies regulating industries have been introduced, they are inadequate and poorly enforced. Moreover, essentially no effort has been made to regulate the marketing and sale of junk food products, especially toward children, nor has there been an attempt to introduce a soda tax. It is as if the central government has been willing to do any and everything *except for* taking on the interests of big industry.

As seen throughout several of the other countries discussed in this book, junk food industries have been able to safeguard their interests and avoid these more threatening policies by using various political and social tactics. In China, junk food industries have utilized China's propitious—and indeed supportive—political context. As I explain with the IPCI analytical framework, it seems that companies such as Coca-Cola, PepsiCo, and Mondeléz have been able to garner political support and policy protection by partnering with the central and provincial governments to create innovative prevention programs. This move has signaled their willingness to be part of the solution to China's NCD problem. At the same time, companies have engaged in informal lobbying practices while clandestinely infiltrating China's Center for Disease Control and Prevention to introduce and sustain their policy interests and secure political support. What's more, these companies have restructured civil society in their favor by partnering with influential academics and providing corporate social responsibility activities, efforts that have helped to bolster their political and social credibility and support.

All the while, IPCI's emphasis on complementary institutions has further augmented junk food industries' influence while safeguarding them from costly regulatory policies. As a developmental state, the central government has consistently viewed these industries as vital partners in the government's ongoing focus to eradicate poverty and accelerate economic growth. To that end, industries have been nurtured and safeguarded by presidential leaders, gaining respect and influence, which, in turn, has facilitated industry's ability to influence policy.

While NGOs and activists have recently emerged to increase society's awareness of China's ongoing obesity and diabetes problem, their willingness and ability to aggressively pressure the government for meaningful regulatory policy reform has been limited. This primarily has to do with society's fears of state repression, a lack of access to representative policy-making institutions, and the government's reluctance to fully incorporate society's views into the policy-making process. Until these challenges are overcome, industries will continue to shape NCD policies in their favor, regardless of their costs to China's most vulnerable and innocent populations.

Rise and Development of the Junk Food Industry

China's junk food industry was slow to develop, troubled by an inhospitable political environment. During the 1940s, China's communist government precluded the presence of foreign companies and investment, which worsened under Chairman Mao's Cultural Revolution. During this period, state-owned enterprises across several sectors dominated the landscape, while foreign beverage brands were prohibited from being sold (see Cendrowski 2014). Such was the case with popular multinational corporations, such as Coca-Cola. Despite entering China's market as early as 1927 and the population enjoying Coca-Cola's special formula (in fact, by 1940, in the city of Shanghai, annual sales reached approximately $1 million), by the late 1940s, the company's heyday came to a swift end (Koetse 2015). In 1949,

Chairman Mao decided to nationalize all of Coca-Cola's bottling operations (Cendrowski 2014). During this time, the company decided to side with the US government's commitment to defeating communism, to promote democratic institutions, while Chinese propaganda viewed Coca-Cola as an imperialist arm of America (Fahs 2019). Coca-Cola was banned from the country, with its product being viewed by Chinese communists as unhealthy, a Western beverage unsuitable for Mao's healthy people. On top of this, local publications referred to the drink as a *"Coca-Colonization,"* a product that "undermined sovereignty and local culture" (1).

It was not until Mao's death and the emergence of Premier Deng Xiaoping and his "Reform and Open Up" free market reforms, such as the Law of the People's Republic of China on Joint Ventures Using Chinese and Foreign Investment (see Yuan and Tsai 2000), that foreign direct investment in the food and beverage sector began to increase. Nevertheless, international companies were still not allowed 100 percent foreign capital ownership and had to partner with local companies, as was the case when McDonald's entered into China (see Ronggang 2017). Full ownership laws would only surface circa 2004 and were restricted to particular sectors (Ronggang 2017). After ongoing negotiations with the government and its state-owned enterprise, National Cereals, Oils, and Foodstuffs Corporation (COFCO), which was in charge of beverage and foodstuff production, in 1978, Coca-Cola was finally allowed market reentry—albeit limited, selling in local hotels and friendship stores—and was the first and only foreign company to gain reentry (Fahs 2019). But the Chinese government also benefited from its partnership with Coca-Cola: a joint-venture bottling-plant was established in Beijing, officials were allowed to learn about Coca-Cola's production technologies, and foreign exchange and cash US dollars floated in the economy because of the soda's sales to local tourists (Fahs 2019). Initially, the soda product was only allowed to be sold in select cities, such as Beijing, Guangzhou, and Shanghai (Cendrowski 2014).

However, there was still an ideological stigma associated with Coca-Cola due to it being perceived as a symbol of Western capitalism (Cendrowski 2014), which seemingly took a while for consumers, and especially politicians, to get over. During the 1970s, Coca-Cola was unwaveringly dedicated to establishing strong ties with influential politicians, such as Deputy Prime Minister Teng Hsiao-ping; to improving its broader image by sponsoring sports teams and even cultural events; and to winning local hearts and minds by at one point offering Harvard scholarships to brilliant students (Williams 2015). Such activities are perfectly understandable if one considers the context. There was stern political resistance. Koetse (2015) reminds us that Coca-Cola had been marketing its product in the early 1980s (inexpensively selling balloons with its product), which was nevertheless frowned upon by leaders who perceived this commercial marketing activity, the first since Chairman Mao's passing, as "introducing American style Commercialism." The government responded by stating in 1983 that "not a single bottle of Coke should be sold to Chinese." Interestingly, however, this vociferous response and mandate ended the following year, in 1984, when Coca-Cola and China established a joint venture (Koetse 2015). But more than ever, the Atlanta company was determined to invest heavily throughout the country, especially because its main competitor, PepsiCo, was already prospering in other nearby countries, such as India (Williams 2015). According to Williams (2015), "Coca-Cola was therefore at the forefront of the expansion of the soft drinks industry, where the total number of soft drink plants across all companies rose considerably from 130 in 1981 to at least 2700 in 1991" (461). Coca-Cola was successful because it was able to "cultivate good political relations " (462), a political cushion, I would argue, that would eventually facilitate the company's ability to enter government and influence policy.

Coca-Cola's reentry paved the way for other multinational food and beverage companies. Kentucky Fried Chicken appeared in 1987, in Qianmen, Beijing (a stone's throw from Tiananmen Square; Zhai et al. 2014), eventually becoming "the largest restaurant branch in China" (Guzman 2017). McDonald's soon opened up shop in Shenzhen in 1990 (Wei 2018; Zhai et al. 2014). With Deng's opening up to trade and investment, coupled with the public's yearning to try previously forbidden fruits, the junk food industry was thriving by the late 1980s. Writing for Eater.com in 2018, reporter Clarissa Wei notes that Professor Arthur Dong of Georgetown University's McDonough School of Business once commented: "You're dealing with a civilization that pretty much closed itself off to the outside world for the greater part of the post–World War II period. . . . And even before WWII, they did not have a lot of exposure to the West. So as a result, there was a huge fascination with foods that are completely foreign to the Chinese palate" (quoted in Wei 2018).

To meet these growing demands, China witnessed a swift expansion in the availability of junk food products in the decades to follow, facilitated by a major increase in urban supermarkets, convenience stores, and international retailers (see Costa-Font and Revoredo-Giha 2019). China's first supermarket opened in 1990, with the country seeing more than fifty-three thousand supermarkets in operation by 2002, "representing the fastest growth rate in the world (30–40% per year sales growth)," according to Hawkes (2007, 153). The number of supermarkets and hypermarkets (which also sell nonfood items) has increased and these markets remain the most important places for purchasing prepackaged foods (Chafea 2019). Hypermarkets are mainly dominated by international multinational companies, such as "Metro, Carrefour, Auchan, and Walmart" (Nogueira et al. 2019, 48), whereas supermarkets are dominated by domestic companies (Chafea 2019). According to Pham (2019), Walmart announced in 2019 that it would "open 500 new stores in China over the next five to seven years." According to Pham (2019), researchers at IGD Asia claimed that in early 2019 "China will overtake the United States to become the world's largest grocery market by 2023, with online sales alone more than quadrupling to $205 billion." Purchasing food online (i.e., e-commerce) is also a thriving industry (see Nogueira et al. 2019).

Small convenience stores, where one can readily pick up sodas and snacks on the go, are also prevalent throughout the country. By the late 1990s, with support from the central government, several domestic convenience stores also emerged on the scene, such as Wumart in Beijing in 1999 and Kuai-ke in Shanghai in 1997 (KPMG and CCFA 2019, 14). Foreign corporations such as 7-Eleven and Family Mart are also present in large cities (Bomi 2019). In Beijing, according to information obtained from Shanghai Securities News, more than seven hundred convenience stores, such as "Bianlifeng, Suning Xiaodian and 7-eleven," were scheduled to open in 2019 (*Xinhua* 2019). Even in other provinces like Shaanxi, in northwest China, in its capital city of Xi'an, *Xinhua* (2019) claimed that the city "is set to have no less than 3,000 chain convenience stores by the end of 2020." Competition has increased among small convenience stores, with no dominant store brand taking the lion's share of the market (see Zhuoqiong 2018). According to KPMG and CCFA (2019), the convenience store chain Easy Joy (with 27,259 stores) is by far the largest, followed by uSmile (19,700), Meiyijia (15,559), Suning (4,508), Tianfu (4,212), Hong Qi (2,817), Family Mart (2,571), C&U, ZHSH (2,141), Lawson (1,973), and 7-Eleven (1,882) (6). Rural areas have also seen a combination of convenience stores and grocery markets selling manufactured foods and beverages (Zhai et al. 2014). Considered to be the fastest growing business model in China (*Xinhua* 2019), analysts note that convenience store sales increased from 154.3 billion CNY in 2016 to 190.5 billion CNY in 2017, ultimately reaching 226.4 billion CNY in 2018 (KPMG and CCFA 2019).

The number of fast food restaurants has also burgeoned, quickly spreading out from major cities to locations close to rural areas (Stony Brook University, n.d.). According to Judy Bankman, a consultant and scholar: "There [was] an allure around these brands because they are from the West and represent something very clean and modern—something that was previously inaccessible when lives were more rural" (quoted in Middlehurst 2019). By the late 1990s, major cities, such as Beijing, were home to a plethora of foreign multinational restaurant chains, such as KFC, McDonald's, Starbucks, Häagen-Dazs, Dunkin' Donuts, and Pizza Hut (Watson 2000, 120). Today, KFC has "more than 5,000 restaurants in 1,100 cities" and is considered by some to be "by far the most popular fast food chain in China" (H. Jacobs 2019). Wei (2018) maintains that "McDonald's, KFC, and Starbucks are growing faster in the Chinese republic than in the U.S." Domestic fast food restaurants are nevertheless becoming more competitive with these giants (see Wei 2018), such as Discos (Wei 2018), Laoxiangji, and Real Kungfu (Koetse 2019). Domestic food restaurant chains, such as Discos and East Dawning, have been emerging in smaller cities, offering similar meals but in a special "Chinese way" (Stony Brook University, n.d.). According to research conducted by Koetse (2019), the most popular restaurant chains in China are KFC (ranked no. 1), followed by McDonald's (no. 2), Burger King (no. 3), Laoxiangji/Home Original Chicken (no. 4), Discos (no. 5), Real Kungfu (no. 6), Country Style Cooking (no. 7), Ajisen Ramen (no. 8), Yonghe King (no. 9), and Yoshinoya (no. 10). Koetse (2019) explains that "from January to August of 2019 alone, China's restaurant industry had a total sales revenue of 2.8 trillion yuan (355 billion US dollars)—making it one of the country's fastest-growing industries according to *Sina Finance*." And between 2013 and 2018, Wei (2018) maintains that revenues from the fast food industry grew "at rate of 11.2 percent annually, compared to 3.1 percent in the U.S. over the same period." The snack food industry has also seen remarkable sales growth, with, according to some analysts, "an estimated output value of 3 trillion yuan ($433 billion) in 2020" (Zhuoqiong 2019).

Snack foods are also popular. Snacking in China reflects its unique history. China does not have a deep history of snacking on sweet candies (Nogueira et al. 2019). Indeed, research by Y. Zhou and colleagues (2015) revealed that when compared to other developing nations and regions, such as Latin America, China and other Asian countries are considerably delayed in the emergence and consumption of packaged and processed foods. Snacking appears to be in its infancy; this in large part reflects the delayed—though escalating—pervasiveness of the ultraprocessed food retail industry. Studies have found that an overall rise in income, particularly in urban centers, was likely to be associated with increased snacking (see Wang et al. 2008). Indeed, according to Professor Barry Popkin of the University of North Carolina at Chapel Hill and world-renowned nutrition expert on China and other developing nations, "China's speed of change in snacking, beverage consumption, [and] meat and oil intake has exceeded every other part of the world" (quoted in Levitt 2014). The rate of snacking, such as beverages, has also been high among China's children (Z. Zhou et al. 2015), with the availability of snacks emerging in rural areas. "You won't find a village or small town where they don't have confectionary and somewhere to buy pastries and soft drinks," argued Professor Popkin (quoted in Levitt 2014). The desire for chocolate confectionary has recently emerged as a sweet delicacy, with brands such as Ferrero, Rocher, Lindt, Cote D'or, Meiji, Hershey, Malteser, and Dove present (see Nogueira et al. 2019). Potato chips produced by local and foreign brands, such as "Doritos, Lays, and Pringles," have also flown off store shelves (17). When comparing food brands, Nestlé appears to be the most popular and profitable, having a total market brand value in 2018 of $US19.37 billion (Clere 2018).

While preparing home meals is still popular in China (Y. Zhou et al. 2015), more and more consumers are eating out. According to Hawkes (2008), the "away-from-home spending on food rose from 8% or [sic] urban household food expenditures in 1992 to nearly 20% in 2004" (154). In 2016, "China's 1.37 billion population spent half a trillion dollars eating out at restaurants" (Huang 2017). Huang (2017) also found that in 2016, China's total dining out tally, $507 billion, was higher than several countries' own gross domestic product—for example, Sweden's (US$496 billion), Nigeria's (US$487 billion), and Poland's (US$477 billion). Spending on dining out is also increasing in rural areas, especially those located near major urban centers, in turn reflecting the emergence of markets and stores in these areas (see Gale et al. 2005).

Food delivery has also become increasingly popular (*Xinhua Net* 2018). The lion's share of the market is mainly controlled by the companies Meituan and Ele.me, "who together have 95 percent of the market" (Bomi 2019). Some analysts believe that food deliveries are the "most important food trend in China today." Bomi (2019) further writes that according to the retailer Meituan-Dianping, "$31.9 billion was spent on food delivery in China in 2017."

Similar to what we have seen in the other emerging economies, the soda and sugar-sweetened beverage market has also grown at an alarming pace, indicating increasing consumer demand for foreign products (Direct China Chamber of Commerce 2018). While some consumers have become more health conscious, turning to tea and dairy products, which some argue are equally as profitable as sodas (China Consumer 2018), soft drinks will continue to be in demand, especially among youth (Marketing to China 2013). In the carbonated soft drinks sector, Coca-Cola is king. It dominates not only because of its aggressive marketing and global reputation, but also because of the company's ongoing creativity. Coca-Cola's creativity has been demonstrated through introducing "more than 60 products under 20 brands" (Jing 2018), convincing analysts that Coca-Cola is the "fastest growing" brand in China (Yu 2019). Trailing Coca-Cola's dominant market share of 63 percent in 2014 was PepsiCo, with approximately 30 percent of the market share (Freifelder 2015). According to research conducted by Clere (2018), in 2018 Coca-Cola had a total brand value of $30.38 billion, followed by PepsiCo with $20.04 billion, Red Bull with $7.64 billion, and Gatorade with $4.92 billion. China is Coca-Cola's "third-largest market," only trailing behind Mexico and the United States (Fahs 2019).

And yet, rising competition from other brands appears to have strengthened Coca-Cola's ongoing competitive spirit, while seeing an increase in sales in China—which has certainly helped (see Giammona 2019). In general, throughout the world, Coca-Cola is concerned about the rise of other competitors; indeed, the CEO of Coca-Cola, James Quincey, once commented that "the bigger and smaller players are being very active—it's a vibrant industry that's growing . . . it means we have to up our game" (quoted in Giammona 2019). China has seen several local carbonated soda brands, such as Master Kong and Wahaha, rise and prosper (Freifelder 2015). Other brands imitate Coca-Cola and Pepsi. If you don't like Dr. Pepper, for the same or cheaper price, you can find a can of Dr. Bob, Dr. Thunder, Dr. Skipper, Dr. Snap, Dr. Perfect, or even Dr. Perky, and if you don't like Mountain Dew, you can find the alternatives Mountain Frost, Mountain Lightning, Mountain Rapids, or even Mountain Shoutin' (Lesniak 2019).

According to analysts from the consulting firm Euromonitor International, in China, Jing (2018) claims that "the total market size of the beverage industry in the nation rose for the seventh consecutive year in 2017 to 570 billion yuan ($83.7 billion)." Moreover, others claim that the volume of the soda industry increased by "7 times" from 2000 to 2012 (Marketing to China 2013, 1). The sale of sugar-sweetened beverages is also taking off, in turn convincing some researchers that this will "become a major component of the diet within the next decade" (Zhai et al. 2014).

The junk food industry's ongoing growth and importance to China's economy will continue to make it both a powerful economic and, by extension, political force. For some, the country's food and beverage sector is the world's largest (Dezan Shira and Associates 2016, 1). Coca-Cola's now iconic and increasingly popular image, benefiting from its recent symbolism as an official sponsor of major sporting events such as the 2008 Olympic Games in Beijing (Chhabara 2008), will certainly contribute to the company's economic and political importance. Nevertheless, the emergence and prosperity of junk foods in China has entailed several public health challenges, such as the ongoing rise of NCDs, especially among its most vulnerable populations.

The Rise of NCDs and China's Most Vulnerable Populations

Indeed, with the increased access and consumption of junk foods has come a rise in NCDs. Since the 1990s, the heightened consumption of unhealthy foods appears to have contributed to a host of NCDs and risk factors in China, including type 2 diabetes, cancer, hypertension, heart disease, and overweight and obesity across age groups, including youth (Dong et al. 2019; Na 2010; Wang 2016; Z. Wang et al. 2018). While other risk factors, such as environmental pollution, excessive tobacco and alcohol consumption, and a decrease in physical activity, have also contributed to these ailments (Hunt 2019; Min et al. 2015; World Health Organization 2016b), China's transition from eating more nutritious, traditional food staples (e.g., grains, plants) to consuming sugary and fatty foods has contributed to the rise of NCDs as well as their associated risk factors, such as overweight and obesity, even among children (Na 2010; UNICEF 2019).

By 2017, China ranked number one (with the United States in second) for

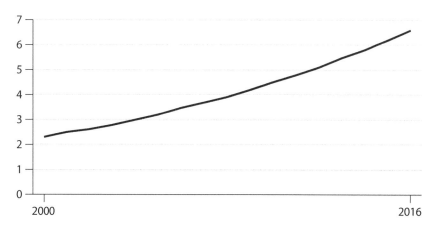

China: prevalence (%) of obesity among adults. *Source*: WHO, 2021. https://
www.who.int/data/gho/data/indicators/indicator-details/GHO/prevalence-of
-obesity-among-adults-bmi-=-30-(crude-estimate)-(-)

having the most overweight people in the world (see Ng 2017). According to
O'Riordan (2019), "From 2004 to 2014, the prevalence of obesity increased
more than threefold across China," with the nation's capital, Beijing, seeing
a higher incidence level (1; on the latter issue, see also Dong 2017). Most
cases of obesity have occurred in major cities (Ang 2019). Nevertheless, with
rising incomes, food expenditures, and access to junk food in rural areas,
obesity is also rising in these poorer areas. Survey analysis conducted by
Shen et al. (2019) on a national level reveals that from 1993 to 2011, the
prevalence of central and general obesity among adults has been increasing in rural areas, narrowing the gap between urban-rural divides. Shen and
colleagues' (2019) survey also found that in 2011, the prevalence of central
obesity was actually higher for adults in rural areas, in turn highlighting a
quickening increase in food consumption. Researchers have recently found
that the rate of obesity is growing faster in rural areas, and that is partly
attributed to a change in food preferences (see Ang 2019).

China's poorer population has also seen a steady rise in overweight and
obesity. That is, in contrast to the United States and other Western industrialized nations, for decades it was the affluent urban upper- and middle-
income classes in urban areas that were consuming the most sodas and
ultraprocessed foods, particularly as fast food (e.g., KFC, McDonald's) garnered high social status. But this situation may be changing in China. In fact,

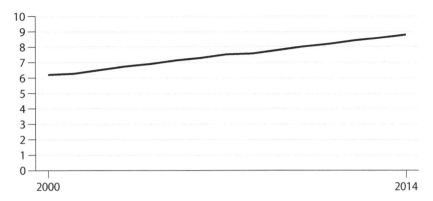

China: prevalence (%) of adult diabetes. *Source*: WHO, 2021. https://www.who
.int/data/gho/data/indicators/indicator-details/GHO/raised-fasting-blood
-glucose-(-=7-0-mmol-l-or-on-medication)(age-standardized-estimate)

Dong and colleagues (2019) mention a study in China that revealed that the consumption of unhealthy foods (e.g., those high in fats) has increased with a rise in income among lower socioeconomic groups, which offers clues into narrowing gaps in obesity between urban and rural areas due to a convergence in dietary patterns between these areas, especially among children. Furthermore, researchers note that the relationship between affluence and obesity is now "breaking, with lower-income urban residents more prone to the problem" (Hancock 2017), and that obesity is now growing faster among low-income households (Levitt 2014).

Referred to by some as "the epicentre of this global diabetes epidemic" (Zimmet et al. 2017), according to Yiwei (2019), China surpassed India in 2011 to become "the country with the highest number of diabetics in the world" (Yiwei 2019, 1; see also Cheung et al. 2018). By 2016, Wang (2016) mentions the WHO's claim that one in three adults with diabetes in the world were located in China. Moreover, Wang (2016) claims that the number of adult diabetics in China "increased from less than 1 per cent in 1980 to 9.4 per cent in 2014." Q. Wang and colleagues (2018) also mentions studies claiming that greater than 10 percent of all adults in China have this ailment, "which is far higher than the world average" (1). By 2017, Hedberg (2020) states that an estimated 113.9 million were diagnosed with diabetes, while referencing a 2017 study by Wang and colleagues that claimed that roughly 50 percent of the population could be prediabetic and 30 percent

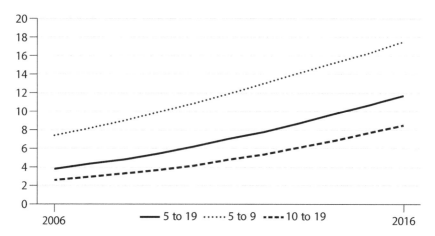

China: prevalence (%) of childhood obesity (ages 5–19). *Source*: WHO, 2021. https://www.who.int/data/gho/data/indicators/indicator-details/GHO/preva lence-of-obesity-among-children-and-adolescents-bmi-2-standard-deviations -above-the-median-(crude-estimate)-(-)

unaware of their condition (for both types 1 and 2). And yet, similar to with obesity, type 2 diabetes appears to be becoming a major problem in rural areas due to its high level of diabetics, a general lack of knowledge about the disease, and its poor management (Q. Wang et al. 2018, 1). The diabetic situation is becoming so grave in China that there is now a great deal of discrimination for those with the disease. In fact, analysts note that some diabetics' employment prospects have been negatively affected, such as in government, where, according to *The Economist* (2019), "the civil service re- fuses to hire people with diabetes" (1).

But obesity in China is not just prevalent among adults—the country's youth is also being affected. China now has the highest cases of childhood obesity in the world (Ang 2019; Pinghui 2017). According to Chen and col- leagues (2019), "In 2002, the rate of overweight and obesity in children and adolescents was 6.6% and increased to 15.8% in 2012" (477), expanding at a growth rate that in recent years has been even higher than in the United States. Pinghui (2017) mentions a study by the Global Burden of Disease, produced by researchers of the University of Washington, that claimed that there were "15 million obese children" in China in 2015. Some analysts ex- pect that by 2030 a quarter of China's children will be overweight (Connor 2017). Chen and colleagues (2019) point to a study by researchers from the

Children's Physical Development Survey Collaboration Team, a group of researchers managed by the Department of Maternal and Child Health on China's National Health and Wellness Committee, which found that after analyzing surveys of children younger than 7 for thirty years from different regions of China, "childhood obesity increased rapidly from 0.91% in 1986 to 3.19% in 2006 and continued to climb to 4.2% in 2016" (477). Zhang and Ma (2018, 3) display data, which they obtained from Ding and others (1989), Li and colleagues (2002), and the Coordinating Group of Nine Cities Study on the Physical Growth and Development of Children (2008), revealing that obesity rates for children between the ages of 0 and 7 increased from 0.93 percent for boys and 0.90 percent for girls in 1986, to 3.82 percent for boys and 2.48 percent for girls in 2006 (measured in percentage of obesity prevalence). Moreover, for children younger than 7 years, Zhang and Ma (2018, 3) also display data, which they obtained from the National Health and Family Planning Commission of the People's Republic of China (2014) and Ma and colleagues (2005), revealing that obesity increased from a prevalence percentage of 1.7 percent for boys and 1.6 percent for girls in 1992 to 3.6 percent for boys and 2.5 percent for girls in 2012. Some maintain that children between the ages of 7 and 12 have seen faster rates of overweight and obesity when compared to adolescents, which may be attributed to greater concerns about body image (Antipolis 2016). Several studies have alluded to boys being more overweight and obese on average over time than girls (Jia et al. 2019; Zhang and Ma 2018). Most childhood overweight and obesity cases have been located in urban areas and those coming from a higher socioeconomic background (Zhang and Ma 2018; Zhu et al. 2019). But this situation is also quickly changing in rural areas (Ang 2019; Dong et al. 2019; Whitten 2016). Hawkins (2016) reports that a twenty-nine-year-old study that took place in rural Shandong revealed that childhood obesity rates were "up 17-fold among boys and 11-fold among girls." Dr. Zhang Yingxiu of the Shandong CDC, who led this study in Shandong, claimed that "the rises in overweight and obesity coincide with increasing incomes in rural households and we expect this trend to continue in the coming decades in Shandong province and other regions of China" (quoted in Hawkins 2016).

There are several reasons for these troubling epidemiological trends. Children simply have more access to pocket money to purchase and consume a vast array of easily accessible unhealthy foods, possibly contributing to overweight and obesity (Jia et al. 2019). Studies find that within some of

China's megacities and big cities, children and teenagers, on average, have substantially higher energy intake from processed foods when compared to their peers in other cities (Z. Zhou et al. 2015). For example, lack of adequate physical activity, fewer public areas available for exercise, and rigorous academic demands, which leave less time for exercise, have also been possible contributing factors (Ang 2019; Pinghui 2017; Zhu et al. 2019). According to researchers, fears and nutritional understanding have also mattered as parents, particularly grandparents historically deprived of having sufficient food, have been more concerned with purchasing as much food as possible, falling short of preparing healthy meals, which impacts what children eat, while having less of an understanding of what it means to eat well in general (see Cerullo 2019). When combined with a one-child policy that for years led to single boys being spoiled by parents and their grandparents, these conditions may have generated an excessive consumption of unhealthy foods.

In addition to weight gain, China's youth are also seeing an increase in diabetes (Hu and Jia 2018; University of North Carolina at Chapel Hill 2012). According to researchers at the University of North Carolina at Chapel Hill (2012), "Chinese teenagers have a rate of diabetes nearly four times greater than their counterparts in the United States" (1). Select studies of several medical centers in China found that the number of type 2 diabetics now exceeds the number of type 1 diabetics among children, and the number of type 2 diabetics among children has doubled (Fu et al. 2013), nearly tripling in number among children under the age of 14 in the past twenty-five years (French 2015b). Children now make up approximately 5 percent of China's diabetic cases, with "the number of juveniles with the potentially fatal condition is rising by 10 percent every year" (Na 2010). National survey data researchers have also found that diabetes and fasting plasma glucose was present among children between 6 and 17 years of age and was higher in urban versus rural areas, potentially due to unhealthy diets among boys and higher obesity (Z. Wang et al. 2018). In addition to these health challenges, young diabetics in China also face a great deal of discrimination, depression, and loneliness (Na 2010).

Policy Response

But how did the central government respond to the rise of obesity and type 2 diabetes? Similar to what we saw in the other nations discussed in this book, the government's approach to controlling NCDs has emphasized the monitoring of disease (through surveys), prevention (e.g., through health education and promotion), and policy interventions focused on at-risk groups (Wu et al. 2017, 4). As we will see, earnestly regulating industry's marketing and sales of their products, especially toward children and the poor, has still not been considered, nor has the introduction of a soda tax.

With respect to NCD prevention, the National Action on Healthy Life-style for All was introduced in 2007 by the Ministry of Health (MoH), China's CDC, and the National Patriotic Health Campaign Committee (Chen and Zhao 2012, 224). Considered the government's primary approach to combat obesity and other diet-related diseases, the focus was to work with commu-nities, families, and employers to be informed and achieve a healthy life-style, with an initial emphasis on balanced diets and physical exercise, sub-sequently expanded to thirty-one provinces (Chen and Zhao 2012). That same year, in 2007, "the Ministry of Health launched the 121 Health Action strategy of 'ten thousand steps a day, the balance of eating and activity and a healthy life'" (Wang and Zhai 2013, 137). The objectives of this program were to inspire individuals to exercise and to have a healthy diet in order to avoid being overweight and obese, as well as to provide new educational and technical tools, achieve national program goals, and disseminate concepts on having a healthy lifestyle (137). In 2010, the government, through the Ministry of Health, also introduced the Nutrition Improvement Work Man-agement Approach initiative to establish national nutritional plans and to improve the population's overall nutrition and health status (136); more-over, it appears that this initiative also emphasized "nutrition surveillance, education, guidance and intervention" (136). Additionally, that same year, in 2010, the MoH created the Comprehensive NCD Prevention and Control Program (Yin et al. 2016). This program introduced initiatives on promoting health and education, detecting NCDs early on and treating them, and es-tablishing standard procedures for managing diseases in communities (130).

The National Plan on NCD Prevention and Treatment (2012–2015), spon-sored by fifteen ministries, also introduced prevention strategies, decentral-ized to the provinces, empowered through primary care providers engaging in multisectoral collaboration and social participation (Min et al. 2015). With respect to food and nutrition, in 2014, the State Council also released the *Outline of the Programme for Food and Nutrition Development in China* (2014–2020) (Zhang and Ma 2018). According to Zhang and Ma (2018), this program provides indicators on, among other issues, nutrient intake and the control of nutrition-related disease. In 2016, the State Council also enacted the Healthy China 2030 initiative (O'Riordan 2019; Zhang and Ma 2018). A total of fifteen goals were introduced, focusing on areas such as decreasing the consequences of secondhand smoking, reducing the number of obesity cases, preventing chronic disease, increasing regular exercise, and establishing a healthy environment and a health industry (O'Riordan 2019; Zhang and Ma 2018). Healthy China 2030 has promoted living a healthy lifestyle and the importance of regular physical exercise (World Health Organization 2016a). Finally, in 2017, the government introduced the 2017–2025 Plan to Control NCDs, a policy that entails, among other goals, "increasing the regular monitoring and self-management rate for diabetes patients from 50% (which is probably an overestimate) to 70% by 2025" (Lou et al. 2020, 48). And to further curb the growth of type 2 diabetes, the MoH introduced several pilot intervention projects, such as the National Demonstration Areas program. Based on applications from local governments, this program allocates federal subsidies to those local governments committed to implementing intervention pilot projects focused on "health promotion, detection and control of chronic diseases" (48).

NCD Prevention among China's Most Vulnerable Populations

With respect to childhood obesity, several national MoH prevention programs were implemented as early as 2007. That year, the *School-Age Children and Teenagers Overweight and Obesity Prevention and Control Guidelines* were introduced (Zhang et al. 2018). And in 2008, in an effort to control the level of childhood obesity, the central government created the *Guidelines on Snacks for Chinese Children and Adolescents* (Zhang et al. 2018). In addition, strategies for reducing childhood obesity, such as improved training for health care personnel and educating parents on nutrition, were also important aspects of the China National Program for Child Development (2011–2020) (Ang 2019). In 2017, the National Nutrition Plan (2017–2030) was introduced, and one of its core objectives was to control the overall prevalence of obesity among school-age children through improvements in general nutrition (Zhang and Ma 2018). Proposed policy initiatives included weight management and policy interventions, with a focus on increasing physical education and nutritional education (Zhang and Ma 2018).

Interestingly, however, the bulk of the government's prevention programs for childhood obesity and type 2 diabetes, and obesity policy in general

(Greenhalgh 2019a), has focused on physical exercise. For example, in 2007, the Sunny Sports Program Supporting Millions of Students across China was created. Managed by the Ministry of Education, the General Administration of Sports, and the Central Committee of the Communist Youth League, this program required schools to organize one hour of daily exercise (Chen and Zao 2012). The endeavor did not go over well with parents, however; they felt that this program distracted their children from studying (Gómez 2018). That same year, in 2007, the State Council released the *Improve the Physical Fitness of Adolescents through Sports*, which included several plans for policy interventions to combat adolescent obesity, as well as the *Guidelines on the Prevention and Control of Obesity and Overweight Among School-Aged Children in China (for Trial)* in an effort to promote a healthy lifestyle and to help children establish the habit of engaging in exercise (Zhang and Ma 2018). These endeavors seemed to suggest that, once again, at the highest level of government, ensuring regular exercise was the basis for combating childhood obesity. In 2011, the State Council again emphasized the same path through its Child Development Outline (2011–2020), but also included strategies to improve nutrition and management of children's health care needs (Zhang and Ma 2018). Through the aforementioned 2016 Healthy China 2030 initiative, the government has also encouraged a minimum of one hour of exercise per day, while also setting a goal of having greater than 25 percent of schoolchildren throughout the nation attain a rating of excellence in physical fitness (Zhu et al. 2019). And finally, a key program falling under the aforementioned National Action on Health Lifestyle program was the 10 Minutes Initiative, which is a program focused on promoting children's exercise in schools (Greenhalgh 2019a, 2019b).

In sum, improving children's exercise in schools appears to have been a repeated priority for the State Council and the MoH. We will explore precisely why this is the case in the following sections.

Policies Targeting Industry

While numerous obesity and type 2 diabetes prevention programs have been introduced, what steps has the government taken to regulate junk food industry activities and their impact on China's most vulnerable populations? And what kinds of policies does this entail? As seen in the other countries discussed in this book, an important regulatory endeavor has been food marketing. Historically, in an effort to protect consumers from false and harmful advertising, the central government enacted several federal advertising regulations, such as the Advertising Law of the Peoples Republic of China (Z. Zhou et al. 2015). Both this Advertising Law and the Food Safety Laws included regulations stating that all advertising should be truthful and legal, and refrain from providing false or exaggerated declarations (Z. Zhou et al. 2015).

Some specific marketing regulations apply to children. According to Z. Zhou et al. (2015), Article 8 of the Advertising Law states that "an advertisement shall not cause any damage to the physical and mental health of underage persons or handicapped persons" (2; see also Chang and McNeal 2003). In 2015, an amendment to the Advertising Law was created, stating that children younger than 10 were not allowed to appear in commercials (Xin 2015). Xin (2015) states that "Zhang Guohua, director of Advertisement Supervision and Management of State Administration of Industry and Commerce (SAIC), said the provision was made since children are deemed incompetent to make their own decisions, and for them to endorse in commercial advertising violates the principle of authenticity in advertisement." Furthermore, this 2015 amendment regulates the usage of any celebrities in advertisements, establishing legal responsibilities and holding celebrities accountable for participating in false advertisements, as well as the producers of these advertisements. The amendment also introduced penalties, such as being banned for three years, for those advertisers found guilty of marketing products that they have not already used themselves (Xin 2015). In July 2016, in response to the rise in online e-marketing activities, China's Administration for Industry and Commerce also introduced online advertising regulation measures (King and Wood Mallesons 2016). These measures clarify how the existing 2015 law applies to online advertisements, such as advertisements provided via text messages and emails for good and services. Ads focused, for example, on health products, medicine, food for medical purposes, and medical treatment are to be regulated before being advertised online (King and Wood Mallesons 2016).

Another regulatory policy targeting the junk food industry's activities is food labeling. Federal regulations regarding this issue were rather delayed when compared to other countries (see Tao et al. 2010). With respect to imported foods, it seems that labeling regulations did not arise in China until the *General Standards for the Labelling of Prepackaged Foods* was introduced (EU SME Centre 2011). These standards stipulated that all prepackaged products contain labels listing, for example, the company's name, address, its trademark, nutritional ingredients, information on weight or volume, and information on expiration dates and use (EU SME Centre 2011, 10). Furthermore, in 2007, the MoH created the Code of Food Nutrition Labeling, which encourages industries to provide food labels on a voluntary basis, highlighting nutritional content and claims (Huang et al. 2014).

The following year, in 2008, the Regulation for Food Nutrition Labeling was also introduced by the MoH, which "encourages food manufacturers to identify nutrient declaration, nutrition claims, and nutrition function claims on sale product labels" (Lv et al. 2011, 117). The labels were supposed to provide information on "calories and four core nutrients: protein, carbohydrate, fat, and sodium" (117). Note, however, that the regulation, according to Lv and colleagues (2011), "encourages" the provision of this information—one could argue, building on the aforementioned voluntary request of the 2007 Code of Food Nutrition Labeling. Indeed, others found that this regulation "recommended" information on sugar, cholesterol, fiber, and vitamins (Tao et al. 2010). Raw fresh foods, such as fruits, vegetables, fish, and meat; food made on site; and smaller packaged foods did not require labels (Tao et al. 2010). All labeling declarations on, for example, trans fat, sodium, carbohydrates, protein, and energy, with the government emphasizing the validity of nutritional claims and reducing exaggerated health benefit claims (Phang 2012), was, it seems, information that was not officially required on food labels until later, in 2011, when the MoH introduced a new regulation (R. Liu et al. 2015). Indeed, Liu and others claim that in 2011, the MoH published the "National Food Safety Standard for Nutrition Labelling of Pre-packaged Foods (GB 28050–2011). This regulation requires that the energy value and the amount of protein, fat, carbohydrate and sodium as well as their percentages in relation to Nutrient Reference Values (NRV) are mandatory items to be labeled on a food nutrition label" (103–104).

And yet, some researchers claim that declared nutritional information on prepackaged foods did not become "mandatory" until January 2013 (see Huang et al. 2016). The 2011 National Food Safety Standard also requires that all labels are truthful and nondeceptive, without any exaggerations on a food's nutritional functions (Meador and Jie 2013). The 2015 version of the Food Safety Law for prepackaged imported and exported products also mandated that packages have nutrition labels providing information on energy (100g/per 100g), protein (100g/per 100g), fat (100g/per 100g), carbohydrates (100g/per 100g), and sodium (100g/per 100g) (CIRS News 2017). Additional required food labeling information for sport, infant, and dietary supplements were provided as well. In 2015, the *General Standard for the Labeling of Food Additives* and the *Labeling of Prepackaged Foods for Special Dietary Uses* were also introduced (Export.gov 2019). More recently, the government has also encouraged the use of a "Healthier Choice logo," through regulation GB 28050, to be placed on products with an alleged reduction in oil, sodium, and sugar content (*Chinafoodlaw* 2020).

Policy Challenges

Despite all of these recent policy efforts, several ongoing challenges remain. Some claim that the government has been focused on obesity prevention through strategies such as health education (e.g., through the Healthy China 2030 initiative), rather than addressing the broader food system, while falling short of implementing needed regulations (see Ng 2017). Indeed, in an article published by Ng (2017), Professor Barry Popkin of the University of North Carolina stated: "For the past 30 years, the Chinese have been misdirected and focused on physical activity instead of the food system as a way to address obesity. . . . One of the major shifts in China has been the massive decline in physical activity and the concurrent increase in the modern retail food sector and consumption of packaged food." Others maintain that there has been inconsistent and insufficient funding for national obesity prevention programs focused on increasing awareness, as well as an ongoing insufficient number of nutritionists (French 2015a). Furthermore, researchers have cautioned that more needs to be done to meet the needs of obese in rural areas (Dong et al. 2019; Zhang et al. 2018).

Existing marketing regulations have also been problematic. First and foremost, there is no existing legislation regulating the marketing of soda and ultraprocessed foods, with scholars underscoring the need to establish these kinds of policies (French 2015a; Huijun and Fengying 2013; Jia et al. 2019). In sharp contrast to what we have seen in Brazil, Mexico, India, and Indonesia, *not a single piece of legislation* exists in China regulating how and when these foods are advertised to children and adolescents (see Z. Zhou et al. 2015; see also Kelly et al. 2019). As Z. Zhou and colleagues (2015) point out, Article 8 of the Advertising Law of the People's Republic of China does state that advertisements "shall not cause any damage to the physical and mental health of underage persons or handicapped persons. However, the stipulation is not operable in the judicial practice because it is relatively abstract" (2). Furthermore, to my knowledge, there has been no effort to prohibit the marketing of junk food in schools. And, all media advertisements are regulated by the central and provincial governments (O'Barr 2007).

The absence of regulations on marketing toward children has generated incentives for industries to engage in predatory media behavior. Industries have targeted children through advertising (Hawkes 2008). Food advertisers have used well-trusted state media sources, such as CCTV, to provide advertisements during children's peak viewing hours, while most of the food ads targeting children promoted unhealthy foods (see S. Li et al. 2016). S. Li and others (2016) found that "a large proportion (71.9%) of advertisements on CCTV were aimed at children, and of these, 47.6% were for food and beverages" (127). With respect to food advertisements targeting children, S. Li and colleagues further note that "unhealthy foods were the largest proportion (86.2%), and included snacks (e.g., savory food and bubble gum), fast food restaurants, desserts (e.g., biscuits and cakes), beverages, and sweets. Beverages made up the largest proportion (39.0%) compared with other food categories" (127). A couple studies conducted by Kelly and colleagues (2010, 2014) also found that the highest volume of advertising for unhealthy foods were during children's peak viewing hours. As D. Li and others (2016) claim: "We speculated that in China, as central TV channels are considered to have greater levels of influence and trust among the public, marketers tend to choose these channels to achieve better publicity and long-term benefits so they broadcast more ads and food ads compared to local TV channels" (6). Researchers have shown, through a survey of nine CCTV and thirty-one PSTV TV channels in 2012, that a considerable portion, roughly one-third, of TV advertisements viewed by children and adolescents are related to food, and that "approximately half of food ads were snack ads" (Z. Zhou et al. 2015, 7). A study by D. Li and colleagues (2016) revealed that in the city of Xi'an, for example, after transcribing 5,527 TV ads on popular children's channels, "25.5% were for food, among which 48.1% were considered to be unhealthy" (1). Others have found a similar pattern. According to Chang (2014), "Similar to previous studies in the West, half of all ads observed in this study for Chinese children are for foods, dominated by sugared candies/sweets, snacks, and cold drinks for convenience stores, and kids' meal with free gift sold at fast food restaurants" (216). These advertisements, in turn, appear to influence children's food preferences and choices in China (see Chang 2014).

Industries have also used popular characters, such as those from Disney and Hollywood movies, to market their products to children (Chang 2014). Coca-Cola has also been creative in its efforts to target teenagers by placing popular numeric symbols on their bottles, which are used by teens to express emotions toward one another (e.g., "521," which for these youngsters translates to "I love you" [Long 2017]). In addition, according to Chang and colleagues (2018), "TV food advertising was dominated by the big food companies' brands: Coca-Cola, PepsiCo (Purchase, NY, USA), Kellogg's (Battle Creek, MI, USA), Mars (McLean, VA, USA), Kraft (Chicago, IL, USA), Nestlé (Vevey, Switzerland), Master Kang (Kangshifu) (Tianjin, China), Tongyi (Shenzhen, China), Yili (Hohhot, China), and the Wahaha (Hangzhou, China)" (8). In the absence of federal regulations limiting these marketing activities, food industries advertising to children have engaged in a form of self-regulation (Ronit and Jensen 2014).

In addition, when it comes to regulating the sale of soda and ultraprocessed food products, to my knowledge, no federal legislation exists. In contrast to the other nations discussed in this book, China does not have any regulations limiting the sale of these products in schools, for example. Additionally, no effort has been made to limit the sale of these products to the poor, who, as mentioned earlier, now have greater access to these foods at a cheaper price.

Yet another challenge has been ensuring industry compliance with the government's food label regulations. According to Huang and others (2014), the aforementioned voluntary 2007 Code of Food Nutrition Labeling regulations have not had as strong of an impact on corporate practices in providing food labeling information on prepackaged foods as was hoped, in turn suggesting that more monitoring and enforcement processes are needed. Indeed, as Huang and colleagues (2014) maintain: "It is likely that widespread compliance will be achieved only if a significant enforcement process is put in place with meaningful sanctions against those that fail to comply" (653). Industry's lackluster compliance may also be the result of industries not being accustomed to adhering to federal guidelines and regulations, as providing labels was entirely voluntary for several years prior to becoming mandatory in 2013 (on this timing of mandatory compliance, see Huang et al. 2014).

Additionally, during the 1990s, the quality and accuracy of labels were limited, with "confusing expressions, inaccurate nutrition claims, and non-standardized labeling language, which have caused serious misunderstandings by consumers" (Zheng et al. 2011, 404). A major (and, quite frankly, alarming) limitation was the *National Food Safety Standard for Nutrition Labeling of Pre-Packaged Foods* and its absence of a requirement that sugar content (Lin et al. 2018) and different types of fat, such as saturated and trans fat, be reported on labels (Ettinger et al. 2019; Huang et al. 2014, 2016). As previously mentioned, listing sugar content is completely voluntary through the 2008 *Chinese Food Nutrition Labelling Regulation*. These limitations have prompted suggestions to update this regulation "to capture four core nutrients, i.e., vitamin A, calcium, sugar and saturated fat" (Ettinger et al. 2019). Yet, the omission of a mandated requirement for providing complete sugar information on labels is astonishing, considering sugar's impact on a host of ailments and the growing consumption of sugary products in China. Studies of several supermarkets in Beijing have found that popularly consumed products, such as noncarbonated, sugar-sweetened beverages (SSBs), have few sugar content specifications on their labels despite having high amounts of sugar in them (Jin et al. 2019). Others have concluded that there has been no government effort to correct the situation and to create additional food labels, especially labels that provide additional warnings about the consumption of products high in sugar and fat (French 2015b). Researchers have advocated for more effective regulations on the nutritional content of labels so that consumers can make wiser, better-informed choices (He et al. 2014).

In this context, when reinforced with a culture where most citizens are not knowledgeable about good nutrition, few proactively and consistently read food labels. When they do, many have reported that labels are unreliable, falling short of providing accurate information (Phang 2012). Surveys conducted in cities such as Wuhu have found that consumers only have a moderate subjective understanding of labels, while reporting an overuse of labels and a positive attitude toward them (Song et al. 2015). Other surveys, conducted in 2012, of consumers in the cities of Beijing and Baoding revealed "a moderate degree of subjective understanding and low degree of objective understanding of nutrition labels" (Liu et al. 2015, 108).

Finally, with respect to fiscal policy, despite being one of the world's leaders in the consumption of SSBs, no effort has been made to introduce a much-needed beverage tax (Hunt 2019; Lin et al. 2018). The situation is so grave in China, especially with respect to childhood obesity, that other researchers have suggested creating a tax on obesogenic foods in general (He et al. 2014). This is an issue that the government continues to essentially ignore, notwithstanding increased evidence from other countries, particularly Mexico, that the tax could help to reduce the consumption of these products. As we'll soon see, a major reason this tax has not emerged in China has to do with the strong connection that the central government has with major soda companies, which have been instrumental in shaping fiscal and other prevention policies in their favor.

In addition, there has been an ongoing inability to effectively enforce existing legislation, even when programs on obesity, diabetes, and nutrition have been introduced by the government (Greenhalgh 2019a). For example, with respect to childhood obesity prevention programs, central government initiatives mandating regular childhood exercise in schools, such as the aforementioned 2007 Sunny Sports Program, which requires one hour of daily exercise, have been ignored by local schools, mainly due to parents complaining that this endeavor takes time away from their child's study time (French 2015b; Luedi 2016). Others write that only a small portion of the federal obesity prevention programs focused on health education have actually been implemented (Huijun and Fengying 2013). This, in turn, smacks of government apathy in ensuring that policies serve their intended purpose. Lastly, with respect to labeling, researchers note that the lack of compliance with federal regulations is mainly due to the absence of policy enforcement, with "meaningful sanctions" in place, which needs to be present if industries are to comply with labeling policies (Huang et al. 2014, 653).

Why is the government failing to create and enforce regulations that take a more aggressive stance against the junk food industry's interests, even after several years since the premier and the State Council's public and international acknowledgment that NCDs are rising in China, and after several years of introducing innovative NCD prevention programs? This is especially interesting in a context where, since the government liberalized the economy in the 1980s, it has proactively regulated the economy through hundreds of administrative regulations and laws (Kennedy 2009). In fact, under the current leader, Xi Jinping, new federal regulatory institutions have been established. An example of these new federal regulatory institutions is the State Administration for Market Regulation, which enforces regulations, including the investigation and prosecution of entities, across several sectors, for instance, food and drugs (Chamorro and Khaw 2018). Once again, it seems that politics has interfered.

Political Action

In accordance with IPCI, interest groups and major multinational industries often engage in a host of political tactics to curry favor with politicians and avoid the specter of aggressive policy regulations. As we saw in other countries, one tactic that these industries use is engaging in policy partnerships with government. In so doing, industries give the impression that they are important solutions to the NCD problem, dedicated to helping the government find ways to safeguard the nation's most vulnerable populations.

In China, major junk food companies have engaged in these types of partnerships. In 2009, for example, through its Mondeléz Hope Kitchen program, Mondeléz International, the producer of popular confectionary (chocolate) candies and other snack foods, worked with the Chinese Youth Development Foundation, the Chinese CDC, and the Mondeléz International Foundation as well as several local governments in rural areas to improve children's nutrition (Pérez-Escamilla 2018). These organizations established school kitchens, training kitchen staff and teachers, with the end goal of improving children's nutritional status in schools, eradicating hunger, and reducing obesity (Pérez-Escamilla 2018). Through Mondeléz's Hope Kitchen program, moreover, the foundation targeted rural schools "to promote healthy lifestyles to young rural students through a three-part strategy of nutrition education, vegetable gardens and active play" (Mondeléz International Foundation 2017, 12). The program emphasized teacher training on nutrition knowledge while providing physical exercise equipment (Pérez-Escamilla 2018). The Mondeléz International Foundation (2017) claimed that "by the end of 2016, 307 MHKs and 50 Delicious Veggie Gardens were completed in 21 provinces and cities across a wide swath of China, benefiting 150,000 rural students" (12). Greatly facilitating the Mondeléz International Foundation's work was its ability to tap into and strategically use the Chinese Youth Development Foundation's vast network of local political leaders and community partners (Pérez-Escamilla 2018).

Beginning in 2006, Coca-Cola also worked with several provincial governments to implement the company's Happy Playtime program (China Daily 2009). Through this program, Coca-Cola organizes a variety of sports activities to help keep children active as well as training for teachers and students to increase their knowledge about good nutrition. According to the China Daily (2009), "Since September 2006, Coca-Cola has been implementing the Happy Playtime program in over 1,300 primary schools from 20 provinces across the country, which inspired more than 1.3 million students ages 6–12 to participate" (1).

More recently, in 2017, Coca-Cola's Exercise is Medicine (EIM) program sought to establish a policy partnership between Coca-Cola and the government (Fields and Greene 2018). Indeed, according to Fields and Greene (2018), "EIM declares that one of its 2017 goals is to 'form an official partnership with government officials in the General Administration of Sport of China and in the Family Planning Commission'" (1). It seems that EIM's goal through this partnership has been to implement policy with an emphasis on exercise as a key obesity prevention strategy. In that vein, EIM has worked with Dr. Wenhua Zhao, a senior health official who is also a high-ranking official within the Chinese CDC, a member of the Chinese EIM National Center Advisory Board, and deputy director of ILSI China, to introduce EIM's activities to university campuses (Fields and Greene 2018).

And finally, in an effort to appease government officials and convince them that industries are a solution to China's NCD problems, several industries have agreed to engage in the self-regulation of their marketing practices. In 2010, several industries, such as through the China Association of National Advertisers, China Advertising Association, and the China Advertising Association of Commerce, jointly agreed, with guidance from the World Federation of Advertisers and other companies, to adopt ethical standards for advertising and self-regulation through the adoption of the China Responsible Marketing Code (Huneke 2011). Moreover, this code was created based on the International Chamber of Commerce's preexisting international code (Huneke 2011). According to Brent Sanders, chairman of the Marketing and Advertising Committee for USCIB (United States Council for International Business): "The new Chinese Code is not only an opportunity for industry to demonstrate its commitment to ethical marketing practice, it will assist industry to engage the Chinese government as it updates and revises its current advertising laws, a process that has been ongoing" (quoted in Huneke 2011, 1). Note the comment on engaging the government.

Lobbying and Largesse

According to IPCI, lobbying and engaging in largesse is yet another political tactic industry uses to manipulate policy in its favor. In China, however, with its absence of democratic elections and therefore any potential for campaign contributions, and because the state consistently seeks to limit the influence of civil society and business interests through formal government channels, the government has been ambivalent toward business lobbying activities (Kennedy 2009). While the central government has periodically allowed for public hearings on major policy issues, the impact on these hearings varies based on what is being discussed. At times, especially for broader policy issues, they are only a formality, with major decisions already being made within government. Furthermore, and as Kennedy (2009) notes, the All-China Federation of Industry and Commerce, which is China's "most influential" chamber of commerce representing private businesses, despite electing its own membership, is still nevertheless influenced by the leadership preferences of the United Front Department of the CCP (Chinese Communist Party). There are also many independent foreign industry associations, although they are technically illegal, spanning across a host of policy sectors (Kennedy 2009). In this context, it appears that the central government is torn between its efforts to remain autonomous and safeguard its national policy priorities, and ensuring civic and corporate participation in defense of public criticism. The central government seems to prefer being consulted by big business rather than acknowledging industry's direct influence over policy (Kennedy 2009).

These limitations notwithstanding, there have been periodic instances of industry associations voicing their opposition to policy proposals introduced in the National People's Congress. In March 2006, after a delegate from the National People's Congress put forth a bill prohibiting children under the age of 12 from participating in food commercials, as well as restricting food advertisements to children under the age of 12, representatives from the World Federation of Advertisers worked with the Chinese Association of National Advertisers to oppose the proposal (Hawkes 2007).

But this does not mean that companies have not engaged in "informal" lobbying tactics. With formal institutional channels and representation limited in China, junk food lobbying may be taking an "informal rout," as seen with other industry groups. Indeed, industries seeking to influence policies through this process have historically organized informal meetings with government officials (i.e., personal connections, or *guanxi*), but these meetings rarely yield direct influence on policies due to the various formal channels that the national policy-making process entails. In addition, these industries have created government affairs offices, often staffed with former government officials, who, in turn, reconnect with their previous colleagues within government (Kennedy 2009).

In China, the media is essentially silent on these lobbying efforts. Major news coverage of these activities in popular newspapers, such as *Xinhua* or the *People's Daily*, is rarely, if at all, mentioned, due in large part to the government not wanting to give the impression that it is being influenced by industry (Kennedy 2009). Of course, one must keep in mind that the government has been unwaveringly committed to reducing corruption and improving transparency in response to heightened international pressure and criticism. As of 2013, thousands of government officials have been persecuted, and this has contributed to "increased scrutiny of political-business ties" (Hancock 2019). In 2009, in Shanghai, a former employee at the Shanghai Shenmei Beverage and Food Company, one of Coca-Cola Pacific's bottling plants, was arrested by police and detained for a corruption investigation that involved approximately 10 million yuan (Reuters 2009).

Despite their limited influence through formal lobbying and largesse, industry remains influential primarily because it shares mutual policy interests with the government. We must keep in mind that the Chinese government is unwaveringly committed to economic development. Consequently, junk food industries continue to have substantial policy leverage, even if informally.

Institutional Infiltration

As I emphasize in IPCI, yet another political tactic that industries use to influence NCD policy is institutional infiltration processes. Indeed, and similar to what we have seen in Mexico, Brazil, and India, industries eager to shape the government's policies in alignment with their interests also seek to infiltrate the federal bureaucracy. Done either formally or informally, industries take advantage of bureaucratic institutions to inculcate them with their scientific research, ideas, and beliefs, gradually converting them to institutions that support industry's mission. In the case of China, this endeavor reflected an informal, clandestine effort, like the informal approaches taken toward policy lobbying by major industries in Mexico.

As Susan Greenhalgh (2019b) explains, Coca-Cola achieved this kind of institutional infiltration process by working through the International Life Sciences Institute, a scientific-based NGO that it created in 1978. Shortly after reentering China's market, Mr. Alex Malaspina, at that time president of ILSI-Global, found an influential nutrition scientist in China that his organization could work with (Greenhalgh 2019a). This reflected Coca-Cola's goal, at the time, of building strong political connections and overcoming any remnants of Coca-Colonization. Malaspina successfully befriended a prominent nutrition scientist, Chen Chunming, who shortly thereafter, in 1983, became president of the Chinese Academy of Preventive Medicine within the MoH (Greenhalgh 2019a). (The Chinese Academy became the CDC in 2002.) Greenhalgh (2019a) notes that after becoming frustrated with the dearth of research funding and bureaucratic red tape, in 1993 Chen created ILSI Focal Point in China, also known as ILSI-China. Even after assuming her role as ILSI-China's director, Chen appears to have still been present within the Chinese Academy of Preventive Medicine and eventually the CDC (see Greenhalgh 2019a). Chen's extensive government connections even after establishing ILSI-China provided her with considerable policy influence (see Greenhalgh's interview discussion on this in Reuell 2019; see also Greenhalgh 2019a). Indeed, Greenhalgh (2019a) states: "The ambiguity in Chen's status as a (now) de facto high official operating in a formally nongovernmental organization to help the MoH shape policy allowed her to wield substantial, mostly behind-the-scenes, policy influence" (8). ILSI-China, in fact, had a presence within the federal agency responsible for implementing policies on obesity-related diseases, the CDC, sharing office space and staff with these government officials (see Jacobs 2019a, 2019b). Furthermore, under Chen, ILSI-China had no governing board of directors (Greenhalgh 2019a). With Chen present within the bureaucracy, ILSI-China could infiltrate China's CDC with their science, ideas, and interests. Chen could shift these ideas and resources in ILSI-China's favor.

It appears that ILSI-China's presence within the CDC essentially aided industry's ability to influence the science and guide China's obesity policies. As Greenhalgh (2019a) explains, Chen's ILSI-China office was eventually able to attend key government meetings and influence the government's policies on chronic diseases. By the early 2000s, ILSI-China's influence was becoming apparent. According to Greenhalgh (2019a), "By 2003, ILSI-China had defined body mass index cutoffs for obesity and created guidelines for obesity prevention and management that were issued in the name of the MoH, firmly establishing it as China's primary obesity-related science and policy-making organization" (9). Nevertheless, according to Karlis (2019), the MoH at the time did not publicly acknowledge their participation in the formulation of these guidelines established by ILSI-China. By 2015, Coca-Cola, in Atlanta, had prioritized the importance of physical exercise, rather than diet, as an important strategy for tackling obesity, in turn supporting research scientists to create the Global Energy Balance Network, to advocate for this idea and approach to obesity prevention (Greenhalgh 2019a). ILSI-China also organized several conferences and workshops with world-renowned scientists, mainly from the United States. The research presented at these conferences examined either obesity or chronic diseases with an emphasis on the importance of physical activity. This focus on physical exercise appeared to gradually crowd out the importance of improved diet. As Greenhalgh (2019a) notes, "From 2010 to 2015, 60% of ILSI-China-sponsored obesity efforts focused primarily on exercise; only 23% dealt with diet" (10). And as she further explains, "Although nutritional approaches promoting healthy foods, dietary guidelines, and nutritional education remained on the books, they had had little (or only corporate) funding, visibility, or active support" (10). During this period, China's MoH began to emphasize physical exercise to tackle obesity. When combined with its powerful, historically based political connections, ILSI-China was able to gradually transform the MoH's anti-obesity and anti-chronic disease programs in its favor (Greenhalgh 2019a). Exercise, exercise, exercise—that was the focus, that was the goal, and that was, as we have seen in earlier chapters, the primary strategy taken by the government to tackle childhood obesity.

A concrete example is the Happy 10 Minutes program discussed earlier in this chapter. Introduced in China 2006, the Happy 10 Minutes program was based on an initiative created by the ILSI's Center for Health Promotion (CHP) in 1999 called Take 10! and associated with none other than Mr. Alex Malaspina, former vice president of Coca-Cola and creator and head of ILSI-Global from 1978 to 2001 (Greenhalgh 2019b). Chen Chunming also served on CHP's governing board of trustees as an unpaid member throughout CHP's entire existence (1999–2004) (140). Shortly after the Take 10! program was launched, Greenhalgh (2019b) found that China's CDC received two grants from the CHP in 2004, "totaling more than US$53,000." Greenhalgh (2019b) further found that "the timing of the grants (on February 6 and May 13, 2004) and the launch of the Happy 10 pilot project (in September 2004) leaves little doubt that some if not all of the funds were earmarked for China to create its own Take 10 program. ILSI-China (in the person of Chen) had served as the intermediary and asked the China CDC to be the implementing agency" (140).

But there were direct consequences to ILSI-China's efforts. First and foremost, ILSI-China had become the authority on China's obesity legislation, as "its role in addressing obesity has been greater than that of China's Ministry of Health" (Greenhalgh 2019a, 6). ILSI's ideas and its policy language "(e.g., 'energy balance,' 'eating and moving in balance,' and 'integrating exercise with medical are') is embedded in national plans and programs" (Greenhalgh 2019a, 12). Over the years, it appears as if a path-dependent process has taken place, where ILSI-China's ideas and policy prescriptions persist and continue to shape the government's position on obesity and other chronic diseases (see Greenhalgh 2019a), as well as more recent MoH health initiatives (e.g., Healthy China 2030), with the bulk of its targeted initiatives focused on physical activity and regulating salt intake for improved nutrition (see Greenhalgh's discussion on this in Lambert 2019). As Greenhalgh (2019a) notes in her article, quoting nutrition scientist Barry Popkin, from an email sent from him to Greenhalgh, this problem has delayed China's broader approach to NCD prevention: "There is now no immediate possibility the government will regulate food, beverage, or sugar in the way countries globally are beginning to work to create healthy diets and address not only obesity but all diet-related noncommunicable diseases. I believe ILSI's influence in promoting the physical activity agenda was extremely detrimental and put China decades behind in efforts to create a healthier diet for its citizens" (13).

Unfortunately, ILSI recently continued to maintain a presence within China's CDC (Jacobs 2019b). Worse still, unlike what we saw with Chen, Junshi Chen simultaneously serves as a senior research professor at the Institute of Nutrition and Food Safety in China's CDC, the "'National Center Director' of Exercise is Medicine in China and the Director of the International Life Sciences Institute's Chinese arm, ILSI Focal Point China" (Fields and Greene 2018, 1). Keep in mind that Coca-Cola was the Exercise is Medicine program's "first founding corporate partner" (Thore 2015). In addition, yet another influential scientist, Wenhua Zhao, serves as "a member of the Chinese CDC's Division of Academic Publication, the Deputy Director of ILSI China, and a member of the Chinese Exercise is Medicine organization's National Advisory Board" (Fields and Greene 2018, 1). Thus, through these senior health officials, ILSI, and by extension the multitude of food industries supporting it, continues to be present among the highest echelons of the bureaucracy.

Restructuring Society

IPCI also highlights the strategies that industries take to restructure civil society in industry's favor. This is accomplished in several ways, such as by building civil societal allies (by partnering with like-minded NGOs or academics in order to champion industry's policy views), in turn amplifying the latter's voice and legitimacy within government, and by working closely with local communities through corporate social responsibility activities, with the ultimate goal of increasing community support for industry.

Perhaps the best example of industry partnerships with academia and NGOs is, once again, Coca-Cola. For example, Coca-Cola provided research grants to prominent US nutrition science professors to conduct research illustrating the importance of physical exercise in weight reduction (Greenhalgh 2019b). Indeed, Greenhalgh (2019b) "discovered that in 2008 (if not earlier) Coke had begun funding Steven Blair to conduct 'energy balance research'. . . [and that] by 2010 Blair had been joined by Gregory A. Hand (also at the University of South Carolina) and James O. Hill" (143–144). Furthermore, by 2015, Greenhalgh found that "since 2008 [Blair] had received $4 million from the company, mostly for work on physical activity, energy balance, and the global network" (144). Steven Blair and James O. Hill also attended several international conferences organized by ILSI-China (Greenhalgh 2019a). Their academic research on the importance of physical exercise to avoid weight gain was displayed and shared with Chinese researchers, with Greenhalgh (2019a) at one point stating that "the ideas of Blair and Hill about energy balance, the neglected importance of physical activity, and of inactivity not obesity being the critical health problem were presented more often than those of other scientists" (11). Influential individuals such as Dr. Chen Chunming, who, as mentioned earlier, founded ILSI-China, harbored academic viewpoints given by Blair at an obesity conference held in China in 2013 (Greenhalgh 2019b). In fact, Greenhalgh (2019b) found that "Chen Chunming, by then ILSI-China's senior advisor and the undisputed leader of China's obesity field, underscored Blair's points, contending that his approach should become a national priority. Her comments revealed that Blair's views had influenced Chinese thinking at the highest level, and that Chen had known him for some time" (141).

China's nutrition scientists and academics have also received, and welcomed, funding, in the form of research grants, from industry (Lambert 2019). When questioned about the ethics involved in this clear conflict of interest, scientists were not concerned by their relationship with Coca-Cola and upheld the integrity of ILSI-sponsored researchers (Jacobs 2019b). Moreover, these scientists argued that Coca-Cola was merely reinforcing an old idea put forth by China's Communist Party: that exercise is fundamental to good health (Jacobs 2019b).

Other scholars also underscore that Coca-Cola and other industries are important and welcomed sources of funding for researchers in China (see Dr. Paulo Serodio's interview in Cockerell and Chwa 2019). Indeed, "Coca-Cola (and other companies in the industry) are important funders in the Chinese market, and academics appreciate the availability of resources to advance their research agendas," explained Dr. Paulo Serodio, a researcher focusing on the corporate sector's influence on health (quoted in Cockerell and Chwa 2019).

And yet, Coca-Cola and other major industries have gone well beyond simply partnering with like-minded academics and NGOs. As seen in other countries discussed in this book, these industries also embed themselves within local communities through various CSR activities. The goal has been to demonstrate compassion in order to win the hearts and minds of local communities, and this further ensures these industries' social and political support.

For example, in addition to investing in schools through the aforementioned Happy Playtime program, Coca-Cola has provided 80 million yuan to the China Youth Development Foundation to help rebuild schools after natural disasters (Wanxian 2009). Moreover, beginning in 2013, Coca-Cola, through its Clean Water 24 program, provided free and clean drinking water to citizens suffering from natural disasters (Coca-Cola Company 2018). At the same time, Coca-Cola, in an effort to help enhance China's sustainable agricultural practices in the area of sugarcane production, worked with sugarcane producers in the Guangxi Autonomous Region to conserve their usage of water so that they could provide for local communities (Coca-Cola Company 2011). Coca-Cola has also worked with the WWF (World Wildlife Fund) to clean up major rivers, such as the Yangtze (Knowledge@Wharton 2010). For policy experts, these activities are important for increasing a company's image in China, a point raised by Piet Klop, senior fellow at the World Resources Institute in Washington, DC: "The last thing a branded company would want . . . is to end up in a newspaper [report] saying it is operating a bottling plant in an area where households cannot even access clean drinking water" (quoted in Knowledge@Wharton 2010, 1).

PepsiCo has also engaged in similar activities. According to analysts, in 2016, "PepsiCo, through its Quaker brand, partnered with the Chinese Nutrition Society (CNS) to give Chinese consumers access to good nutritional advice" (*Global Times* 2016). These consumers resided "in 600 locations in eight provinces and cities across China, including Beijing, Shanghai, and Guangdong" (*Global Times* 2016). Analysts further maintained that, in their work together, Quaker and the CNS were committed to inspiring a healthy, balanced diet among consumers, providing information about important nutritional and scientific concepts while aligning their activities with "the national health goal of 'enjoying healthy life with good nutrition every day'" (*Global Times* 2016). In 2015, the PepsiCo Nutrition in Action Plan was launched through a partnership among Quaker, the China Foundation for Poverty Alleviation, and the CNS. Through this partnership, these entities were able to provide nutritious meals for children in schools located within poor locations, such as Zhaotong, which is located in the Yunnan province (*Global Times* 2016). Thus far, the program has "provided 130,000 Quaker Nutrition Breakfasts to more than 1,600 poor pupils in Zhaotong, and completed nutrition and hygiene knowledge training for 200 teachers and canteen staff" (Xinyi 2016). Others highlight CNS's efforts to work with PepsiCo and Nestlé "to provide healthy meals and promote nutrition education in children across China" (Tabledebates, n.d.). In 2010, PepsiCo also challenged citizens, especially those consumers with high blood cholesterol, to participate in its China Cholesterol Education program by way of the Quaker 30-Day Cholesterol Challenge Program (PepsiCo 2010). The goal has been to raise awareness about the health risks of high cholesterol and encourage exercise and more nutritious diets to reduce cholesterol. In 2018, PepsiCo also helped to improve water quality in China's rural areas by providing $2 million to the China Women's Development Foundation for a program called the Water Cellar for Mothers-Green Village (*Global Times* 2018a). Lastly, PepsiCo introduced projects that helped rural potato farmers increase the efficiency of their water use through the provision of sprinkler irrigation technology (PepsiCo 2017).

These CSR activities have helped to bolster the food industry's popularity and support in communities, and these activities have earned the respect of key politicians. As Paul Haenle, chairman of the Asia-Pacific region for Teneo, once noted, for industries in China, these CSR activities work and should be pursued: "Many companies have taken additional measures through corporate social responsibility efforts to give back to Chinese society, further building their support among powerful Chinese officials and agencies, as well as the Chinese public" (Haenle 2015). China's senior politicians have certainly noticed these efforts. For instance, in 2006, in response to PepsiCo helping farmers use water more efficiently (as mentioned earlier), former premier Wen Jiabao "applauded PepsiCo's 'triple-win model' for the equal benefits delivered to the environment, potato plantation, and the farmers. In October 2011, when visiting the PepsiCo booth at the Canton Fair, Premier Wen once again acknowledge[d] and encouraged PepsiCo's commitment to sustainable agriculture in China" (PepsiCo 2017, 25–26).

The Absence of Civil Societal Division

Nevertheless, in the case of China, little evidence suggests that industries' engagement with civil society is contributing to divisions in society. First and foremost, and as I will discuss in greater detail shortly, it seems that there are very few, if any, NGOs or community-based organizations that are working on the childhood obesity issue or on improving nutritional health in vulnerable populations. Because of this, there has been no conflict of interest between these NGOs and those that are working with industry on particular initiatives. In this context, then, there has been no sense of industry-induced civil societal division and conflict, as IPCI suggests.

Complementary Institutions

IPCI also explains how a supportive general political context can facilitate industry's ability to influence policy. More specifically, IPCI emphasizes the importance of what I call complementary institutions. These institutions arise when political leaders seek to strategically partner with and use industries to achieve politicians' alternative policy, and thus, by extension, political objectives. Because of this, they have an interest in supporting industry development and prosperity. These complementary institutional interests indirectly support industry's interests while helping to increase their political legitimacy and influence within government. Complementary institutions therefore serve as critical intervening variables that supplement industries' aforementioned political and social tactics.

While complementary institutions have been present in several policy and political areas, it is also important to note that the broader political context has been extremely favorable for the junk food industry's development in China. Since the opening up of China's economy, the central government has benefited from having a partnership with a thriving business sector (Kennedy 2009). Indeed, as Kennedy (2009) maintains: "As a pro-development regime, the Chinese state is ideologically oriented towards business. The two are in some sense partners seeking to use the other to achieve their own goals. While the government is in a position to influence business, firms have gained policy leverage because they are central to accomplishing government objectives such as a growing economy" (198). Despite being a socialist government with a communist party at the helm, ironically, the government has also been very pro-business, in turn giving industry—even foreign multinationals—considerable influence.

Poverty reduction has been a key area in which complementary institutions exist. From Deng Xiaoping's reign to the present day, under current president Xi Jinping, poverty alleviation has been a national priority (Westcott and Wang 2019; *Xinhua Net* 2020). Xi has been so committed to broadcasting the state's commitment to this endeavor that he visited Huaxi Village, located in the Shizhu Tujia Autonomous County, to inquire into the community's poverty status and to reassure this community that their needs would be met (Jinping 2020). Xi's focus on the household, on the individual rather than on the broader community, has been known as his targeted poverty alleviation strategy (Diallo 2019). According to news analysts, the central government in Beijing has even "dispatched about 775,000 party officials to drive the anti-poverty campaign. Many are going door-to-door to work out what the government can do to help" (Westcott and Wang 2019). At the same time, poverty has been viewed as a concern of the CCP with respect to its overall legitimacy (Bowie 2019).

In this context, Xi's government viewed partnering with private industry as vital to eradicating poverty by 2020—a policy deadline that he announced in 2015 (Donaldson 2019; Huifeng 2019). Xi's anti-poverty measures appear to rely on the support of businesses and other community members such as government officials and teachers (Donaldson 2019), in turn suggesting that Xi's government is reliant on and is working with industry to achieve his anti-poverty objectives. Donaldson notes: "Government officials are far from the only group mobilized to this effort; the private and state-owned sectors have also responded" (54). Donaldson further claims that "Xi has directed unprecedented amounts of money, both public and ostensibly private, towards this endeavor" (53).

As yet another example, in 2018, the central government partnered with PepsiCo through the former's state-sponsored China Foundation for Poverty Alleviation (*Global Times* 2018b). The goal has been to improve children's nutritional status through the provision of school meals and nutritional knowledge in poor rural areas, such as in Zhaotong in Yunnan province and Qiandongnan in Guizhou, an area that has been described as having "the highest poverty level in China" (*Global Times* 2018b). To achieve this, and as part of its PepsiCo Nutrition in Action initiative, PepsiCo awarded $1 million to the China Foundation for Poverty Alleviation, with the grant funding to be managed by the Give2Asia nonprofit (*Global Times* 2018b). Provincial governments have also worked with Coca-Cola to provide employment opportunities by opening bottling plants in central and western China (Coca-Cola Company 2009). After working with Coca-Cola's bottling partner COFCA Coca-Cola Beverages Limited to open bottling plants in Urumqi, Xinjiang (with a plant also opening up in Nanchang), Wang Lequan, who at the time was party secretary of the CPC's Xinjiang Committee as well as a member of the Political Bureau of the CPC's Central Committee, stated: "I represent the Xinjiang people in welcoming the China National Cereals, Oils and Foodstuffs Corporation (COFCO) and the Coca-Cola Company's investment in Xinjiang and expressing their sincere congratulations in establishing the new bottling plant. . . . This well-known international brand will bring in progressive management concepts and boost the development of the local industry in Xinjiang" (quoted in Coca-Cola Company 2009).

In addition, the central government has also viewed junk food industries as key allies in helping the government achieve its goal of ongoing economic development. While Deng Xiaoping encouraged market reform and foreign investment, his successor, President Jian Zemin (1993–2003), was also committed to fast-paced economic growth (Tisdell 2009). Jian not only viewed industries as key partners in this endeavor, but, believe it or not, he also went so far as to incorporate business entrepreneurs into the CCP under his "Three Represents" CCP modernization strategy (Guo et al. 2013). For the first time in communist China, Jiang viewed private entrepreneurs as a social productive force, part of the honorable working class, joining the ranks of the common worker and intellectuals and fully eligible for CCP membership benefits (Guo et al. 2013; see also Coble 2005). What followed was a myriad of policies that encouraged increased foreign direct investment and free market reforms. In essence, now, under Jiang, "the market would play the primary role in the development of the productive forces" (Brodsgaard and Rutten 2017, 101).

Jiang's successor, President Hu Jintao (2003–2013), was also laser-focused on the economy, but from a more equitable and just perspective (CNN International 2005; Puthenkalam 2009). Under Hu's New Deal initiative, for example, the government remained focused on industrial development and economic growth but in a fairer, more equitable manner (Li 2003). The New Deal entailed efforts to achieve regional equality in economic development and also strove to ensure fairness and equality in society and social justice, as well as to make known the importance of creating a social safety net. Finally, the New Deal sought to increase transparency within government (Li 2003).

More recently, President Xi Jinping (2013–present) sought to sustain the central government's partnership with industry in order to secure economic development, though not as enthusiastically, and with troubling worry from businesses. Unlike his predecessors, Xi entered office in 2013 on a mandate to recentralize political authority, eradicate corruption (with an increased focus on state-business relationships), and increase the state's presence in the market, mainly through greater investment in state-owned enterprises (Hancock 2019; Heilmann 2017). Bank credits to private businesses declined sharply after Xi's arrival (Hancock 2019). Furthermore, his Made in China 2025 initiative emphasized strengthening the capacity of China's industries to manufacture on their own, with an emphasis on tech-intensive industries such as robotics and artificial intelligence, in turn seemingly creating an "uneven playing field" with respect to foreign multinationals (Chamorro and Khaw 2018). And to have some sort of state influence over business, there has been "pressure from party committees to have a seat at the table when executives are making big calls on investment and the like" (McGregor 2019). McGregor (2019) claims that "the party's efforts to place itself inside private companies have been, according to its own figures, very successful." A recent survey conducted by "the party's personnel body found that 68% of China's private companies had party bodies by 2016, and 70% of foreign enterprises." The party's infiltration within business reflected its desire to ensure that the CCP's "revolutionary spirit" remain alive and well within business (McGregor 2019) and that Xi's interests, such as the promotion of " 'Xi Jinping Thought' and driving Beijing's agenda," are consistently represented (Chamorro and Khaw 2018). With this, it ensures that the government can sustain its policy interests and avoid a potential source of alternative power.

In a context of low economic growth in 2018, Xi publicly reassured industries, stating that they had his support (Hancock 2019), while also encouraging more foreign investment (Tse 2018). Xi introduced his "three-sector paralleled development" strategy to reassure businesses and other sectors that the central government was committed to them (Li and Liang 2019). Li and Liang (2019) explain that this three-sector initiative emerged "in response to private sector concerns" and theoretically should have helped to build confidence within the private company sector and foreign firms after the three-sector's focus on the simultaneous development of state-owned enterprises and private and foreign business enterprises (Li and Liang 2019). In addition, Tse (2018) claims that a "three-layered duality" model was introduced by Xi. Under this approach, the central government retains control over the creation of national development policies; at the micro community level, private entrepreneurs are "a main driving force behind the economy," and in the middle, provincial governments periodically partner with business entrepreneurs to compete regionally, in response to the central policy guidance (Tse 2018). As a sign of good faith, Xi authorized a reduction in corporate taxes and authorized more bank loans for small businesses (Hancock 2019; Li and Liang 2019). Recently, Xi has even publicly commented that "private enterprises and private entrepreneurs belong to our own family" (quoted in *Xinhua* 2018). While Xi certainly remains supportive of state-owned enterprises, and while his government prefers CCP influence within industry boards, there is no question that the government has maintained its tradition of viewing major industries as a vital partner in securing China's ongoing growth and prosperity.

China's complementary institutions in the area of poverty reduction and economic growth appear to have contributed to industry's ongoing political and policy influence. By relying on industry to help achieve the government's objectives, industry seems to retain a great deal of support, and thus influence, within government. This context appears to have aided ongoing efforts to have the government focus on protecting and nurturing industry, rather than pursuing regulatory policies that go against its interests.

The Reemergence of Civil Society?

In a context of worsening NCD outcomes for China's most vulnerable populations and in which the government has yet to sternly take on corporate sector interests in defense of its people, civil society in China has responded by helping to increase awareness and engaging in community projects. However, and as seen in the other emerging economies discussed in this book, civil society's emphasis on the regulatory aspects of NCD policy is a new area of policy focus. While NGOs and activists have recently influenced regulatory policy in Mexico and Brazil, China joins India and Indonesia in seeing an activist community that is hampered by the absence of a government seeking to proactively work with and incorporate civil society's policy recommendations.

In recent years, NGOs and activists in China have helped raise public awareness and interest in obesity while providing community interventions. For example, the China Preventive Medicine Association has been active in highlighting the importance of paying attention to obesity in China, notwithstanding government delay in acknowledging the problem (French 2015b). Public charities, such as the Mian Fei Wu Can initiative, established in 2011, have also been credited with raising awareness and helping to draw support for the passage of national legislation, such as the Rural Compulsory Education Nutrition Improvement Plan, introduced by the State Council in 2011 (Liu 2015). Other NGOs, such as the Chinese Nutrition Society, introduced school campaigns like the Eat Smart at School initiative, which had a goal of "cultivating healthy eating practices in schools" (French 2015b). Similar initiatives took place in Hong Kong in 2006, with the EatSmart@school.hk (ESS) initiative (EatSmart@school.hk 2020). This campaign is a partnership between several stakeholders and the Department of Health and the Education Bureau. The ESS initiative provides nutritional guidelines to schools so that they can provide healthier lunches, establish an environment of healthy eating (such as increased fruit consumption), and avoid overweight and any associated ailments due to poor dietary behavior (EatSmart@school.hk 2020). According to some scholars, the Beijing Consumer Association has also focused on consumer rights issues (McBeath and McBeath 2010). This association has also conducted surveys on consumer attitudes (McBeath and McBeath 2010).

The Chinese Nutrition Society, though closely affiliated with the government, has also been vocal about addressing children's malnutrition issues in China, going so far as to work with international organizations, such as UNICEF (United Nations Children's Fund), to host conferences and elevate discussion (UNICEF China 2019). In 2007, the CNS also played an important role in helping to revise federal dietary guidelines, with special attention given to preventing chronic diseases (Huijun and Fengying 2013).

Still, to my knowledge, NGOs and nutrition activists have not been publicly critical of the central government's reluctance to introduce more effective NCDs policies, especially with respect to regulating industry. Compared to the other nations discussed in this book, for the most part, this is an uncharted area of public health activism. Several other issues may be contributing to civil society's lack of aggressive engagement.

First, under the current the Xi Jinping presidency, the state has tried to reassert greater control over NGOs, particularly those with links to international NGOs and funders. In fact, a proposed law was introduced in 2015 to monitor foreign NGOs and their domestic partners, while viewing them as national security risks (Denyer 2015). Furthermore, according to Denyer (2015), this proposed legislation requires that international NGOs be monitored by the Public Security Bureau rather than the Ministry of Civil Affairs (which historically regulated these international entities), and that NGOs must obtain a federal agency sponsor for registration (Denyer 2015). As one can imagine, this conundrum has instigated greater fear for NGOs seeking to partner with international NGOs and funders to advocate for improved regulations and NCD policies.

Second, it appears that the central government still has not remained firmly committed to reaching out to and integrating the views of public health activists, even in the critical area of NCDs among children and the poor. While the state obtains information from the aforementioned NGOs, and public health scientists can provide information and recommendation, essentially no evidence suggests that their ideas have increased attention to needed policy reforms or to industry regulations. Instead, and as high-lighted by Kennedy (2009), the central government only appears to want to be consulted by society, rather than fully integrating their views and policy recommendations.

Ultimately, while NGOs that draw attention to the importance of im-proving children's nutrition exist in China, civil society still has a long way to go with respect to directly confronting the state and aggressively pressur-ing the government to change its policies. Fears of political repercussion, when combined with a government that historically has been apathetic and uncommitted to fully incorporating civil society's views, may be further hin-dering civil society's rise and influence.

Conclusion

While China's government has paid a lot of attention to its ongoing obesity and type 2 diabetes epidemics, especially among children and the poor, the evidence introduced in this chapter suggests that the government has been consistently reluctant to directly challenge the interests of junk food industries. It is as if the government wants to do everything it can to curtail these public health challenges as long as they do not threaten indus-tries' interests and growth potential. While the government's repeated em-phasis on living a healthy lifestyle and engaging in physical exercise is im-portant, China will not make any progress in reducing obesity, diabetes, and protecting its children and the poor from these ailments until stiffer, more effective regulatory policies are in place.

Applying IPCI to the case of China has revealed that once again, junk food industries' ongoing political and social interference has consistently shaped NCD policy in industry's favor. Several political and social strategies have been adopted, ranging from engaging in prevention policy partner-ships with government, informal lobbying, and clandestine infiltration of bureaucratic institutions, to building academic and social allies through ac-ademic partnerships and community investment. Through all of these po-litical, institutional, and social activities, it seems that industries have been able to deepen their political and social support, and thus their ability to avoid stringent regulatory policies. In this context, industries have easily pushed for and sustained the government's focus on general obesity and diabetes prevention programs—such as the importance of regular physical exercise—that fail to get at the heart of the matter: reducing access to fatty foods and protecting those who are incapable of making healthy decisions on their own.

But we must also add to this conundrum the critical role of complementary institutions. Industries are only partly to blame; ambitious presidents, with their broader policy and political ambitions, are also culprits. For decades, China's presidents have strategically partnered with industries to achieve their alternative policy—and thus political—objectives, such as poverty reduction and long-term economic growth. In this context, industries have been essentially protected, nurtured, and at times even incorporated into the governing Chinese Communist Party. This situation, in many regards, has indirectly bolstered the political legitimacy and influence of junk food industries, facilitating their ability to avoid the imposition of stricter regulatory policies.

All the while, civic activists have been there, operating along the margins, calling attention to the ongoing NCD crisis. But until NGOs and activists have no more fear of state repression; until they can have permanent representation within policy-making institutions; and until they can work with international colleagues to establish an alternative policy narrative, civil society's full potential in China will not be unleashed. Therefore, China's ability to catch up to the other emerging economies with greater industry regulation will be an ongoing, and daunting, task.

China: Summary of Chapter Findings

Political Action	Restructuring Society	Complementary Institutions	Regulatory Policy Failure and Absence
Policy partnership Mondelēz International works with the Chinese Youth Development Foundation and the CDC and local governments to improve school kitchens and children's nutrition Coca-Cola's Exercise is Medicine (EIM) program in partnership with the government's General Administration of Sport of China, Family Planning Commission	*Corporate social responsibility* For example, Coca-Cola provides financial support to the China Youth Development Foundation to rebuild schools after natural disasters and provides clean drinking water to communities through Coco-Cola's Clean Water 24 program PepsiCo provides nutritious meals to schoolchildren in poor areas through its PepsiCo Nutrition in Action Plan, in partnership with Quaker, the China Foundation for Poverty Alleviation, and the Chinese Nutrition Society (CNS)	Presidential and government partnerships with industry to eradicate poverty, achieving the president's political objectives Presidential partnership with industry to ensure economic development, an ongoing presidential objective	Absence of federal regulations on the marketing and sale of junk foods to children and the poor Absence of federal regulations (legal mandates) for food labels listing harmful ingredients (e.g., sugar); nevertheless, other ingredients, such as fats, protein, and carbohydrates, are legally required Absence of labeling regulation enforcement and sanctions for noncompliance; lackluster industry compliance with labeling regulations; quality and accuracy of labels limited Absence of sugary beverage and soda tax
Lobbying and largesse Limited by lack of elections and state influence on industry; lobbying mainly by personal political connection	*Partnering with society* Industry has provided research grants to scientists in China		

Political Action	Restructuring Society	Complementary Institutions	Regulatory Policy Failure and Absence
Institutional infiltration ILSI presence within the CDC and influence over NCD policy	*Dividing society* Absent due to the dearth of Chinese NGOs and community-based organizations working on childhood obesity and vulnerable populations		

8

South Africa

In the past two decades, South Africa has joined the other emerging economies discussed in this book in seeing a correlation among increased globalization, the rise of free markets, and the prevalence of obesity and type 2 diabetes. In addition to increasing among the general population, these health care issues have also affected South Africa's most vulnerable populations: children and the poor. To its credit, the government has, in recent years, recognized this ongoing problem and enacted a series of national noncommunicable disease prevention programs. In addition to raising awareness of these diseases, encouraging physical exercise and balanced nutrition, and working with schools, South Africa was the first country on the African continent to introduce a tax on soda and sugar-sweetened beverages. The government, so it seemed, took these NCD issues head-on, unveiling several impressive prevention programs. These programs would aim to reduce obesity and type 2 diabetes cases, safeguard society, and prepare children for ongoing health and prosperity.

Unfortunately, and as we have seen in essentially all of the other emerging economies discussed in this book, the government has yet to introduce aggressive policy regulations that directly hamper junk food industries' ability to market, sell, and distribute their products. Once again, it is as if the government seeks to do everything it can *besides* harm the interests of big industry, and at the expense of its most vulnerable populations.

As I emphasized in IPCI (see chapter 1), when facing the specter of increased regulations on their activity, junk food industries sought to discourage presidents and parliamentarians from adopting not only prevention policies, such as the SSB tax, but also regulatory policies. They did so through several political tactics aimed at increasing their legitimacy and influence among these policy makers. For example, industries were glad to partner with Department of Health (DoH) officials to introduce NCD prevention programs so that they could be viewed as genuine allies with solutions to the problem. While industries or their interest group representatives were less inclined to engage in lobbying tactics and infiltrate the bureaucracy, they engaged in several corporate social responsibility strategies to establish further political credit, while winning the hearts and minds of community members. Industry has also divided society by partnering with NGOs and, in the process, hindering other activists' ability to work with these NGOs and establish a unifying voice in opposition to industry activities.

And yet, industry is not the only culprit—complementary institutions also matter (as IPCI also highlights). That is, since the transition to democracy in 1994, the alternative policy and political preferences of South Africa's presidents have indirectly supported these industries and, in a sense, safeguarded them from further regulatory action. Presidents, to this day, have focused on strengthening the nation's economy, viewing this not only as a means to reduce poverty and provide equal opportunity for all but also as a chief electoral strategy. To this end, presidents have viewed junk food—and other—industries as integral partners in achieving these alternative policies and, hence, political objectives.

When combined, the political strategies of junk food industries and ambitious presidents have facilitated the former's ability to avoid further regulations while also securing their ongoing growth and prosperity. But how and why did these industries become so prosperous and influential in the first place?

The Rise and Influence of Junk Food Industries

Similar to what we saw in the other emerging economies discussed in this book, few multinational junk food industries existed in South Africa in the early twentieth century. Coca-Cola made its way to Cape Town in 1928 (FMCG News South Africa 2018), seemingly viewing South Africa as a gateway to the continent and therefore vital for global expansion. Coca-Cola invested not only in bottling plants, production, and distribution but also in local communities through its sponsorship of sporting and community events (Moses and Vest 2010; Spivey 2009). These activities appeared to help establish the company's reputation for giving back to society; and it also associated its drink with the people—strategies we'll see Coca-Cola use again and again. By the time its main rival, PepsiCo, entered the market in 1946, Coca-Cola dominated South Africa's soda industry (Moses and Vest 2010; Spivey 2009).

And yet, perhaps with the exception of these soda industries, from the 1950s through the early 1990s, there was a considerably low level of foreign direct investment (Arvanitis 2006) in South Africa. This was mainly due to the international political backlash, as well as external sanctions, against the racist Apartheid regime, which took control of the government in 1946 (Arvanitis 2006). Confronting vehement opposition from the international community, US business owners, and the religious community, by the 1970s most foreign multinational enterprises, including Coca-Cola and PepsiCo, withdrew their investments from South Africa, though in varying degrees (Moses and Vest 2010; Spivey 2009). At the time, Coca-Cola also planned to sell and establish contracts with local black-owned bottling companies (Sing 1986) and encouraged the marketing of its product, all while supplying its secret formula from Swaziland, which bordered Mozambique (Moses and Vest 2010; Spivey 2009). In essence, through these endeavors the Atlanta company stayed in South Africa's market through indirect channels, diversifying its investments in other sectors such as food and entertainment (Spivey 2009, 35). As Spivey (2009) writes: "With the absence of Pepsi, Coke's market share in the country actually increased, despite their [Coke's] alleged 'absence'" (35).

For the most part, the emergence of multinational junk food industries did not occur until after South Africa's transition to democracy (and subsequent integration into the global economy) in the mid 1990s. With the transition to democracy in 1994, led by President Nelson Mandela and the African National Congress (ANC), free market reforms were introduced and efforts were made to attract more foreign investment (Musakwa and Odhiambo 2019). In a context of low domestic savings, inadequate capital investment, few job opportunities, and low levels of economic growth, the government liberalized the economy and invited greater FDI (Musakwa and Odhiambo 2019). To incentivize these foreign investments, the government also entered into several regional trade agreements, such as the African Union, the Southern Africa Development Community, and the Tripartite Free Trade Area, and created several national development plans (Musakwa and Odhiambo 2019).

Coca-Cola and PepsiCo resurfaced in South Africa after Apartheid and the lifting of US sanctions (Spivey 2009). However, the former's ability to strategically invest in local bottling companies, as well as market and distribute its product, during Apartheid allowed it to secure the soda market by 81 percent by the mid-1990s, gradually edging out PepsiCo, which commanded a measly 4.7 percent (Moses and Vest 2010, 237). Interestingly, Mandela initially resisted Coca-Cola's reemergence, choosing instead to support PepsiCo (Moses and Vest 2010). Mandela sipped Pepsi products in public when visiting Atlanta—Coke's home turf—in the summer of 1990, shortly after his release from prison, and required that the hotels he was staying at get rid of all Coke products while he was there (Spivey 2009). Furthermore, when visiting Atlanta that summer, a member of Mandela's entourage stated: "They [Coca-Cola] are not the kind of people to do business with. They are making money off of us. Apartheid is good business for Coke" (Moses and Vest 2010, 236; Moses cites Pendergast [2000], who provided the quote). However, because of Coca-Cola's persistence in working closely with Mandela and the ANC, as well as Mandela's concern about the economy, the president appeared to have eventually changed his mind (Spivey 2009). As we will soon see, this set the tone for a close and enduring political relationship between the central government and Coca-Cola, which in turn facilitated the company's ability to influence policy.

Following the reopening of South Africa's economy to foreign and domestic investment, the production and distribution of junk foods proliferated. There are now a host of convenience stores, such as Woolworths Foods (dominating the convenience store market), Shoprite, Pick n Pay, and Forecourt, throughout the nation (Euromonitor International 2020b). Moreover, Pick n Pay and Shoprite's smaller U-Save stores are now highly prevalent in poorer areas (Euromonitor International 2020b). Shoprite, considered by others to be the country's biggest food retailer, and smaller mom-and-pop stores, also known as spaza shops, have also found their way to townships and rural areas and are viewed as important growth areas for these retailers (Ntloedibe 2017). Some of these chains have partnered with local gas stations, such as Pick n Pay and Spar (Briggs 2019). In addition, the number of large retail food stores, such as Shoprite, followed by Pick n Pay, Massmart (which was purchased by Walmart in 2011), Spar, Woolworths, Fruit & Vegie City, and Choppies, has also increased (Ntloedibe 2017). Furthermore, multilateral fast food chains have also burgeoned, with Kentucky Fried Chicken

(KFC) being the most profitable chain in 2017, followed by McDonald's, Wimpy Burger, and Debonairs (Andersen 2018). With respect to sales, in 2018, major fast food restaurants made an estimated R597 billion (Andersen 2018).

The ultraprocessed and packaged foods industry has also grown. The sales of these packaged food products in South Africa are dominated by the following companies, in ranking order (by percentage of contributions to total sales for this industry in 2009): Tiger Brands Ltd (17.2 percent), Unilever Group (4.9 percent), Parmalat Group (4.8 percent), Nestlé SA (4.6 percent), Clover (4.6 percent), DairyBelle (4 percent), Pioneer Food Group Ltd (3.7 percent), Cadbury (2.8 percent), AVI (2.8 percent), and PepsiCo (2.4 percent) (Igumbor et al. 2012, 3). According to Igumbor and colleagues, "The largest ten packaged food companies in South Africa account for 51.8% of total packaged food sales" (2).

With respect to the soda industry, Coca-Cola has become the market leader in South Africa (Igumbor et al. 2012; Soft Drink, n.d.). In 2010, Coca-Cola garnered 49.8 percent of the market, with PepsiCo at 5.5 percent, Tiger Brands at 9.4 percent, and the remaining other brands at a combined 35.3 percent (Statista 2011). Due to a merger that took place in 2014 between SABMiller, Coca-Cola, and the locally owned Coca-Cola SABCO, Coca-Cola now has the largest Coca-Cola bottling company on the African continent, known as Coca-Cola Beverages Africa. Through Coca-Cola Beverages Africa, Coca-Cola distributes its product throughout the continent, with South Africa being the company's largest market (Dludla 2016). Coca-Cola products can also be found in rural areas in small spaza shops (Taylor and Jacobson 2016). Other soda brands, such as Appletiser, Coo-ee, Fer Brew, Jive, Refreshhh, Soda King, Sparletta, and Twizza, are present (Soft Drinks, n.d.), as well as energy drinks, such as MoFaya, which is locally owned and "lauded as the first and only 100% Black-owned beverage brand in South Africa" (Gundan 2015, 1). The soft drink industry has also been highly profitable in recent years. Analysts note that this industry's revenue totaled "$3.3 billion in 2012, representing a compound annual growth rate (CAGR) of 5% from 2008 and 2012" (Soft Drink, n.d., 1).

Over the years, the junk food sector has become increasingly important to the South African economy. Recent analysis also shows that the total size of the country's food and beverage sector was approximately 46.7 billion euros in 2018 (InterGest South Africa 2020). E-commerce in this sector is also developing quickly, with an estimated market value of 84.89 million euros in

2020 (InterGest South Africa 2020). In this context, the junk food industry's economic, and thus political, importance appears to be substantial.

Rise of NCDs in Vulnerable Populations

For several years now, NCDs in South Africa have been attributed to various factors, including increased urbanization, increased disposal income, sedentary lifestyles, unhealthy diets, excessive consumption of alcohol, and tobacco use (Baleta and Mitchell 2014). Obesity and type 2 diabetes in South Africa have been associated with the consumption of foods high in sugar, saturated fat, and calories, a turn to Western-based diets (Kruger et al. 2005; Ronquest-Ross et al. 2015; Stacey et al. 2017b). "South Africans are listed among the top 10 consumers of sugary drinks in the world" (Healthy Living Alliance 2019, 1). Igumbor and colleagues (2012) also found that the consumption of snack foods, street foods, and sodas has increased. For example, they discovered that compared to a global per capita consumption average of 89 Coca-Cola products each year, in South Africa, the per capita yearly consumption average was 254 in 2010 (1). Even more disturbing is Igumbor and others' (2012) claim that "carbonated drinks are now the third most commonly consumed food/drink item among very young urban South African children (aged 12–24 months)—less than maize meal and brewed tea, but more than milk" (1).

In addition to consuming junk food, rising obesity levels have continued due to various cultural factors. For many, being overweight is associated with happiness and prosperity (Mvo et al. 1999; Puoane et al. 2002), while, conversely, being thin, for some, is linked with being sick and even having a life-threatening disease, such as HIV/AIDS (Birrell 2014; Bizcommunity 2017). After interviewing 25,500 individuals in 2013, the Human Sciences Research Council found that 90 percent believed that being fat was "the preferred body type" (Motsoeneng 2014, 1). By 2000, research conducted by Pheiffer and colleagues (2018) explains that an estimated 87 percent of South Africans had type 2 diabetes and that this was attributed to being overweight (see also Rheeder 2019). According to Motsoeneng (2014), some medical doctors believe that NCDs will "soon overtake HIV and tuberculosis as the country's biggest killers" (1). Indeed, analysts note that diabetes has now become the second major cause of death after tuberculosis (Vital Strategies 2019a).

In recent years, prevalence rates of obesity and type 2 diabetes have in-

South Africa: prevalence (%) of obesity among adults. *Source*: WHO, 2021. https://www.who.int/data/gho/data/indicators/indicator-details/GHO/preva lence-of-obesity-among-adults-bmi-=-30-(crude-estimate)-(-)

creased throughout the country. South Africa currently leads sub-Saharan Africa in having the highest levels of overweight or obesity (Rheeder 2019). By the late 1990s, an analysis of the 1998 South African Demographic and Health Survey revealed that approximately 56.6 percent of women and 29.2 percent of men were either overweight or obese (Puoane et al. 2002). In the general adult population, obesity rates increased from 15.7 percent of the population in 1992 to 28.3 percent of the population in 2016 (WHO 2020b). Most cases of overweight and obesity have emerged in urban areas (Puoane et al. 2002). Several studies also indicate that women have reported a higher prevalence of overweight and obesity when compared to men (Baleta and Mitchell 2014; Temple et al. 2001).

The number of type 2 diabetes cases has also increased. In as early as 2012, findings from the Human Science Research Council and the South African Health and Nutrition Examination Survey revealed that 5 percent of adults, out of a sample size greater than twenty-five thousand, reported themselves as having diabetes, and that for those older than 55, 16 percent reported having the disease (Baleta and Mitchell 2014, 687). More recent studies have found that diabetes affects 4.5 million adults in South Africa, and that this was more than double the number of adult diabetic cases esti-mated in 2017, findings that were provided by a report released by the Inter-national Diabetes Federation in 2019 (Kahn 2019). According to Kahn (2019):

South Africa: prevalence (%) of adult diabetes. *Source*: WHO, 2021. https://www
.who.int/data/gho/data/indicators/indicator-details/GHO/raised-fasting
-blood-glucose-(-=7-0-mmol-l-or-on-medication)(age-standardized-estimate)

"It means that SA now has the highest proportion of adult diabetics on the
continent, and the greatest number of deaths due to the disease" (1).

South Africa has also seen an increased number of cases of obesity and
type 2 diabetes among its most vulnerable populations: children and the
poor. According to Jewell (2020), South Africa now leads the regions of East
and Southern Africa with respect to overall levels of childhood obesity, while
the UN Children's Fund claims that South Africa now has the highest rate
of childhood obesity in the world (Persens 2018). Recently, while giving a
speech at the 2019 Child Health Priorities Conference at North West University in South Africa, Dr. Tshepo Motsepe, the First Lady of South Africa,
voiced her concerned that, "by some estimates, by 2025, 3.61 million schoolchildren in South Africa will be clinically obese—a daunting prospect by any
measure" (quoted in SAnews 2019, 1).

In South Africa, childhood obesity is the product of several factors, including heightened consumption of sugary drinks and junk food and sedentary lifestyles as a result of increased TV viewing and internet usage (Feeley
and Norris 2014; Monyeki et al. 2015; Otitoola et al. 2020; Rossouw et al.
2012). This is further complicated by the youth's growing interest in dining out at fast food restaurants, with some 82 percent enjoying the activity
(BusinessTech 2019). But culture also matters, and there appears to be a belief in South Africa that overweight infants are healthy and full of nutrition

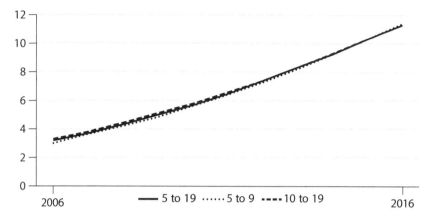

South Africa: prevalence (%) of childhood obesity (ages 5–19). *Source*: WHO, 2021. https://www.who.int/data/gho/data/indicators/indicator-details/GHO /prevalence-of-obesity-among-children-and-adolescents-bmi-2-standard -deviations-above-the-median-(crude-estimate)-(-)

and happiness, so "mothers therefore indulge in overfeeding—often with energy-rich foods" (Rossouw et al. 2012, 2).

Goedecke and Jennings (2005) report that as early as 1998, the South Africa Demographic and Health Survey of thirteen thousand individuals found that obesity was already prevalent among 10 percent of women between 15 and 24 years of age. In 1999, according to research conducted by Pienaar and Kruger (2014), a National Food Consumption Survey found that for children between the ages of 1 and 8, 3.7 percent were obese and 6.7 percent were overweight. According to Otitoola and others (2020), in 2013, the South African National Health and Nutrition Examination Survey reported that 13.5 percent of children between the ages of 6 and 14 were overweight and obese (combined) and that this was higher than the international average of 10 percent for school-age children. In light of these findings, the South African National Health and Nutrition Examination Survey emphasized an urgent need to address this situation, as well as the ongoing challenge of malnutrition (Mchiza and Maunder 2013). By 2016, NGO Pulse (2016) indicated that the Heart and Stroke Foundation of South Africa reported a national survey indicating that approximately 14.2 percent of schoolchildren in primary schools were overweight. Other studies found that the increase in overweight and obese children was also accompanied by a reduction in stunting (Monyeki et al. 2015). Other studies note that approximately 13 percent of children younger than 5 are obese (Chothia 2019; Thebus 2019). Studies further note that on average, girls, especially at the adolescent age, both in urban and rural areas, tend to have a higher prevalence of overweight and obesity (Grobbelaar et al. 2013; Monyeki et al. 2015; Otitoola et al. 2020; Rossouw et al. 2012). Finally, research revealed that the bulk of overweight and obesity cases are among children living in urban areas and that underweight cases are more prevalent in rural areas (Kruger et al. 2005; Monyeki et al. 2015; Pienaar and Kruger 2014); however, more recent studies reveal an ongoing increase in child and adolescent obesity in poorer rural areas (Craig et al. 2016; Kimani-Murage et al. 2011; TimesLIVE 2019) and that this is occurring along with a decline in stunting (Otitoola et al. 2020).

Even more startling, though, is the fact that type 2 diabetes is now occurring among younger populations in South Africa. According to Professor Andre Kengne of Tygerberg Hospital in South Africa: "This used to be an adult condition and now it is not uncommon to see it in 15-year-olds. If we are only targeting adults, we will miss it" (quoted in Keeton 2017, 1).

Obesity and type 2 diabetes are also increasing among the poor. As Kruger and colleagues (2005) maintain, the poor in urban South Africa have experienced both over- and underweight nutritional challenges. As observers note, a major problem is the arrival of cheap, easily accessible processed foods, steeped in sugar and fat, in rural areas (Chothia 2019). Cois and Day (2015) find that rural areas are catching up to urban areas in the number of obese cases. This is due to the arrival of the urban lifestyle, that is, the increased consumption of processed foods and sedentary lifestyles (Cois and Day 2015). And in urban areas, because healthier food options are more expensive, those without a sufficient amount of money tend to consume more processed food products (Park 2010). According to Park (2010), in South Africa's urban food deserts, access to fresh fruit and vegetables has been challenging, as these products often require traveling to purchase them in grocery stores.

But how has the national government responded to this situation? Has the government implemented effective national prevention and, more importantly, regulatory policies that challenge the influence of junk food industries?

Policy Response

South Africa's national government was slow to respond to these challenging NCD circumstances. While several national programs have addressed malnutrition and its double burden since the transition to democracy in 1994, NCD-specific programs on obesity and type 2 diabetes took longer to develop.

In 2011, in a move that signaled the government's commitment to NCD prevention, the Declaration on the Prevention and Control of NCDs was established at the Summit on the Prevention and Control of Non-Communicable Diseases (Delobelle et al. 2016). The goal through this endeavor was to introduce targets focused on reducing tobacco use, salt intake, and alcohol consumption while advocating for increased physical exercise to help people lose weight and avoid diabetes, asthma, and high blood pressure (Delobelle et al. 2016). In recent years, the government took earnest efforts to address NCDs through the DoH's Strategic Plan for NCDs (2013–2017) (Delobelle et al. 2016). In general, this plan was focused on creating policy interventions to reduce NCDs, which included interventions focused on improving diets (Spires et al. 2016). Furthermore, Spires and colleagues note that this plan increased the need to create legislation that improved South Africa's overall food environment: policy ideas such as a potential tax on unprocessed foods, regulations to reduce salt content and trans fat in food, and even regulations to prohibit the advertising of junk food to children.

With respect to nutrition-related NCDs, additional preventive measures were taken when in 2004, the DoH established national food-based dietary guidelines (Goedecke et al. 2006). Later that year, in November, the DoH, through its Directorate of Health Promotions, "launched an inter-sectoral strategy aimed at the Promotion of Healthy Lifestyles and change from risky behaviour, particularly among the youth" (73). Other broader prevention programs, such as the Move for Your Health program and the Vuka-South Africa program (initiated through a partnership between the government and the education sector), encouraged people to increase daily physical exercise in order to sustain a healthy weight (Goedecke et al. 2006).

In 2015, the DoH also created the Strategy for the Prevention and Control of Obesity in South Africa (Claasen et al. 2016). This initiative focused on addressing the obesogenic environment, with an emphasis not only on improving nutrition but also exercise; it also established a goal of reducing obesity by 10 percent by 2020 (Claasen et al. 2016). Importantly, the plan further addresses the broader factors that contribute to obesity, such as the environment, policy, and context (in line with a population-based approach) rather than stressing individual responsibility and behavioral change (Claasen et al. 2016). As Claasen and colleagues (2016) outline, this program entails six overall objectives, which include: (1) an improved and enabling environment; (2) more physical exercise; (3) improved community education, awareness, and collective action; (4) avoidance of childhood obesity; (5) improved monitoring and evaluation of the obesity situation; and (6) intersectoral policy engagement. In addition, this plan introduced the idea of a tax on SSBs (15). Furthermore, the DoH's Strategy for the Prevention and Control of Obesity in South Africa gave special attention to childhood obesity (NGO Pulse 2016).

In regard to children's health, as early as 1994, the DoH began to address children's nutritional challenges through the Primary School Nutrition Program (Monyeki et al. 2015). The idea was simple: provide better nutritional education and dietary guidelines for children in order to avoid malnutrition. The program was also focused on kids from low-income households and considered to be a school feeding program. According to Monyeki and colleagues (2015), it "benefited approximately 5 million children" from 1994 to 2002 (1169). This program was later renamed the National School Nutrition Programme and implementation responsibilities fell under the Department of Education in 2004. The program provides free school meals to children in low-income areas (Nortje et al. 2017). Additionally, in 2012, the DoH and the Department of Education created the Integrated School Health Policy (Nortje et al. 2017). This policy provides a framework that focuses on improving the overall health and food environment within schools (Nortje et al. 2017; see also Molelekwa 2018).

While impressive, the government's overall response to NCDs continues to exhibit several shortcomings. While the DoH paid increased attention to type 2 diabetes, it still does not have its own budget, falling instead under the general NCD budget (Ruder 2016). In addition, Spires and colleagues (2016) note that there is also an inherent contradiction in the government's response to NCDs and lack of intersectoral coordination between the departments for national initiatives. With respect to Spires and colleagues' (2016) highlighted contradiction, they claim that, on the one hand, the government is seeking to implement NCD policies while, on the other hand, it is permitting the increased inflow of FDI from fast food companies, in turn "giving free rein to fast food companies like McDonalds [sic] and Burger King" (38).

But when it comes to safeguarding South Africa's most vulnerable populations from junk food products, which kinds of regulatory policies have been pursued?

Advertising

Let us first consider the advertising of junk food products. To date, the South African government has never enacted federal regulations in this policy area, especially toward children (Claasen et al. 2016; Cassim 2010; Hawkes 2004). Instead, there have only been suggested "plans" and "ideas" to consider this legislation.

For example, the aforementioned 2013 Strategic Plan for NCDs (2013–2017) considered regulations that would not allow industries to market their food on popular children's TV channels (Spires et al. 2016). The closest the government came to proposing this kind of regulation came in 2007, when it "included restrictions on food advertising to children under 16 years old in a draft Foodstuffs, Cosmetics & Disinfectants Act" (Igumbor et al. 2012, 5)—namely Regulation R 642, on the Labelling and Advertisements of Foodstuffs, Section 15(1) (Cassim 2010, 184). This regulation, according to Igumbor and others (2012), would have also prohibited the promotion or marketing of "nonessential" foods, such as sodas, fast food, and potato chips, "in any manner" (5). This regulation would have also stopped the use of any cartoons or gifts in advertisements to children (Igumbor et al. 2012). And yet, this regulation was merely a "draft" for public comment for three months, published in the *Government Gazette* (Cassim 2010; Mills 2016). The Department of Health put the idea "on hold" due to the "much heated debate in view of the many severe restrictions that they contained and their potential far-reaching effects" (Igumbor et al. 2012, 6, quoting Smit and Thompson 2010). The DoH decided to wait until the WHO weighed in on the matter in its 2010 *Set of Recommendations on Marketing Food and Non-Alcoholic Beverages to Children* (Igumbor et al. 2012; see also Cassim 2010). Unfortunately, even after the WHO's publication, it appears that no further action was taken by the DoH shortly thereafter (Igumbor et al. 2012). As Cassim and Bexiga (2007) maintain, however, there is an existing code, namely the Code of Advertising Practice, that "contains a general prohibition against misleading, offensive and untruthful advertising and makes specific reference to children within the Code regarding specific issues" (152). Nevertheless, Cassim and Bexiga also state that there is "no specific code for the regulation of advertising to children" (151).

In May 2014, yet another attempt was made to introduce regulations on the advertisement of junk food to children. Regulation R 429 was published in the *Government Gazette*, in an attempt to obtain comments on the proposed legislation (Koen et al. 2016). R 429 stated that "unhealthy food may not be marketed to schoolchildren from grade 0–12, while child actors aged < 18 years, using celebrities or sports stars, cartoon characters, puppets, or any form of computer animation, and the use of competitions, gifts or collectable items, may also not be used to market unhealthy foods to children" (19). Analysts also note that this proposed regulation was also going to enforce restrictions on where junk food products could be advertised, for instance, at sports activities and in schools (Lexology 2016). This proposal also included a ban on the advertising of such products on TV between the times of 6 a.m. and 9 p.m. (Lexology 2016). But, yet again, no legislation was pursued.

Instead, the government appears to have encouraged industry self-regulation. In fact, in the aforementioned 2015 Strategy for the Prevention and Control of Obesity in South Africa, the government made it a goal to ensure that food industries are creating and adhering to a pledge and code of conduct with respect to advertising (Claasen et al. 2016).

Similar to what we saw in Brazil, India, and China, South Africa's industries have instead agreed to formal codes of conduct when marketing to children. In 2009, the Consumer Goods Council of South Africa created the South African Marketing to Children pledge (Claasen et al. 2016; see also Igumbor et al. 2012). Approximately twenty-four companies signed this pledge, promising to refrain from advertising their products to children, mainly those younger than 12, on TV as well as in and near schools (Claasen et al. 2016).

The absence of formal legal regulations on the marketing of junk food to children has prompted calls for a new public awareness campaign emphasizing this regulatory effort (Thebus 2019). And for good reason: McHiza and Maunder (2013) found that on South Africa's major TV broadcasting channels 1 and 2, "the advertising of food of poor nutritional value to children is prominent. Less than 50% of advertisements concentrate on healthy food" (102). According to Claasen and others 2016), some of the top junk food advertisers have been Unilever, ranked first overall, followed by Coca-Cola in the seventeenth spot and Tiger Brand in the twentieth spot (9). Work by Igumbor and colleagues (2012) also highlights a study conducted in 2006 that noted that 16 percent of advertisements were committed to food during 37.5 hours of children's TV viewing; moreover, roughly "55% of these food-related advertisements were for foods of poor nutritional value such as re-fined breakfast cereals, sweets, and high-sugar drinks" (5). Igumbor and others (2012) also underscore a more recent study conducted by academics at the University of Western Cape in 2012 that revealed "eight food adver-tisements [appeared] in 7 hours of children's TV programming," and that, worse still, this advertising was found on the national television channel SABC1 (5). Beyond TV marketing, Bahuguna (2016) discusses a report, pub-lished by the Center for Science in the Public Interest, that found that soda industries such as Coca-Cola have advertised their products at the entrance of schools. Research by Tugendhaft and Hofman (2015) also cites a study by Moodley and colleagues (2015) that found that in the Soweto province, half of all billboards focused on selling SSBs were strategically located near schools, with easy access to these products at local vendors. As Goldstein (2016) maintains: "These campaigns run despite South Africa's voluntary marketing pledge under which the food and beverage industry has promised not to advertise unhealthy products to children under the age of 12" (4). In this context, international agency officials note that the government needs to, and can, regulate industry advertising toward children (Persens 2018). Indeed, according to Alison Feeley of UNICEF (United Nations Children's Fund): "There are various things government can do about restricting the marketing of these processed foods to children, they can look at restrict-ing certain advertising on TV or other media channels" (quoted in Persens 2018, 1). Furthermore, Ruder (2016) has argued that ongoing advertising by major food and beverage industries is contributing to South Africa's type 2 diabetes epidemic.

Claasen and colleagues (2016) found that despite industries' commitment to the 2009 self-regulatory South Africa Pledge, to this day, no monitoring and enforcement mechanisms exist. "The pledge focuses only advertising on television and in schools to children less than 12 years old, but no specific commitments or monitoring of the pledge are in place" (9). Claasen and col-leagues (2016) mention research by Steyn and others (2014) suggesting that the South African Broadcast Corporation take the extra step of creating a "pre-screening committee," staffed by nominees from the Department of Nutrition, to monitor advertisers and "to ensure advertising [meets] the required criteria" (9).

Sales

But how about policy regulations limiting the sale of junk food products to children and the poor? For now, it appears as if no federal or state policy regulations exist that prohibit the sale of these products in or around schools, nor do any regulations appear to exist specifying the types of foods that can be sold in schools. In this context, experts have demanded a ban on fizzy drinks and junk foods sold near schools, while some university professors have also publicly acknowledged their support for such a ban (Govender et al. 2018). According to Steve Mabona, a spokesperson from the Gauteng Department of Education, his department "has published tuck shop guidelines to assist schools in ensuring that healthy foods are sold within the school premises" (quoted in Molelekwa 2018, 1). But these guidelines are the closest the government has come to addressing this issue. Analysts nevertheless find that these types of guidelines are challenged by the absence of adequate facilities, that children still prefer unhealthy options, and that these options are also much cheaper (Nortje et al. 2017).

Not only has the sale of junk food to schoolchildren increased, but it has also led to unethical practices by some schools. Nortje and colleagues (2017) mention a study conducted by De Villiers and others (2012) that claims that "in more than 60% of surveyed schools in the Western Cape, the school name was displayed on a branded food or beverage advertisement board" (77). Nevertheless, findings of De Villiers and colleagues reveal that principals from these schools claim that they have not benefited financially from this activity.

In this context, demands for regulating the sale of these foods in schools—particularly at tuck shops—have only increased, and students have planned to take action on their own (Govender 2019). In the Gauteng province, several pupils went as far as a proposed one-month boycott of purchasing carbonated drinks in their schools, an endeavor that was supported by NGOs (Govender 2019). On the other hand, some schools, such as in Vhembe-Mutale, have taken action on their own, banning the sale of sugary drinks entirely (Lisa 2017).

Research by Monyeki and colleagues (2015) finds that, in general, government policies toward childhood obesity are not very effective. They further note that there is an ongoing need for programs focused on improving school feeding programs and physical education. Moreover, Nortje and others (2017) discovered that unhealthy foods continue to be found and sold in and around schools—and even in school vending machines (Govender et al. 2018). This finding complements Pienaar and Kruger's (2014) discussion that children continue to purchase unhealthy foods from tuck shops, and that they are provided money from parents to do so. Findings by Govender and colleagues (2018) also confirm that schoolchildren are still purchasing food at tuck shops. Monyeki and others (2015) discovered that there were several problems with implementing the aforementioned National School Nutrition Programme, such as poor allocation of resources and neglecting to ensure that schools adequately adopted the program's dietary guidelines. Claasen and others (2016) also cited Faber and colleagues' (2014) survey findings that stated, in general, the quality of food served in school is still low, especially with respect to fresh fruit and vegetables provided by the National School Nutrition Programme.

Labeling

In South Africa, all food labels have been regulated by the 1972 Foodstuffs, Cosmetics and Disinfectants Act, Regulation 146 (Claasen et al. 2016). Surprisingly, however, Claasen and colleagues (2016) claim that "nutrition labelling remains voluntary but regulations require a standard format if nutrition labels are used" (25). In 2014, Regulation 429 was introduced to officially mandate the use of nutrition labels and to regulate the health claims made on product labels (Bursey et al. 2019; Koen et al. 2016). But as Koen and others (2016) claim, these were regulations published in the *Government Gazette* for comments. To this date, labels are not mandatory for food manufacturers.

In 2010, further amendments were made to the R146 of the 1972 Foodstuffs, Cosmetics and Disinfectants Act—namely, the Regulations Related to the Labelling and Advertising of Foodstuffs. Taking effect on March 1, 2012, this regulation maintains that the reporting of nutritional content on labels is "voluntary" unless the product makes nutritious claims. This regulation also prohibits the use of deceptive phrases such as "fat-free" and "balanced nutrition" while only permitting the following terms: "a source of," "high in," "low in," and "free of," as long as specific criteria are being met by the manufacturers (Igumbor et al. 2012). Additionally, this amendment required that the labels adopt a standard format and that these labels include information on serving sizes (Igumbor et al. 2012; Koen et al. 2016). Finally, unlike what we have seen in Mexico, in South Africa, guideline daily amount labels (listing the amount of specific nutrients and daily recommended allowance) appear to be provided on a voluntary basis (Igumbor et al. 2012). Interestingly, it has been the biggest food industries—namely, Coca-Cola, Spar, and Tiger Brands—that have volunteered to provide this information (Igumbor et al. 2012).

There are currently no federal regulations mandating the reporting of high sugar content on labels (Stacey et al. 2017). According to Stacey and colleagues (2017), in 2014, the National Department of Health did draft regulations and guidelines introducing a three-colored traffic light system for labeling products with high, medium, and low levels of sugar, fat, sodium, and energy content, but this has yet to be established.

In 2019, the national department of health claimed that it would impose regulations requiring front-of-package warning labels in the near future. These labels will require that producers display information on the sugar, fat, and salt content of their products (Mbhele 2019; Zama 2019). This proposal mainly emerged due to reports that consumers were having difficulty understanding labels (Zali 2019). However, there will be no required specification on the amount of each ingredient (e.g., fat and salt) present (Zama 2019). In 2019, the DoH stated that it was investigating the type of label that would be most effective for the consumer (Zali 2019). Indeed, according to Lynn Moeng, the DoH's chief director of nutrition: "The department started a process of researching what would work best for the South African consumer. We are still in that process . . . and a research organization is [looking into] what consumers will understand best. When that is done, we can start the process of regulating how food products should be labelled specifically in front" (quoted in Zali 2019, 1). To this day, however, no final label has been approved, and no mandate has been enforced. It appears that the department is still conducting research.

The overall quality and effectiveness of existing food labels is still lacking. Claasen and colleagues (2016) refer to survey research conducted by Jacobs and others (2011) in the North West province of South Africa that shows that consumers still have difficulty using food labels because of inadequate information provided, small font sizes, and confusing terms about listed ingredients (on this issue, see also Zama 2019). In an interview for a radio show, the DoH's Lynn Moeng-Mahlangu stated that "the current labels are very small and not user-friendly for consumers. They are often written in small letters at the back of the pack and the consumer has to read all those small details" (quoted in Zama 2019, 1). Koen and colleagues (2016) have argued that there has been a need, since the 1990s, for more updated food label policies that are aligned with international scientific research and standards.

Soda Tax

As we saw in the other emerging economies discussed in this book, introducing taxes on SSBs has been an arduous political task. Though being the first country in the African continent to take on this bold endeavor (Chutel 2019), South Africa faced a similar uphill battle. In fact, the idea of introducing a tax on mineral water and sodas emerged and was adopted but ultimately was rescinded by 2002 (Hofman et al. n.d.). It was not until several years later that the government reconsidered the issue (Motsoeneng 2014; Stacey et al. 2019). As noted earlier, the tax was introduced as part of the 2015 National Strategy for Prevention and Control of Obesity (Stacey et al. 2019). For the most part, this tax was sold on its fiscal and public health benefits: the tax not only contributed to the government's tax revenue, but the revenues were also supposed to be used to help defray the price of healthier foods (Stacey et al. 2019).

Following the National Strategy, the idea of a tax was introduced yet again in a national budget speech provided by finance minister Pravin Gordhan in February 2016 (Wilkinson and Bhardwaj 2016). The initial goal was to introduce a 20 percent tax on soda (Cullinan 2017). The idea was to use this tax to incentivize a reduction in SSB consumption and encourage manufacturers to alter the sugar content of their products (Stacey et al. 2019). In the summer and fall of 2016, the idea was introduced within the parliament and National Treasury for public commentary, though the Treasury ultimately delayed adopting the tax, which led to further parliamentary hearings and discussion in 2017 (Hofman et al. n.d.). The 20 percent tax was also introduced based on the idea, informed by academic researchers, that it would contribute a nice portion to the federal revenue purse, providing an estimated yearly R7 billion, while helping reduce the prevalence of obesity (Spires et al. 2016).

After several rounds of negotiation that spanned over a year (Cullinan 2017; Stacey et al. 2019), a tax was due to be implemented on April 1, 2017 (Spires et al. 2016). However, there appeared to be a yearlong delay, and the tax was not implemented until April 2018, introduced via the 2017/2018 Rates and Monetary Amounts Bill (Stacey et al. 2019). Titled the Health Promotion Levy, it agreed to exempt "the first 4 g of sugar per 100 ml from taxation, and taxed each gram over the 4 g threshold at 0.021 ZAR" (2). However, Stacey and colleagues (2019) claim that this adjustment equated to approximately a 10–11 percent tax on the price of popular sodas, lower than the initial 20 percent tax on its price. Analysts claim that the tax provided an additional US$202 million for the National Treasury in its first year (Vital Strategies 2019a). Furthermore, in what appeared to be an adjustment for inflation, in February 2019, the National Treasury decided to increase the existing tax by 5 percent. Several products are subject to this tax, such as sodas, sports drinks, energy drinks, fruit drinks, and teas (Sikuka 2019).

Still, there are several limitations with the soda tax. Activists claim that the tax is simply not enough. According to Tracey Malawana of the Healthy Living Alliance (HEALA), "While the tax is a victory for public health, it is around 11% on a can and we would like it to be strengthened to 20% to really deter people" (quoted in Cullinan 2017, 1).

Thus, in sum, it appears that South Africa's government has not been successful in introducing regulations meant to curb the junk food industry's ability to market and sell their products, especially to vulnerable populations. While a soda tax has been adopted, it, too, has been seemingly insufficient in achieving its goals. But why have we seen these ongoing challenges? Why, after the government's recent commitment to introducing impressive national NCD programs, do we see industry regulation taking a back seat? Once again, politics matters.

Political Action

As I emphasize in IPCI, junk food industries in the emerging economies have adopted a variety of strategies to influence NCD policies in their favor. Industry political interference has surfaced through processes such as engaging in policy partnerships with government, lobbying and largesse, institutional infiltration, and CSR tactics. While junk food industries and their representatives varied in their strategies and influence in each of the countries discussed in this book, they facilitated industry's ability to discourage government from pursuing regulatory policies that would threaten corporate sector interests. And yet, industries were only partly to blame. Much of their success rested on the presence of complementary institutions: that is, presidents committed to partnering with industry in order to achieve alternative policy and, thus, political objectives.

Policy Partnerships and Its Limits

As I explain in IPCI, one of the strategies that industries take to influence NCD policy is engaging in policy partnerships with government. The main objective of these efforts is to convince the government that industries are committed to working with them. This will result in businesses being perceived as a vital 'solution to the problem' while cultivating political allies and support.

South Africa's private business sector, among other stakeholders in society, also appears to have been involved in partnering with the government to formulate policy. According to Ndinda and Hongoro (2017), for example, in South Africa, businesses were involved in government programs focused on sports. As the authors go on to explain, "Subsequent approaches to sports policy and programme formulation were more inclusive and reached out to stakeholders beyond the competitive sport fraternity. Stakeholders include the health sector, NGOs, and business" (60).

In the area of obesity prevention, Coca-Cola South Africa has also entered into a partnership with the DoH. As Zipporah Maubane, former communications director for Coca-Cola, once put it: "Coca-Cola, along with other players in the beverage industry, is committed to working with the government to find effective solutions that address the obesity challenge in South Africa, taking health and economic needs fully into account" (quoted in Ismail 2016a, 1). Coca-Cola also partnered with the government through industry's Healthy Food Options Forum. Through this forum, Coca-Cola and other companies work with government on potential policy solutions in response to obesity (*Mail & Guardian* 2016).

As we saw in China and Mexico, an important focus for these industries has been partnering with government to encourage physical exercise as a strategy for leading healthy lives. For example, Coca-Cola partnered with the Department of Sport and Recreation to host the Big Walk initiative, which encourages individuals to join outdoor walking campaigns (*Mail & Guardian* 2016). As Vukani Magubane, director of communications and public affairs for Coca-Cola South Africa once commented: "Together with Coca-Cola Beverages South Africa and Coca-Cola Peninsula Beverages, we also support non-mainstream, family-oriented, active, healthy living programmes. We support the Big Walk, which we host in partnership with the department of sport and recreation. It attracted over 16,000 participants in Pretoria last year and will be led by Minister of Sport and Recreation Fikile Mbalula again this year on October 2" (quoted in *Mail & Guardian* 2016, 1). Magubane was quoted in another article as stating that "Coca-Cola, along with other players in the beverage industry, is committed to working with the government to find effective solutions that address the obesity challenge in South Africa, taking health and economic needs fully into account" (quoted in Ismail 2016a, 1). Mpho Thothela, who is the Beverage Association of South Africa's (BEVSA) general manager for corporate services, also underscored industry's commitment to working with the government in promoting exercise and health education: "Not only did we reformulate products but [also] embarked on a number of different initiatives in partnership with the department of sports and recreation, such as the national recreation day and big walk, to drive increased education to all South Africans" (quoted in Holmes 2018, 1).

Other junk food industries established a partnership with government. Since 2013, Nestlé has worked with the Department of Basic Education and local primary schools to provide instructional education for students, such as learning from chefs about preparing healthy meals and running workshops for staff who provide school meals and for teachers, as part of the government's National Nutrition Week and other celebrations, such as the Mandela Day commemoration (Nestlé 2017). This program also provides free exercise programs for students, including Zumba. In 2018, Nestlé South Africa worked with the Department of Basic Education's National School Nutrition Programme to host seventeen hundred students from the Dr. Nhlapo Intermediate and the Phuthulla Primary Schools, which are both located in the township of Boipatong, in order to commemorate Mandela Day (Nestlé 2018a). Nestlé issued a press release on July 18, 2018, stating that this celebration was "under the auspices of the global Nestlé for Healthier Kids programme (N4HK) and the Department of Basic Education's (DBE) National School Nutrition Program" (1). Furthermore, and this is telling, according to Nestlé, the "N4HK was officially launched in May 2018 at the DBE" (1). Through the N4HK program, Nestlé South Africa has partnered with the

Department of Basic Education to "teach primary school children about the importance of healthy nutrition and physical activity as part of a balanced lifestyle" (1). N4HK also worked with the Department of Basic Education to provide healthier school meals, in an effort to provide nutritional education to students, an endeavor that comports with the national historic effort to improve the nutritious value of school meals, as mentioned earlier.

In the area of NCD prevention, these partnerships with government have helped to increase the legitimacy and influence of junk food industries (interview with anonymous source, August 29, 2020; interview with Nzama Lawrence Mbalati, HEALA South Africa, August 20, 2020; interview with Nicholas Stacey, PRICELESS South Africa, August 14, 2020). Industry's views have also been valued and respected (interview with anonymous source, August 29, 2020). Because of these partnerships with government, industries are viewed as genuine partners in striving to tackle NCDs. Industries are seen by politicians as providing goodwill for the people, offering food for children, and, in the end, helping save lives (interview with Nzama Lawrence Mbalati, HEALA South Africa, August 20, 2020). Worse still, because of these partnerships, health officials are reluctant to pursue more stringent regulations targeted at these industries (interview with Nzama Lawrence Mbalati, HEALA South Africa, August 20, 2020); others believe that there is only a risk of these regulations not being pursued (interview with Nicholas Stacey, PRICELESS South Africa, August 14, 2020). It seems that the government believes these industries are doing their part through these partnerships, and because of this, the government does not see the need to pursue further industry regulations.

With respect to other areas of food regulation, however, it appears as if the government may not have been as consultative and cooperative, especially in the eyes of industry. A good example was the regulations imposing compulsory limits on salt content in food products. In March 2013, the Regulations Relating to the Reduction of Sodium in Certain Foodstuffs and Related Matters, Reg No. 214, which is part of the Foodstuffs, Cosmetics and Disinfectants Act of 1972, was adopted into law and mandated these limitations on industry (Kaldor et al. 2018). However, Kaldor and colleagues (2018) claim that in a context of international consensus for policy action, such as the 2011 UN General Assembly meeting on NCDs, which generated a sense of urgency, information from academic nutrition scientists, and bureaucratic resolve, the Ministry of Health ultimately enacted this regulation without adequate consultation from industry, notwithstanding industry being initially involved in discussions with government officials about whether to pursue ardent government regulations or an industry self-regulatory approach. Some within government and civil society were of the view that industry had had adequate time to adjust their products, to self-regulate, in response to years of federal nutritional guidelines but had not yet taken action. In response to the Ministry of Health's decision, industry felt as if it had not been adequately consulted, and that the government's pursuit of a regulation was "predetermined" (Kaldor et al. 2018, 1320). As an industry individual that Kaldor and others interviewed commented: "One moment we're still brainstorming and the next moment, there's a regulation!" Another individual mentioned that "the Minister signed off the new regulations, in the middle of a consultative process!" (1320). Thus, unlike what we saw with the other aforementioned regulations on sweetened junk food products, when it came to an initiative that may not have been as politically sensitive (i.e., gaining considerable media attention), or perhaps one that did not pose as much of a financial strain on the junk food industry, the government appeared to be more autonomous and a bit more reluctant to engage in a consultative process that industry considered to be fair and adequate on their part. It is nevertheless still interesting to note that this industry was willing to work with the government on this policy issue.

Finally, one must also keep in mind that the government had imposed taxes and advertising regulations on the tobacco and alcohol sector several years prior (Myers et al. 2015). This similarly suggests that the government was unwilling to engage in policy partnerships on other products that were not aligned with the junk food industries' interests, and that the government was more concerned with the interests of the latter than with the alcohol and tobacco sector's interests.

Lobbying and Largesse

IPCI also highlights the importance of industry lobbying and largesse. These processes are often considered the bread and butter of industry politics and policy manipulation: they serve as both a direct and indirect means of influencing policy in industry's favor. As seen in several of the other countries discussed in this book, these processes were also present in South Africa and contributed to the delayed and watered-down effort to introduce a tax on SSB products.

The idea of introducing a tax on SSBs was initially met with staunch industry resistance. Due to intensive industry lobbying in opposition, the tax was delayed for several months beginning in 2016 (Holmes 2018). Coca-Cola, for example, questioned the idea, claiming that it was not the best and only solution (Ismail 2016a). As Zipporah Maubane, Coca-Cola's former communications director, once put it: "It is clear that there is no one 'silver bullet' to solving the obesity problem; it is a complex problem that requires collaboration across many different government departments and between the public and private sector" (quoted in Ismail 2016a, 1). Taxes are not very effective, particularly on an individual's body mass index, Maubane went on to claim, also stating that taxes should not be implemented simply because they are easy to pursue (Ismail 2016a). According to Maubane, there were other potential solutions that needed to be considered, "such as education campaigns, and Coca-Cola's commitment to reduce calories by double the amount the tax aims to achieve and to subject that reduction to independent verification" (1). Public education and even Coca-Cola's efforts to improve the quality of their products, such as reducing the amount of sugar, were also viable alternative solutions, argued Maubane (Ismail 2016a).

Major industries were apparently surprised with the soda tax proposal in 2017—mind you, industry coalitions had thwarted a tax attempt in the past. Indeed, according to Pfister (2016), Coca-Cola was taken by surprise and "quickly shifted it's astroturf [sic] 'responsible marketing' coalition into an anti-tax coalition" (1). Michael Goltzman, a representative from Coca-Cola, in a leaked email, stated that "the Coca-Cola Company has a seat at the table in on-going regulatory discussions with the Ministry of Health, which did not know of [the] tax the night prior to its introduction. With the announcement, the BU has *shifted industry coalition work on responsible marketing to engagement with this tax threat*, but details on the actual tax have not been published" (quoted in Pfister 2016, 1).

BEVSA, by far the largest lobbying group representing the SSB industry, also rallied hard against the tax. Its point of contention was focused on several issues. First, the tax focused too much on penalizing the content of sugar, claiming that this only represented roughly 3 percent of a South African's daily nutritional intake (Food Ingredients 1st 2017), and that because of this, the tax was discriminatory, as other food products contained just as many, if not more, calories (Beverage Association of South Africa 2016). Second, there was no concrete evidence from other countries that a soda tax would lead to a reduction in weight gain. Third, there would be enormous economic costs, mainly because of unemployment and reduced economic growth, and the competitiveness of the nonalcoholic beverages industry would be undermined (Beverage Association of South Africa 2016). Coca-Cola South Africa complained that the tax would equate to greater than one thousand lost workers (Chutel 2019). BEVSA asked the MoH to first engage in a serious process of research and negotiation with them and other parties, prior to agreeing to the tax being considered, and that the beverage industry could be seen as part of the policy solution to obesity (Food Ingredients 1st 2017; on the need for consultation, see also Beverage Association of South Africa 2016). In fact, Mapule Ncanywa, the executive director of BEVSA, commented:

> Surely such a win-win as a South African solution should be given an opportunity. To do this full consultation across unions, civil society, Government and business is required and more information and research would assist such deliberation, we urge the Government to pause legislative action until such research is available and such engagement and consultation processes have run their course . . . to be clear, obesity is a problem and we can be part of the measures toward addressing this problem, but singling out one beverage category and taxing it punitively does not make sense, especially as we are offering up an alternative solution that unions and civil society are discussing with us. (quoted in Food Ingredients 1st 2017, 1)

Furthermore, analysts point out that the industry had previously taken voluntary measures to reduce by 15 percent the number of calories that one consumes from SSB products, as well as introducing low-calorie foods and altering the size of its prepackaged products (Food Ingredients 1st 2017).

All of the lobbying efforts, bickering, and disagreements led to a delayed adoption of the tax as well as a watered-down version of it, as mentioned earlier. It took two years for it to be adopted, and when it was, the tax had been reduced from an initial 20 percent to 10 percent (Stacey et al. 2017).

In February 2019, a further increase in the soda tax was proposed. The Treasury Department called for an approximate 5 percent increase in the SSB tax due mainly, the agency claimed, to inflation. The soda industry resisted once again, claiming that the existing tax had already taken an economic toll; the sugar cane industry, for example, had seen a reduction in local sugar produced and sold (Sikuka 2019). But to date, it seems that this tax increase will still take place.

Part of the junk food lobbies' success also has to do with its greater access to resources and institutions compared to others. As Thow and colleagues (2018) maintain, industries have had a much larger budget to spend on lobbying activities and have had access to forums where they can voice their concerns, which has been particularly advantageous in the area of food supply policy. The converse situation has been seen among civil societal activists.

However, to my knowledge, industries in South Africa have not tried to engage in a process of institutional infiltration. That is, they have not established a physical presence, either directly or indirectly through NGOs (e.g., the International Life Sciences Institute, as seen in China), the DoH, or any other federal agency. The DoH and other agencies focusing on NCD policy appear to be autonomous from industry's direct presence and influence within their agencies.

Restructuring Society

Consistent with IPCI, engaging in CSR tactics is yet another strategy that industries have used in South Africa to curry favor with civil society. For example, Nestlé has been committed to simultaneously strengthening worker skills while improving the health of its workers. In South Africa, for example, Nestlé is not only providing job training but also HIV/AIDS testing, treatment services, and counseling (Nestlé 2005). At the same time, through its Nestlé Community Nutrition Awards, created in 1993, the company has recognized those who have contributed to reducing hunger and malnutrition and improving food security, particularly in poor rural areas (Nestlé, "Nestlé Community Nutrition Awards"). One focus is on gardening organic foods and establishing a gardening culture. Women's projects, particularly in rural areas and in "per-urban communities" and schools, have been targeted for this award (Nestlé, "Nestlé Community Nutrition Awards").

Coca-Cola has also participated in CSR activities. Interestingly, just days after the United Nations organized a National Conference on NCDs in New York, Myers and colleagues (2015) wrote that UN Women and Coca-Cola engaged in a public-private partnership agreement. In South Africa, this program entailed providing funding for women to start up small businesses.

Specifically, and as Myers and colleagues (2015) explain, this program "involve[s] providing business training, mentoring and capital to 'a total of 25,000 women entrepreneurs, many of whom are running small retail businesses [e.g., so-called "spaza shops"] within the Coca-Cola value Chain'" (11). This program not only empowers women but also serves to "improve its [industry's] public relations" (11). In addition, "the juxtaposition of the UN imprimatur and [the] Coca-Cola logo is a huge asset for the company in terms of promoting its brand, particularly in remote rural areas" (11). Coca-Cola has also sought to empower women entrepreneurs through its 5by20 initiative in South Africa (*Mail & Guardian* 2016). As Vukani Magubane, Coca-Cola South Africa's public affairs and communications director, once explained: "This initiative aims to help women entrepreneurs such as spaza shop owners to overcome the barriers they face to succeeding in business. One 5by20 partnership is with UN Women; in the programme we are addressing barriers facing women entrepreneurs by providing them with business skills training, mentoring, and peer networking skills" (quoted in *Mail & Guardian* 2016, 1).

As we saw in several other countries, Coca-Cola has also invested in environmental sustainability. In addition to committing to replenishing the same amount of water that it has used for production by 2020, it has invested in several water treatment plants throughout South Africa (*Mail & Guardian* 2016). The Atlanta company has also invested in programs that supply clean water to local communities, as seen with its Clean Water Supply Project in the Modderspruit Village, which is located in the North West province of South Africa (Buckley 2010, 63). Coca-Cola partnered with Water for All, a local NGO, to implement this program (Buckley 2010). In 2009, the Foundation also provided funding, through its RAIN Water for Schools project, to increase, by 2012, access to water and to improve sanitation as well as education on proper hygiene to students throughout South Africa (Coca-Cola Company 2011b).

And finally, with respect to health care, Coca-Cola has worked with South Africa's DoH to ensure increased access to health care services. Through its Project Last Mile initiative, Coca-Cola has built on its expertise in supply chain management and "worked with USAid and the South Africa Department of Health to revolutionize access to chronic medication and antiretroviral treatment for more than two-million [*sic*] people through the development of patient-friendly, alternative pick-up points" (Creamer Media's

Engineering News 2019, 1). According to the USAID (n.d.), South Africa's DoH realized that it would benefit from the private sector's expertise in the areas of planning businesses, providing logistics, and managing franchises (1). Moreover, the USAID claimed that "as these are all key strengths of the Coca-Cola System, Project Last Mile was engaged by USAID South Africa to adapt and integrate private sector business practices into CCMDD in 27 Presidents' Emergency Plan for AIDS Relief (PEPFAR) funded districts and six National health Insurance (NHI) priority districts" (1). The Central Chronic Medicines Dispensing and Distribution (CCMDD) program provides medical pickup points to facilitate access to lifesaving medicines, such as HIV medication (1). Throughout the African continent in general, Project Last Mile's intentions have been to provide "lifesaving medicines and health services available wherever and whenever needed" (Creamer Media's *Engineering News* 2019, 1). Interestingly, Project Last Mile was a partnership between Coca-Cola; the Coca-Cola Foundation; the Global Fund to Fight AIDS, Tuberculosis, and Malaria; the Bill and Melinda Gates Foundation, and USAID (1).

Coca-Cola South Africa also worked with the NGO 46664 to provide support for HIV/AIDS initiatives. For instance, through its Message in a Bottle campaign, Coca-Cola South Africa provided assistance by randomly distributing one million empty Coke bottles throughout the country with messages from Mandela inside of them. This endeavor was initiated during an outdoor campaign two weeks prior to 46664's World AIDS Day concert (Crossroads' Global Hand 2020). In response, Tim Massey, the international director of 46664, commented: "The Hello Campaign illustrates the power of partnerships between corporates and charities to realize a common goal—in this case to increase awareness about HIV/AIDS. Coca Cola's generous donation will be used to fund the 46664 outreach activities, while the TV commercial and the outdoor activation will ensure that the 46664 campaign remains highly visible, and that Mr. Mandela's appeal for help is heard by most South Africans" (quoted in Crossroads' Global Hand 2020, 1).

These CSR activities have served to increase these industries' social acceptability. Through these activities, it appears that these industries now have more support among local communities because they are widely perceived as giving back to the community and are committed to improving the population's health and well-being.

Creating a Divided Society

And yet, as I explain in IPCI, junk food industries' involvement in civil society has entailed serious ramifications with respect to the latter's ability to mobilize and resist industry's policy influence. This challenge arises when industries partner with strategic civil societal actors, such as academics or NGOs, which in turn offers few additional partners for civil societal activists, who sternly defend the public's interests, to work with and use to increase their voice and collective resistance to industry's policy activities. Conflicting views between these civil societal actors also emerge due to their differing policy positions, with those supporting industry's views staunchly resisting the views of activists and academics defending the public's health care interests and needs.

In South Africa, it seems that industry has also partnered with think tanks to bolster industry's policy position. For example, in 2016, when the soda tax was being discussed within government, Coca-Cola was accused of funding a research paper titled "A Stealth Tax, Not a Health Tax" at the African Institute for Race Relations (Cameron 2016; Ismail 2016b). This paper highlighted the economic impact that the tax would have as well as general doubts about its effectiveness in reducing obesity, ultimately suggesting that the tax be abandoned (Ismail 2016b).

Furthermore, industries' activities with NGOs have also hindered activists' ability to create a unifying voice and mobilize against the former's activities. A good example is the soda industry's relationship with an NGO in South Africa (interview with Nzama Lawrence Mbalati, August 20, 2020). This NGO is dedicated to eradicating hunger through the provision of foods to those in need. According to Mr. Nzama Lawrence Mbalati of HEALA, an NGO in South Africa, however, this NGO has been reluctant to work with HEALA because the former receives funding from the soft drink industry (interview with Nzama Lawrence Mbalati, August 20, 2020). Nzama has also had disagreements with this NGO's leadership over the provision of Coca-Cola products when providing free food. Moreover, Nzama was of the view that it seems as if industry is pitting NGOs against each other. This situation appears to have generated a sense of conflict between them, while hampering Nzama's ability to create a unifying voice and social movement in opposition to industry. More than ever, Nzama and HEALA believe that civil society needs to be unified and committed to working together (interview with Nzama Lawrence Mbalati, August 20, 2020).

Complementary Institutions

While all of the aforementioned political strategies that industries have taken in South Africa have bolstered their ability to influence NCD policy in their favor, industries' activities, on their own, are insufficient for explaining their policy influence. Indeed, as IPCI emphasizes, governments are also to blame. Presidents and their interest in strategically partnering with and using industries to achieve their alternative policy and political objectives also matter. As IPCI explains, this dynamic represents the presence of complementary institutions. These institutions arise when presidents have a preexisting personal history with the fast food industry, either by way of former employment or investment in it, which in turn influences their perception and support of industry, viewing them as beneficial while maintaining some degree of allegiance and support. Moreover, complementary institutions arise when presidents strive to directly or indirectly use industries to achieve alternative policy and political objectives. In South Africa, and in all the other emerging economies discussed in this book, complementary institutions have aided junk food industries in their mission to influence policy and avoid stringent policy regulations.

In South Africa, complementary institutions have been most visible in two policy domains: economic growth (primarily) and food security. With respect to the economy, ever since the transition to democracy in 1994, presidents have prioritized economic growth and prosperity as a means to not only reduce poverty but also to provide new opportunities for previously marginalized populations (Cheru 2001; Mosala et al. 2017). For example, one of President Mandela's policy priorities was achieving these types of objectives through economic reforms and development (Drogin 1994). These policy prescriptions included the Reconstruction and Development Program and the subsequent Growth, Employment and Redistribution program of 1996, which included establishing an investment environment, providing employment opportunities, reducing fiscal deficits, and engaging in international trade and privatization (Drogin 1994; Mosala et al. 2017). Through the Growth, Employment and Redistribution program, economic growth was perceived as the principal means through which to reduce poverty and inequality (Cheru 2001). Toward the end of his administration, Mandela was also focused on job creation and held summits, such as his Presidential Job Summit in October 1998, in which he revealed his dedication to this issue, working with civil society through its National Economic Development Labor Council on achieving this objective (Cheru 2001). Some considered these neoliberal policy ideas a continuation of the previous Apartheid regime's focus on market-based reforms (Cheru 2001), principles that for some, such as the Tripartite Alliance (comprised of the ANC party, the Congress of South African Trade Unions, and the South African Communist Party), betrayed the principles established through the National Democratic Revolution: for example, its emphasis on the equitable distribution of income and avoiding economic exploitation (Mosala et al. 2017). Nevertheless, Mandela soon realized that businesses (foreign and domestic) served to meet his broader economic priorities, in turn allowing him to achieve his larger political objective of poverty alleviation, development, and prosperity for his citizens.

Let us recall for a moment Mandela's shifting relationship with Coca-Cola. As noted earlier, at the very beginning of his administration, Mandela resisted Coca-Cola's presence in South Africa (Moses and Vest 2010). However, it appears that Mandela may have eventually realized the importance of Coca-Cola's ongoing expansion in providing jobs for thousands of South Africans (Spivey 2009), seeing the company as a key partner in achieving these endeavors and, by extension, achieving his poverty-alleviation objectives. In fact, Mandela returned to Atlanta, Georgia, in 1993, accompanied by Carl Ware (Coca-Cola's vice president) on one of Coca-Cola's corporate jets, and during his visit received an honorary degree from Clark Atlanta University. When on the podium, Mandela publicly stated his support for Coke and its vice president (Spivey 2009). In fact, Mandela was quoted at this event as stating: "Carl Ware has shown quite a commitment to the problems that bear on our country. . . . He has quietly helped the ANC stand on its feet. I want to acknowledge publicly that he has done this" (quoted in Spivey 2009, 41–42).

Subsequent presidents held the same views, not only toward Coca-Cola but also toward the role of industry in general. Presidents Thabo Mbeki (1999–2008) and Jacob Zuma (2009–2018) also prioritized economic growth with a focus on employment, both viewing this, again, as a means to not only rejuvenate the economy but also reduce poverty. As part of his commitment to tackling poverty and underdevelopment, Mbeki's 2005 Accelerated and Shared Growth Initiative for South Africa was focused on investing in the provision of jobs to eradicate poverty, while reducing most people's (with the exception of the most vulnerable) dependency on social welfare programs in the long run, because he did not see this as sustainable for societal development (VOANews 2009). At a 2003 Growth and Development Summit, Mbeki emphasized the importance of providing jobs for all (Pollin et al. 2006). His policy was also focused on the ease of doing business, such as reducing small busines regulations, while proactively displaying South Africa's investment opportunities (Mosala et al. 2017; South African Government, 2004). Importantly, Mbeki also believed in achieving these economic objectives through partnership with businesses, as well as society, working with government in achieving these objectives. Indeed, at a Growth and Development Summit held on July 6, 2003, Mbeki's speech stated the following: "After more than a year of consultations, we have finally assembled to seal the common agreement between government and business, labour and community organisations about the steps we need to take to speed up economic growth and development" (quoted in Polity 2003, 2). Mbeki appeared to have viewed this partnership as the key to providing more jobs and economic opportunities for his citizens (Polity 2003).

Zuma was of the same mind. Through his National Development Plan and New Growth Path, similar to Mbeki, in addition to reducing poverty (mainly through the provision of several social welfare grants) and inequality, Zuma was focused on increasing employment and economic growth (Cook 2013). The New Growth Plan aspired to create new jobs and reduce unemployment by 10 percent in 2020 (Dallimore et al. 2017). Once again, as seen under Mandela, and Mbeki before him, economic growth was perceived as the principle means through which to eradicate unemployment, poverty, and inequality, a goal that Zuma introduced through his New Growth Path program (Mosala et al. 2017). Zuma was also focused on ease of doing business and created the One Stop Shop centers throughout several cities, which were created to help overcome the red tape involved in the creation of new business ventures (Presidency, Republic of South Africa 2018). Zuma viewed establishing partnerships with industry as important when attempting to address the challenges of ensuring job growth (Aboobaker 2013). At one point, when discussing the fruits of his goal of attracting foreign investment to his National Assembly in 2013, he acknowledged Unilever, one of the world's largest food industries, in this process, stating: "Our tax relief incentives, announced in 2011, have resulted in an increase in foreign direct investment. We can count the recent investment of R800 million in Boksburg by Unilever, which is one of (its) largest investments globally" (quoted in Aboobaker 2013, 2). He even brought his views about the importance of investing in South Africa to the United States, stating that his country was a good place to invest in at the US–South Africa Business and Investment Forum meeting held in Washington, DC, in August 2014 (*fin24* 2014). At this forum, Zuma claimed: "Our country is also a great location for growing your business in other parts of the African continent" (quoted in *fin24* 2014, 1). Representatives of several US investors, such as Coca-Cola, Sasol, Pfizer, and Standard Bank, among others, were also present at this event (*fin24* 2014). At this meeting, Zuma shared his view that US businesses are "an important partner in the journey towards growth and prosperity" (quoted in *fin24* 2014, 1).

But perhaps no other president in recent South African history has been as committed as the current president, Cyril Ramaphosa, in working with and through industries to achieve his alternative economic and political objectives. While joining his predecessors in warring against ongoing unemployment, inequality, and poverty (see ANA reporter and staff reporter 2019), and similar again to his presidential predecessors, Ramaphosa's priority was to focus on creating new jobs and opportunities for South Africans (Cameron 2017), overcoming what he once referred to as a "job loss tsunami" (quoted in Mining Journal 2020). According to Signé and Schneidman (2019), at a 2018 job summit in South Africa that he organized, Ramaphosa set the ambitious goal of creating 275,000 jobs per year. Ramaphosa went so far as to create a New Deal for Jobs, Growth, and Transformation, which was focused on unifying the state, government, and society to achieve these economic objectives (Cameron 2017). Ramaphosa's priority through his New Deal was, as he put it, to "place the creation of decent jobs at the centre of our every policy, programme and action. . . . All social partners—labour, government and business—need together to lead a national initiative to create at least one million jobs in 5 years" (quoted in Cameron 2017, 1). He reminded investors (domestic and foreign) to sustain their commitments to the economy (Mining Journal 2020). Ramaphosa was laser-focused on bringing in more foreign direct investment, with a goal of attracting an estimated $100 billion (Corcoran 2018; Signé and Schneidman 2019).

To achieve his objectives, Ramaphosa sought to partner with the private sector. According to Terence Creamer (2019), Ramaphosa "urged business leaders to partner with government to put in place the building blocks required for achieving growth rates of higher than 5%" (1). To solidify this process, Minister in the Presidency Dr. Nkosazana Dlamini-Zuma headed the Public-Private Growth Initiative, which, according Creamer, sought to "build a closer relationship between government and [the] private sector in support of government's aspiration to facilitate new investments worth $100 billion over a five-year period" (3). Indeed, at the second South African Investment Conference held in Johannesburg in November 2019, Ramaphosa discussed the importance of big businesses remaining committed to investing in the nation: "The commitments made at last year's conference and those made today have placed us firmly on the path to achieve our ambitious target of securing $100 billion [about R1.5 trillion] over five years. We do this not as a gimmick, we do this after close and deep collaboration with the various companies" (quoted in Gqubule 2019, 1). According to Gqubule (2019), Coca-Cola (as well as several other major companies making their own pledges) made a pledge of R14.7 billion toward this endeavor.

Furthermore, at a jobs summit held in Midrand, South Africa, Ramaphosa called on businesses (as well as consumers and the government) to purchase products locally in order to ensure that jobs are kept and created (African News Agency 2018). At this summit, Ramaphosa stated: "Government has undertaken to simplify and speed up the process for the designation of products for local procurement, and organised labour, in partnership with Proudly SA, will proactively identify opportunities for new designations. As part of this agreement, a number of companies have made specific commitments to local procurement initiatives as part of their operational strategies" (quoted in African News Agency 2018, 1). "The companies mentioned by Ramaphosa include Adcock Ingram, Anglogold Ashanti, Clientele, Coca Cola [*sic*] SA, Edcon, First Rand, Lixil, Mondi, Nandos, Nestle, AB InBev, Sappi, Sasol, Standard Bank and Tsogo Sun" (1). This, in turn, suggests that Coca-Cola, Nestlé, and other food companies, such as Nandos, have agreed to partner with the president in achieving his goal of creating jobs. Ramaphosa made plans to publicly acknowledge and celebrate the contributions of these industries, stating: "They will be the first to be invited to join a 'BuySA Circle', which recognizes companies that are leaders in buying local and have demonstrated in practice their commitment to supporting South African enterprise. Companies that sign up to this commitment will, among other things, be celebrated at an annual dinner convened by the President" (quoted in African News Agency 2018, 1).

But where did Ramaphosa's interest in strategically using and working with big business come from? Similar to what we saw with President Vicente Fox of Mexico, Ramaphosa's interests appeared to have been shaped by his previous experience working in the private sector. Interestingly, despite his history of working as a famous labor union representative, founding the National Union of Mineworkers, as well as being a parliamentarian, in 1997, he left government to create his own consulting firm, the Shanduka Group (Sayed 2018). Jacobs and Fogel go so far as to claim that the "ANC 'deployed' him to the private sector and South Africa's white captains of industry decided he was a man with whom they could do business. As a result he was catapulted into the boardrooms of mega-corporations like McDonald's and Coca-Cola" (1). While heading the Shanduka Group, Ramaphosa invested in Coca-Cola and McDonald's shares (1). Among his assets was ownership of a Coca-Cola bottling plant (QSRweb 2011). In fact, at one point, he bought a twenty-year McDonald's franchise in South Africa, an agreement that nevertheless was perceived as unconventional because it also allowed him asset ownership (QSRweb 2011; see also Bond 2018). Ramaphosa was no stranger to business. He prospered from it—becoming a multimillionaire (estimated at $450 million) and making it on the *Forbes* list as one of Africa's top fifty richest people in 2015 (Sayed 2018). He eventually returned to government in 2014, becoming the deputy president, and was elected leader of the ANC in 2017 (Sayed 2018). It is very likely that Ramaphosa's background in business incentivized him to view and support the growth and development of junk food industries, believing that they would be an important part in helping him achieve his goal of providing thousands of new jobs, and hence, economic growth and prosperity.

However, the government has also seen industry as a major partner in achieving broader policy and political goals in the area of food security. In 2010, President Zuma emphasized his support for increasing food security. A particular goal was encouraging people to return to farming and to invest in this sector. Through his administration's Fetsa Tlala initiative, moreover, he encouraged people to start planting fresh fruit and vegetables again, in a sense returning to the traditional ways of farming (South African Government 2013).

During this period, the Department of Agriculture, as well as the Independent Development Trust and several other groups, engaged in a strategic partnership with Nestlé South Africa to assist rural farmers through a Black Economic Empowerment agricultural program (Nestlé, "AGRI-BEE Maluti Window Initiative"). Through this program, located in Harrismith, Free State Province, "Nestlé procures milk from these farms and helps them with funding, procurement, milk tanks, dairy infrastructure and the necessary certification to enable the farmers to compete in the market" (1). In addition, this initiative was "commended by the South African government as a true example of a public-private partnership" (1). These efforts appeared to have helped achieve Zuma's objective of returning to and strengthening the farming sector.

In sum, complementary institutions in South Africa appear to have provided yet another source of legitimacy and indirect support for junk food industries. Since the Mandela administration, presidents have viewed these industries as partners in achieving their broader economic and, by extension, political objectives. In fact, according to longtime activists in South Africa, presidents throughout the country's recent history have never publicly spoken out against industry (interview with Nzama Lawrence Mbalati, HEALA, South Africa, August 20, 2020). This has provided a propitious context for industry. They have indirect presidential backing and leaders who have electoral incentives to see these industries prosper and thrive. Industries are therefore not the only culprits in politicizing NCD policy. Ambitious presidents are also to blame.

The Rise of Civil Society

In this context, the role of civil society has become increasingly important. As we have seen with publicly contested health epidemics in the past, such as HIV/AIDS, obesity, and even tuberculosis (Gómez 2015), civil society has been significant not just for raising awareness about the importance of creating more effective policies but also highlighting their shortcomings. Yet, in South Africa, when it comes to the politics of public health nutrition, the presence of well-organized, influential civil societal activists and organizations has been considerably delayed. While new organizations have recently risen to address the importance of preventing and regulating junk food products, they have only recently emerged and are still in need of greater resources, attention, and political support.

In recent years, for example, HEALA has emerged to raise awareness and to bring attention to these issues. HEALA activists were at the forefront of raising awareness about the importance of the soda tax (interview with Nicholas Stacey, August 14, 2020). HEALA has initiated several public awareness campaigns, focusing on issues such as the importance of front-of-package warning labels, healthy eating, and campaigns targeted at schools (Healthy Living Alliance 2020).

At the same time, think tanks have been established within major research universities to conduct research, publish resources, and advocate for the importance of effective NCD policies. One good example has been PRICELESS SA, which is located within the University of Witwatersrand in Johannesburg, South Africa. Several researchers there have worked on topics such as the soda tax and other related NCD policies.

Nevertheless, while civil societal activists have done a commendable job of raising awareness about the need for more effective NCDs in response to South Africa's ongoing obesity and type 2 diabetes epidemics, it is important to emphasize that this work is new and has not been as influential. Because of this, these organizations have experienced several challenges, such as insufficient financial and organizational support. Indeed, Ruder (2016) claims that NGOs working on type 2 diabetes have not received sufficient funding for diabetic supplies or education and prevention services.

Despite these challenges, as we saw in response to HIV/AIDS and other diseases, with time, activists and NGOs working on NCDs will thrive and have a stronger impact on policy. These activists and organizations will build on the country's rich history of public contestation in areas such as human rights and justice. As South Africa's children and the poor continue to suffer from the challenges of obesity and type 2 diabetes, it is inevitable that these civil societal organizations will become more influential.

Conclusion

Despite the burgeoning growth of NCDs in South Africa, even among the nation's most innocent children and the poor, junk food industries once again succeeded in avoiding regulatory policies that served to challenge their ongoing prosperity. This was achieved by engaging in several political strategies that bolstered industries' political legitimacy and influence, in turn incentivizing government to refrain from aggressively regulating the marketing and sale of their products and introducing effective food labels. While these companies and their interest group allies eventually lost their fight against the soda tax, essentially no concrete effort has been made to introduce these other equally, if not more, important regulatory measures. Industries' involvement in civil society through partnerships with NGOs also contributed to creating divisions in society, where partnering with NGOs has hampered activists' ability to work with them and establish a unifying voice in opposition to industry's political interference and policy influence.

But industries were only partly to blame. As IPCI explains, complementary institutions also mattered. Presidents, from Mandela to Ramaphosa, have viewed partnering with industries as a means to achieve their broader economic and political agendas. Industry has served to help these presidents achieve their goal of increasing growth and employment while reducing poverty and inequality. In this context, junk food industries have, in essence, been safeguarded from constricting regulatory measures while being encouraged to thrive and prosper in South Africa's growing market economy.

And yet, there is hope. Building on South Africa's strong roots of civil societal activism and demands for social justice, activists and NGOs are now, more than ever, appearing with gusto to increase awareness and challenge industries' policy interference. While new to the political game, they will play a critical role in holding the president, parliament, and the DoH accountable for their repeated unwillingness to seriously tackle obesity and type 2 diabetes, and, more importantly, to protect the health and well-being of South Africa's most vulnerable populations.

South Africa: Summary of Chapter Findings

Political Action	Restructuring Society	Complementary Institutions	Regulatory Policy Failure and Absence
Policy partnership Coca-Cola and other industries working with government to find policy solutions to obesity, such as through the Healthy Foods Options Forum Coca-Cola working with government to organize public exercise events, such as the Big Walk campaign Nestlé working with government to provide nutritional education, training for staff, improved school meals, and school exercise programs	*Corporate social responsibility* Nestlé providing job training, health care services, and community nutrition awards Coca-Cola providing funding support to women to start small businesses, as well as business training and mentoring through its 5by20 global program	Presidents Mandela, Mbeki, Zuma, and Ramaphosa partnering with industry to achieve their alternative economic and antipoverty objectives	Absence of regulations on the sale of junk foods in schools Absence of regulations on marketing junk food products to children Absence of effective food labels and labels that warn consumers about products high in sugar, fat, and salt Soda tax passed, though lowered due to industry opposition
Lobbying and largesse Industry pressures to question and delay the soda tax	*Partnering with society* Coca-Cola's financial support to think tanks for studies investigating the efficacy of a soda tax		
Institutional infiltration Not present	*Dividing society* Soda industry's partnership with NGOs hampers other NGOs' (e.g., HEALA's) ability to establish a broad civil societal coalition in response to industry's policy influence		

Conclusion

I began this book with a discussion about a keynote address that former WHO director Margaret Chan gave to the National Academy of Medicine in 2016. During her speech, Director Chan emphasized that if the world was going to make any progress on tackling the obesity and type 2 diabetes epidemics, then governments must be more committed to taking on the power and influence of major industries. Her remarks suggested that this was the only way that we could ever safeguard our societies, especially our most vulnerable populations, from the ongoing challenges of these ailments, and put them on the path toward health and prosperity.

At the beginning of my research, I was optimistic that the emerging economies were paying heed to Director Chan's recommendations, taking concrete actions to truncate the power and influence of junk food industries. Why? Because, for the most part, several of these economies had already implemented impressive noncommunicable disease prevention programs. Recall that in 2010, Brazil was recognized by the international community for its impressive track record on combating obesity—along with the United Kingdom. Mexico introduced a soda tax in 2013. India, China, South Africa, and Indonesia had also done their part in implementing impressive NCD prevention programs.

Despite these accomplishments, throughout the course of my research an interesting paradox had emerged, one that inspired the crafting of this book. Despite these impressive NCD policies, with many focused on children and the poor, most of these governments have not been equally as committed to creating effective regulatory policies that limit junk food industries' ability to market and sell their products to these vulnerable populations.

While some countries have made progress along these lines, these poli-cies have either never been adequately enforced or have only recently been introduced—as seen in Mexico and Brazil. In India, China, Indonesia, and South Africa, essentially no serious attempt has been made to implement these regulatory policies.

Adding further credence to these shortcomings is the simple fact that the epidemiological profiles of these countries appear to be worsening. Rates of obesity and type 2 diabetes continued to surge even after impressive NCD prevention policies were adopted, and worse still, these ailments have surged among children and the poor. In fact, today, the childhood obesity epidemic is mainly concentrated in the developing world (WHO 2020). Type 2 diabe-tes, a medical condition that has historically been found among older adults, is now increasingly common among young adolescents in several of these countries. At the same time, the poor are seeing a heightened increase in these health care challenges, due to several factors, such as having greater disposable income through anti-poverty cash transfer programs and easier access to junk food.

To return to Director Chan's calling, the deeper I dug into the case stud-ies of Mexico, Brazil, India, Indonesia, China, and South Africa, the more I realized that junk food industries are, unfortunately, *more* powerful today than they have ever been. My central argument in this book has been that in a context of fear and opportunity, junk food industries have emerged as powerful political and social forces in these emerging economies. These industries have engaged in a host of political, institutional, and civil societal tactics with the unwavering goal of increasing and sustaining their political and social legitimacy, and thus, policy influence. But at the same time, I have argued that these industries are only partly to blame. Governments are also at fault. Ambitious presidents have benefited from working closely with these industries and have, in the process, indirectly contributed to industry's po-litical and policy influence. In all of the countries discussed in this book, presidents have pursued and accepted junk food industries as vital partners in helping these leaders achieve their alternative political, economic, and so-cial welfare objectives.

Junk food politics is a two-way street. Industries' and government's interests have collided in mutually reinforcing and beneficial ways. But this has occurred at the expense of impairing the health and prosperity of our most innocent and vulnerable populations.

Why is this the case? In an attempt to thoroughly address this question, I introduced the Industry Politics and Complementary Institutions analytical framework. This framework brings together several theoretical concepts in political science and public health policy to provide an in-depth explanation for why and how junk food industries continue to influence politics, institutions, and civil society in ways that obstruct governments' ability to either create or effectively implement NCD regulatory policies. In applying theoretical concepts, while generating new ones, IPCI revealed that in a context of fear and opportunity, industries are consistently engaged in a host of political and social strategies to achieve these policy objectives.

Applying the works of several scholars, such as Hillman and Hitt (1999), Savell and colleagues (2014), Moodie and colleagues (2013), Miller and Harkins (2010), and Gómez (2019a), IPCI emphasizes that industries in essentially all of the emerging economies discussed in this book have engaged in innovative policy partnerships with health officials from federal and state governments. These partnerships have, for the most part, motivated policy makers to refrain from pursuing aggressive regulatory policies (in the areas of marketing, sales, and food labeling), mainly due to the latter's belief that these industries are important allies that are doing their part to help solve the obesity and type 2 diabetes problem. For as Hastings (2012) reminds us, industries, through their corporate social responsibility activities, continuously strive to be perceived as "part of the solution rather than the problem" (27). At the same time, IPCI applies political science and health policy "insider" interest group theories (Berry 1977; Hall and Deardorff 2006; Hillman and Hitt 1999; McSpadden and Culhane 1999; Milbrath 1963; Savell et al. 2014) to emphasize that industries and their representatives are continuously engaged in their traditional bread-and-butter tactics of lobbying and largesse to manipulate regulatory policies in their favor. They have done so by not only meeting with policy makers—often clandestinely, behind closed doors (Culpepper 2011)—but also by strategically infiltrating bureaucratic institutions.

In all of the countries examined in this book, industries eagerly engaged in these partnerships. In Mexico, Brazil, India, China, and South Africa, several major soda and ultraprocessed food industries engaged in partnerships with federal and state health departments in order to provide health and educational programs in schools and local communities. These efforts helped industries build political capital, if you will, with political leaders, convincing them that industries were committed to tackling the childhood obesity and diabetes problems. But in several cases, as seen in Brazil and South Africa, these efforts also generated few incentives for policy makers to pursue stringent regulations. At the same time, industry and lobbying groups in Mexico, Brazil, India, and South Africa incessantly lobbied congressional and bureaucratic committees, using their vast resources and information to either delay soda tax legislation or disrupt the creation of regulatory policies.

Industries have also engaged in what IPCI refers to as institutional infiltration processes. Building on the works of Klein and Lee (2019), Falleti (2009), and Goldfrank (2011), institutional infiltration occurs when industries establish their presence within national bureaucratic committees for the purposes of not only lobbying and pressuring government for policy reform but, perhaps more importantly, introducing and establishing their particular policy beliefs and ideas, educating and convincing policy makers over time about the importance and effectiveness of particular NCD policy strategies. This infiltration process helps to firmly establish industries' policy ideas within government, continuously supported by health officials who, in turn, view these ideas as legitimate and effective. This institutional infiltration process can lead to industry's ongoing policy influence over the government's approach to obesity and type 2 diabetes prevention, such as the importance of regular physical exercise as a national strategy for tackling childhood obesity.

As we saw in Mexico, Brazil, India, and China, institutional infiltration processes were used to occupy strategic positions within national bureaucratic committees and policy hearings. Either by being present themselves or by working through affiliated NGOs, such as the International Life Sciences Institute, industry representatives strategically used these venues to present and defend their policy ideas either about specific prevention programs or to question and delay regulations. In Brazil and especially China, however, industries and their representatives infiltrated national bureaucratic agencies, such as Anvisa in Brazil and the Center for Disease Control and Prevention in China (Greenhalgh 2019a), with their policy ideas while incessantly striving to ensure that these ideas were adopted into legislation. As the seminal works of Greenhalgh (2019a) explain, this process was most prominent in China, where the International Life Sciences Institute's historic and ongoing partnership with leading CDC officials led to the inculcation of ideas and eventually several national prevention programs emphasizing the importance of physical education as a national strategy to reduce childhood obesity.

At the same time, IPCI emphasizes the fact that industries are also engaged in several strategies to restructure civil society in their favor. That is, these industries have engaged in what the literature describes as corporate social responsibility tactics (Fooks and Gilmore 2013; Hastings 2012; Moodie et al. 2013; Vogel 2008; Walker and Rea 2014), which serve to deepen industry's social legitimacy and acceptability. In all the countries discussed in this book, industries have provided health care, agricultural, and employment programs, and even human rights campaigns, to contribute to society and to establish strong social support networks. These industries have not only achieved these objectives, but their endeavors have helped to increase their acceptability and influence within government, contributing to policy makers' views that industries are genuine partners in their commitment to improving the health and well-being of society and vulnerable populations.

Nevertheless, IPCI also emphasizes that industries' restructuring of society has entailed serious ramifications for collective social movements—an issue that has not been thoroughly addressed in the literature. That is, and building on the work of Gómez (2019a), by working with civil societal actors, particularly influential academic researchers, think tanks, and NGOs, junk food industries can divide society and its ability to collectively mobilize in opposition to industry's political and policy tactics. By establishing allies with these influential actors, industries can restrict the number of potential civic allies that those activists and NGOs working for the general public's health concerns can potentially work with in order to successfully unify and hold industries and government accountable while impressing the need for effective regulatory policies. These NGOs serving the public also have fewer individuals to work with on the importance of safeguarding the health and well-being of children and the poor. IPCI emphasizes that industries are seemingly engaged in these activities in order to intentionally disrupt civil society's ability to effectively mobilize, hold industries accountable, and pressure the government for the introduction of effective NCD regulatory policies.

This process was clearly evident in the cases of Mexico, Brazil, India, Indonesia, and South Africa. In all of these countries, industries' efforts to partner with prestigious academic researchers and ideologically supportive NGOs ultimately reduced the number of influential individuals and organizations that activists striving to defend the health and well-being of children and the poor could work with. Differences in policy opinion between these groups also emerged, at times generating conflict between them. Due to the absence of well-organized NGOs in China, however, as well as increasingly restrictive political conditions discouraging civic mobilization on nutrition and other areas, these challenges were not present.

IPCI has also emphasized the importance of better understanding the role that government plays in this process. In essence, IPCI explains that junk food politics is a two-way street: that is, while big business is committed to reaching out to and influencing government, at the same time, political leaders may at times reach out to businesses to achieve politicians' alternative policy and political objectives. Indeed, IPCI emphasizes that political leaders' interests and objectives can serve to indirectly augment junk food industries' political tactics and policy influence.

To better understand this process, I introduced the concept of complementary institutions in IPCI. Complementary institutions arise when (1) presidents' previous personal connections and experiences with industry motivate them to support industry's development; (2) presidents view these industries as vital partners in achieving their alternative economic and social welfare objectives, in turn bolstering their political influence; and (3) presidents build institutions in order to ensure that these partnerships endure. Altogether, complementary institutions serve as an intervening variable indirectly complementing and supporting these industries' political activities, legitimacy, and policy influence.

These complementary institutions were clearly present in all of the emerging economies discussed in this book. For example, in Mexico and South Africa, presidents Vicente Fox and Cyril Ramaphosa, respectively, had previously worked with industries and had personal interests and connections that appeared to motivate them to support major companies. In all of the countries I examined, presidents also established partnerships with industries to achieve their broader economic and, in many instances, social welfare objectives, in turn providing these leaders with political popularity and support. And in some instances, as seen under President Lula in Brazil, presidents went so far as to create federal institutions to solidify this partnership with industry in the area of poverty alleviation; this greatly benefited Lula's effort to expand his popular Bolsa Família program.

Thus, in sum, the application of IPCI to the cases of Mexico, Brazil, India,

Indonesia, China, and South Africa helps to reveal and explain the various political, institutional, and civil societal strategies that industries pursue to achieve their policy objectives. And yet, this framework also revealed that ambitious presidents also play their part in indirectly aiding industry in these endeavors. Whether they realize it or not, regardless of the innovative NCD prevention programs that they introduce and are proud to display, these presidents indirectly contribute to industry's political and policy influence and, in the end, indirectly contribute to the ongoing challenge of obesity and type 2 diabetes among children and the poor.

IPCI's Broader Theoretical Significance

But how does IPCI relate to the existing literature? What new theoretical insights have we learned, and why is it necessary? First, IPCI advances the literature on the politics of the commercial determinants of health because it is the first to apply and combine political science interest group and institutional change theory with health policy research on corporate political activity and corporate social responsibility. IPCI underscores the fact that political scientists have neglected to explore the extent to which their theories about interest group behavior, institutions, and corporate strategies can be combined with the CPA/CSR literature to provide a more thorough explanation of the various ways that junk food industries shape NCD regulatory policy in their favor while establishing strong support networks at the community level. To my knowledge, IPCI, and this book in general, is also the first effort to thoroughly apply this political science literature to NCD policy making in several emerging economies. As we saw in chapter 1, most of the political science literature on interest groups and industry political behaviors has focused on advanced industrialized nations.

With respect to the political science literature on interest groups and institutional theory, IPCI advances this work by emphasizing the importance of combining interest group with institutional infiltration and change theoretical perspectives. IPCI emphasizes that focusing on interest group behaviors and tactics is insufficient (De Bruycker and Beyers 2019), and that we must combine this approach with the institutional theory literature emphasizing the importance of repeated access to congressional and governmental institutions as areas providing additional space for lobbying and pressure tactics within government (Hacker 1998). But at the same time, and building on the institutional infiltration and change literature (Falleti 2009; Goldfrank 2011; Klein and Lee 2019), IPCI stresses that we must explore how interest groups strategically infiltrate bureaucratic institutions, often working with and through NGOs (international and domestic) to gradually implant their ideas and interests and build policy coalitions that sustain industry's policy views. IPCI therefore underscores that political science interest group theory must be combined with two important aspects of institutions: using institutions to amplify lobbying efforts and to implant policy ideas and build supportive coalitions around them.

IPCI also addresses recent calls in political science to further explore the relationship between interest groups and their broader political context. As Hojnacki and colleagues (2012) maintain, we need to learn more about how interest groups interact with legislatures, political parties, and the bureaucracy, and how the design of institutions, such as decentralization, shapes industries' political activities. Hojnacki and others (2012) further emphasize that interest group researchers need to do a better job of engaging the theoretical literature. IPCI addresses these needs by not only applying interest group and institutional theory to empirical case studies in the developing world but also by emphasizing how and why junk food industries, as well as their supportive interest groups, strategically work with and within government institutions to strategically use them toward their policy advantage.

But IPCI also advances the literature by underscoring the importance of complementary institutions. To date, political scientists and health policy experts have not thoroughly addressed why and how political leaders, such as presidents, reach out to and strategically use junk food industries to meet their alternative policy, and thus political, objectives. IPCI emphasizes the importance of revealing why, when, and how political leaders use industries for these reasons; in the process, this reveals that industries are not the only culprit in working the politics to sustain their policy preferences. To my knowledge, the existing research addressing the politics of public health policy has failed to acknowledge the complementary role of institutions. This is particularly problematic in a context where, as seen in the emerging economies discussed in this book (many of which are either nascent democracies or nondemocratic [e.g., China]), the power and influence of presidents are arguably much stronger than their counterparts' in advanced, industrialized—mainly democratic—nations. In essence, this reflects the longer history of democratic consolidation and checks-and-balances systems in the latter.

But how does my analytical framework build on the recent literature on CPA in public health policy? While IPCI and the findings in this book certainly corroborate the myriad of political and social tactics that industries use to influence NCD policy in this literature, several shortcomings abound. First, the literature is essentially silent on exploring the importance of national institutions, such as the federal health care bureaucracy and NCD policy-making committees, and more importantly, how to combine a political analysis of these institutions with CPA political tactics. As revealed in this book, IPCI provides greater insight into why industries have more power and influence within government. Both by having repeated access to these institutions (Gómez 2019a) and by gradually inculcating industry's policy ideas through institutional representation, IPCI offers greater insight into why and how industries continue to shape the policy agenda-setting process in their favor. Furthermore, this approach goes beyond the mere act of lobbying, policy framing discourse, and the like as forms of corporate power and policy influence (Jaichuen et al. 2018; Lima and Galea 2018; Martino 2017; Miller and Harkins 2010).

Second, the CPA literature has also been silent on the broader historical factors accounting for why industries engage in myriad political tactics in the first place. While industry's motivation is always to deepen its profits, as we saw in chapter 2, we must also acknowledge the broader historical contextual importance of fear and opportunity as motivational forces merging with these profit motives to instigate political action within industry. We must also combine this approach with the deep historical economic and political factors leading to these industries' early presence in emerging economies, at times decades before the emergence of NCD challenges such as obesity and type 2 diabetes—as seen in Mexico, South Africa, India, and Brazil. In contrast to the CPA literature, this broader historical perspective can provide a more compelling explanation for why CPA tactics have emerged and why they continue to be influential.

Finally, IPCI, as well as the comparative case study approach taken in this book, suggests that the CPA literature is too descriptive in nature. Scholars have done a commendable job of applying, evaluating, and modifying the literature highlighting the various political and policy tactics that industries use to influence NCD policy (Fooks and Gilmore 2013; Gilmore et al. 2011; Jaichuen et al. 2018; Mialon et al. 2015; Miller and Harkins 2010). They have also done a commendable job of showing how this literature can be used to monitor and hold industries accountable for their actions (Jaichuen et al. 2018; Sacks et al. 2013). And yet, none of this literature has explored how political science and public policy agenda-setting theory can be applied and used to propose new questions and empirical approaches, and, in the process, provide a more in-depth and compelling explanation. As IPCI demonstrates, the application of political science interest group and institutional theory generates questions that reveal the importance of institutional change processes and complementary institutions while also illustrating the political and policy tactics emphasized by the CPA literature.

When taken together, IPCI advances the literature by providing a conceptual analytical framework that delivers a more in-depth explanation of the broader political and social influence of junk food industries in emerging economies, as well as the complementary role of presidential institutions. It is the first systematic attempt to combine the political science literature on interest groups, institutions, and the CPA/CSR health policy literature to offer an alternative framework that allows for a more thorough explanation of the rise and ongoing policy influence of junk food industries in these countries. The utility of this interdisciplinary analytical perspective further underscores the need for political scientists and public health policy experts to work together to devise new theoretical and methodological approaches to addressing the politics of the commercial determinants of health.

Policy Lessons

My analytical approach to explaining the complex world of junk food politics also provides several empirical lessons for policy makers. These lessons are centered on two areas: government-industry relations and NCD policy processes.

Government-Industry Relations

With respect to government-industry relations, findings from this book suggest that governments should establish stricter limits on the extent to which industries can partner with government officials to devise NCD policies. Considering how easy it has been for industry to inculcate their ideas and policy preferences within government—as we saw with the institutional infiltration process mentioned earlier—and for industries to manipulate politicians' interests and actions (or, rather, inactions) through policy partnerships, governments should refrain from engaging in these activities, a view that comports with other scholars' claims that there is scant evidence supporting the efficacy of these public-private partnerships (Moodie et al. 2013). Furthermore, governments should refrain from these activities *especially* when it comes to creating obesity and type 2 diabetes prevention programs focused on children and the poor. As we have seen in this book, yet another reason governments should refrain from these partnerships is because these partnerships can help to bolster industry's political legitimacy and influence. While industry research and partnerships with government can be fruitful in the area of improving the overall quality of food through research and innovation, industry involvement should not extend to the area of NCD prevention, such as working with governments to provide nutritional information to the public, emphasizing the importance of exercise, and engaging in any related policies that impact individual's direct behaviors.

In addition, findings from this book suggest that industries should not be permitted to work with government on the design of public health policies. This would entail prohibiting industries and their representatives, either unions or aligned international and domestic NGOs, from being represented on national policy-making committees. As we saw in several countries in this book, industries and their representatives often outweigh the representation and influence of public health activists and nutrition scientists. Going forward, governments should restrict industry access to policy-making institutions.

Finally, my discussion about complementary institutions suggests that presidents should not be proactively working with junk food industries on health, economic, or any other social welfare programs. Why? While the intentions of these political leaders might be admirable, partnering with industry in these policy domains can further bolster the political and social acceptability of these industries. Instead, presidents should ideally be partnering with federal- or state-level health departments, NGOs, and activists that are committed to addressing obesity and type 2 diabetes among vulnerable populations. This, in the process, reveals that these political leaders are genuinely committed to addressing the root causes of these ailments rather than just meeting alternative policy objectives, such as anti-poverty programs, and thus advancing their political careers.

Policy Priority and Implementation

Several key lessons also emerge with respect to public health policy and implementation. First, empirical findings from the case studies discussed in this book suggest that NCD prevention policies, such as soda taxes, nutritional awareness, exercise promotion, and communication campaigns (e.g., food labels), will not be enough to combat the burgeoning growth of obesity and type 2 diabetes among children and the poor. While these policies certainly do their part in positively influencing individuals' downstream behaviors, all of the case studies in this book reveal that these policies *must* be combined with a variety of effective regulatory policies aimed at truncating industries' ability to market and sell their products to these populations. In other words, *effective* NCD policies must be *wholistic* in nature: that is, not only focused on helping individuals make wiser choices and be better informed about good food and nutrition but also safeguarding these individuals from industry manipulation and influence through the power of government law.

Second, the case studies in this book suggest that while governments have been very innovative and, to a certain extent, timely in their creation of NCD prevention policies, they have not been nearly as committed to enforcing or creating policies on food labeling, marketing, and sales. While some governments have made more progress along these lines, as seen in Mexico and Brazil, even then, we have learned that these policies have not been adequately enforced. Industries either tend to ignore these regulations altogether or are willing to pay the fines associated with policy noncompliance. To address this issue, governments must find creative ways to enforce existing regulations. This can be achieved either through the creation of stiffer financial penalties for noncompliance or the usage of public accountability mechanisms such as sharing information about industry's willful avoidance of government regulations—especially those focused on vulnerable populations. Such an approach could potentially affect industry's social reputation and generate incentives for industry regulatory compliance.

In the absence of effective government regulations, governments have also permitted industries to engage in acts of self-regulation, particularly in the area of advertising. However, as we saw in several countries discussed in this book, these efforts simply do not work. Time and time again, despite their public pledges to limit the marketing of their products to children, industries have repeatedly broken their promises, through a variety of processes, ranging from TV and social media advertisements that target children, to consistently posting advertisements near schools. For the most part, these self-regulatory practices have been used by industry to reveal to the government, and society in general, that companies are unwaveringly committed to reducing the childhood obesity and type 2 diabetes problems. Consequently, as we saw in several countries discussed in this book, governments have neglected to pursue alternative regulatory policies precisely because they believe that industry is sacrificing and doing its part in working with government to safeguard the health and well-being of children and the poor. What these findings therefore suggest is that governments should refrain from endorsing these kinds of self-regulatory policies. Or, at a very minimum, governments must be fully committed to holding industries accountable for their promises, either by introducing penalties for breaking marketing pledges or publicly disclosing these activities; the latter, in turn, can tarnish a company's reputation and generate incentives to maintain their marketing pledges.

Finally, more than ever, findings from this book suggest that national governments need to work closely with state health departments to create prevention and regulatory policies. The states or provinces should not wait or look to the national government for policy ideas and innovations. With the exception Brazil, where states were early innovators in NCD prevention programs, and even at the city level in the United States, essentially all of the other state governments in the other countries discussed in this book have not taken the initiative to create prevention and, especially, regulatory policies. In this context, it behooves national governments to make the effort to work more closely with the state governments to create effective regulatory policies targeting junk food industries.

The Way Forward

I do not want to leave you with the impression that I am direly opposed to the presence of free markets and their provision of delicious foods. Free markets should certainly be allowed to develop, prosper, and meet the public's needs. While history has shown us that not everyone benefits equally from fast-paced economic growth (Szreter 2003), markets also instigate development and provide new opportunities and incentives, while generating individual aspirations (Osnos 2015). And this is especially the case with the emerging economies discussed in this book, which have seen a burgeoning middle-income class and thousands lifted out of poverty through a combination of aggressive anti-poverty programs and economic opportunity. Furthermore, in this context, individuals should have the right to choose which foods they want to consume. This represents our most cherished principles of democratic liberalism, which guarantees individuals the right and opportunity to act and behave as they wish within the confines of public law.

However, in this context, I am vehemently opposed to *any* and *all* forms of commercial industry efforts to strategically take advantage of those individuals who are limited in their ability to make responsible and healthy choices on their own. Unlike adults, children often do not have the mental maturity and cognitive capacity needed to make healthy choices (Harris and Graff 2011). Countless studies—as well as the case studies discussed in this book—reveal that children are easily manipulated by the junk food industry's aggressive, highly innovative marketing strategies. We have also learned that these industries often strategically target children, incessantly taking advantage of the absence of federal regulations limiting the marketing and sale of their products. This activity has to stop. And it has to stop even if state intrusion via stern government regulations targeting food industries cuts against the grain of our most cherished free market principles.

The same goes for the poor. In emerging economies today, most of the poor, either in urban or rural areas, continue to face socioeconomic and infrastructural conditions that make it difficult for them to make healthy food choices. Low incomes, stress from employment, and inadequate infrastructural conditions continue to incentivize the poor to purchase foods that are easier to access but are also cheap and unhealthy. As we saw in essentially all of the countries examined in this book, industries have strategically taken advantage of this context by ensuring that their products reach the poorest of the poor, even sending their own corporate boats throughout Brazil's vast Amazonian rivers to reach them. This, too, must stop.

So, then, in this context, what should the government's priorities be in emerging economies? If these nations care about their international reputation, striving to show the world that they truly care about the health and well-being of their citizens while pushing to reveal to the world that they can overcome disease and prosper, then it behooves political leaders to *dramatically* transform their relationship with junk food industries and implement policies that limit their impact on society. Governments can use these efforts to show the world that the sign of a truly innovative and prosperous emerging economy is not just the presence of government resolve to diversify markets, provide opportunity, and alleviate poverty but, more importantly, a commitment to enacting legislation that simultaneously safeguards their future children and the poor from nutrition-related disease. And, above all else, an unwavering commitment to ensuring that vulnerable populations have the health and opportunities needed to prosper.

References

Aboobaker, Shanti. 2013. "President Appeals for Unity." *Pressreader*, February 22. https://www.iol.co.za/dailynews/news/president-appeals-for-unity-1475041.

Aceves-Martins, Magaly, Elisabet Llauradó, Lucia Tarro, Rosa Solà, and Montse Giralt. 2016. "Obesity-Promoting Factors in Mexican Children and Adolescents: Challenges and Opportunities." *Global Health Action* 9 (1): 29625. https://doi.org/10.3402/gha.v9.29625.

ACN Correspondent. 2019. "Nestlé India, SM Sehgal Foundation Join Hands for Project 'Vriddhi.'" Asian Community News, April 6. https://www.asiancommunitynews.com/nestle-india-and-sm-sehgal-foundation-join-hands-for-project-vriddhi/.

ACT Promoção da Saúde. 2019. *Doenças Crônicas Não Transmissíveis no Brasil*. https://actbr.org.br/uploads/arquivos/Relatório-sombra-DCNT.pdf.

Adukia, Rajkumar. 2019. *Food Processing Industry in India*. Adukia and Associates. Unpublished manuscript. http://www.caaa.in/Image/food%20processing%20book.pdf.

Africa News Agency. 2018. "Buy Local to Save Jobs in South Africa, Says Ramaphosa." *Polity*, October 4. https://www.polity.org.za/article/buy-local-to-save-jobs-in-south-africa-says-ramaphosa-2018-10-04.

Afrida, Nani. 2013. "Reinventing Posyandu." *Jakarta Post*, April 24. https://www.thejakartapost.com/news/2013/04/24/reinventing-posyandu.html.

Agarwal, Vibhuti. 2010. "What Is the Future of Lobbying in India?" *Wall Street Journal*, December 16. https://www.wsj.com/articles/BL-IRTB-8728.

Agencia EFE. 2016. "Peña Nieto inaugura planta Nestlé en Jalisco de 245 millones de dólares." October 6. https://www.efe.com/efe/america/mexico/pena-nieto-inaugura-planta-de-nestle-en-jalisco-245-millones-dolares/50000545-3061331.

———. 2019. "ONG: Industria de comida 'chatarra' opera come crimen organizado en México." May 13. https://www.efe.com/efe/america/mexico/ong-industria-de-comida-chatarra-opera-como-crimen-organizado-en-mexico/50000545-3975354.

Agência Estado. 2003. "Presidente da Nestlé Anuncia April ao Programa Fome Zero." *Tribuna*, April 2. https://tribunapr.uol.com.br/noticias/presidente-da-nestle-anuncia-apoio-ao-programa-fome-zero/.

Agren, David. 2020. "Mexico State Bans Sale of Sugary Drinks and Junk Food to Children." *The Guardian*, August 6. https://www.theguardian.com/food/2020/aug/06/mexico-oaxaca-sugary-drinks-junk-food-ban-children.

Aguilar, A., E. Gutiérrez, and E. Seira. 2015. "Taxing Calories in Mexico." Preliminary and incomplete draft. Instituto Tecnológico Autónomo de México. http://cie.itam.mx/sites/default/files/cie/15-04.pdf.

Aguilar-Rivera, N., D. A. Rodríguez, R. Enríquez, A. M. Castillo, and S. Herrera. 2012. "The

Mexican Sugarcane Industry: Overview, Constraints, Current Status and Long-Term Trends." *Sugar Tech* 14 (3): 207–222. https://doi.org/10.1007/s12355-012-0151-3.

AIMS Institutes. 2020. "Rise of the Restaurant Industry in India." Executive summary. https://theaims.ac.in/resources/rise-of-the-restaurant-industry-in-india.html.

Aizawa, Toshiaki, and Matthias Helble. 2016. "Rapid Growth of Overweight and Obesity in Indonesia: Increasing Risk for the Poor." *Asia Pathways* (blog), March 22. https://www.asiapathways-adbi.org/2016/03/rapid-growth-of-overweight-and-obesity-in-indonesia-increasing-risk-for-the-poor/.

———. Forthcoming. *Socioeconomic Related Inequity in Excessive Weight in Indonesia*. ADBI Working Paper Series. Asian Development Bank Institute. Tokyo, Japan.

Aliança pela Alimentação Adequada e Saudável. n.d. "Quem Somos." https://alimentacao saudavel.org.br/a-alianca/quem-somos/ (accessed on January 7, 2021).

Alianza por la Salud Alimentaria. 2013. *Gobierno del Distrito Federal con Coca-Cola contra la Salud Pública de Los Capitalinos*. June 27. https://alianzasalud.org.mx/2013/06/gobierno-del-distrito-federal-con-coca-cola-contra-la-salud-publica-de-los-capitalinos/.

All That's Interesting. 2017. "India Considers a 'Fat Tax' for Junk Food." May 17, updated on May 15, 2018. https://allthatsinteresting.com/india-fat-tax.

Alliance against Conflict of Interest (AACI). 2014. "Conflict of Interest: A Case for Legislation." February 4. http://www.aaci-india.org/ACCI-news/AACI%20Update%204.pdf.

Allison, Elton. 2018. "Drivers of the Obesity Epidemic in Brazil." Agência FAPESB News, September 19. https://agencia.fapesp.br/drivers-of-the-obesity-epidemic-in-brazil/28742/.

Almeida, Celia, Claudia Travassos, Silvia Porto, and Maria Eliana Labra. 2000. "Health Sector Reform in Brazil: A Case Study of Inequity." *International Journal of Health Services* 30 (1): 129–162.

Al-Mendalawi, M. 2016. "The Study of Obesity among Children Aged 5–18 Years in Jaipur, Rajasthan." *Muller Journal for Medical Sciences and Research* 8 (10): 60.

Alpert, Bill. 2017. "How Sweet It Is: Rising Sales Could Lift Mondelez." *Barron's*, November 25. https://www.barrons.com/articles/how-sweet-it-is-rising-sales-could-lift-mondelez-1511577542.

Alves, Gabriel. 2016. "Indústrias de Alimentos Criam Regras de Publicidade Para Crianças." *Folha de São Paulo*, December 16. https://www1.folha.uol.com.br/equilibrioesaude/2016/12/1841887-industrias-de-alimentos-criam-nova-regra-de-publicidade-para-criancas.shtml.

———. 2018. "Empresas de Alimentos Reduzem Propagandas Voltadas para Crianças." *Folha de São Paulo*, March 21. https://www1.folha.uol.com.br/equilibrioesaude/2018/03/empresas-de-alimentos-reduzem-propagandas-voltadas-para-criancas.shtml.

Alves, Lise. 2018. "Brazil's KFC and Pizza Hut Consolidated with R$135 Million Investment." *Rio Times*, January 9; https://www.riotimesonline.com/brazil-news/rio-business/brazilian-mogul-to-invest-r135-million-in-kfc-pizza-hut/.

ANA reporter and staff reporter. 2019. "#SONA2019: Ramaphosa Outlines 7 Priorities and 5 Goals." IOL News, June 20, 2019. https://www.iol.co.za/news/politics/sona2019-ramaphosa-outlines-7-priorities-and-5-goals-26870427.

Anand, Geeta. 2017. "One Man's Stand against Junk Food as Diabetes Climbs across

India." *New York Times*, December 26. https://www.nytimes.com/2017/12/26/health/india-diabetes-junk-food.html.

Anbalagan, Amresh. 2018. "Unique Battle between International and Local Convenience Stores in Indonesia." *The Low Down, Momentum Works* (blog), October 26. https://thelowdown.momentum.asia/unique-battle-between-international-and-local-convenience-stores-in-indonesia/.

Andersen, Nic. 2018. "The South African Fast Food Franchises That Make the Most Money." *The South African*, August 3. https://www.thesouthafrican.com/news/south-african-fast-food-franchises-profits/.

Andoko, Effendi, and Aurellia Candida Doretha. 2019. "Analysis of Indonesian Government Strategies to Food Security: Harnessing the Potential of Natural and Human Resources." FFTC Agricultural Policy Articles, September 20. https://ap.fftc.org.tw/article/1588.

Andrade, Giovanna Calixto, Maria Laura da Costa Louzada, Catarina Machado Azeredo, Camila Zancheta Ricardo, Ana Paula Bortolleto Martins, and Renata Bertazzi Levy. 2018. "Out-of-Home Food Consumers in Brazil: What Do They Eat?" *Nutrients* 10 (2): 218. https://www.doi.org/10.3390/nu10020218.

Ang, Timothy. 2019. "Bursting at the Seams: Obesity in China." CKGSB Knowledge, October 2. https://english.ckgsb.edu.cn/knowledges/obesity-in-china/.

Anitharaj, M. S. 2018. "Global Fast Food Retailing in India—a Way Ahead." *IOSR Journal of Business and Management* 20, no. 2 (2018): 38–43. https://www.iosrjournals.org/iosr-jbm/papers/Vol20-issue2/Version-2/F2002023843.pdf.

Antipolis, Sophia. 2016. "China Pays Price of Western Lifestyle with Soaring Childhood Obesity." European Society of Cardiology. April 27. https://www.sciencedaily.com/releases/2016/04/160426215327.htm.

Antlöv, Hans, Derick Brinkerhoff, and Ehlke Rapp. 2010. "Civil Society Capacity Building for Democratic Reform: Experience and Lessons from Indonesia." *Voluntas: International Journal of Voluntary and Nonprofit Organizations* 21 (3): 417–439. https://www.doi.org/10.1007/s11266-010-9140-x.

Antono, Lina, Astri Kurniati, Amelinda Angela, Kamalita Pertiwi, and Susana. 2013. "The Incidence of Diabetes in Indonesian Young Adults: The Importance of Lifestyle Compared to Family History." International Conference on Food and Agricultural Sciences, *IPCBEE* 55: 62–66. http://www.ipcbee.com/vol55/012-ICFAS2013-G2015.pdf.

Aparecida Borges, Camila, William Cabral-Miranda, and Patricia Constante Jaime. 2018. "Urban Food Sources and the Challenges of Food Availability according to the Brazilian Dietary Guidelines Recommendations." *Sustainability* 10 (12): 4643. https://www.doi.org/10.3390/su10124643.

Aranha, Adriana, Alexandra da Costa Lunas, Carlos Américo Banco, Celso Marcatto, Crispim Moreira, Elisabetta Recine, and Francesco Pierri. 2009. *Building Up the National Policy and System for Food and Nutrition Security*. Brasília: CONSEA, Office of the President.

Aristegui, Carmen. 2019. "El Etiquetado." *La Reforma*, May 10. https://sihena.iib.unam.mx/index.php/Detail/Object/Show/page/1/facetname_0/faceta_tema_general/criteria_0/salud+pública/object_id/13063/facet_browse/1.

Aristegui Noticias. 2019. "Protector de la Corte sober Etiquetado de Alimentos Respalda a la Industrial: El Poder del Consumidor." May 6. https://aristeguinoticias.com/0605 /mexico/proyecto-de-la-corte-sobre-etiquetado-de-alimentos-respalda-a-la-industria -el-poder-del-consumidor/.

Arjun, Kharpal. 2013. "Fast Food Giants Locked in Battle for Brazilian Market." CNBC, November 8. https://www.cnbc.com/2013/11/08/fast-food-giants-locked-in-battle -for-brazilian-market.html.

Arokiasamy, Perianayagam. 2018. "India's Escalating Burden of Non-Communicable Diseases." *The Lancet Global Health* 6 (12): e1262–e1263. https://www.doi.org/10.1016 /S2214-109X(18)30448-0.

Arora, Manish, Swapnil Shinde, and R. P. Patwardhan. 2017. "Prevalence of Overweight or Obesity in Adolescent School Children from Pune, India." *Imperial Journal of Inter-disciplinary Research* 3: 1272–1276.

Arredondo, Elva M. 2007. "Predictors of Obesity among Children Living in Mexico City." *Journal of the American Dietetic Association* 107 (1): 41–45. https://doi.org/10.1016/j .jada.2006.11.018

Arvanitis, Athanasios. 2006. "Foreign Direct Investment in South Africa: Why Has It Been So Low?" In *Post-Apartheid South Africa: The First Ten Years*, edited by Michael Nowak and Luca Antonio Ricci, 64–79. Washington, DC: International Monetary Fund.

Asociación Mexicans de Diabetes. 2017. "Ejericio y Diabetes." June 21. https://fmdiabetes .org/category/ejercicio/.

Astudillo, Olaya. 2014. "Country in Focus: Mexico's Growing Obesity Problem." *The Lancet Diabetes and Endocrinology* 2 (1): 15–16. https://doi.org/10.1016/S2213-8587 (13)70160-8.

Atlanta Business Chronicle. 2015. "Coca-Cola Expands in Indonesia, $500M Investment." March 31. https://www.bizjournals.com/atlanta/news/2015/03/31/coca-cola-expands -in-indonesia-500m-investment.html.

Ávila, Mauricio Hernández, and Olga Georgina Martínez Montañez. 2011. "General Guide-lines for the Sale and Distribution of Food and Beverages Consumed by Students in Basic Education Establishments." *Boletín Médico del Hospital Infantil de México* 68 (1): 1–6.

Baby Milk Action. 2013. "Conflicts of Interest Threaten Mexico's Hunger Project— Industry's Poison Chalice." Press release, April 9. http://www.babymilkaction.org /archives/493.

Bahuguna, Karnika. 2016. "Soft Drink Companies Investing Heavily in Developing Coun-tries, Says Report." *DownToEarth*, February 10. https://www.downtoearth.org.in /news/health/soft-drink-companies-investing-heavily-in-developing-countries-says -report-52775.

Baird, Marcelo Fragano. 2015. "O Lobby na Regulação da Publicidade de Alimentos da Agência Nacional de Vigilância Sanitária." *Revista de Sociologia e Política* 24 (57): 67–91.

Baker McKenzie. 2018. *Asia Pacific Food Law Guide*. https://apacfoodlawguide.baker mckenzie.com/asia-pacific-food-law-guide/.

Baker, Phillip, Alexandra Jones, and Anne Marie Thow. 2018. "Accelerating the Worldwide Adoption of Sugar-Sweetened Beverages Taxes: Strengthening Commitment and

Capacity." *International Journal of Health Policy and Management* 7 (5): 474–478. https://www.doi.org/10.15171/ijhpm.2017.127.

Baker, Philip, and Sharon Friel. 2016. "Food Systems Transformations, Ultra-Processed Food Markets and the Nutrition Transition in Asia." *Globalization and Health* 12 (80): 1–15. https://globalizationandhealth.biomedcentral.com/articles/10.1186/s12992-016 -0223-3.

Balch, Oliver. 2012. "India: Food, Marketing and Children's Health." *The Guardian*, July 10. https://www.theguardian.com/sustainable-business/fast-food-marketing-childrens -health.

Baleta, Adele, and Fiona Mitchell. 2014. "Country in Focus: Diabetes and Obesity in South Africa." *The Lancet* 2 (9): 687–688. https://doi.org/10.1016/S2213-8587(14)70091-9.

Balisacan, Arsenio, Ernesto Pernia, and Abuzar Asra. 2002. "Revisiting Growth and Poverty Reduction in Indonesia: What Do Subnational Data Show?" ERD Working Paper No. 25. Economics and Research Department. Asian Development Bank. https:// www.adb.org/sites/default/files/publication/28320/wp025.pdf.

Ballard, John. 2018. "Is Coca-Cola a Buy?" *The Motley Fool*, November 30. https://www .yahoo.com/now/coca-cola-buy-022100203.html.

Banerjee, A. 2019. "Noncommunicable Diseases in India: Challenges and the Way For-ward." *Journal of Post-graduate Medicine* 65 (1): 5–6. https://www.doi.org/10.4103 /jpgm.JPGM_157_18.

Bankman, Judy, and Ross Miranti. 2013. "Junk Food Marketing Makes Big Move in Developing Countries." Foodtank, October 2. https://foodtank.com/news/2013/10 /junk-food-marketing-makes-big-moves-in-developing-countries/.

Barquera, Simón, Ismael Campos, and Juan A. Rivera. 2013. "Mexico Attempts to Tackle Obesity: The Process, Results, Push Backs and Future Challenges." *Obesity Reviews* 14 (52): 69–78. https://www.doi.org/10.1111/obr.12096.

Bassette, Fernanda. 2019. "Está na Hora de Tratarmos o Açúcar como Lidamos com o Tobaco?" *BBC*, July 21. https://www.bbc.com/portuguese/geral-48959819.

Basu, Moni. 2017. "India, Notorious for Malnutrition, Is Now a Land of Obesity." CNN. https://www.cnn.com/interactive/2017/10/health/i-on-india-childhood-obesity/.

Basu, Saurav, Neha Dahiya, and Damodar Bachani. 2017. "Sugar and Fat Taxes as Means to Halt Obesity and Prevent Lifestyle Diseases: Opportunities and Challenges in the Indian Context." *International Journal of Noncommunicable Diseases* 2 (2): 56–59.

Baumgartner, Frank. and Bryan Jones. 1993. *Agendas and Instability in American Politics*. Chicago: University of Chicago Press.

BBC. 2001. "India predicts diabetes explosion," February 6. http://news.bbc.co.uk/2/hi /health/1156218.stm.

———. 2014. "The Profusion of Temporarily Brazilian-Themed Products." June 18. https://www.bbc.com/news/magazine-27879430.

———. 2018. "Sugar Tax: Are Mexicans the Fattest People in the World?" April 6. https:// www.bbc.com/news/world-43668927.

Beaubien, Jason. 2017. "How Diabetes Got to Be the No. 1 Killer in Mexico." NPR, April 5. https://www.npr.org/sections/goatsandsoda/2017/04/05/522038318/how-diabetes -got-to-be-the-no-1-killer-in-mexico.

Belloni, Luiza. 2018. "Coca-Cola vs. Temer: Como a Redução do IPI no Setor de Refriger-antes Irritou a Gigante." *HuffPost Brasil*, August 21.

Bernhagen, Patrick, and Natalka Patsiurko. 2015. "Grooming for Politics: How Corpora-tions Combine Lobbying with Social Responsibility." Paper prepared for the 73rd Annual Meeting of the Midwest Political Science Association, April 16–19. https://www.semanticscholar.org/paper/Grooming-for-Politics%3A-How-Corporations-Combine-Bernhagen/d4616a6f055423f74490431219e94446632e6391.

Berry, J. M. 1977. *Lobbying for the People: The Political Behavior of Public Interest Groups.* Princeton, NJ: Princeton University Press.

Beverage Association of South Africa. 2016. *Response to Taxation of Sugar-Sweetened Bev-erages Policy Paper.*

Beverage Marketing Corporation. 2018. *What Is America Drinking? US Market Trends.* The Packaging Conference, February 5. https://www.beveragemarketing.com/docs/packagingconference2018.pdf.

Bhat, Prajwal. 2017. "India Has the Second Highest Number of Obese Children in the World." DownToEarth, June 16. https://www.downtoearth.org.in/news/health/india-has-the-second-highest-number-of-obese-children-in-the-world-58115.

Bhatnagar, Nidhi, Ravneet Kaur, and Puja Dudeja. 2014. "Food Marketing to Children in India: Comparative Review of Regulatory Strategies across the World." *Indian Journal of Pediatrics* 81: 1187–1192. https://link.springer.com/article/10.1007/s12098-014-1480-x.

Bhattacharya, Deya. 2016. "Food and Beverage Alliance Policy Guidelines Are a Good Step, but India's Public Health Framework Is a Worry." Firstpost, December 15. https://www.firstpost.com/india/food-and-beverage-alliance-policy-guidelines-are-a-good-step-but-indias-public-health-framework-is-a-worry-3156864.html.

Bhushan, Chandra. 2018. "The Politics of Samosa-versus-Burger." *Financial Express*, April 25. https://www.financialexpress.com/opinion/the-politics-of-samosa-versus-burger/1144548/.

Bhushan, Ratna. 2015. "Small Local Brands with Deeper Reach and Lower Price Give Pepsi, Coke a Run for Their Fizz." *Economic Times*, July 1. https://economictimes.indiatimes.com/industry/cons-products/food/small-local-brands-with-deeper-reach-lower-price-give-pepsi-coke-a-run-for-their-fizz/articleshow/47887949.cms?from=mdr.

———. 2016. "India Sells the Cheapest, Most Accessible Coke: President and COO of Coca Cola James Quincy." *Economic Times*, June 18. https://economictimes.indiatimes.com/industry/cons-products/food/india-sells-the-cheapest-most-accessible-coke-president-and-coo-of-coca-cola-james-quincey/articleshow/52803742.cms.

———. 2017a. "Hold Your Board Meeting Here to Get a Sense of Changing India, PM Modi Urges Food MNCs." *Economic Times*, November 6. https://economictimes.indiatimes.com/news/economy/policy/hold-your-board-meetings-here-to-get-a-sense-of-changing-india-pm-modi-urges-food-mncs/articleshow/61522991.cms?from=mdr.

———. 2017b. "Coca-Cola India to Flavour a Bigger Portfolio with Ethnicity." *Economic Times*, October 28. https://economictimes.indiatimes.com/industry/cons-products

/food/coca-cola-india-to-flavour-a-bigger-portfolio-with-ethnicity/articleshow /61280714.cms?from=mdr.

Bicchieri, Cristina. 2019. "Clean India Mission Shows That Flexibility Is Key to Even Poo Healthy." *Quartz India*, October 1. https://qz.com/india/1718798/why-narendra -modis-swachh-bharat-mission-is-working-in-india/.

Bill and Melinda Gates Foundation. 2011. "Coca-Cola Foundation Indonesia Launches 'PerpuSeru' Project." Press release. https://www.gatesfoundation.org/Media-Center /Press-Releases/2011/10/CocaCola-Foundation-Indonesia-Launches-PerpuSeru -Project.

Binderkrantz, Anne Skorkjaer, Peter Munk Christiansen, and Helene Holboe Pedersen. 2015. "Interest Group Access to the Bureaucracy, Parliament, and the Media." *Governance: An International Journal of Policy, Administration, and Institutions* 28 (1): 95–112. https:www.doi.org/10.1111/gove.12089.

Birrell, Ian. 2014. "South Africa's Obesity Crisis: The Shape of Things to Come?" *Mosaic*, September 8. https://mosaicscience.com/story/south-africas-obesity-crisis/.

Bizcommunity. 2017. "Study Finds Large Number of South Africans Happy to Be Overweight." August 29. https://www.bizcommunity.com/Article/196/323/166643.html.

Bland, Ben. 2014. "Drinks Groups Lose Some Fizz in Indonesia." *Financial Times*, November 4. https://www.ft.com/content/b2eafa70-601a-11e4-98e6-00144feabdc0.

Block, Jane Mara, Adriana Pavesi Arisseto-Bragotto, and Maria Manuela Camino Feltes. 2017. "Current Policies in Brazil for Ensuring Nutritional Quality." *Food Quality and Safety* 1 (4): 275–288. https://www.doi.org/10.1093/fqsafe/fyx026.

Bloom, D. E., C. Fonseca, V. Candeias, E. Adashi, L. Bloom, L. Gurfien, E. Jané-Llopis, A. Lubet, E. Mitgang, C. O'Brien, and A. Saxena. 2014. *Economics of Non-Communicable Diseases in India*. World Economic Forum. Boston: Harvard School of Public Health.

Bomi, Truong. 2019. "Food and the Megacity: How Urbanization and Technology Are Changing the Way China Eats (Space10)." *Medium*, March 30. https://medium.com /@truonghang297/food-and-the-megacity-how-urbanisation-and-technology-are -changing-the-way-china-eats-space10-ea51379aa4c3.

Bond, Patrick. 2018. "For South Africa's New President, 'Black Economic Empowerment' Is All about Personal Enrichment." *The Nation*, February 27. https://www.thenation .com/article/archive/for-south-africas-new-president-black-economic-empowerment -is-all-about-personal-enrichment/.

Bonilla-Chacín, M., R. Iglesias, S. Agustino, T. Claudio, and M. Claudio. 2016. *Learning from the Mexican Experience with Taxes on Sugar-Sweetened Beverages and Energy-Dense Foods of Low Nutritional Value: Poverty and Social Impact Analysis*. Washington, DC: World Bank Group.

Borges Aparecida, Camila, William Cabral-Miranda, and Patricia Constante Jaime. 2018. "Urban Food Sources and the Challenges of Food Availability According to the Brazilian Dietary Guidelines Recommendations." *Sustainability* 10 (12): 4643.

Bose, Nandita, and Tatiana Bautzer. 2018. "Walmart Sells Majority of Brazil Unit, Takes $4.5 Billion Charge." *Reuters*, June 4. https://www.reuters.com/article/us-walmart -brazil/walmart-sells-majority-of-brazil-unit-takes-4-5-billion-charge-idUSKCN 1J01L0.

Bourke, Emily Jane, and J. Lennert Veerman. 2018. "The Potential Impact of Taxing Sugar Drinks on Health Inequality in Indonesia." *BMJ Global Health* 3: e000923.

Bowie, Julia. 2019. "Introduction: Scrambling to Achieve a Moderately Prosperous Society." In *Party Watch Annual Report 2019: Scrambling to Achieve a Moderately Prosperous Society*, edited by Julia Bowie, 1–5. Washington, DC: Center for Advanced China Research.

BQ Desk. 2019. "How 'Swachh' Did India Get in the Last Five Years?" Bloomberg Quint, October 2. https://www.bloombergquint.com/economy-finance/how-swachh-did -india-get-in-the-last-five-years.

Branford, Sue. 2015. "Free Trade and Mexico's Junk Food Epidemic." Grain, March 2. https://grain.org/article/entries/5170-free-trade-and-mexico-s-junk-food-epidemic.

Brasil de Fato. 2017. "Conflicts de Interesse: JBS Financiou 36% da actual Bancada do Congress Nacional." May 22. https://www.brasildefato.com.br/2017/05/22/conflitos -de-interesse-jbs-financiou-36-da-atual-bancada-do-congresso-nacional.

Brazil, Ministry of Health. 2008. *Política Nacional de Alimentação e Nutrição*. Brasília: Ministry of Health. http://bvsms.saude.gov.br/bvs/publicacoes/politica_nacional _alimentacao_nutricao_2ed.pdf.

———. 2012. *Programa Saúde na Escola—PSE*. Brasília: Ministry of Health.

———. 2015. "Da Saúde se Cuida Todos os Dias." July 3.

———. 2017. "INCA Apoia Campanha 'Você Tem o Director de Saber o que Come.'" *Brasil, Ministério de Saúde* (blog), December 6.

Brazil, Presidency of the Republic. 2018. "Temer Stresses Importance of Industrial Sector for National Growth." July 3.

Breuer, Luis, Jaime Guajardo, and Tidiane Kinda. 2018. *Realizing Indonesia's Economic Potential*. Washington, DC: International Monetary Fund.

Briggs, Fiona. 2019. "South Africa's Fastest Growing Convenience Retail Brand, FreshStop, Turns 10." *Retail Times*, March 6. https://www.retailtimes.co.uk/south-africas-fastest -growing-convenience-retail-brand-freshstop-turns-10/.

Brodsgaard, Kjeld Erik, and Koen Rutten. 2017. "The Emergence and Development of the Socialist Market Economy (1992–2003)." In *From Accelerated Accumulation to Socialist Market Economy in China*, edited by Kjeld Erik Brodsgaard and Koen Rutten, 94–127. Netherlands: Koninklijke Brill NV.

Bruce, Ian. 2003. "Ask President Lula da Silva of Brazil." BBC, July 15. http://news.bbc.co .uk/2/hi/talking_point/3055286.stm.

Buchholz, Katharina. 2019. "Vast Majority of Americans Interested in Health Foods." Statista, January 25. https://www.statista.com/chart/16796/us-interest-in-healthy -food/.

Buckley, Lisa Keegan. 2010. "Corporate Citizenship in South Africa: A Case-Study of Coca-Cola South Africa." Master's thesis, University of the Witwatersrand, Johannesburg, South Africa.

Bühler, Thomas, Deborah Buschor, Lorena Kreis, and Lukas Tanner. 2010. "Food Security." Unpublished manuscript, Universität St. Gallen, May 10. http://www.msdconsult.ch /wp-content/uploads/2017/07/Food_Security_Endversion.pdf.

Bundhun, Rebecca. 2017. "Coca-Cola Losing Its Fizz in India." *The National*, March 25;

https://www.thenationalnews.com/business/coca-cola-losing-its-fizz-in-india-1.72443.

Bursey, Andrea Susan, Nicola Laurelle Wiles, and Chara Biggs. 2019. "The Nutrient Quality and Labelling of Ready-to-Eat Snack Foods with Health and/or Nutrition Claims." *South African Journal of Clinical Nutrition* 34: 65–71. https://doi.org/10.1080/16070658.2019.1682242.

BusinessTech. 2019. "Here's How Many South Africans Are Overweight According to Discovery." July 25. https://businesstech.co.za/news/lifestyle/331389/heres-how-many-south-africans-are-overweight-according-to-discovery/.

Business Today. 2021. "Coca Cola, Shell, IBM, Lockheed Martin CEOs Hail PM Modi's 'Come to India' Speech." September 26. https://www.businesstoday.in/current/economy-politics/coca-cola-shell-ibm-lockheed-martin-ceos-hail-pm-modi-come-to-india-speech/story/381387.html.

Business Wire. 2009. "Coca-Cola Accelerates Expansion in China: Two Plant Openings Mark New Wave of Investment in China." June 24.

Buzzanell, Peter. 2010. "Sugar in Mexico: An Industry Overview." Agweek.com, May 2. https://www.agweek.com/sugarbeet/sugar-in-mexico-an-industry-overview-by-peter-buzzanell.

BW Online Bureau. 2017. "Hindustan Coca-Cola Beverages Recognized for Its Efforts to Train 50,000 Women towards Economic Empowerment." http://bwpeople.businessworld.in/article/Hindustan-Coca-Cola-Beverages-recognized-for-its-efforts-to-train-50-000-women-towards-economic-empowerment/29-08-2017-125022/.

Calvillo, Alejandro, and Peterander Sonja. 2018. "Sugar Crisis in Mexico." Development and Cooperation, March 13. https://www.dandc.eu/en/article/mexico-consumer-protection-organisation-campaigns-against-food-lobby-and-fights-sensible.

Câmara, M. C. C., C. L. C. Marinho, M. C. Guilin, and A. M. C. B. Bragg. 2008. "A Produção acadêmica sober a Rotulagem de Alimentos no Brasil." *Revista Panamericana de Salud Pública* 23 (1): 52–58.

Cameron, Jackie. 2016. "Sugar Tax Research Funding Scandal: Investigation Exposes Sickly Coca-Cola, IRR Links." *BizNews*, December 7. https://www.biznews.com/health/2016/12/07/sugar-tax-research-funding.

———. 2017. "Ramaphosa: My New Deal for SA—and 10-Point Action Plan for Jobs, Growth, Transformation." *BizNews*, November 14. https://www.biznews.com/thought-leaders/2017/11/14/ramaphosa-new-deal-for-sa.

Campbell, Charlie. 2014. "India Just Asked PepsiCo to Help Improve the Diet of the Nation's Children." *TIME*, August 27. https://time.com/3185579/narendra-modi-diet-nutrition-india-pepsi-children-pepsico/.

Campos, Elisa. 2009. "Nestlé Aposta Suas Fichas em Venda Porta a Porta Para Conquistar Baixa Rena no País." *Negócios*, March 26. https://epocanegocios.globo.com/Revista/Common/0,,EMI65809-16355,00-NESTLE+APOSTA+SUAS+FICHAS+EM+VENDA+PORTA+A+PORTA+PARA+CONQUISTAR+BAIXA+REND.html.

Campos, H., and M. Abreu. 2010. "Fome Zero e as Parcerias: Dos Alimentos Amos Telecentros." In *Fome Zero: Uma História Brasileira*, edited by Heliana Kátia Campos and Fátima Abreu, 152–163. Brasília: Ministério do Desenvolvimento Social e Combate á Fome.

Canella, Daniela, Ana Paula Martins, Hutu F. R. Silva, Adriana Passanha, and Bárbara Lourenço. 2015. "Food and Beverage Industries' Participation in Health Scientific Events: Consideration and Conflicts of Interest." *Revista Panamericana de Salud Pública* 38 (4): 339–343.

Carriedo, Angela, Adam Koon, Luis Manuel Encarnación, Kelley Lee, Richard Smith, and Helen Walls. 2021. "The Political Economy of Sugar-Sweetened Beverage Taxation in Latin America: Lessons from Mexico, Chile, and Colombia." *Globalization and Health* 17 (1): 5. https://www.doi.org/10.1186/s12992-020-00656-2.

Carriedo-Lutzenkirchen, Ana Angela. 2018. "A Policy Analysis of the 2014 Mexican Soda Tax." PhD diss., London School of Hygiene and Tropical Medicine. https://www.doi.org/10.17037/PUBS.04648204.

Cassim, Shahida. 2010. "Food and Beverage Marketing to Children in South Africa: Mapping the Terrain." *South African Journal of Clinical Nutrition* 23 (4): 181–185.

Cassim, S. B., and D. Bexiga. 2007. "The Regulation of Advertising to Children: A Comparative Assessment." *Alternation* 14 (1): 137–165.

Castellanos, Lourdes. 2019. *Mexico: Food Processing Ingredients 2019*. GAIN report. Washington, DC: USDA Foreign Agricultural Services. https://apps.fas.usda.gov/new gainapi/api/report/downloadreportbyfilename?filename=Food%20Processing%20 Ingredients_Mexico%20City%20ATO_Mexico_3-27-2019.pdf.

Cecil, Andrea Maria. 2017. "Big Soda: Buying Chronic Disease." *CrossFit Journal*, June 26. https://journal.crossfit.com/article/soda-cecil-2017-2.

Cendrowski, Scott. 2014. "Opening Happiness: An Oral History of Coca-Cola in China." *Fortune Magazine*, September 11. https://fortune.com/2014/09/11/opening-happiness -an-oral-history-of-coca-cola-in-china/.

Centeno, Miguel Angel. 1997. *Democracy within Reason: Technocratic Revolution in Mexico* College Park: Penn State University Press.

Centre for Science and Environment. 2015. "CSE Welcomes Delhi High Court Order on Junk Food." Press release. March 18. https://www.cseindia.org/cse-welcomes-delhi -high-court-order-on-junk-food-5393.

Cerullo, Megan. 2019. "For Fashion Industry, China's Child Obesity Problem Could Be Big Business." *CBS News*, May 21. https://www.cbsnews.com/news/child-obesity -overweight-children-in-china-represent-massive-opportunity-for-fashion-industry/.

Chafea (Consumers, Health, Agriculture and Food Executive Agency). 2019. *The Food and Beverage Market Entry Handbook: The People's Republic of China: A Practical Guide to the Market in China for European Agri-food Products and Products with Geographical Indications*. Brussels: European Commission. https://ec.europa.eu/chafea/agri/sites /default/files/handbook-china-052018_en.pdf.

Chakrovorty, Joyeeta. 2019. "India is No. 2 among Countries with Most Deaths Caused by Poor Food Prices." *Times of India*, April 24. https://timesofindia.indiatimes.com /life-style/health-fitness/health-news/india-is-no-2-among-countries-with-most -deaths-caused-by-poor-food-choices/articleshow/69019345.cms.

Chamorro, Dane, and Bliss Khaw. 2018. "China: What Xi Jinping Means for Your Business." *Forbes*, October 9. https://www.forbes.com/sites/riskmap/2018/10/09/china -what-xi-jinping-means-for-your-business/?sh=5f9c9b6f1fe6.

Chan, Margaret. 2017. "Obesity and Diabetes: The Slow-Motion Disaster." *Milbank Quarterly* 95. https://www.milbank.org/quarterly/articles/obesity-diabetes-slow-motion-disaster/.

Chang, Angela Wen-Yu. 2014. "Advertising and Childhood Obesity in China." In *Strategic Urban Health Communication*, edited by Charles Okigbo, 211–219. New York: Springer Press.

Chang, Angela, Peter Schulz, Tony Schirato, and Brian Hall. 2018. "Implicit Messages Regarding Unhealthy Foodstuffs in Chinese Television Advertisements: Increasing the Risk of Obesity." *International Journal of Environmental Research and Public Health* 15 (1): 1–15. https://www.doi.org/10.3390/ijerph15010070.

Chang, Kara, and James McNeal. 2003. "Parental Concern about Television Viewing and Children's Advertising in China." *International Journal of Public Opinion Research* 15 (2): 151–166.

Charities Aid Foundation India. 2015. "NDTV Coca Cola SMS." Press release. https://cafindia.org/media-center/caf-latest-news/press-release/item/66-ndtv-coca-cola-sms.

Chatenay, Patrick H. 2013. *Government Support and the Brazilian Sugar Industry*. American Sugar Alliance, April 17. Arlington, VA: https://sugaralliance.org/wp-content/uploads/2021/01/gov-support.pdf.

Chaturvedi, Sanjay. 2019. "Silent Drivers of Childhood Obesity in India." *Indian Journal of Public Health* 63: 91–93. https://www.doi.org/10.4103/ijph.IJPH_155_19.

Chen, Jing, Chaoyiing Hu, Guozhang Zeng, Chao Xu, Lijun Xu, Junxia Shi, Conway Niu, and Liangwen Zhang. 2019. "Trends and Prevalence of Overweight and Obesity among Children Aged 2–7 from 2011 to 2017 in Xiamen, China." *Obesity Facts* 12 (4): 476–488. https://www.doi.org/10.1159/000501722.

Chen, Junshi, and Wenhua Zhao. 2012. "Diet, Nutrition, and Chronic Disease in Mainland China." *Journal of Food and Drug Analysis* 20 (1): 222–225.

Cheng, Fuzhi. 2009. "The Nutrition Transition and Obesity in China (3–9)." In *Case Study in Food Policy for Developing Countries*, edited by Per Pinstrup-Anderseon and Fuzhi Cheng, 103–114. Ithaca, NY: Cornell University Press.

Cheru, Fantu. 2001. "Overcoming Apartheid's Legacy: The Ascendancy of Neoliberalism in South Africa's Anti-Poverty Strategy." *Third World Quarterly* 22 (4): 505–527. https://www.jstor.org/stable/3993354.

Cheung, Lorena, Ruth Chan, Gary Ko, Eric Lau, Francis Chow, and Alice Kong. 2018. "Diet Quality Is Inversely Associated with Obesity in Chinese Adults with Type 2 Diabetes." *Nutrition Journal* 17 (1): 63, https://nutritionj.biomedcentral.com/articles/10.1186/s12937-018-0374-6.

Chhabara, Rajesh. 2008. "Olympics 2008: Beijing Games—Sponsors Enter Rings of Fire." Reuters Events, May 8. https://www.reutersevents.com/sustainability/business-strategy/olympics-2008-beijing-games-sponsors-enter-rings-fire.

Chibber, Ankush. 2012. "No Ban on Junk Foods in Indian Schools, but There Will Be New Standards." *Food Navigator-Asia*, January 12. https://www.foodnavigator-asia.com/Article/2012/01/12/No-ban-on-junk-foods-in-Indian-schools-but-there-will-be-new-standards.

Chilkoti, Avantika. 2016. "Asian Nations Sweeten to Idea of Sugar Taxes on Fizzy Drinks."

Financial Times, February 14. https://www.ft.com/content/7d733946-a864-11e5-955c
-1e1d6de94879.

China Consumer. 2018. "Turning Soft: Wanglaoji Is Brewing a Cola-Like Herbal Version."
Week in China, February 9. https://www.weekinchina.com/2018/02/turning-soft/.

China Daily. 2009. "Coca-Cola, MOH Tout 'Keeping Healthy Weight.'" May 18. http://
www.chinadaily.com.cn/bw/2009-05/18/content_7785381.htm.

Chinafoodlaw (blog). 2020. "China's Healthier Choice." April 30. https://chinafoodlaw.blog
/2020/04/30/chinas-healthier-choice/.

Chipman, Andrea. 2019. *Addressing Non-Communicable Diseases in Adolescents*. Economist
Intelligence Unit report. London: The Economist. https://www.younghealthprogram
meyhp.com/content/dam/young-health/Resources/research/EIU%202019%20FINAL
.PDF.

Chothia, Andrea. 2019. "Child Obesity Study: 13% of South African Children under Five
Are Obese." *The South African*, December 11. https://www.thesouthafrican.com
/lifestyle/health-fitness/child-obesity-growing-in-south-africa/.

Christian. 2011. "Indonesia Needs a Framework for Responsible Political Lobbying." Association of Accredited Public Policy Advocates to the European Union. Policy report,
November 11. http://www.aalep.eu/indonesia-needs-framework-responsible-political
-lobbying.

———. 2014. "Public Policy Advocacy in Mexico." Association of Accredited Public Policy
Advocates to the European Union, July 17. http://www.aalep.eu/public-policy
-advocacy-mexico.

Chutel, Lynsey. 2019. "South Africa's Sugar Tax is Pitting Job Losses against National
Health." *Quartz Africa*, March 15. https://qz.com/africa/1573448/sugar-tax-pits-jobs
-versus-health-diabetes-in-south-africa/.

CIAA (Confederation of the Food and Drink Industries of the EU). 2002. *Industry as a
Partner for Sustainable Development*. Brussels: CIAA Press. https://www.worldcat
.org/title/industry-as-a-partner-for-sustainable-development-food-and-drink/oclc
/60130208.

CIRS News. 2017. "Label Review and Translation of Pre-packaged Food." June 14. https://
www.cirs-reach.com/news-and-articles/What-is-a-Compliant-Chinese-Label-for
-Imported-Pre-packaged-Food.html.

Claasen, Nicole, Marinka van der Hoeven, and Namukolo Covic. 2016. "Food Environments, Health and Nutrition in South Africa: Mapping the Research and Policy Terrain." Working Paper 34. Cape Town: PLAAS, UWC, and Center of Excellence on Food
Security. https://www.africaportal.org/publications/food-environments-health-and
-nutrition-in-south-africa-mapping-the-research-and-policy-terrain/.

Claro, Rafael Moreira, Maria Aline Siqueira Santos, Tais Porto Oliveira, Cimar Azeredo
Pereira, Célia Landmann Szwarcwald, and Deborah Carvalho Malta. 2015. "Unhealthy
Food Consumption Related to Chronic Non-communicable Diseases in Brazil: National Health Survey, 2013." *Epidemiologia e Serviços de Saúde* 24: 257–265. https://
www.doi.org/10.5123/S1679-49742015000200008.

Clay, Jason. 2005. *Exploring the Links between International Business and Poverty Reduction: A Case Study of Unilever in Indonesia*. Oxfam GB, Novib, Unilever, and Unilever

Indonesia joint research project. https://www.unilever.com/Images/slp_oxfam
-exploring-business-poverty-reduction-unilever-indonesia_tcm244-419293_en.pdf.

Clere, Alex. 2018. "Yili Climbs Ahead in Ranking of Food and Soft Drinks Brands." *Foodbev
Media*, June 26. https://www.foodbev.com/news/yili-climbs-ahead-in-ranking-of
-food-and-soft-drinks-brands/.

CNN International. 2005. "China Sets 2020 Growth Goal." May 18. http://www.cnn.com
/2005/WORLD/asiapcf/05/17/eyeonchina.hujintao.target/.

Coble, Parks M. 2005. "Is China Going Capitalist? The Debate over Admitting Private
Entrepreneurs to the Membership in the Chinese Communist Party." *Studies on Asia*
3 (2): 20–27.

Coca-Cola Amatil. 2017. *Sustainability Report*. http://s3.amazonaws.com/arena-attachments
/2576570/af7bab72dde3e09c925c7bb55b84f73b.pdf?1534769613.

———. 2018. *Sustainability Report*. https://www.ccamatil.com/getmedia/d80d077e-2f8a
-4ecc-8e4e-e0dcf028df8b/2018-sustainability-report.pdf.

Coca-Cola Company. n.d. *Transforming Schools, Transforming Lives*. Final program report.
https://www.coca-colaindia.com/content/dam/journey/in/en/private/smartwater
/SMS-Final-Program-Report_LowRes.pdf.

———. 2009. "Coca-Cola Accelerates Expansion in China." June 24. https://investors.coca
-colacompany.com/news-events/press-releases/detail/164/coca-cola-accelerates
-expansion-in-china.

———. 2011a. "Coca-Cola Helps Improve Lives of African Women and Girls." Corporate
Social Responsibility Newswire, March 22. https://www.csrwire.com/press_releases
/31839-coca-cola-helps-improve-lives-of-african-women-and-girls.

———. 2011b. *The Water Stewardship and Replenish Report*. January. https://www.nature
.org/media/companies/coke_replenish_report_2011.pdf.

———. 2013. "Coca-Cola India Set to Install 1000 'eKOcool' Solar Coolers to Drive Energy
Efficiency." May 6. https://www.coca-colaindia.com/newsroom/coca-cola-india-set
-install-1000-ekocool-solar-coolers-drive-energy-efficiency.

———. 2014. *2013/2014 Sustainability Report*. http://globalsustain.org/files/2013-2014
-coca-cola-sustainability-report-pdf.pdf.

———. 2016. "The Coca-Cola Company's 5by20 Initiative Reaches More Than 1.2 Million
Women Entrepreneurs." April 12. https://www.coca-colacompany.com/press-releases
/5-by-20-initiative-reaches-more-1-2-million-women-entrepreneurs.

———. 2017. "CSR Activities." December 9. https://www.coca-colaindia.com/about-us
/csr-activities.

———. 2018. *2018 Business & Sustainability Report*. https://www.coca-colacompany.com
/content/dam/journey/us/en/policies/pdf/safety-health/coca-cola-business-and
-sustainability-report-2018.pdf.

Coca-Cola FEMSA. 2016. *Accelerating towards Excellence*. Sustainability report. https://
coca-colafemsa.com/wp-content/uploads/2019/12/Coca-Cola-FEMSA-Sustainability
-Report-2016.pdf.

Coca-Cola India. 2004. "Coca-Cola India." https://www.ibef.org/download/CocaColaIndia
.pdf.

———. 2015. "Support My School Initiative Completes 500 Schools." April 21. https://

www.coca-colaindia.com/newsroom/support-school-initiative-completes-500
-schools.

———. 2020. "Coca-Cola India Partners with Save the Children to Provide Relief Assiso
tance to Cyclone AMPHAN Impacted in West Bengal." July 7. https://m.dailyhunt.in
/news/africa/english/the+times+of+bengal+english-epaper-timbanen/coca+cola
+india+partners+with+save+the+children+to+provide+relief+assistance+to+cyclone
+amphan+impacted+in+west+bengal-newsid-n196638994.

Cockerell, Emma, and Jason Chwa. 2019. "Public Health Scholar on China's Research
Partnerships with Coca-Cola." *US-China Today,* July 8. https://china.usc.edu/public
-health-scholar-china's-research-partnerships-coca-cola.

Cois, Annibale, and Candy Day. 2015. "Obesity Trends and Risk Factors in the South
African Adult Population." *BMC Obesity* 2 (1): 42. https://doi.org/10.1186/s40608
-015-0072-2.

Coitinho, Denise, Carlos A. Monteiro, and Barry M. Popkin. 2002. "What Brazil is Doing
to Promote Healthy Diets and Active Lifestyles." *Public Health Nutrition* 5 (1a):
263–267. https://www.doi.org/10.1079/PHN2001302.

Collier, David. 1993. "The Comparative Method." In *Political Science: The State of the
Discipline II*, edited by Ada W. Finifter. Washington, DC: American Political Science
Association.

Confectionery Production. 2019. "Brazil's Leading Confectioners Prepare for Sweets and
Snacks Expo." May 14. https://www.confectioneryproduction.com/news/26320
/brazils-leading-confectioners-prepare-for-sweets-and-snacks-expo/.

Connelly, Aaron. "Joko Widodo's Indonesia: Control and Reform." In *Hopes and Doubts:
Perspectives on the Long Road to Indonesia's Economic Development*, 9–14. *The Economist*,
Intelligence Unit.

Connor, Neil. 2017. "One in Four Chinese Children Expected to be Overweight by 2030
amid Obesity Epidemic." *The Telegraph*, May 12. https://www.telegraph.co.uk/news
/2017/05/12/one-four-china-children-expected-overweight-2030-amid-obesity/.

CONSEA. 2017. "Instituto Nacional do Câncer Apoia Campanha 'Você Tem o Direito de
Saber o Que Come.'" Presidência da República, June 12.

Cook, Nicolas. 2013. *South Africa: Politics, Economy, and US Relations*. Washington, DC:
Congressional Research Service.

Coordinating Group of Nine Cities Study on the Physical Growth and Development of
Children. 2008. "A National Epidemiological Survey on Obesity of Children under
7 Years of Age in Nine Cities of China." 2008. *Chinese Journal of Pediatrics* 46 (3):
174–178.

Corcoran, Bill. 2018. "Ramaphosa's First 100 Days in Power: Building Trust an Immediate
Goal." *Irish Times*, June 7. https://www.irishtimes.com/news/world/africa/ramaphosa
-s-first-100-days-in-power-building-trust-an-immediate-goal-1.3521383.

Corporations and Health Watch. 2012. "Coke and Pepsi in China: The New Opium Trade?"
April 18. https://corporationsandhealth.org/2012/04/18/a-different-kind-of-urban
-rural-linkage/.

Correio do Brasil. 2004. "Lula Convoca Empresários a Apoiar o Desenvolvimento." https://
www.correiodobrasil.com.br/lula-convoca-empresarios-a-apoiar-o-desenvolvimento/.

Cortes, P. 2009. *The Mexican Market for Soft Drinks*. GAIN report. Washington, DC: USDA Foreign Agricultural Service.

Costa, E. A. 2013. "Regulação e Vigilância Sanitária para a Proteção da Saúde." In *A Regulação de Medicamentos no Brasil*, edited by F. P. Vieira, C. F. Rediguieri, and C. Fracalossi, 21–37. Porto Alegre: Artmed.

Costa-Font, Montserrat, and Cesar Revoredo-Giha. 2019. "Introduction of New Food Products in China: Is There a Trend towards Healthier and Safer Products?" *Social Sciences* 8 (51): 1–22. https://www.doi.org/10.3390/socsci8020051.

Craig, E., J. J. Reilly, and R. Bland. 2016. "Risk Factors for Overweight and Overfatness in Rural South African Children and Adolescents." *Journal of Public Health* 38 (1): 24–33. https://doi.org/10.1093/pubmed/fdv016.

Creamer, Terence. 2019. "Ramaphosa Identifies Growth as the 'One Goal' of His Presidency." Creamer Media's *Engineering News*, January 29. https://www.engineering news.co.za/article/ramaphosa-2019-01-29.

Creamer Media's *Engineering News*. 2019. "Coca-Cola Facilitates Health Services Delivery." March 15. https://www.engineeringnews.co.za/article/coca-cola-facilitates-health -services-delivery-2019-03-15/rep_id:4136.

Crossroads' Global Hand. 2020. "Coca-Cola Joins with 46664 in the Fight against HIV/ AIDS." https://www.globalhand.org/en/search/video/document/20694.

Cruz, F., and M. Durán. 2017. *Los Depredadores: La Historia Oscura del Presidencialismo en México*. Mexico City: Temas de Hoy.

CSR News. 2012. "$10.5 Million in New Grants from the Coca-Cola Foundation Will Spark Sustainability Efforts on Six Continents." August 30. https://www.coca-colacompany .com/press-releases/coca-cola-foundation-grants-10-5-mil-to-spark-sustainability -efforts-on-six-continents.

Cucolo, Eduardi. 2019. "Bolsonaro Eleva Benefício Fiscal para Indústria de Refrigerantes." *Folha de Pernamboco*, July 2. https://www1.folha.uol.com.br/mercado/2019/07 /bolsonaro-eleva-beneficio-fiscal-para-industria-de-refrigerantes.shtml.

Cullinan, Kerry. 2017. "Parliament Finally Passes Sugary Drinks Tax." *Health24*, December 5. https://www.news24.com/health24/diet-and-nutrition/beverages/parliament -finally-passes-sugary-drinks-tax-20171205.

Culliney, Kacey. 2018. "Mondeléz School Programs Prove Power in Public-Private Collaboration, Says Researcher." Food Navigator-Latham. September 11. https://www .foodnavigator-latam.com/Article/2018/09/11/Mondelez-International-Foundation -Healthy-Lifestyle-school-programs-analysis.

Culpepper, Pepper. 2011. *Quiet Politics and Business Power: Corporate Control in Europe and Japan*. New York: Cambridge University Press.

Dabas, Maninder. 2017. "Here's the Story of 'Double Seven', the Sarkari Cola That Was Launched for 'Achhe Din' in 1977." *India Times News*, May 23; https://www.india times.com/news/india/here-s-the-story-of-double-seven-the-sarkari-cola-that-was -launched-for-achhe-din-in-1977_-322249.html.

Dallimore, Anthea, Motshidisi Mokoena, and Zulaikha Brey. 2017. *Political Economy Analyses of Countries in Eastern and Southern Africa. A Case Study—South Africa Political Economy Analysis*. New York: UNICEF.

Dangl, Benjamin. 2010. "Dilma Rousseff: In Lula's Shadow." *The Nation*, December 29. https://www.thenation.com/article/archive/dilma-rousseff-lulas-shadow/#.

Dantas, Iuri, and Tom Mulier. 2010. "Nestlé to Sail Amazon Tributaries to Reach Consumers." *Seattle Times*. June 21. https://www.seattletimes.com/business/nestl-to-sail-amazon-tributaries-to-reach-consumers/.

De Bruycker, Iskander. 2014. "How Interest Groups Develop Their Lobbying Strategies: The Logic of Endogeneity." Paper presented at the ECPR General Conference, Glasgow, Scotland. https://ecpr.eu/Events/Event/PaperDetails/21351.

De Bruycker, Iskander, and Jan Beyers. 2019. "Lobbying Strategies and Success: Inside and Outside Lobbying in European Union Legislative Politics." *European Political Science Review* 11 (1): 57–74. https://www.doi.org/10.1017/S1755773918000218.

De Jesus, Vincent. 2014. "FDA Food Labeling Regulations for Trans Fat." In *Trans Fats Replacement Solutions*, edited by D. Kodali, 61–69. AOCS Press.

De Marco Lawyers. n.d. "Advertising Regulation in China." https://demarco.com.au/de-marco-thinks/international-advertising-law-advertising-regulation-in-china (accessed May 16, 2020).

De Villiers, Anniza, Nelia Steyn, Catherine Draper, Jean Fourie, Gerhard Barkhuizen, Carl Lombard, Lucinda Dalais, Zulfa Abrhams, and Estelle Lambert. 2012. "'HealthKick': Formative Assessment of the Health Environment in Low-Resource Primary Schools in the Western Cape Province of South Africa." *BMC Public Health* 12 (1): 794, https://doi.org/10.1186/1471-2458-12-794.

Debroy, Sumitra. 2014. "Diabetes Epidemic on Rise in India." *Times of India*, February 17. https://timesofindia.indiatimes.com/city/mumbai/Diabesity-epidemic-on-rise-in-India/articleshow/30533494.cms.

DelGrossi, Mauro, Gala Dahlet, Paulo de Lima, and Saulo Ceolin. 2019. "Brazil's Fome Zero Strategy." In *From Fome Zero to Zero Hunger: A Global Perspective*, edited by J. Graziano da Siva, 21–43. Rome: FAO.

Delobelle, Peter, David Sanders, Thandi Puoane, and Nicholas Freudenberg. "Reducing the Role of the Food, Tobacco, and Alcohol Industries in Noncommunicable Disease Risk in South Africa." *Health Education & Behavior* 43, no. 15 (2016): 705–815. https://www.doi.org/10.1177/1090198115610568.

Del Rosso, Joy Miller, and Rina Arlianti. 2009. *Investing in School Health and Nutrition in Indonesia*. Policy report. Jakarta, Indonesia: World Bank.

Dennis, Chelsea. 2019. "Coca-Cola Takes Its Obesity Philanthropy to China." Nonprofit Quarterly. China Food and Healthy Eating, January 16. https://nonprofitquarterly.org/coca-cola-takes-its-obesity-philanthropy-to-china/.

Denyer, Simon. 2015. "NGOs in China Fear Clampdown as Xi Jinping Plans New Security Controls." *The Guardian*, March 30.

Deshpande, Shailesh, A. G. Unnikrishnan, and Tushima Mashelkar. 2015, May. "Tackling Childhood Obesity: A Novel School-Based Programme in India." Diabetes Voice Online.

Desidério, Mariana. 2018. "Por que a Coca-Cola Colocou Temer na Parede." *Negócios*, August 21.

Development Solutions. 2016. *The Food and Beverage Market Entry Handbook: Indonesia. European Commission*. European Union Press, 2016.

Devulapalli, Rohan Saketh. 2019. "Combating Childhood Obesity in India." Scholastic Kids Press, April 15. https://kpcnotebook.scholastic.com/post/combating-childhood -obesity-india.

Dey, Sushmi. 2016. "22% of Indian Kids Are Obese, Face Health Risks." *Times of India*, January 28.

Dezan Shira and Associates. 2011. *Master Plan: Acceleration and Expansion of Indonesia Economic Development 2011–2015, Indonesia.*

———. 2016. "Q&A: Investing in China's Food and Beverage Industry." China Briefing, November 11.

Diallo, Fatoumata. 2019, March. "China's Anti-Poverty Efforts: Problems and Progress." Institute for Security and Development. Focus Asia.

Dias, Laércio Fidelis, Jouliana Jordan Nohara, and Thaís da Costa Pio dos Reis. 2012. "Alimentação Propagandas e Saúde Infanto—Juvenil." REMark-Revista Brasileira de Marketing 11 (1): 3–28. https://www.redalyc.org/pdf/4717/471747527002.pdf.

Dias, Patricia Camacho, Patrícia Henrique, Luiz Antonio dos Anjou, and Luciene Burlandy. 2017. "Obesity and Public Policies: The Brazilian Government's Definitions and Strategies." *Cadernos de Saúde Pública* 33 (7): 1–11.

Diela, Tabita. 2015. "Sugary Drinks Industry: Sugar Good, Tax Bad." *Jakarta Globe*, December 15.

———. 2016. "Businesses Warn Gov't against 'Misplaced' Plastic Bottle Tax." *Jakarta Globe*, May 16.

digitalLEARNING Network News. 2014. "Centre Invites PepsiCo to Partner for R&D in Processed Food Products." August 26.

Dillman Carpentier, Francesca R., Teresa Correa, Marcela Reyes, and Lindsey Smith Taillie. 2020. "Evaluating the Impact of Chile's Marketing Regulation of Unhealthy Foods and Beverages: Preschool and Adolescent Children's Changes in Exposure to Food Advertising on Television." *Public Health Nutrition* 23 (4): 747–755.

Ding, Z. Y., R. Zhang, and Z. Huang Z. 1989. "Epidemiological Survey of Simple Obesity among Children Aged 0–7 Years in Urban Areas of China." *Acta Nutrimenta Sinica* 3: 255–266.

Dipa, Arya. 2019. "Obesity Continues to Haunt Indonesia Despite Campaign." *Jakarta Post*, February 3.

Direct China Chamber of Commerce. 2018. "Soft Drinks in China Market." February 21. https://www.dccchina.org/news/soft-drinks-china-market-import-soft-drinks-to -china-chinese-importers/.

Discurso do Presidente da República. 2004. *Discurso do Presidente da República, Luiz Inácio da Silva, na Cerimônia Oficial de Inaguração da Nova Fábrica de Café Solúvel da Nestlé.* Presidential speech, April 1. http://www.biblioteca.presidencia.gov.br/presidencia /ex-presidentes/luiz-inacio-lula-da-silva/discursos/10-mandato/2004/01-04-2004 -discurso-do-presidente-da-republica-luiz-inacio-lula-da-silva-na-cerimonia-oficial -de-inauguracao-da-nova-fabrica-de-cafe-soluvel-da-nestle.

DLA Piper. 2016. *Advertising & Marketing to Children: Global Report*. London: DLA Piper Press.

Dludla, Nqobile. 2016. "South Africa Approves SABMiller, Coke Bottling Deal with Conditions." *Reuters*, May 10.

Doctor, Mahrukh. 2010. "Brazil's Rise and the Role of Big Business." BCJIA Editors, December 29. https://core.ac.uk/download/pdf/151162681.pdf.

Donaldson, John. 2019. "For Ye Have the Poor Always with You: Exploring China's Latest War on Poverty." In *Party watch Annual Report 2019: Scrambling to Achieve a Moderately Prosperous Society*, edited by Julia Bowie, 50–60. Washington, DC: Center for Advanced China Research.

Dong, Liu. 2017. "Tipping the Scale: Beijing Leads in Obesity Rate." *China Daily*, June 28.

Dong, Yanhui, Yinghua Ma, Bin Dong, Zhiyong Zou, Peijin Hu, Zhenghe Wang, Yide Yang, Yi Song, and Jun Ma. 2019. "Geographical Variation and Urban-Rural Disparity of Overweight and Obesity in Chinese School-Aged Children between 2010 and 2014: Two Successive National Cross-Sectional Surveys." *BMJ Open* 9 (4): e025559. http://dx.doi.org/10.1136/bmjopen-2018-025559.

Douglas, Bruce. 2015. "Brazil Bans Corporations from Political Donations amid Corruption Scandal." *The Guardian*, September 18.

Drogin, Bob. 1994. "Mandela Outlines His Vision for South Africa: Democracy, President Sets Health Tone in State of Nation Speech. He Balances Blacks' Needs, Whites' Fears." *Los Angeles Times*, May 25.

DT Next. 2017. "Coca-Cola India, FSSAI Join Hands to Train Street Food Vendors." March 28. https://www.dtnext.in/News/Business/2017/03/28210718/1030071/CocaCola -India-FSSAI-join-hands-to-train-street-food-.vpf.

Dubashi, Jagannath. 1984. "Indian Soft Drink Industry Goes on Advertising and Sales Promotion Spree." *India Today*, May 31.

Duncan, Bruce Bartholow, Maria Inês Schmidt, Ewerton Cousin, Maziar Moradi-Lakeh, Valéria Maria de Azeredo Passos, Elisabeth Barboza França, Fátima Marinho, and Ali H. Mokdad. 2017. "The Burden of Diabetes and Hyperglycemia in Brazil-Past and Present: Findings from the Global Burden of Disease Study 2015." *Diabetology and Metabolic Syndrome* 9 (1): 18. https://www.doi.org/10.1186/s13098-017-0216-2.

Durairaj, Amialya. 2018, June. "Diabetes Is on the Rise in India: Is Fast Food to Blame?" FoodTank. https://foodtank.com/news/2018/06/diabetes-india-fast-food-nutrition/.

Dutt, Anonna, and Puja Pednekar. 2017. "How Safe Are Our Kids: Tall Order to Keep Them Away from Junk Food." *The Hindustan Times*, February 8. https://www.hindustan times.com/india-news/how-safe-are-our-kids-tall-order-to-keep-them-away-from -junk-food/story-03mlmBkYLIl1RJHeWU8PiL.html.

Dwyer, Liz. 2015. "India's Obesity Problem Is So Huge, Officials Want to Ban Junk-Food Sales to Students." Takepart, August 21. https://www.yahoo.com/entertainment/s /indias-obesity-problem-huge-officials-want-ban-233111649.html.

EatSmart@school.hk. 2020. "Background." https://school.eatsmart.gov.hk/en/content .aspx?id=6001

Eckstein, Harry. 1960. *Pressure Group Politics: The Case of the British Medical Association*. London: Allen and Unwin.

Economic Times. 2011. "All India Food Processors Association Moves Delhi HC on Junk Food Ban in Schools." November 2.

———. 2017. "FSSAI Ties Up with Coca-Cola to Train 50,000 Food Vendors." March 27. https://economictimes.indiatimes.com/industry/cons-products/food/fssai-ties

-up-with-coca-cola-to-train-50000-food-vendors/articleshow/57858671.cms?from
=mdr.

Economic Times Bureau. 2014. "Make in India: How PM Modi's Ambitious Plan Will Make
India a Manufacturing Superpower." November 10. https://economictimes.india
times.com/news/economy/policy/make-in-india-how-pm-modis-ambitious-plan
-will-make-india-a-manufacturing-superpower/articleshow/43382742.cms.

The Economist. 2019. "As China Puts On Weight, Type-2 Diabetes is Soaring." December 12.
https://www.economist.com/china/2019/12/12/as-china-puts-on-weight-type-2
-diabetes-is-soaring.

Economist Intelligence Unit. 2017. "The Impacts of Banning Advertising Directed at
Children in Brazil." London: Economist Intelligence Unit. http://graphics.eiu.com
/upload/pp/EIU-Alana-Report-WEB-FINAL.pdf.

Edmonds-Poli, Emily, and David A. Shirk. 2020. *Contemporary Mexican Politics.* Lanham,
MD: Rowman and Littlefield.

EIBN. 2014. *EIBN Sector Reports, Food & Beverage.* https://www.flandersinvestmentand
trade.com/export/sites/trade/files/news/637150602213204/637150602213204_1.pdf.

Elver, Hilal. "Fome Zero: How Brazil's Success Story Became a Model for Achieving the
Right to Food." In *From Fome Zero to Zero Hunger: A Global Perspective*, edited by
J. Graziano da Siva, 98–110. Rome: FAO. http://www.fao.org/3/ca5524en/ca5524en.pdf.

Embassy of the People's Republic of China in the United States of America. 2011. "Xinhua:
China Raises Poverty Line by 80 PCT to Benefit over 100 MLN." November 29.

Endahayu, Cahyani. 2019. "Indonesia-Food and Drugs Supervisory Agency Unifies
Processed Food Label Provisions." Conventus Law. September 20. https://www
.conventuslaw.com/report/indonesia-food-and-drugs-supervisory-agency/

EP Staff. 2017. "Coca-Cola Will Use Gov't Partnership to Promote Unhealthy Products,
Experts Say." *Business and Economy*, March 30.

Equipe BeffPoint. 2018. "Empresas de Alimentos Reduzem Propagandas Voltadas para
Crianças." March 22. https://www.beefpoint.com.br/empresas-de-alimentos-reduzem
-propagandas-voltadas-para-criancas/.

Erlanger, Steven. 1998. "The Fall of Suharto: The Legacy; Suharto Fostered Rapid Economic Growth, and Staggering Graft." *New York Times*, May 22.

Erwidodo. 2017. *Funding Heifer Importation in Indonesia.* ICASEPS, Ministry of Agriculture.
Workshop on Importing Dairy Heifers into Indonesia: Opportunity and Challenges
for Growing National Herd, Hotel Santika, Bogor, September 28.

Esworthy, Emily. 2018. "National Nutrition Communications Campaign Turns Advocacy
Targets into Champions to Influence Stunting Policies in Indonesia." IMA World
Health, May 2.

ETBrandEquity. 2019. "Nestle India Commemorates 10 Years of Its Flagship 'Health Kids
Programme.'" ETBrandEquity.com, September 30. https://brandequity.economic
times.indiatimes.com/news/marketing/nestle-india-commemorates-10-years-of
-its-flagship-healthy-kids-programme/71377675.

ET Bureau. 2014. "Private, Public Companies like Dabur, TCS, Indian Oil, GAIL and Others
Pledge Support to Swachh Bharat Mission." *Economic Times*, November 10. https://
economictimes.indiatimes.com/news/company/corporate-trends/private-public

-companies-like-dabur-tcs-indian-oil-gail-and-others-pledge-support-to-swachh
-bharat-mission/articleshow/44144497.cms.

Ettinger, David, Wilfred Feng, Jenny Xin Li, Chen Hu, and Yin Dai. 2019. "China Food and Food Packaging Laws." *National Law Review*. March 21.

Euphrasio, Andre. 2017. "Are Smaller Formats T. H. Key to Boosting Brazil's Grocery Market?" February 7. https://www.mintel.com/blog/retail-market-news/smaller -formats-boost-brazils-grocery-market.

EU-Indonesia Business Network. 2017. EIBN Sector Reports: Food and Beverage.

EU SME Centre. 2011. *Food and Beverages Technical Requirements and Labelling*. EUSME Centre Publication.

———. 2015. *Food and Beverage Technical Requirements and Labelling*. EUSME Centre Publication.

Euromonitor International. 2020a, February. "Convenience Stores in Brazil." Country report, February 2020.

———. 2020b, March. "Convenience Stores in South Africa." Market research report.

European Commission. n.d. "Developments and Forecasts of Growing Consumerism." Knowledge for Policy. https://ec.europa.eu/knowledge4policy/foresight/topic /growing-consumerism/more-developments-relevant-growing-consumerism_en (accessed August 29, 2020).

European Society of Cardiology. 2016. "China Pays Price of Western Lifestyle with Soaring Childhood Obesity." *ScienceDaily*, April 26.

Evia-Viscarra, María Lola, Rodolfo Guardado-Mendoza, and Edel Rafael Rodea-Montero. 2016. "Clinical and Metabolic Characteristics among Mexican Children with Different Types of Diabetes Mellitus." *PLOS One* 11 (12): 0168377. https://doi.org/10.1371 /journal.pone.0168377.

ExpokNews. 2012. "Coca-Cola presenta su plataforma de bienestar integral como eje para contribuir a reducir la obesidad y el sedentarismo." October 12.

Export.gov. 2019. "China-Labeling/Marking Requirements." November 14.

EY. 2017. "High Growth Segments of the Delicious Indian Food and Beverage Industry." *India Forbes*, November 21. https://www.forbesindia.com/blog/business-strategy /high-growth-segments-of-the-delicious-indian-food-and-beverage-industry/.

Faheem, Hadiya. 2009. *Coca-Cola India's Corporate Social Responsibility Strategy*. OIKOS Foundation for Economy and Ecology. OIKOS Sustainability Case Collection. https:// oikos-international.org/wp-content/uploads/2013/10/oikos_Cases_2009_Coca_Cola _India.pdf.

Fahs, Ramsey. 2019. "How Coca-Cola Came to China, 40 Years Ago." *China Channel*, February 6.

Faizal, Elly Burhaini. 2012. "Indonesia Announces Wide Ranging Actions to Address Non-Communicable Diseases." *Jakarta Post*, January 9, 2012.

Falleti, Tulia. 2009. "Infiltrating the State: The Evolution of Health Care Reforms in Brazil, 1964–1988." In *Explaining Institutional Change: Ambiguity, Agency, and Power*, edited by James Mahoney and Kathleen Thelen, 38–62. New York: Cambridge University Press.

Farina, Elizabeth. 2001. "Challenges for Brazil's Food Industry in the Context of Globalization and Mercosur Consolidation." *The International Food and Agribusiness Management Review* 2 (3–4): 315–330.

Farina, Elizabeth Mercier Querido, and Cláudia Assunção dos Santos Viegas. 2003. "Foreign Direct Investment and the Brazilian Food Industry in the 1990s." *International Food and Agribusiness Management Review* 5 (2): 1–16.

Feeley, A. B., and S. A. Norris. 2014. "Added Sugar and Dietary Sodium Intake from Purchased Fast Food, Confectionary, Sweetened Beverages and Snacks among Sowetan Adolescents." *South American Journal of Child Health* 8 (3): 88–91. http://www.doi .org/10.7196/SAJCH.678.

Fernald, Lia C., Juan Pablo Gutierrez, Lynnette M. Neufeld, Gustavo Olaiz, Stefano M. Bertozzi, Michele Mietus-Snyder, and Paul J. Gertler. 2004. "High Prevalence of Obesity among the Poor in Mexico." *Jama* 291 (21): 2544–2545. https://www.doi .org10.1001/jama.291.21.2544.

Fernandez, Belen. 2020. "Neoliberal Obesity and Coronavirus I Mexico." *Al Jazeera*, September 19.

FGV Projetos. 2016. *Food Industry in Brazil and South America: Structure of Distribution and Retail Chains Inclusion in International Trade Main Market Tendencies and Perspectives Taxes and Tariffs*, FGV, no. 25. Rio de Janeiro, Brazil. https://fgvprojetos.fgv.br/sites /fgvprojetos.fgv.br/files/food_industry_eng.pdf.

Fields, Derek, and Russ Greene. 2018. "How America's Soda Industry Conquered China's Public Health Agency." Keep Fitness Legal, January 11.

Figueiredo, Ana Virginia Almeida, Elisabetta Recine, and Renata Monteiro. 2017. "Food Risk Regulation: The Tensions of the Brazilian Health Surveillance System." *Ciência and Saúde Coletiva* 22 (7): 2353–2366. doi:10.1590/1413-81232017227.25952015.

Figueiredo, John, and Brian Kelleher Richter. 2014. "Advancing the Empirical Research on Lobbying." *Annual Review of Political Science* 17: 163–165.

fin24. 2014. "Zuma: South Africa is Open for Business." August 4. https://www.news24 .com/fin24/zuma-south-africa-is-open-for-business-20140804.

Finnigan, Christopher. 2019. "Has Modi's Swachh Bharat Campaign Been a Success?" LSE blog, May 16. https://blogs.lse.ac.uk/southasia/2019/05/16/has-modis-swachh-bharat -campaign-been-a-success/.

FirstPost. 2017. "PepsiCo, Nestle, ITC, et al Devise Plans to Fight Back Govt's Higher Tax, Stringent Rule Proposals." March 16. https://www.firstpost.com/business/pepsico -nestle-itc-et-al-devise-plans-to-fight-back-govts-higher-tax-stringent-rule-proposals -3337938.html.

Fitriyanti, Azizah, and Aria Cindya. 2019. "Jokowi-Ma'ruf Pair Prepares Three Cards to Promote Social Welfare." *Antara News*, April 13. https://en.antaranews.com/news /123586/jokowi-maruf-pair-prepares-three-cards-to-promote-social-welfare.

FMCG News South Africa. 2018. "Nine Decades of Coca-Cola in Africa." *Biz Community*, May 11.

Fonseca, Fabiana. 2018. *Brazil: Retail Foods*. GAIN Report No. BR18011. Washington, DC: USDA Foreign Agricultural Service. https://apps.fas.usda.gov/newgainapi/api/report /downloadreportbyfilename?filename=Retail%20Foods_Sao%20Paulo%20ATO_Brazil _6-29-2018.pdf.

Fonseca, Fabiana, and Eros Nascimento. 2018. *Brazil: Food Processing Ingredients*. GAIN Report No. BR18007. Washington, DC: USDA Foreign Agricultural Service. https://usdabrazil.org.br/wp-content/uploads/2020/06/food-processing-ingredients-2018.pdf.

Food Business Africa. 2019. "South Africa Increases Tax on Sugary Drinks amid Struggling Sugary Industry." February 26. https://www.foodbusinessafrica.com/south-africa -increases-tax-on-sugary-drinks-amid-struggling-sugar-industry/.

Food Export Association. 2019. "Mexico Country Profile." https://www.foodexport.org /get-started/country-market-profiles/north-america/mexico-country-profile.

Food Ingredients 1st 2017. "BevSa Responds to Revised Tax Proposal on Sugar Sweetened Beverages." April 5. https://www.foodingredientsfirst.com/news/bevsa-responds-to -revised-tax-proposal-on-sugar-sweetened-beverages.html.

Food and Land Use Coalition. 2019. *Action Agenda for a New Food and Land Use Economy in Indonesia*. Jakarta: Food and Land Use Coalition. https://www.foodandlanduse coalition.org/wp-content/uploads/2019/11/17th-November-FOLU-Indonesia-Action -Agenda.pdf.

Fooks, Gary, and Anna Gilmore. 2013. "Corporate Philanthropy, Political Influence, and Health Policy." *PLOS One* 8 (11): 1–11. https://doi.org/10.1371/journal.pone.0080864.

Forbes India (blog). 2017. "High Growth Segments of the Delicious Indian Food and Beverage Industry," by EY posted on November 21. https://www.forbesindia.com/blog /technology/high-growth-segments-of-the-delicious-indian-food-and-beverage -industry/.

Foreign Agricultural Service. 2019. *Food and Agricultural Import Regulations and Standards Country Report*. United States Department of Agriculture, February 11. https://apps .fas.usda.gov/newgainapi/api/Report/DownloadReportByFileName?fileName=Food %20and%20Agricultural%20Import%20Regulations%20and%20Standards%20 Country%20Report_Jakarta_Indonesia_12-31-2019.

Fountaine, Tim, Jessica Lembong, Raajesh Nair, and Claudia Süssmuth-Dyckerhoff. 2016. *Tackling Indonesia's Diabetes Challenge: Eight Approaches from Around the World*. McKinsey and Company.

Fradkin, Chris, and Maria Angela Mattar Yunes. 2014. "Childhood Obesity in Brazil: Lessons to be Learned from the Northern Hemisphere." *Educação, Ciência e Cultura* 19 (2): 117–122.

Fradkin, Chris, Nadia C. Valentini, Glauber C. Nobre, and João OL dos Santos. 2018, April. "Obesity and Overweight among Brazilian Early Adolescents: Variability across Region, Socioeconomic Status, and Gender." *Frontiers in Pediatrics* 6 (2018): 81. http:/ www.doi.org/10.3389/fped.2018.00081.

Fraser, Barbara. 2013. "Latin American Countries Crack Down on Junk Food." *The Lancet* 382 (9890): 385–386. https://www.doi.org/10.1016/S0140-6736(13)61657-8.

Freifelder, Jack. 2015. "Beverage Battle in China Goes Beyond Colas." *China Daily USA*, May 12.

Freitas, Daniel Antunes, Árlen A. Sousa, and Kimberly Jones. 2014. "Development, Income Transfer Strategies, and the Nutrition Transition in Brazilian Children from a Rural and Remote Region." *Rural and Remote Health* 14 (1): 2632.

Freitas, Gerson, Jr. 2019. "Whoppers Sizzle in Steak Land as Burger King Rises in Brazil."

Bloomberg, January 9. https://www.bloombergquint.com/business/whoppers-sizzle
-in-land-of-steak-as-burger-king-surges-in-brazil.

French, Paul. 2015a. "Fat China: How Are Policymakers Tackling Rising Obesity?" *The Guardian*, February 12.

———. 2015b. "How Are Policymakers Tackling Rising Obesity in China?" NDTV Food News, February 15. https://food.ndtv.com/health/how-are-policymakers-tackling
-rising-obesity-in-china-739335.

Fu, Jun-Fen, Li Liang, Chun-Xiu Gong, Feng Xiong, Fei-Hong Luo, Gi-Li Liu, Pin Li, Li Liu, Ying Xin, Hui Yao, Lan-Wei Cui, Xing Shi, Yu Yang, Lin-Qi Chen, and Hai-Yan Wei. 2013. "Status and Trends of Diabetes in Chinese Children: Analysis of Data from 14 Medical Centers." *World Journal of Pediatrics* 9 (2): 127–134. https://doi.org/10.1007
/s12519-013-0414-4.

Fukuoka, Yuki. 2019, July. *Indonesia's Jokowi to Commence Second Term: Challenges of Becoming a Leading Economy by 2045*. Global Strategic Studies Institute Monthly Report. Mitsui and Co.

Gaiha, Raghav, Raghbendra Jha, and Vani Kulkarni. 2011. "Affluence, Obesity and Non-communicable Diseases in India." January 5. https://papers.ssrn.com/sol3/papers
.cfm?abstract_id=1735687.

Gais, T. L., and J. L. Walker Jr. 1991. "Pathways to Influence in American Politics." In *Mobilizing Interest Groups in America*, edited by J. L. Walker Jr., 103–122. Ann Arbor: University of Michigan Press.

Gale, Fred, Ping Tang, Xianhong Bai, and Huijun Xu. 2005. *Commercialization of Food Consumption in Rural China*. Washington, DC: United States Department of Agriculture.

Games, P., and P. Hut. 2010. "Brazil Fast Food: A Restaurant Chain with Staying Power." Seeking Alpha, June 8.

Gandhi, Feroze Varun. 2017. "A Necessary Reform: On Conflict of Interest." *The Hindu*, December 30.

Garceau, Oliver. 1941. *The Political Life of the American Medical Association*. Cambridge, MA: Harvard University Press.

Garza-Montoya, B., and M. Ramos-Tovar. 2017. "Cambios en los Patrones de Gasto en Alimentos y Bebidas de Hogares Mexicanos." *Salud Publica de Mexico* 59 (6): 612–620.

Gasnier, Annie. 2010. "Brazil Ponders Future of Successful Hunger Relief Program." *The Guardian*, September 21.

Gauba, Vaishali. 2015. "India's Fast-Food Industry is Becoming a Major Market." CNBC, April 2.

Gauri, Varun, and Peyvand Khaleghian. 2002. "Immunization in Developing Countries: Its Political and Organizational Determinants." *World Development* 30 (12): 2109–2132.

Gayanti, Mentari Dwi, and Yuni Arisa. 2019. "Pepsi Leaves Indonesia Due to Increasingly Strict Regulations: GAPMMI." Antara News, October 3. https://en.antaranews.com
/news/134058/pepsi-leaves-indonesia-due-to-increasingly-strict-regulations-gapmmi.

George, Nirmala. 2016. "India Says Number of Obese Teens Nearly Doubles in Five Years." *Medical Press*, March 9.

———. 2017. "A Wealthier India Sees Alarming Rise in Adolescent Diabetes." *Medical Express*, June 1.

Geromel, Ricardo. 2012. "What Is Brazil's Most Attractive Sector?" *Forbes*, November 14.

Ghosh, Palash. 2013. "Fat of the Land: In India, Obesity Affects the Affluent, Not the Poor." *International Business Times*, May 29. https://campbellmgold.co.uk/archive _blowing_in_the_wind/obesity_in_india_may_2013.pdf.

Giammona, Craig. 2019. "Coca-Cola Jumps on Profit Beat as China Fuels Beverage Sales." *Bloomberg*, April 23.

Gilmore, Anna, Emily Savell, and Jeff Collin. 2011. "Public Health, Corporations and the New Responsibility Deal: Promoting Partnerships with Vectors of Disease?" *Journal of Public Health* 33 (1): 2–4.

Giuntella, Osea, Matthias Rieger, and Lorenzo Rotunno. 2020. "Weight Gains from Trade in Foods: Evidence from Mexico." *Journal of International Economics* 122: 103277. https://doi.org/10.1016/j.jinteco.2019.103277.

Global Times. 2016. "PepsiCo Promotes Nutrition and Dietary Balance." May 15.

———. 2018a. "PepsiCo: In China, for China, with China." June 19. https://www.global times.cn/page/201806/1107446.shtml.

———. 2018b. "PepsiCo Donates Additional $1 Million Plus New Quaker Kids Nutrition Products to China Foundation for Poverty Alleviation." July 23.

Goedecke, Julia, and Courtney Jennings. 2005. "Ethnic Differences in Obesity." *CME* 23 (11): 546–550.

Goedecke, Julia H., Courtney Jennings, and Estelle Lambert. 2006. "Obesity in South Africa." In *Chronic Diseases of Lifestyle in South Africa since 1995–2005. Technical report*, edited by Krisela Steyn, Jean Fourie, and Norman Temple, 65–79. Cape Town: South African Medical Research Council.

Goldfrank, Benjamin. 2011. *Deepening Local Democracy in Latin America: Participation, Decentralization, and the Left*. University Park: Pennsylvania State University Press.

Goldstein, Susan. 2016. "Children Must be Protected from Robust Marketing If They're Going to Eat Well." *The Conversation*, August 28.

Gomes, Fabio S. 2015. "How the Brazilian Dietary Guidelines Work with the Promotion of Fruits and Vegetables." *The Global Food Network*, no. 3 (October). https://www.half yourplate.ca/wp-content/uploads/2015/02/GFVN_-3_Food_regulation_and_FV _promotion_Brazil_10_2015.pdf.

Gómez, Eduardo J. 2013. "What Reverses Decentralization? Failed Policy Implementation, Civic Supporters, Policy Ideas, or Central Bureaucrats' Expertise? The Case of Brazil's AIDS Program." *Administration and Society* 20 (2): 1–31. https://www.doi.org/10.1177 /0095399712469199.

———. 2015a. *Contested Epidemics: Policy Responses in the BRICS and US and What the BRICS Can Learn*. London: Imperial College Press.

———. 2015b. "Understanding the United States and Brazil's Response to Obesity: Institutional Conversion, Policy Reform, and the Lessons Learned." *Global Health* 11(24): 1–14.

———. 2018. *Geopolitics in Health: Confronting AIDS, Obesity, and Tuberculosis in the Emerging BRICS Economies*. Baltimore: Johns Hopkins University Press.

———. 2019a. "Coca-Cola's Political and Policy Influence in Mexico: Understanding the Role of Institutions, Interests, and Divided Society." *Health Policy and Planning* 34 (7): 520–528. https://www.doi.org/10.1093/heapol/czz063.

———. 2019b. "Let Them Eat Junk: Snack and Soda Companies Seek Political Cover in the Developing World." *Foreign Affairs*, July 31.

———. 2021, September. "The Politics of Ultra-Processed Foods and Beverages Regulatory Policy in Upper-Middle-Income Countries: Industry and Civil Society in Mexico." *Global Public Health*. https://www.doi.org/10.1080/17441692.2021.1980600.

Gómez, Eduardo J., and Claudio Méndez. 2021. "Institutions, Policy, and Non-Communicable Diseases (NCDs) in Latin America." *Journal of Politics in Latin America* 13 (1): 114–137. https://doi.org/10.1177/1866802X20980455.

Gómez, Luis, Enrique Jacoby, Lorena Ibarra, Diego Lucumí, Alexandra Hernandez, Diana Parra, Alex Florindo, and Pedro Hallal. 2011. "Sponsorship of Physical Activity Programs by the Sweetened Beverages Industry: Public Health or Public Relations?" *Rev Saúde Pública* 45 (2): 423–427.

Gonçalves, Tamara Amoroso. 2012. "Advertisement to Children in Brazil: Tensions between Regulation and Self-Regulation." Paper presented at the 5th International Conference on Multidisciplinary Perspectives on Child and Teen Consumption, Milano, Italy.

Gonzalez-Rossetti, A. 2001. *The Political Dimension of Health Reform: The Case of Mexico and Colombia*. PhD diss. London School of Hygiene and Tropical Medicine.

Gorbiano, Marchio Irfan. 2019a. "Rip 10.3 Trillion Allocated for Jokowi's Preemployment Cards." *The Jakarta Post*, July 17.

———. 2019b. "2020 Budget Reflects Jokowi's Campaign Promises." *Jakarta Post*, July 17. https://www.thejakartapost.com/news/2019/07/17/2020-budget-reflects-jokowis-campaign-promises.html.

Gossett, Alexandra. 2011. "Brazil's Utilization of Self-Regulation to Control the Advertising Industry." *Law and Business Review of the Americas* 17 (1): 121–132.

Govender, Karina, Ashika Naicker, Carin Napier, and Deepak Singh. 2018. "School Snacking Preferences of Children from a Low Socio-Economic Status Community in South Africa." *Journal of Consumer Sciences* 3: 1–10.

Govender, Prega. 2019. "Ban Junk Food and Fizzy Drinks from Schools." *Times Live*, December 20.

Government of India. n.d. "Sector Survey: Food Processing." Make in India.

Government of Indonesia. 2010. "The Minister of National Development Planning Head of National Development Planning Agency." National Plan of Action for Food and Nutrition 2011–2015. Jakarta, Indonesia: Government of Indonesia.

Government Regulation No 69/199 on Food Labels and Advertisements. 2019. Office of the President of the Republic of Indonesia. http://www.flevin.com/id/lgso/translations/JICA%20Mirror/english/30.PP_NUMBER%2069%20OF%201999.eng.html.

Gqubule, Duma. 2019. "Jobs Won't Materialise until Investment Pledges Do." *New Frame*, November 14. https://www.newframe.com/jobs-wont-materialise-until-investment-pledges-do/.

GRAIN. 2015. "Free Trade and Mexico's Junk Food Epidemic." March 2. https://www.grain.org/article/entries/5170-free-trade-and-mexico-s-junk-food-epidemic.

Gray, Virginia, and David Lowery. 1996. *The Population Ecology of Interest Representation: Lobbying Communities in the American States*. Ann Arbor: University of Michigan Press.

Graziano da Silva, J., ed. 2019. *From Fome Zero to Zero Hunger: A Global Perspective*. Rome: FAO. http://www.fao.org/3/ca5524en/ca5524en.pdf.

Green, Mackenzi, Dian Hadihardjono, Alissa Pries, Doddy Izwardy, Elizabeth Zehner, and Sandra Huffman. 2019. "High Proportions of Children under 3 Years of Age Consume Commercially Produced Snack Foods and Sugar-Sweetened Beverages in Bandung City, Indonesia." *Maternal and Child Nutrition* 15 (S4): e12764. http://www.doi.org/10.1111/mcn.12764.

Greenhalgh, Susan. 2019a. "Soda Industry Influence on Obesity Science and Policy in China." *Journal of Public Health Policy* 40 (1): 5–16. https://doi.org/10.1057/s41271-018-00158-x.

———. 2019b. "Science and Serendipity: Finding Coca-Cola in China." *Perspectives in Biology and Medicine* 62 (1): 131–152.

Grobbelaar, H. H., C. E. Napier, W. N. Oldewage-Theron. 2013. "Nutritional Status and Food Intake Data on Children and Adolescents in Residential Care Facilities in Durban." *South African Journal of Clinical Nutrition* 26 (1): 29–36. https://doi.org/10.1080/16070658.2013.11734437.

Grossman, Matt. 2012. "Interest Group Influence on US Policy Change: An Assessment Based on Policy History." *Interest Groups and Advocacy* 1 (2): 171–192.

Gulati, Seema, and Anoop Miura. 2014. "Sugar Intake, Obesity, and Diabetes in India." *Nutrients* 6: 5955–5974. https://www.doi.org/10.3390/nu6125955.

Gundan, Farai. 2015. "Made in Africa: Beverages from Africa and Produced in Africa." *Forbes*, March 18.

Guo, Di, Kun Jiang, Byung-Yeon Kim, and Chenggang Xu. 2013. "Political Economy of Private Firms in China." *Journal of Comparative Economics* 42 (2): 286–303. https://doi.org/10.1016/j.jce.2014.03.006.

Gupta, Rajeev, and Denis Xavier. 2018. "Hypertension: The Most Important Non-Communicable Disease Risk in India." *India Heart Journal* 70: 565–572. https://www.doi.org/10.1016/j.ihj.2018.02.003.

Gupta, Setu, Swati Kalra, Jaya Shankar Kaushik, and Piyush Gupta. 2017. "Content of Food Advertising for Young Adolescents on Television." *Indian Journal of Community Medicine* 42: 43–45.

Guruprasad's Portal. n.d. "Part 4: Thums Up story: Govt launches 77 Double Seven Cola." guruprasad.net/posts/part-4-thums-up-story-govt-launches-77-double-seven-cola/ (accessed September 23, 2019).

Gustafson, Timi. 2017. "Younger Consumers Are More Health Conscious Than Previous Generations," *Huffington Post*, January 23. https://www.huffingtonpost.ca/timi-gustafson/younger-consumers-are-mor_b_14290774.html.

Guterres, Estefania Pinto. 2018. *Internship Report in Coca-Cola Amatil, Indonesia Balinusa*. International Industrial Engineering Study Program, Faculty of Industrial Technology, University of Atma Jaya Yogyakarta.

Guzman, Emily. 2017. "The Day in History: China's First KFC Opens by Tiananmen Square." That's News, November 28. https://www.thatsmags.com/shanghai/post/21133/this-day-in-history-first-kfc-in-china.

H. T. 2013. "Eating Themselves to Death: Waistlines Are Growing, and with Them Diabetes." *The Economist*, April 10.

Hacker, Jacob. 1998. "The Historical Logic of National Health Insurance: Structure and Sequence in the Development of British, Canadian, and US Medical Policy." *Studies in American Political Development* 12: 57–130.

Haenle, Paul. 2015. "Mounting Difficulties for Doing Business in Xi Jinping's China." *Teneo*, September 17. https://www.teneo.com/mounting-difficulties-for-doing -business-in-xi-jinpings-china/.

Halder, Arpita. 2019. "Nestlé Healthy Kids Programme Completes Ten Years of their Societal Initiative." *Deccan Chronicle*, October 3.

Hall, Richard, and Alan Deardorff. 2006. "Lobbying as Legislative Subsidy." *American Political Science Review* 100 (1): 69–84. https://www.jstor.org/stable/27644332.

Hanan, Ardi. 2018. "Unique Battle between International and Local Convenience Stores in Indonesia." *The Low Down News* (blog), October 26. https://thelowdown.momentum .asia/unique-battle-between-international-and-local-convenience-stores-in-indonesia/.

Hancock, Tom. 2017. "Obesity in China Loses Link with Affluence." *Financial Times*, June 3.

———. 2019. "Xi Jinping's China: Why Entrepreneurs Feel Like Second-Class." *Financial Times*, May 13.

Haning, Mohamad Thahir, Andi Imam Arundhana, and Asry Dwi Muqni. 2016. "The Government Policy Related to Sugar-Sweetened Beverages in Indonesia." *Indian Journal of Community Health* 28 (3): 222–227.

Harbuwono, Dante, Laurentius Pramono, Em Yuniar, and Imam Subikti. 2018. "Obesity and Central Obesity in Indonesia: Evidence from a National Health Survey." *Medical Journal of Indonesia* 27 (2): 114–120. https://doi.org/10.13181/mji.v27i2.1512.

Harris, Jennifer, and Samantha Graff. 2011. "Protecting Children from Harmful Food Marketing: Options for Local Government to Make a Difference." *Preventing Chronic Diseases* 8 (5): A92.

Hastings, Gerard. 2012, August 21. "Why Corporate Power Is a Public Health Priority." *BMJ* 345: 1–5. https://www.doi.org/10.1136/bmj.e5124.

Hawkes, Corinna. 2004. *Marketing Food to Children: The Global Regulatory Environment.* Geneva: World Health Organization Press.

———. 2007. *Marketing Food to Children: Changes in the Global Regulatory Environment 2004–2006.* Geneva: World Health Organization. https://apps.who.int/iris/bitstream /handle/10665/43693/9789240682122_eng.pdf?sequence=1.

———. 2008. "Agro-food Industry Growth and Obesity in China: What Role for Regulating Food Advertising and Promotion and Nutrition Labelling?" *Obesity Reviews* 9 (1): 151–161.

Hawkins, Laurie. 2016. "Explosion in Childhood Obesity in China 'Worst Ever', Expert Says of New Study Findings." April 28. https://www.linkedin.com/pulse/explosion -childhood-obesity-china-worst-ever-expert-hawkins-2-500-/.

He, Wei, Sherman James, Giovanna Merli, and Hui Zheng. 2014. "An Increasing Socioeconomic Gap in Childhood Overweight and Obesity in China." *American Journal of Public Health* 104 (1): e14–e22. https://www.doi.org/10.2105/AJPH.2013.301669.

Healthy Living Alliance. 2019. "HPL Anniversary Press Release." Press release, July 26. https://heala.org/hpl-anniversary-press-release/.

———. 2020. "Our Campaigns." HEALA. https://heala.org/campaigns/.

Hedberg, Tom. 2020. "The Silent Epidemic of Diabetes in China." Kinexum.

Heilmann, Sebastian. 2017, November 21. "How the CCP Embraces and Co-opts China's Private Sector." Mercator Institute for China Studies.

Heitshusen, V. 2000. "Interest Group Lobbying and US House Decentralization: Linking Informational Focus to Committee Hearing Appearances." *Political Research Quarterly* 53 (1): 151–176.

Heneghan, Carolyn. 2016. "Why Kellogg's Acquisition of Brazil's Parati Made Financial Sense." Brief. Food Dive, October 13.

Hennessy, Maggie. 2014. "Mexico Restricts Junk Food Ads; Time for Rethinking on Advertising?" Food Navigator-usa.com, July 21. https://www.foodnavigator-usa.com/Article/2014/07/22/Mexico-restricts-junk-food-ads-time-for-rethink-on-advertising.

Henriques, Isabella, and Pedro Hartung. 2014. "Sim, a publicidade voltada ás crianças é abusiva e ilegal." Migalhas de Peso, June 25. https://www.migalhas.com.br/depeso/203254/sim--a-publicidade-voltada-as-criancas-e-abusiva-e-ilegal.

Hérick de Sá, Thiago. 2014. "Can Coca Cola Promote Physical Activity?" *The Lancet* 383: 9934. http://www.doi.org/10.1016/S0140-6736(14)60988-0.

Hernández-Cordero, S., Lucía Cuevas-Nasu, M. C. Morales-Ruán, I. Méndez-Gómez Humarán, Marco A. Ávila-Arcos, and J. A. Rivera-Dommarco. 2017. "Overweight and Obesity in Mexican Children and Adolescents during the Last 25 years." *Nutrition and Diabetes* 7, no. 3 (2017): e247. https://doi.org/10.1038/nutd.2016.52.

Hillman, A. J., and M. A. Hitt. 1999. "Corporate Political Strategy Formulation: A Model of Approach, Participation, and Strategy Decisions." *Academy of Management Review* 24 (4): 825–842. http://www.jstor.com/stable/259357.

Hindu Business Line. 2017. "Nooyi to PM: Will Support Development Goals." March 2. https://www.thehindubusinessline.com/companies/nooyi-to-pm-will-support-development-goals/article9567333.ece.

Hindustan Times. 2020. "Fit India Movement 2020: PM Narendra Modi in Conversation with India's Fitness Enthusiasts Including Virat Kohli, Milind Soman." September 22. https://www.hindustantimes.com/fitness/fit-india-movement-2020-pm-narendra-modi-in-conversation-with-india-s-fitness-enthusiasts/story-l1hzOFyp2roxOWJUyNOAtK.html.

Hofman, Karen, Anne Marie Thow, Agnes Erzse, Aviva Tugendhaft, and Nicholas Stacey. n.d. "The Political Economy of Sugar-Sweetened Beverage Taxation in South Africa: Lessons for Policy Making." Unpublished manuscript. https://pmac2019.com/uploads/poster/A183-AGNESERZSE-3da6.pdf.

Hojnacki, Marie, David C. Kimball, Frank R. Baumgartner, Jeffrey M. Berry, and Beth L. Leech. 2012. "Studying Organizational Advocacy and Influence: Reexamining Interest Group Research." *Annual Review of Political Science* 15: 379–399. https://www.doi.org/10.1146/annurev-polisci-070910-104051.

Holmes, Thalia. 2018. "Sweets for My Sweet, Sugar for My Levy." *Mail and Guardian, Africa's Best Read*, November 23.

Holzendorff, Denise. 2013. "Living on the Coke Side of Thirst: The Coca-Cola Company and Responsibility for Water Shortage in India." *Journal of European Management and Public Affairs Studies* 1 (1): 1–4.

Hu, Cheng, and Weiping Jia. 2018. "Diabetes in China: Epidemiology and Genetic Risk Factors and Their Clinical Utility in Personalized Medication." *Diabetes* 67 (1): 3–11. https://doi.org/10.2337/dbi17-0013.

Huang, Echo. 2017. "The Amount China Spends Eating Out Is Greater Than the GDP of Sweden." *Quartz*, May 12.

Huang, Liping, Bruce Neal, Elizabeth Dunford, Guansheng Ma, Jason Wu, Michelle Crino, and Helen Trevena. 2016. "Completeness of Nutrient Declarations and the Average Nutritional Composition of Pre-Packaged Foods in Beijing, China." *Preventive Medicine Reports* 4: 397–403. https://doi.org/10.1016/j.pmedr.2016.08.002.

Huang, L., N. Li, F. Barzi, G. Ma, H. Trevena, E. Dunford, M. A. Land, and B. Neal. 2014. "A Systematic Review of the Prevalence of Nutrition Labels and Completeness of Nutrient Declarations on Pre-Packaged Foods in China." *Journal of Public Health* 37 (4): 649–658. https://doi.org/10.1093/pubmed/fdu091.

Huber, Bridget. 2016. "Welcome to Brazil, Where a Food Revolution is Changing the Way People Eat." *The Nation*, July 28.

Hughes, Sam. 2013. "Thums Up for Indian Cola." Serious Eats. July 23.

Huifeng, He. 2019, November. "China's Subsidies Lifting Rural Villages Out of Poverty, but Is Xi Jinping's Plan Sustainable?" *South China Morning Post*.

Hula, K. W. 1999. *Lobbying Together: Interest Group Coalitions in Legislative Politics*. Washington, DC: Georgetown University Press.

Huneke, Jonathan. 2011, June. "China Embraces Self-Regulation of Marketing." *World Commerce Review*.

Hunt, Katie. 2019. "One in Five Chinese Children is Overweight or Obese, and the Booming Economy May Be to Blame, Study Reveals." CNN, March 19.

IANS. 2016. "India Provides Huge Opportunity for Swiss Business: Narendra Modi." *Business Today*, June 6. https://www.businesstoday.in/current/economy-politics/india-provides-huge-opportunity-for-swiss-business-modi/story/233419.html.

IDEOS. 2018. "Know More about Advertising Standards Council of India." November 13. http://ideosstartup.com/knowledge-hub/know-more-about-advertising-standards-council-of-india.

Igumbor, Ehimario, David Sanders, Thandi Puoane, Lungiswa Tsolekile, Cassandra Schwarz, Christopher Purdy, Rina Swart, Solang Durão, and Cornia Hawkes. 2012. "'Big Food,' the Consumer Food Environment, Health, and the Policy Response in South Africa." *PLOS Medicine* 9 (7): 1–7. https://doi.org/10.1371/journal.pmed.1001253.

Imenda, Sitwala. 2014. "Is There a Conceptual Difference between Theoretical and Conceptual Frameworks?" *Journal of Social Sciences* 38 (2): 185–195.

Immergut, Ellen. 1992. *Health Politics: Interests and Institutions in Western Europe*. New York: Cambridge University Press.

India CSR Network. 2017. "Nestlé Healthy Kids Program Celebrates 3 Years of Partnership with Magic Bus." India Corporate Sustainability and Responsibility, November 16.

https://indiacsr.in/nestle-healthy-kids-program-celebrates-3-years-of-partnership
-with-magic-bus-in-kochi/.

India, Government. 2006. *Recommendations for a National Plan of Action for the Implementation of WHO's Global Strategy on Diet, Physical Activity, and Health in India*. New
Delhi: Government of India.

India, Ministry of Health and Family Welfare, Government of India. n.d. "National Action
Plan and Monitoring Framework for Prevention and Control of Non-Communicable
Diseases (NCDs) in India." https://www.iccp-portal.org/system/files/plans/India%20
-%20National_Action_Plan_and_Monitoring_Framework_Prevention_NCD_2013
.pdf (accessed January 23, 2021).

India Resource Center. 2017a. "India Applies Sin Tax on Sweetened Carbonated Beverages:
40% Tax on Colas to Discourage Consumption and Protect Health," India Resource
Center, August 17; accessed on-line on January 25, 2021; http://www.indiaresource
.org/news/2017/1007.html

———. 2017b. "Gov't Tie-up with Coca-Cola on Food Safety and Nutrition Misguided:
Coca-Cola Will Use Gov't Partnership to Promote Unhealthy Products." March 29.
http://www.indiaresource.org/news/2017/1006.html.

Indonesia Government. *Government Regulation No. 69/1999 On Food Labels and Advertisements*. President of the Republic of Indonesia, 1999.

Indonesia Investments. n.d. "Masterplan for Acceleration and Expansion of Indonesia's
Economic Development." https://www.indonesia-investments.com/projects
/government-development-plans/masterplan-for-acceleration-and-expansion-of
-indonesias-economic-development-mp3ei/item306 (accessed March 5, 2021).

———. n.d. "Susilo Bambang Yudhoyono Administration." https://www.indonesia
-investments.com/culture/politics/reformation/susilo-bambang-yudhoyono/item
7596 (accessed March 4, 2021).

———. 2018a. "Indonesia Sets Realistic Investment Target for Food and Beverage Industry." March 27. https://www.indonesia-investments.com/news/news-columns
/indonesia-sets-realistic-investment-target-for-food-beverage-industry/item8686.

———. 2018b. "Outlook on the Food Service Industry in Indonesia." October 11. https://
www.indonesia-investments.com/business/business-columns/outlook-on-the-food
-service-industry-in-indonesia/item9001?.

Institute for Health Metrics and Evaluation. 2019a. "India." https://www.healthdata.org
/india.

———. 2019b. "Mexico." http://www.healthdata.org/mexico.

———. 2020. "Brazil." http://www.healthdata.org/brazil.

Instituto Nacional de Câncer. 2017. "INCA apoia campanha 'Você Tem o Direito de Saber o
que Come." December 1. https://www.inca.gov.br/noticias/inca-apoia-campanha-voce
-tem-o-direito-de-saber-o-que-come.

InterGest South Africa. 2020. *Overview of the Food and Beverage Industry in Africa and
Opportunities for European Companies*. Opportunities for European Companies:
Africa's Food and Beverage Industry. https://intergest.co.za/2021/05/11/overview
-of-the-food-and-beverage-industry-in-africa-and-opportunities-for-european
-companies/.

Irwin, Rachel. "Chronic Diseases and Marketing to Children in India." Paper presented at the Roundtable on Global Health Diplomacy in Asia, London School of Hygiene and Tropical Medicine, November 17.

Ishio, Yoshito. 1999. "Interest Groups' Lobbying Tactics in Japan and the US: The Influence of Political Structures and Conflict on Tactical Choices." *Southeastern Political Review* 27 (2): 243–264.

Ismail, Adiel. 2016a. "Coca-Cola Explains the Sour Side of a Sugary Tax on SSBs." *Fin24*, December 7.

———. 2016b. "Exposed: Coca-Cola Bankrolls IRR Research on Sugary Tax in South Africa." *Fin24*, December 7.

Jack, Andrew. 2011. "Brazil's Unwanted Growth." *Financial Times*, April 8.

Jacobs, Andrew. 2019a. "How Chummy are Junk Food Giants and China's Health Officials? They Share Offices," *New York Times*, January 9. https://www.nytimes.com /2019/01/09/health/obesity-china-coke.html.

———. 2019b. "A Shadowy Industry Group Shapes Food Policy Around the World." *New York Times*, September 16. https://www.nytimes.com/2019/09/16/health/ilsi-food -policy-india-brazil-china.html.

Jacobs, Andrew, and Matt Richtel. 2017. "How Big Business Got Brazil Hooked on Junk Food." *New York Times*, September 16.

Jacobs, Harrison. 2019. "KFC Is by Far the Most Popular Fast Food Chain in China and It's Nothing Like the US Brand—Here's What It's Like." *Business Insider*, March 8.

Jacobs, Sean, and Benjamin Fogel. 2018. "From Zuma to Ramaphosa." *Jacobin*, February 22.

Jacobs, S. A., H. De Beer, and M. Larney. 2011. "Adult Consumers' Understanding and Use of Information on Food Labels: A Study among Consumers Living in the Potchefstroom and Klerksdorp Regions, South Africa." *Public Health Nutrition* 14 (3): 510–522.

Jacobsen, Jessica. 2019. "2019 Soft Drink Report: Occasional Consumer Offers Potential for Market." Beverage Industry. April 19.

Jaichuen, Nongnuch, Sirinya Phulkerd, Nisachol Certthkrikul, Gary Sacks, and Viroj Tangcharoensathien. 2018. "Corporate Political Activity of Major Food Companies in Thailand: An Assessment and Policy Recommendations." *Globalization and Health* 14: 1–11.

Jaime, P. C., C. F. da Silva, P. C. Gentility, R. M. Claro, and C. A. Monteiro. 2013. "Brazilian Obesity Prevention and Control Initiatives." *Obesity Review* 14 (2): 88–95. https:// www.doi.org/10.1111/obr.12101.

Jain, Anjali, Ashish Jain, J. P. Pankaj, B. N. Sharma, and A. Paliwal. "The Study of Obesity among Children Aged 15–18 Years in Jaipur, Rajasthan." *Muller Journal of Medical Sciences and Research* 7 (2016): 125–130.

Jakarta Post. 2015. "Unilever Commits to Investment Plan." February 28. https://www .thejakartapost.com/news/2015/02/28/unilever-commits-investment-plan.html.

———. 2019. "'We're Unstoppable', Says Jokowi-Ma'ruf Team." March 7. https://www .thejakartapost.com/news/2019/03/07/were-unstoppable-says-jokowi-maruf-team .html.

Jayanna, Krishnamurthy, N. Swarovski, Arin Kar, Satyanarayana Ramnaik, Manoj Kumar Pati, Ashwini Punjab, Prathibha Rai, Suresh Chitrapu, Gururaj Patil, Preeti Aggarwal,

Shivla Saksena, Hemanth Madegowda, S. Rekha, and H. L. Mohan. 2019. "Designing a Comprehensive Non-Communicable Diseases (NCD) Programme for Hypertension and Diabetes at Primary Health Care Level: Evidence and Experience from Urban Karnataka, South India." *BMC Public Health* 19: 409.

Jayaswal, Rajeev. 2020. "Over 400 Million Poor Now Have Access to Banks Due to Pradhan Mantri Jan Dhan Yojana: Finance Ministry," *Hindustan Times*, August 28. https://www.hindustantimes.com/india-news/over-400-million-poor-now-have -access-to-banks-due-to-pradhan-mantri-jan-dhan-yojana-finance-ministry/story -V7ZTGA4VES6PqUIbG8kAOJ.html.

Jeffery, Anthea. 2016. *A Stealth Tax, Not a Health Tax*. Johannesburg: South African Institute of Race Relations.

Jember University with IIED. 2019. *Indonesia's Triple Burden of Malnutrition: A Call for Urgent Policy Change*. Research Paper. Jember University and IIED. https://pubs.iied .org/pdfs/16662IIED.pdf.

Jewell, Jo. 2020. "Childhood Obesity: A Sustainable Development Issue." UNICEF blog, March 20.

Jia, Peng, Shuang Ma, Xin Qi, and Youfa Wang. 2019. "Spatial and Temporal Changes in Prevalence of Obesity among Chinese Children and Adolescents, 1985–2005." *Preventing Chronic Disease* 16: 190290. https://www.doi.org.10.5888/pcd16.190290.

Jin, Chuyao, Lizi Lin, Chenxiong Li, Yuanzhou Peng, Graham MacGregor, Fengjun He, and Haijun Wang. 2019. "The Sugar and Energy in Non-Carbonated Sugar-Sweetened Beverages: A Cross-Sectional Study." *BMC Public Health* 19 (1): 1141. https://www.doi .org/10.1186/s12889-019-7486-6.

Jing, Shi. 2018. "Coca-Cola Embarks on 'Healthy' Growth Rate." *China Daily*, August 30.

Jinping, Xi. 2020. "Speech at a Symposium on Revolving Prominent Problems in Poverty Alleviation." *Qiushi Journal*, updated on January 13. http://english.qstheory.cn/2020 -01/13/c_1125443359.htm.

Johns, Paul, and Ana Paula Bortoletto. 2016. "Obesity Follows Soda Consumption Like Night Follows Day." *The NCD Alliance* (blog), March 10. https://ncdalliance.org/news -events/blog/obesity-follows-soda-consumption-like-night-follows-day.

Johnson, Krista. 2004. "The Politics of AIDS Policy Development and Implementation in Postaparteid South Africa." *Africa Today* 51 (2): 107–128.

Journey Staff. 2017. "Witnessing Woman Empowerment through the Eyes of Women." Coca-Cola India, April 3.

Juárez, S. 2017. "Dos Presiones desde el Lobby: El Cabildero Legislativo en la Aprobación del Impuesto al Refresco en México em 2013." In *El Proceso Legislative en México*, edited by L. Lazi, 179–303. Mexico City: UNAM-La Biblioteca.

Kahn, Tamar. 2019. "Diabetes Rates Soar in SA." *Business Day*, November 14.

Kaldor, Jenny Claire, Anne Marie Thow, and Hettie Schönfeldt. 2018. "Using Regulation to Limit Salt Intake and Prevent Non-communicable Diseases: Lessons from South Africa's Experience." *Public Health Nutrition* 22 (7): 1316–1325.

Kalra, Aditya. 2017. "Food, Drink Giants Plot Fightback as India Looks to Tighten Rules." Reuters News, March 16. https://www.reuters.com/article/us-india-fastfood/food -drink-giants-plot-fightback-as-india-looks-to-tighten-rules-idUSKBN16N0UH.

Kalra, Sanjay, and Mudita Dhingra. 2018. "Childhood Diabetes in India." *Annals of Pediatric Endocrinology and Metabolism* 23 (3): 126–130. https://www.doi.org/10.6065/apem.2018.23.3.126.

Kamal, Neel. 2019. "Nestlé 'Health Kids' Programme Commemorates 10 Years of Impacting Nearly 300,000 Beneficiaries." *Times of India*, September 30. https://timesofindia.indiatimes.com/business/india-business/nestl-healthy-kids-programme-commemorates-10-years-of-impacting-nearly-300000-beneficiaries/articleshow/71379020.cms.

Kannan, Shilpa. 2014. "How McDonald's Conquered India." *BBC News*, November 19.

Kar, Stanshu Sekhar, and Subhranshu Sekhar Kar. 2015. "Prevention of Childhood Obesity in India: Way Forward." *Journal of Natural Science, Biology and Medicine* 6 (1): 12–17. https://www.doi.org/10.4103/0976-9668.149071.

Karawang New Industry City. 2019. "Development of Food Manufacturing in Indonesia." July 11. https://www.knic.co.id/development-of-food-manufacturing-in-indonesia.

Karlis, Nicole. 2019. "How Coca-Cola Manipulated Chinese Public Health Policy for Its Own Gain." Salon, January 16.

Kasotia, Vijaylaxmi. 2008. "Food Processing: New Era in the Indian Economy." *Rediff India Abroad News*, April 10.

Kassahara, Aline, and Flavia Mori Sarti. 2018. "Publicidade de Alimentos e Bebidas no Brasil: Rivisão de Literatura Científica sober Regulação e Autorregulação de Propagandas." *Interface-Comunicação, Saúde, Educação* 22 (65): 589–602.

Kaul, Rhythma. 2019. "After PM Narendra Modi's Fit India, Govt Focuses on Eat Right Initiatives, Launches 'Poshan Maah.'" *Hindustan Times*, September 6. https://www.hindustantimes.com/india-news/after-pm-narendra-modi-s-fit-india-govt-launches-eat-right-india-campaign/story-k6eGXadvgKeJI5pD3O7RVP.html.

Kaur, Harminder, and Gazal Aggarwal. 2012. "A Paradox on Corporate Social Responsibility—Case Study on Coca Cola." *International Journal of Physical and Social Sciences* 2 (9): 264–274. https://www.ijmra.us/project%20doc/IJPSS_SEPTEMBER2012/IJMRA-PSS1654.pdf.

Kaye, Jennifer. 2004. *Coca-Cola India. Case Study No. 1-0085*. Tuck School of Business, Dartmouth University.

Kazmin, Amy. 2014. "India Pressures Pepsi to Reduce Sugar in Drinks and Snacks." *Financial Times*, August 27.

Keeton, Claire. 2017. "SA's Diabetes Epidemic is Growing at an Alarming Rate." *Sunday Times*, November 22.

Keller, Eileen. 2018. "Noisy Business Politics: Lobbying Strategies and Business Influence after the Financial Crisis." *Journal of European Public Policy* 25 (3): 287–306. https://doi.org/10.1080/13501763.2016.1249013.

Kelly, Bridget, Jason C. G. Halford, Emma J. Boyland, Kathy Chapman, Inmaculada Bautista-Castaño, Christina Berg, Margherita Caroli, B. Cook, J. G. Coutinho, T. Effertz, and E. Grammatikaki. 2010. "Television Food Advertising to Children: A Global Perspective." *American Journal of Public Health* 100 (9): 1730–1736.

Kelly, Bridget, Lana Hebden, Lesley King, Yang Xiao, Yang Yu, Gengsheng He, L. Liangli, L. Zeng, H. Hadi, T. Karupaiah, and N. S. Hoe. 2014. "Children's Exposure to Food

Advertising on Free-to-Air Television: An Asia-Pacific Perspective." *Health Promotion International* 31 (1): 144–152. https://doi.org/10.1093/heapro/dau055.

Kelly, Bridget, Stefanie Vandevijvere, SeeHoe Ng, Jean Adams, Lorena Allemandi, Liliana Bahena-Espina, Simon Barquera, E. Boyland, P. Calleja, I. C. Carmona-Garcés, and L. Castronuovo, et al. 2019. "Global Benchmarking of Children's Exposure to Television Advertising of Unhealthy Foods and Beverages across 22 Countries." *Obesity Reviews* 20: 116–128. https://www.doi.org/10.1111/obr.12840.

Kennedy, Scott. 2009. "Comparing Formal and Informal Lobbying Practices in China: The Capital's Ambivalent Embrace of Capitalists." *China Information* 23 (2): 195–222.

Keshari, Priya, and C. P. Mishra. 2016. "Growing Menace of Fast Food Consumption in India: Time to Act." *International Journal of Community Medicine and Public Health* 3 (6): 1355–1362.

Khandelwal, S., and K. S. Reddy. 2013. "Eliciting a Policy Response for the Rising Epidemic of Overweight-Obesity in India." *Obesity Reviews* 14 (2): 114–125. https://www.doi .org/10.1111/obr.12097.

Khurana, Amit, and Indu Dhangar. 2014. *Junk Food Targeted at Children: Regulatory Action Required to Limit Exposure and Availability*. New Delhi: Centre for Science and Environment. https://www.cseindia.org/junk-food-targeted-at-children-5464.

Killer Coke. N.d. "Coke's Crimes in India." http://killercoke.org/crimes_india.php#:~:text =Overexploitation%20and%20pollution%20of%20water,firestorm%20of%20criticism %20and%20protest (accessed November 5, 2019).

Kilpatrick, Kate. 2015. "Childhood Obesity in Mexico: US Sends Its Supersized Diet to Kids South of the Border." *Al Jazeera*, August 15. http://projects.aljazeera.com/2015 /08/mexico-obesity/.

Kimani-Murage, Elizabeth, Kathleen Kahn, John Pettifor, Stephen Tollman, Kerstin Klipstein-Grobusch, and Shane Norris. 2011. "Predictors of Adolescent Weight Status and Central Obesity in Rural South Africa." *Public Health Nutrition* 14 (6): 1114–1122. https://www.doi.org/10.1017/S1368980011000139.

King and Wood Mallesons. 2016. "China's E-Commerce Regulatory Tsunami Continues: New Advertising and Food Safety Regulations." July 29. https://www.lexology.com /library/detail.aspx?g=77e07e1f-6619-4df0-a2a3-e6e19a7cd290.

Klein, Steven, and Cheol-Sung Lee. 2019. "Towards a Dynamic Theory of Civil Society: The Politics of Forward and Backward Infiltration." *Sociological Theory* 37 (1): 62–88.

Klüver, Heineken, and Elizabeth Zeidler. 2019. "Explaining Interest Group Density across Economic Sectors: Evidence from Germany." *Political Studies* 67 (2): 459–478. https:// doi.org/10.1177/0032321718774685.

Knowledge@Wharton. 2010. "Coca-Cola on the Yangtze: A Corporate Campaign for Clean Water in China." August 18. https://knowledge.wharton.upenn.edu/article/coca-cola -on-the-yangtze-a-corporate-campaign-for-clean-water-in-china/.

———. 2017. "Will Coca-Cola's New India Strategy Have Fizzy or Go Flat?" November 17. https://knowledge.wharton.upenn.edu/article/will-coca-colas-new-india-strategy -fizz-go-flat/.

Koen, N., R. Blaauw, and E. Wentzel-Viljoen. 2016. "Food and Nutrition Labelling: The

Past, Present and the Way Forward." *South African Journal of Clinical Nutrition* 19 (1): 13–21. https://doi.org/10.1080/16070658.2016.1215876.

Koetse, Manya. 2015. "Coca Cola in China: 'Not a Bottle of Coke Should be Sold to Chinese.'" What's on Weibo, September 24. https://www.whatsonweibo.com/coca-cola-in-china/.

———. 2019. "China's Best Fast-Food Restaurants: These Are the 11 Most Popular Chains in the PRC." What's on Weibo, October 24. https://www.whatsonweibo.com/chinas -best-fast-food-restaurants-these-are-the-11-most-popular-chains-in-the-prc/.

Koopman, Jacob, David van Bodegom, Juventus Ziem, and Rudi Westendorp. 2016. "An Emerging Epidemic of Noncommunicable Disease in Developing Populations Due to a Triple Evolutionary Mismatch." *American Journal of Tropical Medicine and Hygiene* 94 (6): 1189–1192. https://www.doi.org/10.4269/ajtmh.15-0715.

Kowsalya, R., and R. Parimalavalli. 2014. "Prevalence of Overweight/Obesity among Adolescents in Urban and Rural Areas of Salem, India." *Journal of Obesity and Metabolic Research* 1 (3): 152–155.

KPMG and CCFA. 2019, May. *2019 China Convenience Store Development Report*. https:// assets.kpmg/content/dam/kpmg/cn/pdf/en/2019/05/china-convenience-stores -developement-report.pdf.

Krishnakumar, T. n.d. "Message from our Leadership." In *Transforming Schools, Transforming Lives*. Final program report, Coca-Cola/NDTV Support My School, 2010–2017. https://www.coca-colaindia.com/content/dam/journey/in/en/private/smartwater /SMS-Final-Program-Report_LowRes.pdf.

Kruger, H. Salome. 2018. "Obesity among Women: A Complex Setting." *South African Journal of Clinical Nutrition* 31 (4): 4–5.

Kruger, H. Salome, Thandi Puoane, Marjanne Senekal, and M-Theresa van der Merwe. 2005. "Obesity in South Africa: Challenges for Government and Health Professionals." *Public Health Nutrition* 8 (5): 491–500. https://www.doi.org10.1079/PHN2005785.

Kulkarni, Pankaj. n.d. "Pepsico-Corporate Social Responsibility." CSR World: Forum for Corporate Social Responsibility. https://landmatrix.org/media/uploads/csrworldnet pepsicoe28093corporate-social-responsibilityasp.pdf.

Kumari, Santosh, and Tanu Sharma. 2014. "Corporate Social Responsibility: A Study of Pepsico India." Paper presented at the National Level Seminar on CSR, Bahra University, School of Management, Waknaghat, Solan, Himachal Pradesh. https://www .researchgate.net/publication/282272797_Corporate_Social_Responsibility_A_study _of_Pepsi_Co_India.

La Información. 2010. "Calderón quieted convertir a México en el major destiny para las inversions." January 20.

LA Times Archives. 1996. "McDonald's Debuts in India—Sans Beef." October 14, https:// www.latimes.com/archives/la-xpm-1996-10-14-fi-53776-story.html.

Lakhani, Nina. 2013. "Mexico Obesity Bulges on Diet Concerns." *Al Jazeera*, April 26.

Laksmi, P. W., C. Morin, J. Gandy, L. A. Moreno, S. A. Kavouras, H. Martinez, J. Salas-Salvado, and I. Guelinckx. 2018. "Fluid Intake of Children, Adolescents and Adults in Indonesia: Results of the 2016 Liq.In National Cross-Sectional Survey." *European Journal of Nutrition* 57 (3): 89–100. https://www.doi.org/10.1007/s00394-018-1740-z.

Lambert, Jonathan. 2019. "Study: Coca-Cola Shaped China's Efforts to Fight Obesity."
    NPR, January 10.

Lancet Diabetes and Endocrinology. 2017. "Sweet Success: Will Sugar Taxes Improve Health?"
    The Lancet Diabetes and Endocrinology 5 (4): 235. https://www.thelancet.com/pdfs
    /journals/landia/PIIS2213-8587(17)30070-0.pdf.

Laporta, Tais. 2016. "Entenda a atual situação das contas públicas e possíveis medidas."
    Economia, May 21. https://g1.globo.com/economia/noticia/2016/05/entenda-atual
    -situacao-das-contas-publicas-e-possiveis-medidas-maio.html.

Lara, Bruna de. 2018. "Como Coca-Cola, Bunge e 110 Empresas Ganham com o Pior da
    Bancada Ruralista." *The Intercept, Brasil*, September 11.

Latnovic, L., and L. Rodriguez Cabrera. 2013. "Public Health Strategy against Overweight
    and Obesity in Mexico's National Agreement for Nutritional Health." *International
    Journal of Obesity Supplements* 3 (1): 12–14. https://www.doi.org/10.1038/ijosup
    .2013.5.

Lawton, Thomas, Steven McGuire, and Tazeeb Rajwani. 2012. "Corporate Political Activity:
    A Literature Review and Research Agenda." *International Journal of Management Re-
    view* 15 (1): 86–105.

Le Ker, Heineken. n.d. "The Diabetic." Spiegel. Accessed October 4, 2019.

Leme, Ana Carolina Barco, Regina Mara Fisberg, Debbe Thompson, Sonia Tucunduva
    Philippi, Theresa Nicklas, and Tom Baranowski. 2019. "Brazilian Children's Dietary
    Intake in Relation to Brazil's New Nutrition Guidelines: A Systematic Review." *Current
    Nutrition Reports* 8 (2): 145–166. https://www.doi.org/10.1007/s13668-019-0261-6.

Lesniak, Sandra. 2019. "10 Hilarious Knock Off Soda Drinks Only in China." Click Mag,
    August 3. https://babbletop.com/top-10-chinese-knock-off-sodas/.

Levitt, Tom. 2014. "China Facing Bigger Dietary Health Crisis Than the US." *China
    Dialogue*, July 4.

Lexology. 2016. "New Limitations on Marketing Foodstuffs to Children in 2016: South
    Africa Update Vol 1, #3." May 5. https://www.lexology.com/library/detail.aspx?g
    =9799cabf-4985-4263-aa43-e24b81acf590.

Li, Cheng. 2003. "The 'New Deal': Politics and Policies of the Hu Administration." *Journal
    of Asians and African Studies* 38 (4–5): 329–346.

Li, Cheng, and Diana Liang. 2019, Spring. "Rule of the Rigid Compromiser." *The Cairo
    Review of Global Affairs*.

Li, Danyang, Ting Wang, Yu Cheng, Min Zhang, Xue Yang, Zhonghai Zhu, Danli Liu,
    Wenfang Yang, and Lingxia Zeng. 2016. "The Extent and Nature of Television Food
    Advertising to Children in Xi'an, China." *BMC Public Health* 16 (1): 1–9.

Li, H., X. Zhang, and G. F. Yan. 2002. "Prevalence and Trend of Obesity in Preschool
    Children in China 1986 to 1996." *Chinese Journal of Child Health Care* 10 (5): 316–318.

Li, Shiying, Jialu Ye, Mark Blades, and Caroline Oates. 2016. "Foods Shown on Television
    in China: Content Analysis and Impact Estimation." *Chinese Sociological Dialogue* 1 (2):
    120–139. https://www.doi.org/10.1177/2397200916686761.

Lieberman, Evan. 2009. *Boundaries of Contagion: How Ethnic Politics Have Shaped Govern-
    ment Response to AIDS*. Princeton, NJ: Princeton University Press.

Lima, Joana Madureira, and Sandro Galea. 2018. "Corporate Practices and Health: A

Framework and Mechanisms." *Globalization and Health* 14 (21): 1–12. https://doi
.org/10.1186/s12992-018-0336-y.

Lin, Lizi, Chenxiong Li, Chuyao Jin, Yuanzhou Peng, Kawther Hashem, Graham Mac-
Gregor, Feng He, and Haijun Wang. 2018. "Sugar and Energy Content of Carbonated
Sugar-Sweetened Beverages in Haidian District, Beijing: A Cross-Sectional Study."
BMJ Open 8 (8): e022048. http://dx.doi.org/10.1136/bmjopen-2018-022048.

Lira, Ivette. 2018. "La Salud de los mexicanos se ha decidido desde el sector privado durante
años, dicen especialistas." Sinembargo.mx, August 7. https://www.sinembargo.mx/08
-07-2018/3437225.

Lisa. 2017. "South African Sugary Beverage Policies Effective for Rural Schools." Salud-
America, March 10. https://salud-america.org/south-african-government-implements
-sugar-tax-to-rural-schools/.

Little, Matthew, Sally Humphries, Kirin Patel, and Cate Dewey. 2017. "Decoding the Type2
Diabetes Epidemic in Rural India." *Medical Anthropology* 36 (2): 96–110. https://www
.doi.org/10.1080/01459740.2016.1231676.

Liu, Ji. 2015. "What Shapes Policy Formulation in China? A Study of the National Student
Nutrition Policies." *FIRE: Forum for International Research in Education* 2 (3): 1–20.
http://dx.doi.org/10.18275/fire201502031031.

Liu, Rongduo, Christine Hoefkens, and Wim Verbeke. 2015. "Chinese Consumers' Understanding and Use of a Food Nutrition Label and Their Determinants." *Food Quality
and Preference* 41: 103–111. https://doi.org/10.1016/j.foodqual.2014.11.007.

LiveMint. 2017. "Coca-Cola Ties Up with FSSAI to Train Street Food Vendors." FSSAI In
News, March 28. https://www.livemint.com/Industry/SyGFqv4Udcab2UN20116DO
/CocaCola-ties-up-with-FSSAI-to-train-street-food-vendors.html.

———. 2019. "PM Modi Urges Global CEOs to Leverage 'Startup India' Platforms." September 26. https://www.livemint.com/news/india/pm-modi-urges-global-ceos-to
-leverage-startup-india-platforms-1569493507552.html.

"Lobbying with Social Responsibility." 2015. Paper presented at the 73rd Annual Midwest
Political Science Association Meeting, April 16–19, Chicago.

Long, Danielle. 2017. "How Coca-Cola is Targeting China's 355 Million Teens to Share a
Coke." *The Drum News*, June 28.

Lopez, Oscar, and Andrew Jacobs. 2018. "Coca-Cola Could Be Causing a Diabetes Epidemics in This Town." *The Independent*, July 23.

Lorenz, Geoffrey Miles. 2019. "Prioritized Interests: Diverse Lobbying Coalitions and
Congressional Committee Agenda Setting." *The Journal of Politics* 82 (1): 225–240.

Lou, Zhen, Guilhem Fabre, and Victor Rodwin. 2020. "Meeting the Challenge of Diabetes
in China." *International Journal of Health Policy and Management* 9 (2): 47–52. https://
www.doi.org/10.15171/ijhpm.2019.80.

Luedi, Jeremy. 2016. "Why China's Obesity Crisis Is Great News for Investors." Global Risk
Insights, May 10.

Luhar, Shammi, Poppy Alice Carson Mallingson, Lynda Clarke, and Sanjay Kinra. 2018.
"Trends in the Socioeconomic Patterning of Overweight/Obesity in India: A Repeated
Cross-Sectional Study Using National Representative Data." *BMJ Open* 8 (10): 1–9
https://www.doi.org/10.1136/bmjopen-2018-023935.

Lumanauw, Novy, and Edi Hardum. 2015. "Jokowi: Indonesia Can Attain Food Self-Sufficiency in Next Four Years." *Jakarta Globe*, February 13. https://jakartaglobe.id /business/jokowi-indonesia-can-attain-food-self-sufficiency-next-four-years/.

Luo, Lucy. 2016. "The New Chinese Dietary Guidelines—What Do They Really Say on Meat Consumption and Sustainability?" *FCRN* (blog), April 25.

Lv, Jun, Yong Chen, Shengfeng Wang, Qingmin Liu, Yanjun Ren, Sara Karrar, and Liming Li. 2011. "A Survey of Nutrition Labels and Fats, Sugars, and Sodium Ingredients in Commercial Packaged Foods in Hangzhou, China." *Public Health Reports* 126 (1): 116–122. https://www.doi.org/10.1177/003335491112600116.

Ma, G. S., Y. P. Li, Y. F. Wu, F. Y. Zhai, Z. H. Cui, X. Q. Hu, et al. 2005. "The Prevalence of Body Overweight and Obesity and Its Changes among Chinese People during 1992 to 2002." *Chinese Journal of Preventive Medicine* 39(5): 311–315.

Mabiyan, Rashmi. 2019. "Nearly 3 Lakh Beneficiaries in 22 States Impacted through Healthy Kids Programme: Sanjay Khajuria, Nestlé India." *Economic Times*, September 30.

Macari, Marisa, Liliana Bahena, Fátima Torres, Rebecca Berner, and Alejandro Calvillo. 2019. "Improving the School Food Environment through Policy: A Case Study of Challenges and Recommendations from Mexico." In *Food Environments: Where People Meet the Food System*, edited by Christine Campeau, Denis Costa Coitinho Delmué, and Stineke Oenema, 107–114. Rome: United Nations Systems Standing Committee on Nutrition.

Maehara, Masumi, Jee Jyun Rah, Airin Roshita, Julia Suryantan, Asrinisa Rachmadewi, and Doddy Izwardy. 2019. "Patterns and Risk Factors of Double Burden of Malnutrition among Adolescent Girls and Boys in Indonesia." *PLOS One* 14 (8): e0221273. https://doi.org/10.1371/journal.pone.0221273.

Mail & Guardian. 2016. "Coca-Cola Is a Household Name, but What Has It Been Doing to Stay That Way?" September 30. https://mg.co.za/article/2016-09-30-coca-cola-is-a -household-name-but-what-has-it-been-doing-to-stay-that-way/.

Make in India. n.d. "Sector Survey: Food Processing." https://www.makeinindia.com /article/-/v/sector-survey-food-processing (accessed on February 4, 2021).

Maldonado, Mario. 2019. "Dos Bocas: El Error del Sexenio." *El Universal*, May 10. https:// www.eluniversal.com.mx/columna/mario-maldonado/cartera/dos-bocas-el-error-del -sexenio.

Malhotra, Amit. n.d. "Fast Food Grows in India." *DesiBlitz News*. https://www.desiblitz .com/content/fast-food-grows-in-india (accessed September 23, 2019).

Malta, D. C., O. L. D. Morris Neto, and J. B. D. Silva Junior. 2011. "Apresentação do Plano de ações estratégicas para o enfrentamento das doenças crônicas não transmissíves no Brasil, 2011 a 2022." *Epidemiological e Serviços de Saúde* 20: 425–438.

Mani, Radha, and Varun Anthony. 2017. *India's Food Processing Sector Poised for Growth*. GAIN report. US Department of Agriculture, December 31. https://apps.fas.usda.gov /newgainapi/api/report/downloadreportbyfilename?filename=Food%20Processing %20Ingredients_New%20Delhi_India_1-3-2018.pdf.

Mariath, Aline Brandão, and Ana Paula Bortoletto Martins. 2020. "Ultra-Processed Products Industry Operating as an Interest Group." *Revista de Saúde Pública*, 54: 107.

Marinho F., V. de Azeredo Passos, D. Carvalho Malta, E. Barbosa França, D. M. X. Abreu, et al. 2018. "Burden of Disease in Brazil 1990–2016." *The Lancet* 392 (10149): 760–775.

Market Research.com. "Brazil Savory Snacks Market Assessment and Forecasts to 2025—Analyzing Products Categories and Segments, Distribution Channel, Competitive Landscape, Packaging and Consumer Segmentation." https://www.marketresearch .com/GlobalData-v3648/Brazil-Savory-Snacks-Assessment-Forecasts-30351249/.

Marketing to China. 2013. *China Beverage Market*. September 20. https://marketingto china.com/china-beverage-market-report/.

Marketing Consultancy Division. n.d. *Export Study: Labelling, Marking and Packaging Regulations*. https://ajng3zwvtrj9.wpcdn.shift8cdn.com/wp-content/uploads/2019 /12/2004-ES-Labelling-Marking-and-Packaging-Regulations-Part1.pdf.

Marks, Jonathan. 2019. *The Perils of Partnership: Industry Influence, Institutional Integrity, and Public Health*. Oxford: Oxford University Press.

Marmor, T., and D. Thomas. 1972. "Doctors, Politics and Pay Disputes: 'Pressure Group Politics' Revisited." *British Journal of Political Science* 2 (4): 421–442.

Martinko, Katherine. 2011. "Brazil's Junk Food Culture is Driven by Big Business." Treehugger, October 18.

Martino, Florentine Petronella, Peter Graeme Miller, Kerri Coomber, Linda Hancock, and Kypros Kypri. 2017. "Analysis of Alcohol Industry Submissions against Marketing Regulation." *PLOS ONE* 12 (4): e0175661.

Martins, Ana Paula Bortoletto. 2015, October. "Food Labeling in Brazil." *The Global Fruit and Veg Newsletter*, no. 3. https://www.halfyourplate.ca/wp-content/uploads/2015 /02/GFVN_-3_Food_regulation_and_FV_promotion_Brazil_10_2015.pdf.

Martucci, Livio. 2018. "Healthy Eating Trends in Europe: Food Wellness in Europe." INC International Nut and Dried-fruit, July 20.

Mathai, Palakunnathu. 1984. "Processed Food Industry in India Starts Invading Indian Homes." *From the Magazine*, August 31.

Mathew, Joe. 2019. "BT Buzz: FSSAI Plans to Make Indians 'Eat Right'; Food Companies in No Mood to Relent." *Business Today*, July 23. https://www.businesstoday.in/bt -buzz/news/industry-food-service-sees-trouble-in-regulators-attempt-sweet-salty -dishes-fssai-india/story/366661.html.

Mathiason, Nick. 2006. "Coke 'Drinks India Dry.'" *The Guardian*, March 18.

Maulida, Rizka, Keiko Nanishi, Joseph Green, Akira Shibanuma, and Masamin Jimba. 2016. "Food-Choice Motives of Adolescents in Jakarta, Indonesia: The Roles of Gender and Family Income." *Public Health Nutrition* 19 (15): 2760–2768. https://www .doi.org/10.1017/S136898001600094X.

Mazui, Guilherme. 2019. "Bolsonaro altera lei e extingue atribuções do conselho de segurança alimentar." *O Globo*, March 1. https://g1.globo.com/politica/noticia /2019/01/03/bolsonaro-muda-regras-e-retiraatribuicoes-do-conselho-de-seguranca -alimentar.ghtml.

Mbhele, Thabile. 2019. "Warning Labels to be Introduced on Food Packaging." *SABC News*, August 1.

McBeath, Jenifer Huang, and Jerry McBeath. 2010. *Environmental Change and Food Security in China*. New York: Springer Dordrecht Heidelberg.

McGrath, Conor. 2007. "Framing Lobbying Messages: Defining and Communicating Political Issues Persuasively." *Journal of Public Affairs* 7: 269–280. https://www.doi .org/10.1002/pa.267.

McGregor, Richard. 2019. "How the State Runs Business in China." *The Guardian*, July 25.

McGuire, James. 2010. *Wealth, Health, and Democracy in East Asia and Latin America*. New York: Cambridge University Press.

Mchiza, Zandile, and Eleni Maunder. 2013. "Fighting Childhood Obesity." *South African Journal of Clinical Nutrition* 26 (3): 100–102.

McMillan, T. 2015. "How NAFTA Changed American (and Mexican) Food Forever." National Public Radio, February 13. https://www.npr.org/sections/thesalt/2015 /02/13/385754265/how-nafta-changed-american-and-mexican-food-forever.

McSpadden, Lettie, and Paul Culhane. 1999. "The Strategies and Tactics of Interest Groups: The Case of the Environmental and Energy Policy Arena." *Southeastern Political Review* 27 (2): 223–242.

Meador, M., and Ma Jie. 2013. *General Rules for Nutrition Labeling of Prepackaged Foods*. USDA Foreign Agricultural Service, GAIN Report (USDA).

Mehandra, Bharat, Sanjeev Sharma, Govind Singhal, and Dilip Kumar L. 2017. "Overweight and Obesity: A Rising Problem in India." *International Journal of Community Medicine and Public Health* 4 (12): 4548–4552.

Menon, Ramesh. 2013. "Obesity: Are Parents Responsible?" indiatogether, June 27; https://indiatogether.org/obesity-health.

Mexican Health Foundation. 2019. "Nestlé Nutrition Fund."

Mialon, M., B. Swinburn, and G. Sacks. 2015. "A Proposed Approach to Systematically Identify and Monitor the Corporate Political Activity of the Food Industry with Respect to Public Health Using Publicly Available Information," *Obesity Reviews* 16 (7): 519–530.

Middlehurst, Charlotte. 2019. "How America's Junk Food Problem Made Its Way to China." *HuffPost*, updated January 24.

Mietzner, Maracus. 2007. "Democratising Indonesia: The Challenges of Civil Society in the Era of Reformasi." Book review by Mikaela Nyman. *Contemporary Southeast Asia: A Journal of International and Strategic Affairs* 29 (3): 535–537.

Mihardja, Laurentia, and Uken Soetrisno. 2012. "Prevalence and Determinant Factors for Overweight and Obesity and Degenerative Diseases among Young Adults in Indonesia." *Journal of the ASEAN Federation of Endocrine Societies* 27 (1): 77–81.

Milbrath, L. W. 1963. *The Washington Lobbyists*. Chicago: Rand McNaly.

Miller, David, and Claire Harkins. 2010. "Corporate Strategy, Corporate Capture: Food and Alcohol Industry Lobbying and Public Health." *Critical Social Policy* 30 (4): 1–26. https://www.doi.org/10.1177/0261018310376805.

Mills, Lize. 2016. *Considering the Best Interests of the Child When Marketing Food to Children: an Analysis of the South African Regulatory Framework*. PhD diss., Faculty of Law, Stellenbosch University.

Min, Yan, Li-Xiin Jiang, Li-Jing L. Yan, Lin-Hong Wang, Sanjay Basu, Yang-Feng Wu, and Randall Stafford. 2015. "Tackling China's Noncommunicable Diseases: Shared Origins,

Costly Consequences and the Need for Action." *Chinese Medical Journal* 128 (6): 839–843. https://www.doi.org/10.4103/0366-6999.152690.

Mining Journal. 2020. "Honour Investment Commitments: Ramaphosa." June 23. https://www.mining-journal.com/covid-19/news/1389466/honour-investment-commitments-ramaphosa.

Ministerio da Saude Blog da Saúde (blog). 2016. "Ações do Governors Combatem Obesidade e Sobrepeso." Last updated April 11.

Ministry of Foreign Affairs of the People's Republic of China. 2020. "General Secretary Xi Jinping Talks about the Economy When Meeting CPPCC Members from the Economic Sector." May 24. https://www.fmprc.gov.cn/mfa_eng/topics_665678/kjgzbdfyyq/t1782258.shtml.

Ministry of Health. 2013. *Inclusion of Sugar, Salt and Contents as Well as Health Message in Processed Foods and Fast Foods*. Jakarta, Indonesia: Ministry of Health.

Miryala, Ramesh. 2016. "Advertisements' Effect on Food Habits of Children—an Empirical Study." Unpublished manuscript. SSRN, November 16. https://papers.ssrn.com/sol3/papers.cfm?abstract_id=2691462.

Misra, P., R. Upadhyay, A. Misra, and K. Anand. 2011. "A Review of the Epidemiology of Diabetes in Rural India." *Diabetes Research and Clinical Practice* 92 (3): 303–311. https://www.doi.org/10.1016/j.diabres.2011.02.032.

Misra, Suresh, and Mamta Pathania. N.d. *A Report on Evaluation of the Effect of Junk Food on the Health of the School Children in Delhi*. Delhi: Center for Consumer Studies, Indian Institute of Public Administration. https://vdocuments.mx/reader/full/conducted-by-a-report-on-evaluation-of-the-effect-of-junk-food-on-the-health-of.

Mitra, Sounak. 2017. "The Evolution of FSSAI." LiveMint, October 18. https://www.livemint.com/Industry/NbljKgRzQhChgGZhtFPBoL/The-evolution-of-FSSAI.html.

Moeloek, Nila. 2017. "Indonesia National Health Policy in the Transition of Disease Burden and Health Insurance Coverage." *Medical Journal of Indonesia* 26 (1): 3–6. https://www.doi.org/10.13181/mji.v26i1.1975.

Moelyo, A. G., I. W. Himawan, V. Pateda, and R. Fadil. 2013. "Indonesian National Registry of Children with Type 2 Diabetes Mellitus," *International Journal Pediatric Endocrinology* (1 Suppl): P8.

Molelekwa, Thabo. 2018. "Unhealthy Offerings at SA's School Tuck Shops." *Health-E News*, June 29.

Mondeléz International Foundation. 2017, April. *Helping Communities Thrive through Public-Private Partnerships: Impact Report on Healthy Lifestyles Programs*. https://www.mondelezinternational.com/~/media/MondelezCorporate/uploads/downloads/impact-report-healthy-lifestyles-programs.pdf.

Monsanto Fund. 2017. "INMED Announce 3-Year Program for Food and Nutrition Security in Brazil." Press release, March 15.

Monteiro, Carlos, and Geoffrey Cannon. 2017. "The Impact of Transnational 'Big Food' Companies on the South: A View from Brazil." *PLOS Medicine* 9 (7): 1–5. https://www.doi.org/10.1371/journal.pmed.1001252.

Monteiro, Carlos, and Maria Laura da Costa Louzada. N.d. "Ultra-Processed Foods and

Chronic Diseases: Implications for Public Policy." Unpublished manuscript, Department of Nutrition, University of São Paulo. http://capacidadeshumanas.org/oich sitev3/wp-content/uploads/2018/10/07_Ultra-processed-foods-and-chronic-diseases _implications-for-public-policy1.pdf.

Monteiro, Carlos, Wolney Conde, and Barry Popkin. 2002. "Is Obesity Replacing or Adding to Undernutrition? Evidence from Different Social Classes in Brazil." *Public Health Nutrition* 5: 105–12. https://www.doi.org/10.1079/PHN2001281.

Monyeki, Makama Andries, Adedapo Awotidebe, Gert Strydom, J. Hans de Ridder, Ramoteme Lesly Mamabolo, and Han Kemper. 2015. "The Challenges of Underweight and Overweight in South African Children: Are We Winning or Losing the Battle? A Systematic Review." *International Journal of Environmental Research and Public Health* 12 (2):1156–1173. https://www.doi.org/10.3390/ijerph120201156.

Moodie, Rob, David Stuckler, Carlos Monteiro, Nick Sheron, Bruce Neal, Thaksaphon Thamarangsi, Paul Lincoln, and Sally Casswell. 2013. "Profits and Pandemics: Prevention of Harmful Effects of Tobacco, Alcohol, and Ultra-processed Food and Drink Industries." *The Lancet* 381: 670–79. https://doi.org/10.1016/S0140-6736(12)62089-3.

Moodley, Gillian, Nicola Christofides, Shane Norris, Thomas Achia, and Karen Hofman. 2015. "Obesogenic Environments: Access to and Advertising of Sugar-Sweetened Beverages in Soweto, South Africa, 2013." *Preventing Chronic Disease: Public Health Research, Practice, and Policy* 12: 1–9. https://www.doi.org/10.5888/pcd12.140559.

Morone, James. 1992. "The Bias of American Politics: Rationing Health Care in a Weak State." *University of Pennsylvania Law Review* 140: 1923–1938.

Morton, Rebecca, and Charles Cameron. 1992. "Elections and the Theory of Campaign Contributions: A Survey and Critical Analysis." *Economics and Politics* 4 (1): 79–108.

Mosala, S. J., C. M. Venter, and E. G. Bain. 2017. "South Africa's Economic Transformation Since 1994: What Influence Has the National Democratic Revolution (NDR) Had?" *Review of Black Political Economy* 44: 327–340. https://www.doi.org/10.1007/s12114 -017-9260-2.

Moses, Charles Thurman, and Donald Vest. 2010. "Coca-Cola and PepsiCo in South Africa: A Landmark Case in Corporate Social Responsibility, Ethical Dilemmas, and the Challenges of International Business." *Journal of African Business* 11 (2): 235–251. https://www.doi.org/10.1080/15228916.2010.509166.

Motsoeneng, Tiisetso. 2014. "Obesity, South Africa's Emerging Health Crisis." *Reuters*, December 10.

Moubarac, Jean-Claude. 2015. *Ultra-Processed Food and Drink Products in Latin America: Trends, Impact on Obesity, Policy Implications*. Pan American Health Organization and the World Health Organization. https://iris.paho.org/bitstream/handle/10665.2/7699 /9789275118641_eng.pdf.

Mudur, G. S. 2008. "Overnight, Many Overweight Indian Figures Revised to Tone up Flab Fight." *Telegraph* (London), November 26. https://www.telegraphindia.com/india /overnight-many-overweight-indian-figures-revised-to-tone-up-flab-fight/cid/524451.

Muetzberm, Marcus. 2007. "Democratising Indonesia: The Challenges of Civil Society in the Era of Reformasi." *Contemporary Southeast Asia: A Journal of International and Strategic Affairs* 29 (3): 535–537. https://www.doi.org/355/cs29-3k.

Mukherjee, P. K. 2019. "Non-obese and Lean Indians Also Prone to Type-2 Diabetes." downtoearth.org, January 21.

Mukherji, Rahul. 2009. "The State, Economic Growth, and Development in India." *India Review* 8 (1): 81–106. https://www.doi.org/10.1080/14736480802665238.

Musakwa, Mercy, and Nicholas Odhiambo. 2019. "Foreign Direct Investment Dynamics in South Africa: Reforms, Trends and Challenges." *Studia Universitatis Economics Series* 29 (2): 33–53. https://www.doi.org/10.2478/sues-2019-0007.

Mvo, Z., J. Dick, and K. Steyn. 1999. "Perceptions of Overweight African Women about Acceptable Body Size of Women and Children." *Curationis* 22 (2): 27–31.

My Digital Media. 2016. "Women Entrepreneurs in India Make a "Splash" in Their Neighbourhoods." http://mydigitalmediaa.blogspot.com/2016/05/coca-cola-women-entrepreneurs-in-india.html.

Myers, Alex, David Fig, Aviva Tugendhaft, Jessie Mandle, Jonathan Myers, and Karen Hofman. 2015. "Sugar and Health in South Africa: Potential Challenges to Leveraging Policy Change." *Global Public Health* 12 (1): 98–115. http://dx.doi.org/10.1080/17441692.2015.1071419.

MYSA news. 2009. "Mexican President Says Poverty Now First Priority." November 26. https://www.mysanantonio.com/news/mexico/article/Mexican-president-says-poverty-now-first-priority-857611.php

Na, He. 2010. "Diabetes Threatens Children." *China Daily*, May 31.

Nagarajan, Rema. 2019. "Food Regulator Sleeping with 'Enemy.'" *Times of India*, October 8. https://timesofindia.indiatimes.com/india/food-regulator-sleeping-with-enemy/articleshow/71485212.cms.

Nair, Harish V. 2013. "99% NGOs Are Fraud, Money-Making Devices: HC." *The Hindustan Times*, March 6. https://www.hindustantimes.com/delhi/99-ngos-are-fraud-money-making-devices-hc/story-2AMyh5VMGAoedUtvtRnAMP.html.

Narain, Sunita. 2017. "Sin Tax for Redemption." DownToEarth, July 31. https://www.downtoearth.org.in/blog/health/sin-tax-for-redemption-58278.

National Action Plan for Food and Nutrition, 2006–2010. National Development Planning Board. 2007. Jakarta: Government of Indonesia. https://extranet.who.int/nutrition/gina/sites/default/filestore/IDN%202006%20National%20Action%20Plan%20for%20Food%20and%20Nutrition.pdf.

National Council of Food and Nutrition Security. 2017. "Obesity Campaign Draws Attention to Lack of Clear Information on Labels." January 11.

National Development Planning Board. 2007. *National Action Plan for Food and Nutrition, 2006–2010.* Jakarta: Government of Indonesia. https://extranet.who.int/nutrition/gina/sites/default/filestore/IDN%202006%20National%20Action%20Plan%20for%20Food%20and%20Nutrition.pdf.

National Health and Family Planning Commission of the People's Republic of China. 2014. *Report on Chinese Residents' Chronic Disease and Nutrition.* http://en.nhc.gov.cn/2015-06/15/c_45788.htm.

Navarro, Vincente. 2008. "Why Congress Did Not Enact Health Care Reform." *Health Policy: Crisis and Reform in the US Health Care Delivery System* 3 (2008): 414–418.

Nayar, Lola, Smruti Koppikar, Pragya Singh, Anuradha Raman, Arindam Mukherjee, and

Sunit Arora. 2010. "Favourite Lobby Horses: Shadow Warrior Once, the Lobbyist Is a Frontman Today, Working the Government to Get Corporate Leeway." *Outlook*, May 17.

Ndinda, C., and C. Hongoro. 2017. *Analysis of Non-Communicable Diseases Prevention Policies in Africa (ANPPA)—a Case Study of South Africa*. Technical research report. African Population and Health Research Centre (APHRC).

Neilson, J., M. Morrison, A. Dwiartama, R. Utsumi, A. Patnuru, and B. Pritchard. 2018. *Food Processing and Value Chain Development in Indonesia*. Technical report, the Australia-Indonesia Centre, August 1.

Nestlé. n.d. "AGRI-BEE Maluti Window Initiative." Nestle in Society. https://www.nestle -esar.com/csv/rural-development/agri-bee-maluti-window-initiative (accessed August 15, 2020).

———. n.d. "Nestlé Community Nutrition Awards." https://www.nestle-esar.com/csv /nutrition/nestle-community-nutrition-awards (accessed August 1, 2020).

———. n.d. "Nestlé Healthy Kids Programme." https://www.nestle.in/csv/individuals -families/nestle-healthy-kids-programme (accessed February 1, 2021).

———. n.d. *Nestlé's Commitments to Every Woman Every Child*. Background report. Nestlé Corporation. https://www.who.int/pmnch/topics/part_publications/pmnch2011 _summ_nestle.pdf.

———. n.d. "Village Women Dairy Development Programme." Nestlé in Society. https:// www.nestle.in/csv/rural-development/milk/dairy-development-programme-for -village-women (accessed February 2, 2021).

———. 1993. *Nestlé's Commitment to Every Woman Every Child*. Policy report. Nestlé Corporation.

———. 2005. *The Nestlé Commitment to Africa: Report and Summary*. Vavey, Switzerland: Nestle.

———. 2007. "President Luiz Inácio Lula da Silva and Swiss Economic Affairs Minister Doris Leuthard Open New Nestlé Plant in Brazil." February 9. https://www.nestle .com/media/pressreleases/allpressreleases/brazilfactory-09feb07.

———. 2015a. "Nestlé India Implements over 260 Water and Sanitation Projects Bene-fitting 180,000 Village Students." September 1. https://www.nestle.in/media/news -feed/nestle-india-implements-over-260-water-and-sanitation-projects-benefitting -180000-village-students.

———. 2015b. "Nestlé Waters Mexico—Supporting the Community." YouTube video, 2:09. January 13. https://www.youtube.com/watch?v=ZmuMeDwXLpo.

———. 2016. "Nestlé India Participates in Make In India Week." June 8. https://www .nestle.in/featuredstories/nestle-india-participates-in-make-in-india-week-news.

———. 2017. "Basic Education in Partnership with Nestlé South Africa Host Mandela Day Commemoration at Makeneng Primary School in Phuthaditjhaba." Press release, July 27.

———. 2018a. "Nestlé and DBE Celebrate Mandela Day in Boipatong." Press release, July 18. https://www.nestle-esar.com/media/pressreleases/nestle-dbe-celebrate-mandela-day.

———. 2018b. "Helping 30,000 Pacific Alliance Youth Join the Labour Market." June 29. https://www.nestle.com/media/news/pacific-alliance-youth-labour-market.

Nestle, Marion. 2015. *Soda Politics: Taking on Big Soda (and Winning)*. New York: Oxford University Press, 2015.

Nestle-Nespresso. n.d. "Lilia Vidal Vargas in Mexico: Strengthening Community Ties through the Nespresso AAA Sustainability Quality Program." https://nestle -nespresso.com/news/lilia-vidal-vargas-in-mexico (accessed March 10, 2022).

Neuman, William. 2010. "Save the Children Breaks with Soda Tax Effort." *New York Times*, December 14. https://www.nytimes.com/2010/12/15/business/15soda.html.

News Desk. 2018. "Lessons from Mexico: 'Our Sugar Tax Hasn't Worked,' Says Beverage Association." *Foodbev Media*, April 4. https://www.foodbev.com/news/lessons-mexico -sugar-tax-hasnt-worked-says-beverage-association/.

News24. 2015. "Zuma: South Africa is Open for Business." May 31.

Ng, Brady. 2017. "Obesity: The Big, Fat Problem with Chinese Cities." *The Guardian*, January 9.

NGO Pulse. 2016. "Childhood Obesity in South Africa." October 13.

Nieburg, Oliver. 2012. "Ferror Plans First Production Site in Mexico." February 27. https:// www.confectionerynews.com/Article/2012/02/27/Ferrero-plans-first-production -site-in-Mexico.

Nieto, Claudia, Alejandra Castillo, Jacqueline Alcalde-Rabanal, Carmen Mena, Ángela Carriedo, and Simon Barquera. 2020. "Perception of the Use and Understanding of Nutrition Labels among Different Socioeconomic Groups in Mexico: A Qualitative Study." *Salud Publica Mex* 62: 288–297.

Nieto, Claudia, Estefania Rodríguez, Karina Sánchez-Bazán, Lizbeth Tolentino-Mayo, Angela Carriedo-Lutzenkirchen, Stefanie Vandevijvere, and Simón Barquera. 2019. "The INFORMAS Healthy Food Environment Policy Index (Food-EPI) in Mexico: An Assessment of Implementation Gaps and Priority Recommendations." *Obesity Reviews* 20: 67–77. https://doi.org/10.1111/obr.12814.

Nilson, Eduardo August Fernandez. 2015. "The Strides to Reduce Salt Intake in Brazil: Have We Done Enough?" *Cardiovascular Diagnosis and Therapy* 5 (3): 243–247. https:// www.doi.org/10.3978/j.issn.2223-3652.2015.04.03.

Nitahara, Akemi. 2019. "Ministério da Saúde Lança Campanha para Prevenir a Obesidade Infantil." *A Tarde*, November 15. https://atarde.uol.com.br/saude/noticias/2108572 -ministerio-da-saude-lanca-campanha-para-prevenir-a-obesidade-infantil.

Nogueira, Daniel J. Pedraza, Domenico Di Liello, Giulia De Paolis, and Liam Jazcii. 2019, January. *The Snacks Market in China*. EU SME Centre.

Noll, Matias, Luiz Carlos de Abreu, Edmund Chada Baracat, Erika Aparecida Silveira, and Isabel Cristina Esposito Sorpreso. 2019. "Ultra-processed Food Consumption by Brazilian Adolescents in Cafeterias and School Meals." *Scientific Reports* 9 (1): 1–8. https://doi.org/10.1038/s41598-019-43611-x.

Nortje, Nico, Mieke Faber, and Anniza de Villiers. 2017. "School Tuck Shops in South Africa—an Ethical Appraisal." *South African Journal of Clinical Nutrition* 30 (3): 74–79. https://doi.org/10.1080/16070658.2017.1267401.

Nos, Ação Social das Empresas. 2018. "Negras Potências." November 10. https://revistanos .com.br/probono/negras-potencias/.

Ntloedibe, Margarte. 2017. *South Africa Retail Food Industry*. GAIN report. Washington, DC: US Department of Agriculture, Foreign Agricultural Service.

Nunes, Mônica. 2018. "Negras Potências: Projetos em crowdfunding podem receber financiamento dobrado contra desigualdade social." Conexão Planeta, October 15; https://conexaoplaneta.com.br/blog/negras-potencias-projetos-em-crowdfunding -podem-receber-financiamento-dobrado-contra-desigualdade-social/.

Nurwanti, Esti, Hamam Hadi, Jung-Su Chang, Jane C-J Chao, Bunga Astria Paramashanti, Joel Gittelsohn, and Chyi-Huey Bai. 2019. "Rural-Urban Differences in Dietary Behavior and Obesity: Results of the Riskesdas Study in 10–18-Year-Old Indonesian Children and Adolescents." *Nutrients* 11 (2813): 1–14. https://www.doi.org/10.3390 /nu11112813.

Nusaresearch Team. 2014. *Report of Soft Drink Consumption Habits in Indonesia.* Jakarta, Indonesia: Nusaresearch Team.

Nutrição em Pauta. 2008. "Fundação Nestlé Anuncia os dez Projetos Sociais Contemplados Perla Promoção 'Nestlé Torce Por Voce." https://www.nutricaoempauta.com.br /noticias/noticias110.html.

Nutrition Connect. 2019. *Support to Indonesian National School Meals Programme.* Case Study. Geneva, Switzerland: Global Alliance for Improved Nutrition.

O'Barr, William M. 2007. "Advertising in China." *Advertising and Society Review* 8 (3): 2–46.

O'Connor, Anahad. 2016. "How the Sugar Industry Shifted Blame to Fat." *New York Times*, September 12.

O'Riordan, Michael. 2019. "Obesity Prevalence Triples in China over 10-Year Span." TCTMD, October 28.

Oberlander, Lisa. 2018. *TV Exposure, Food Consumption, and Health Outcomes—Evidence from Indonesia.* Working paper, Paris School of Economics and INRA, January 31.

Obermeier, Kylie. 2019. "When India Kicked Out Coca-Cola, Local Sodas Thrived." Atlas Obscura, February 15. https://www.atlasobscura.com/articles/what-is-thums-up.

Octoboni, Jéssica. 2013. "Coca-Cola veta comerciais direcionados para crianças." Veja, May 13. https://veja.abril.com.br/economia/coca-cola-veta-comerciais-direcionados-para -criancas/.

Oddo, Vanessa, Masumi Maehara, Doddy Izwardy, Anung Sugihantono, Pungkas B. Ali, and Jee Hyun Rah. 2019. "Risk Factors for Nutrition-Related Chronic Disease among Adults in Indonesia." *PLOS One* 14 (8): e0221927. https://doi.org/10.1371/journal.pone .0221927.

Oddo, Vanessa, Masumi Maehara, and Jee Hyun-Rah. 2019. "Overweight in Indonesia: An Observational Study of Trends and Risk Factors among Adults in Children." *BMJ Open* 9 (9): e031198. http://dx.doi.org/10.1136/bmjopen-2019-031198.

Ojeda, Enai, Christian Torres, Ángela Carriedo, Mélissa Mialon, Niyati Parekh, and Emanuel Orozco. 2020. "The Influence of the Sugar-Sweetened Beverage Industry on Public Policies in Mexico." *International Journal of Public Health* 65: 1037–1044.

Oliver, Thomas, and Emery Dowell. 1994. "Interest Groups and Health Reform: Lessons from California." *Health Affairs* 13(2): 123–141.

Olson, Georgina. 2014. "Peña Nieto atestigua inversiones para México por 7 mil 350 mdd en Davos." Excelsior, January 24. https://www.excelsior.com.mx/nacional/2014/01 /24/940094.

Olvera, Por Dulce. 2019. "Las Refresqueras Frenanaron en la Cámara de Diputados Iniciativa de Etiquetado: Alianza por la Salud." *Sinembargo.mx*, June 2.

OMICS International. 2019. Type-2 Diabetes in Children.

O'Neil, Shannon. 2013. "Campaign Financing in Mexico." Latin America's Moment and Latin America Studies Program, July 10. https://www.cfr.org/blog/campaign -financing-mexico.

ONICRA. 2007. *Food Processing Industry in India: Adding Value by Creating Synergy between Agriculture and Industry*. ONICRA Credit Rating Agency of India.

ONU Mulheres, Brasil. 2019. "ONU Mulheres traz para o Brasil a Aliança sem Estereótipo para Promover Igualdade de Gênero na Publicidade," February 26. www.onumulheres .org.br/noticias/onu-mulheres-traz-para-o-brasil-a-alianca-sem-estereotipo-para -promover-igualdade-de-genero-na-publicidade/.

Osnos, Evan. 2015. *Age of Ambition: Chasing Fortune, Truth, and Faith in the New China*. New York: Farrar, Straus and Giroux.

Otitoola, Olufunmilola, Wilna Oldewage-Theoron, and Abdul Egal. 2020. "Prevalence of Overweight and Obesity among Selected Schoolchildren and Adolescents in Cofimvaba, South Africa." *South African Journal of Clinical Nutrition* 34: 97–102. https://doi.org/10 .1080/16070658.2020.1733305.

Otto, Ben. 2013. "US Companies Plan to Speed Pace of Investing in Indonesia." *Wall Street Journal*, October 2. https://www.wsj.com/articles/SB10001424052702303492504579111 293739139448.

Otto, Ben, and Anita Rachman. 2015. "Indonesian Sugar-Tax Talks Chills Drinks Industry." *Wall Street Journal*, November 27.

Oxford Business Group. 2018. *Sustained Growth Makes Indonesia's Food and Beverages Industry a Priority for Spending: Analysis*.

PAHO. 2012. *Mexico*. Health in the Americas. Washington, DC: PAHO. https://www3.paho .org/salud-en-las-americas-2012/index.php?option=com_docman&view=download &category_slug=health-americas-2012-edition-42&alias=77-health-americas-2012 -edition-for-print-with-registration-marks-7&Itemid=231&lang=en.

———. 2016. "PAHO Director Lauds Mexico's Soda Tax as a Model Measure to Fight Diabetes." PAHO news, April 7. https://www.paho.org/hq/index.php?option=com _content&view=article&id=11893:paho-director-lauds-mexico-soda-tax-to-fight -diabetes&Itemid=1926&lang=pt.

Pandit, Sadaguru. 2016. "17 Million Obese Children in India by 2025: International Journal." *The Hindustan Times*, October 11. https://www.hindustantimes.com/mumbai -news/17-million-obese-children-in-india-by-2025-international-journal/story -vTSZnYhFIWTjgKwSg5J2AL.html.

Park, Madison. 2010. "Growing in Wealth, South Africa Battles Obesity." CNN, July 9.

Parker, Edward. 2019. "What Does Jokowi's Win Mean for Indonesia's Economy? *The Diplomat*, April 19.

Parra, Diana C., Christine M. Hoehner, Pedro C. Hallal, Rodrigo S. Reis, Eduardo J. Simoes, Deborah C. Malta, Michael Pratt, and Ross C. Brownson. 2013. "Scaling Up Physical Activity Interventions in Brazil: How Partnerships and Research Evidence

Contributed to Policy Action." *Global Health Promotion* 20 (4): 5–12. https://doi.org
/10.1177/1757975913502368.

Parth, Shubhendu. 2008. "Nutrition Policy for Healthy India on Cards." iGovernment
News, April 24.

Partnership for Maternal, Newborn & Child Health. 2013. *Strengthening National Advocacy
Coalitions for Improved Women's and Children's Health.* https://www.who.int/pmnch
/knowledge/publications/cso_report/en/.

Paster, Thomas. 2018. "How Do Business Interest Groups Respond to Political Challenges?
A Study of the Politics of German Employers." *New Political Economy* 23 (6): 674–689.
https://doi.org/10.1080/13563467.2018.1384453.

Patashnik, Eric. 2003. "After the Public Interest Prevails: The Political Sustainability of
Policy Reform." *Governance* 16 (2): 203–234.

Pati, Sanghamitra, Rajeshwari Sinha, and Puranas Mahapatra. 2019. "Non-Communicable
Disease Risk Reduction Teaching in India: A Curricular Landscape." *Frontiers in Public
Health* 7: 133. https://www.doi.org/10.3389/fpubh.2019.00133.

Patil, Shailaja S., Jamie E. Ports, Mallikarjun C. Yadavannavar, and Solveig A. Cunning-
ham. 2016. "Physicians' Perceptions about the Emergence of Adolescents Overweight
in India." *Journal of Krishna Institute of Medical Sciences University* 5 (2016): 37–44.

Peixinho, Albaneide Maria Lima. 2013. "A trajetória do Programa Nacional de Alimentação
Escolar no período de 2003–2010: Relato do Gestor Nacional." *Ciência and Saúde
Coletiva* 18 (4): 909–916.

Peng, Ziewn, Zhongyan Zheng, Hongying Han, Chenjji Dong, Jingjing Liang, Jianping
Lu, and Zhen Wei. 2019. "Imbalance in Obesity and Mental Health among 'Little
Emperors' in China." *PLOS One* 14 (4): e0207129, https://doi.org/10.1371/journal
.pone.0207129.

Penteado, Claudia. 2003. "Brazil's New Leaders Launches Ad Campaign against Hunger."
AdAge News, March 10. https://adage.com/article/news/brazil-s-leader-launches-ad
-campaign-hunger/50080.

PepsiCo. 2010. *Performance with Purpose: The Promise of PepsiCo. Sustainability Summary
2010.* https://www.pepsico.com/docs/album/sustainability-report/2010-csr/pepsico
_2010_sustainability_summary.pdf?sfvrsn=ff237334_4.

———. 2017. *Performance with Purpose: PepsiCo Greater China Region, Sustainability Report.*
Updated September 1. https://www.pepsico.com.cn/downloads/pdfs/report_en
_201709.pdf.

———. 2018. *Performance with a Purpose: Sustainability Report 2017.* PepsiCo International.
https://www.pepsico.com/docs/album/sustainability-report/2017-csr/pepsico_2017
_csr.pdf.

———. 2019. "The PepsiCo Foundation Partners with CARE to Tackle Gender Inequality
in Agriculture with an US18.2 Million Investment in She Feeds the World." Press
release, April 3. https://www.pepsico.com/news/press-release/the-pepsico-foundation
-partners-with-care-to-tackle-gender-inequality-in-agriculo3042019.

Peres, João. 2018a. "Crescem Reações á Relação entire Ciência e Indústrias de Ultraproces-
sados." *O Joio e o Trigo*, February 1. https://outraspalavras.net/ojoioeotrigo/2018/02
/crescem-reacoes-relacao-entre-ciencia-e-industria-de-ultraprocessados/.

———. 2018b. "Indústria de Alimentos Ocupa Espaços da Universidade na ANVISA." *O Joio e o Trigo*, June 4. https://outraspalavras.net/ojoioeotrigo/2017/11/industria-de -alimentos-ocupa-espacos-da-universidade-na-anvisa/.

Peres, João, and Moriti Neto. 2018. "Coca-Cola é Investigada Por Esquema Bilionário para Não Pagar Impostos." *The Intercept Brasil*, December 12. https://theintercept.com /2018/12/21/coca-cola-impostos/

Pérez-Escamilla, Rafael. 2018. "Innovative Healthy Lifestyles School-Base Public-Private Partnerships Designed to Curb the Childhood Obesity Epidemic Globally: Lesson Learned from the Mondeléz International Foundation." *Food and Nutrition Bulletin* 39: S3–S21.

Pérez-Ferrer, Carolina, Tonatiuh Barrientos-Guiterrez, Juan A. Rivera-Dommarco, Francisco Javier Prado-Galbarro, Alejandra Jiménez-Aguilar, Carmen Moralees-Ruán, and Teresa Shamah-Levy. 2018. "Compliance with Nutrition Standards in Mexican Schools and Their Effectiveness: A Repeated Cross-Sectional Study." *BMC Public Health* 18: 1411. https://onlinelibrary.wiley.com/doi/full/10.1111/obr.12096.

Persens, Lizell. 2018. "SA Has Among the Highest Rates of Obese Children in the World." *EWN Eyewitness News*. https://ewn.co.za/2018/10/13/sa-has-among-the-highest -rates-of-obese-children-in-the-world-un.

Pfister, Kyle. 2016. "New #CokeLeak: Soda Tax Opposition in 8 More Countries." *Medium*, October 19.

Pham, Sherisse. 2019. "Walmart Is Doubling Down on China with 500 New Stores." CNN, November 21.

Phang, Jennifer. 2012. "China Standardizes Nutrition Labelling Guidelines." *Food Navigator Asia*, January 10.

Pheiffer, Carmmen, Victoria Pillay-van Wyk, Jané D. Joubert, Naomi Levitt, Mweete Nglazi, and Debbie Bradshaw. 2018. "The Prevalence of Type-2 Diabetes in South Africa: A Systematic Review Protocol." *BMJ Open* 8 (7): e021029. https://www.doi .org/10.1136/bmjopen-2017-021029.

Phillips, Dom. 2016. "Ounce Underfunded, Brazil's Poor Have a New Problem: Obesity." *Washington Post*, November 26.

Phuong, Nam. 2018. "The Curious Case of Mini Marts and Convenience Stores in Indonesia and Vietnam." *Vietnam Investment Review*, March 20.

Phuong, Thao, and Deva Rachman. 2017. *CSR Landscape in Indonesia: The Past, Present and the Future*. Sustainable Square. October 5. https://sustainablesquare.com/evolution -csr-landscape-indonesia/.

Picasso, Ana Paula. 2015. "This Country Is on Track to Dethrone the US as the Most Obese in the World." *Business Insider*, October 4.

Pienaar, Anita. 2015. "Childhood Obesity in South Africa." BMC Blog Network, April 7. https://blogs.biomedcentral.com/bmcseriesblog/2015/04/07/world-health-day -blog/.

Pienaar, A. E., and G. Kruger. 2014. "Prevalence of Overweight and Obesity in Grade 1 Learners in the North West Province of South Africa: The NW-Child Study." *South African Journal of Sports Medicine* 26 (4): 109–114. https://www.doi.org/10.7196/ SAJSM.519.

Pingali, Prabhu, Ankara Aiyar, Mathew Abraham, and Andaleeb Rahman. 2019. *Transforming Food Systems for a Rising India*. London: Palgrave Press.

Pinghui, Zhuang. 2017. "China Has the Largest Number of Obese Children in World, Study Says." *South China Morning Post*, June 13.

Pioneer, The. 2016. "WHO, India Concerned over Rising Obesity." January 28.

PISAgro. 2019. "List of Members." www.pisagro.org/members/list-members (accessed March 6, 2021).

PISAgro News. 2019, September. "Public-Private Collaboration for Human Capital Development Agenda in Agriculture: Scaling up PISAgro's Model through Agricultural Development Polytechnic." Quarterly newsletter, PISAgro, Issue No. 18.

Pisani, Elizabeth. 2014, July/August. "Indonesia in Pieces: The Downside of Decentralization." *Foreign Affairs*, July/August.

Polity. 2003. "Mbeki: Growth and Development Summit (07/06/2003)." Speeches, June 7.

Pollin, Robert, Gerald Epstein, James Heintz, and Léonce Ndikumana. 2006. *An Employment-Targeted Economic Program for South Africa*. New York: UNDP Press.

Popkin, B., and T. Reardon. 2018. "Obesity and the Food System Transformation in Latin America." *Obesity Reviews* 19 (8): 1028–1064. https://www.doi.org10.1111/obr.12694.

Pradeepa, R., and V. Mohan. 2017. "Prevalence of Type 2 Diabetes and Its Complications in India and Economic Costs to the Nation." *European Journal of Clinical Nutrition* 71 (7): 816–824. https://www.doi.org/10.1038/ejcn.2017.40.

Pradeepa, Rajendra, Ranjit Mohan Anjana, Shashank Joshi, Anil Bhansali, Mohan Deepa, Prashant Joshi, Vinay Dhandania, Sri Venkata Madju, Paturi Vishnupriya Rao, Loganathan Geetha, Radhakrishnan Subashini, Ranji Unnikrishnan, Deepak Kumar Shukla, Tanvir Kaur, Viswanathan Mohan, Ashok Kumar Das, and the ICMR-INDIAB Collaborative Study Group. 2015. "Prevalence of Generalized and Abdominal Obesity in Urban & Rural India—the ICMR-INDIAB Study (Phase 1) [ICMR-INDIAB-3]." *Indian Journal of Medical Research* 142 (2): 139–150. https://www.ncbi.nlm.nih.gov/pmc/articles/PMC4613435/

Prasad, Vandana. 2014. "The Fast Food Bomb." *Hindu*, August 1. https://www.thehindu.com/in-school/views/the-fast-food-bomb/article6271357.ece.

Praveen, Pradeep A., and Nikki Tandon. 2016. "Childhood Obesity and Type 2 Diabetes in India." *WHO South-East Asia Journal of Public Health* 5 (1): 17–21. http://www.who-seajph.org/text.asp?2016/5/1/17/206547.

Presidência da República Planalto. 2018. "Presidente ressalta importância do setor industrial para o crescimento do País." July 3.

Presidency, Republic of South Africa. 2018. "Achievements and Milestones during the Tenure of President Jacob Zuma." Press release, February 15.

Press Trust of India. 2019a. "FSSAI Proposes Ban on Junk Food Promotion in and around School Premises." *Business Standard*, June 13. https://www.business-standard.com/article/pti-stories/fssai-proposes-ban-on-junk-food-advertisements-in-and-around-schools-119061300550_1.html.

———. 2019b. "India's Welfare Schemes Give World a New Hope for Better Future, Says PM Modi at UNGA." *India Today*, September 27. https://www.indiatoday.in/india

/story/india-s-welfare-schemes-give-world-a-new-hope-for-better-future-says-pm
-modi-at-unga-1604010-2019-09-27.

Prijosoesilo, Triyono, and Harry Sanusi. 2018. "Food and Beverage: Soft Drink Market
of Indonesia Contracted in 2017." *Indonesia Investments*, January 23. https://www
.indonesia-investments.com/news/news-columns/food-beverage-soft-drink-market
-of-indonesia-contracted-in-2017/item8529.

Proceso. 2008. "Obesidad, Corrupción, y Complicidad Oficial." April 6. https://www
.proceso.com.mx/89928/obesidad-corrupcion-y-complicidad-oficial.

———. 2017. "Plan Nacional Antiobesidad y Diabetes, un Fracaso en Proteger Los
Derechos de la Infancia." April 27. https://www.proceso.com.mx/nacional/2017/4
/27/plan-nacional-antiobesidad-diabetes-un-fracaso-en-proteger-los-derechos-de
-la-infancia-183198.html.

PTI. 2014a. "'Make India' Promises to Fast-Track Economic Growth Trajectory: India Inc."
Financial Express, September 25. https://www.financialexpress.com/archive/make-in
-india-promises-to-fast-track-economic-growth-trajectory-india-inc/1292759/.

———. 2014b. "Narendra Modi Asks Pepsi, Coke to Blend Fruit Juices in Fizzy Drinks."
Economic Times, September 24. https://economictimes.indiatimes.com/industry/cons
-products/food/narendra-modi-asks-pepsi-coke-to-blend-fruit-juices-in-fizzy-drinks
/articleshow/43330216.cms?from=mdr.

———. 2017. "PM Narendra Modi Invites US CEOs to Invest in India, Says GST a Game-
changer." *The Indian Express*, June 26. https://indianexpress.com/article/india/pm
-narendra-modi-invites-us-ceos-to-invest-in-india-says-gst-a-game-changer-4722155/.

Pulungan, Aman, Ireska Tsaniya, and Diadra Annisa. 2018. "Type 2 Diabetes Mellitus in
Children and Adolescents: An Indonesian Perspective." *Annals of Paediatric Endocrinology and Metabolism* 23 (3): 119–125. http://www.doi.org/10.6065/apem.2018.23.3.119.

Puoane, Thandi, Krisela Steyn, Debbie Bradshaw, Ria Laubscher, Jean Fourie, Vicki
Lambert, and Nolwazi Mbananga. 2002. "Obesity in South Africa: The South African
Demographic and Health Survey." *Obesity Research* 10 (10): 1038–1048. https://doi
.org/10.1038/oby.2002.141.

Puthenkalam, John Joseph. 2009. "Emerging China's Economic Visions during the Five
Year Plans and the Evolution of the Doctrine of 'the Scientific Concept of Development.'" 上智経済論集 (*Economic Review*) 54 (1): 29–45.

PWC. 2015. *The Retail and Consumer Industry in Brazil—Navigating the Downturn*. https://
www.pwc.com/gx/en/growth-markets-centre/publications/assets/The%20R&C%20
Industry%20in%20Brazil%20-%20Navigating%20the%20Downturn.pdf.

Qima. 2019. "October 2019 Regulatory Update: Indonesia Publishes New Food Packaging
Regulation." https://www.qima.com/regulation/10-19/oct2019-indonesia-food
-packaging-reg.

QSRweb. 2011. "New Leadership at McDonald's South Africa." March 17.

Rachmi, Cut Novianti, Kingsley Emwingyore Agho, Mu Li, and Louise Alison Baur. 2016.
"Stunting Coexisting with Overweight in 2.0–4.9-year-old Indonesian Children: Prev-
alence, Trends, and Associated Risk Factors from Repeated Cross-Sectional Surveys."
Public Health Nutrition 19 (15): 2698–2707.

Rachmi, C. N., M. Li, and Alison Baur. 2017. "Overweight and Obesity in Indonesia:

Prevalence and Risk Factors—a Literature Review." *Public Health* 147: 20–29. https://doi.org/10.1016/j.puhe.2017.02.002.

Rais, Mohammad, Shatroopa Acharya, and Neenah Sharma. 2013. "Food Processing Industry in India: S&T Capability, Skills and Employment Opportunities." *Journal of Food Processing and Technology* 4 (9): 1–13. http://www.doi.org/10.4172/2157-7110.1000260.

Raj, Pritish. 2020. "Sprite Is Most Selling Soft Drink Brand of India Followed by Thums Up & Pepsi." NBB (Next Big Brand), April 16. https://www.nextbigbrand.in/sprite-is-most-selling-soft-drink-brand-of-india-followed-by-thums-up-pepsi/.

Rajan, Michael Anjello Jothi, R. Srinivasan, and Arockiam Thaddeus. 2018. "Childhood Obesity: The Indian Scenario Compared with World Wide." *Current Research in Diabetes and Obesity Journal* 5 (5): 555672.

Ramachandran, Ambadyl, Ananth Samith Sherry, Arun Nanditha, and Chamukuttan Snehalatha. N.d. "Type 2 Diabetes in India: Challenges and Possible Solutions," Chapter 40. https://citeseerx.ist.psu.edu/viewdoc/download?doi=10.1.1.671.3857&rep=rep1&type=pdf.

Ramadurai, Charukesi. 2017. "Homegrown Indian Beverage Industry Takes on Cola Giants with Nostalgic Flavors." NPR, April 27.

Raman, V. R., and Arundati Muralidharan. 2019. "Closing the Loop in India's Sanitation Campaign for Public Health Gains." *The Lancet* 393 (10177): P1184–1186. https://www.thelancet.com/journals/lancet/article/PIIS0140-6736(19)30547-1/fulltext.

Ramesh, Randeep. 2004. "Soft-Drink Giants Accused over Pesticides." *The Guardian*, February 5.

Rangkuti, Fahwani. 2018. *Indonesia: Retail Foods*. GAIN report: Global Agricultural Information Network. Washington, DC: USDA Foreign Agricultural Service.

Ranjani, Harish, Rajendra Pradeepa, T. S. Mehreen, Ranjit Mohan Anjana, Krishnan Anand, Renu Garg, and Viswanathan Mohan. 2014. "Determinants, Consequences and Prevention of Childhood Overweight and Obesity: An Indian Context." *Indian Journal of Endocrinology and Metabolism* 18(Suppl 1): S17–S25.

Rastogi, Vasundhara. 2017. "The Food Processing Industry in India: Investment Prospects." *India Briefing*, May 9.

Rathi, Neha, Lynn Riddell, and Anthony Worsley. 2017. "Food Environment and Policies in Private Schools in Kolkata, India." *Health Promotion International* 32: 340–350. https://www.doi.org/10.1093/heapro/daw053.

Ray, Daryll, and Harwood Schaffer. 2013. "*Sugar Policies of US and Brazil*." TN: Agricultural Policy Analysis Center. http://www.agpolicy.org/weekpdf/669.pdf.

Ray, Shantanu Guha. 2012. "Changing Lives: The 'Support My School' Project in India." Coca-Cola, November 2.

Reis, Caio Eduardo G., Vasconcelos, Ivana Aragão, and Juliana Farias de N. Barros. 2011. "Políticas Pública de Nutrição para o Controle da Obesidad Infantil." *Revista Paulista de Pediatria* 29 (4): 625–633.

Republic of Indonesia. 2013. *National Nutrition Strategy Paper of Indonesia*. Report prepared for the FAO/WHO 2nd International Conference on Nutrition ICN 2, Jakarta, Indonesia, December 27.

Research and Markets. 2017. *Research Report on Soft Drink Industry in China, 2017–2021*.

Report, March 10. https://www.businesswire.com/news/home/20170310005254/en
/Research-Report-on-Soft-Drink-Industry-in-China-2017-2021---Research-and
-Markets.

Retail Brief Africa. 2019. "South Africa's Fastest Growing Convenience Retail Brand FreshStop, Turns 10." June 3.

Retail News Asia. 2018. "Here Are Indonesia's Top 10 Retailers according to Euromonitor." February 10. https://www.retailnews.asia/here-are-indonesias-top-10-retailers -according-to-euromonitor/.

Reuell, Peter. 2019. "Researcher Finds Coke's Fingerprints on Health Policy in China." *Harvard Gazette*, January 10.

Reuters. 2009. "Coca Cola Says China Ex-Employee Held over Corruption." September 13.

Reuters Staff. 2014. "Indonesia's New President Targets Food Sustainability within 4 Years." Reuters News, October 20. https://www.reuters.com/article/indonesia -president-agriculture/indonesias-new-president-targets-food-sustainability-within -4-yrs-idUSJ9N0PJ01620141020.

Revista ABIR. 2019. "Brasil É o 2 Maior Mercado de Bebidas Não Alcoólicas." August 28. https://abir.org.br/abir/wp-content/uploads/2019/01/REVISTA-ABIR-2019.pdf.

Rheeder, Paul. 2019. "World Diabetes Day—'Obesity Is the Main Driver of South Africa's Type 2 Diabetes Epidemic.'" *Health 24 News*, November 14.

Rich, Jessica, and Eduardo J. Gómez. 2012. "Centralizing Decentralized Governance in Brazil." *Publius: The Journal of Federalism* 42 (4): 636–661. https://doi.org/10.1093 /publius/pjs002.

Rivera, Juan A., Lilia S. Pedraza, Tania C. Aburto, Carolina Batis, Tania G. Sánchez-Pimienta, Teresita González de Cosío, Nancy López-Olmedo, and Andrea Pedroza-Tobías. 2016. "Overview of the Dietary Intakes of the Mexican Population: Results from the National Health and Nutrition Survey 2012." *The Journal of Nutrition* 146 (9): 1851–1855. https://doi.org/10.3945/jn.115.221275.

Rivera, Juan, Onofre Muñoz-Hernández, Martín Rosas-Peralta, Carlos Aguilar-Salinas, Barry Popkin, and Walter Wilett. 2008. "Consumo de bebidas para una vida saludable: Recomendaciones para la población Mexicana." *Salud Pública de México* 50 (2): 173–195.

Rocha, Cecilia, Patricia Constante Jaime, and Marina Ferreira Rea. 2016. *Global Nutrition Report* (blog). "Nutrition for Growth: How Brazil's Political Commitment to Nutrition Took Shape." August 1. https://globalnutritionreport.org/blog/nutrition-for-growth -how-brazils-political-commitment-to-nutrition-took-shape/.

Rodriguez, David Avelar, Erick Manuel Toro Monjaraz, Karen Rubi Ignorosa Arellano, and Jaime Ramirez Mayans. 2018. "Childhood Obesity in Mexico: Social Determinants of Health and Other Risk Factors." *BMJ Case Reports*. https://www.doi.org/10.1136/bcr -2017-223862.

Ronggang, Chen. 2017. "Why Once-Loved McDonald's Now Has an Image Problem in China." *Sixth Tone*, December 13. https://www.sixthtone.com/news/1001386/why -once-loved-mcdonalds-now-has-an-image-problem-in-china.

Ronit, K., and J. D. Jensen. 2014. "Obesity and Industry Self-Regulation of Food and Beverage Marketing: A Literature Review." *European Journal of Clinical Nutrition* 68: 753–759. http://www.doi.org/10.1038/ejcn.2014.60.

Ronquest-Ross, Lisa-Claire, Nick Vink, and Gunnar Sigge. 2015. "Food Consumption Changes in South Africa since 1994." *South African Journal of Science* 111 (9–10): 1–12. http://dx.doi.org/10.17159/SAJS.2015/20140354.

Rosa, Paula. n.d. "Ação Contra Obesidade Infantil Atingirá 50 Mil Escolas Públicas." http://www.pensesaudavel.com.br/noticias/89-acao-contra-obesidade-infantil-atingira-50-mil-escolas-publicas.html (accessed January 1, 2021).

Rosdiana, Dian. 2013. *Nestlé HealthyKids: Bringing Healthier Indonesian Children into Reality*. Case study. Jakarta: Company-Community Partnerships for Health in Indonesia [CCPHI] Press.

Rosenberg, Tina. 2015. "How One of the Most Obese Countries on Earth Took on the Soda Giants." *The Guardian*, November 3.

Rossotti, Tommaso. 2019. "Indonesian Political Economy: A Historical Analysis." *The Rest: Journal of Politics and Development* 9 (1): 34–43.

Rossouw, H. A., C. C. Grant, and M. Viljoen. 2012. "Overweight and Obesity in Children and Adolescents: The South African Problem." *South African Journal of Science* 108 (5–6): 31–37.

Rowland, Paul. 2016. "Cognitive Dissonance; Unclear Signals about Foreign Investment from Indonesia." In *Hopes and Doubts: Perspectives on the Long Road to Indonesia's Economic Development, Intelligence Unit*, 21–24. *The Economist*, Intelligence Unit

Royani, Rosalia. 2009. "The Indonesian Economy Battles to Reduce Unemployment and Poverty." *AsiaNews.It*, October 31.

Ruder, Sundeep. 2016. "How South Africa Can Beat Its Sugar-Fueled Diabetes Epidemic." *The Conversation*, November 23.

Rull, Juan A., Carlos A. Aguilar-Salinas, Rosalba Rojas, Juan Manuel Rios-Torres, Francisco J. Gómez-Pérez, and Gustavo Olaiz. 2005. "Epidemiology of Type 2 Diabetes in Mexico." *Archives of Medical Research* 36 (3): 188–196. https://doi.org/10.1016/j.arcmed.2005.01.006.

Sacks, G., B. Swinburn, V. Kraak, S. Downs, C. Walker, S. Barquera, S. Friel, C. Hawkes, B. Kelly, S. Kumanyika, M. L'Abbé, T. Lobstein, J. Ma, J. Macmullan, S. Mohan, C. Monteiro, B. Neal, M. Rayner, D. Sanders, W. Snowdon, and S. Vendevijvere. 2013. "A Proposed Approach to Monitor Private-Sector Policies and Practices Related to Food Environments, Obesity and Non-Communicable Disease Prevention." *Obesity Review* 14 (1): 38–48.

Salama. 2019. "Indonesia Has Strong Demand in Packaged Food." *FnBNews.com*, August 1.

Salim, Zamroni. 2010. *Food Security Policies in Maritime Southeast Asia*. Series on Trade and Food Security. Policy report. https://www.iisd.org/system/files/publications/food_security_policies_indonesia.pdf.

Samanta, Pranab Dhal. 2019. "How Modi's Schemes Were Shaped by Examples from East Asia." *Economic Times*, May 26. https://economictimes.indiatimes.com/news/economy/policy/view-narendra-modis-growth-model-needs-to-address-unique-indian-problems/articleshow/69499389.cms.

Sanchez, Luis. 2019. "How Coca-Cola is Thriving Despite Declining Soda Consumption." *The Motley Fool*, February 12.

Sánchez, Verenise. 2015. "Apuesta Coca-Cola por científicos Mexicanos." Cienciamx Noticias, June 23.

SAnews. 2019. "Obesity among SA Children a Concern." November 28.

Sanger-Katz, Margot. 2015. "The Decline of 'Big Soda.'" *New York Times*, October 2.

Sanghera, Tish. 2018. "For Rich and Poor Indians Alike, Diabetes Epidemic Shows No Sign of Abating." Business Standard, April 17. https://www.business-standard.com/article/current-affairs/for-rich-and-poor-indians-alike-diabetes-epidemic-shows-no-sign-of-abating-118041700101_1.html.

SANGONet. 2016. "Childhood Obesity in South Africa." October 13.

Santarelli, Mariana, Luciana Marques Vieira, and Jennifer Constantine. 2018. *Learning from Brazil's Food and Nutrition Security Policies*. Institute of Development Studies. https://opendocs.ids.ac.uk/opendocs/bitstream/handle/20.500.12413/13582/Learning-from-Brazilian-Food-and-Nutrition-Security-Policies_final_clean_rev_FF.pdf?sequence=1.

Savell, Emily, Anna Gilmore, and Gary Fooks. 2014. "How Does the Tobacco Industry Attempt to Influence Marketing Regulations? A Systematic Review." *PLOS One* 9 (2): 1–10. https://doi.org/10.1371/journal.pone.0087389.

Sayed, Nawal. 2018. "Profile: Meet South Africa's New President Cyril Ramaphosa." *Egypt Today*, February 16.

Schaffer, Regina. 2017. "Burden of Childhood Obesity Shifting to Poorer Families in Mexico." https://www.healio.com/news/endocrinology/20170317/burden-of-childhood-obesity-shifting-to-poorer-families-in-mexico.

Schmidt, Fabian. 2014. *Ministério da Saúde Lança Guia Alimentar para o População Brasilera*. Brazil: Ministry of Health, November 5.

Schoen, John, W. 2013. "New Global Middle Class Hungers for Good ol' US Fast Food." *CNBC*, August 9.

Schonhardt, Sara. 2016. "Indonesia Aims to Cut Red Tape—and Investor Skepticism." *Wall Street Journal*, January 7.

Schroeder, Eric. 2016. "Investment Firm Acquires Stake in Brazilian Snacks and Candy Maker." *Food Business News*, November 22.

Seale and Associates. 2018, June. *Fast Food Industry Report*. http://mnamexico.com/wp-content/uploads/2018/09/Fast-Food.pdf.

Secretaría de Salud. 2016. *Nestlé Waters y la Secretaría de Salud Federal firman Programa Nacional de Hidratación Familiar*. Official Secretary of Health Press Release, July 20. https://www.nestle-waters.com/sites/g/files/pydnoa611/files/asset-library/documents/press%20releases/2016/press-release-mexico-family-hydration.pdf.

Secretary of Health, IMSS. 2015. *La Obesidade en el Menor de Salud*. Mexico City: Secretary of Health.

SejaTrainee. 2019. "Seja Trainee Nestlé 2019: Material Completo Para Se Preparar."

Sen, Ronojoy. 2019. "Everyone Thinks the Economy Is Issue No. 1 for India's Modi. It's Not." *Foreign Policy*, September 21. https://foreignpolicy.com/2019/09/21/everyone-thinks-the-economy-is-issue-no-1-for-indias-modi-its-not/.

Sentalin, Priscilla Bueno Rocha, Andreia de Oliveira Pinheiro, Robson Rocha de Oliveira, Renato Amaro Zângaro, Luciana Aparecida Campos, and Ovidiu Constantin Baltatu.

2019. "Obesity and Metabolic Syndrome in Children in Brazil." *Medicine* 98 (19): e15666. http://www.doi.org/10.1097/MD.0000000000015666.

Servín, Fernando Camacho. 2017. "Plantea ONG ampana obesidad basidia en dates, no en prohibiciones." Sociedad, August 31.

Shannawaz, Mohd, and P. Arokiasamy. 2018. "Overweight/Obesity: An Emerging Epidemic in India." *Journal of Clinical and Diagnostic Research* 12 (11): LC01–LC05. https://www.doi.org/10.7860/JCDR/2018/37014.12201.

Sharma, Dinesh. 2019. "Not in Safe Hands." *The Tribune*, October 12. https://www.tribuneindia.com/news/archive/comment/not-in-safe-hands-845940.

Sharma, Neetu Chandra. 2018. "Most Indians Eat Unbalanced Diet, Says National Family Health Survey." Livemint.com, January 16. https://www.livemint.com/Politics/4x1Py35VFQqA3yzg0KMrPO/Most-Indians-eat-unbalanced-diet-says-national-family-healt.html.

Sharma, S. 2017. "One in Every Four of India's Youth Suffer from Deadlier Type-2 Diabetes." *The Hindustan Times*, November 14. https://www.hindustantimes.com/health/world-diabetes-day-one-in-every-four-of-india-s-youth-suffer-from-the-deadlier-type-2/story-LP4ugRJ5qqLNITYg24xCbO.html.

Sheingate, A. D. 2001. *The Rise of the Agricultural Welfare State: Institutions and Interest Group Power in the United States, France, and Japan.* Princeton, NJ: Princeton University Press.

Shen, Chi, Zhongliang Zhou, Sha Lai, Xingxing Tao, Dantong Zhao, Wanyue Dong, Dan Li, Xin Lan, and Jianmin Gao. 2019. "Urban-Rural-Specific Trend in Prevalence of General and Central Obesity, and Association with Hypertension in Chinese Adults, Aged 18–65 Years." *BMC Public Health* 19 (1): 661, https://doi.org/10.1186/s12889-019-7018-4.

Sidaner, Emilie, Daniel Balaban, and Luciene Burlandy. 2012. "The Brazilian School Feeding Programme: An Example of an Integrated Programme in Support of Food and Nutrition Security." *Public Health Nutrition* 16 (6): 989–994. https://www.doi.org/10.1017/S1368980012005101.

Signé, Landry. 2019. "Africa's Emerging Economies to Take the Lead in Consumer Market Growth." The Brookings Institution, *Africa in Focus* (blog), April 3. https://www.brookings.edu/blog/africa-in-focus/2019/04/03/africas-emerging-economies-to-take-the-lead-in-consumer-market-growth/.

Signé, Landry, and Witney Schneidman. 2019. "Post-Election South Africa: Top Priorities for the Administration." The Brookings Institution, *Africa in Focus* (blog), June 12. https://www.brookings.edu/blog/africa-in-focus/2019/06/12/recommendations-for-south-africa-after-its-elections/.

Sikuka, Wellington. 2019. *South Africa Sugar Industry Crushed by Not So Sweet Tax.* GAIN report, No. SA1904. Washington, DC: US Department of Agriculture.

Silaen, Linda, and Ben Otto. 2013. "Coca-Cola to Step Up Spending in Indonesia." *Wall Street Journal*, April 16.

Silva, A. C., G. A. Bortolini, and P. C. Jaime. 2013. "Brazil's National Programs Targeting Children Obesity Prevention." *International Journal of Obesity Supplements* 3 (Suppl 1): S9–S11. https://www.doi.org/10.1038/ijosup.2013.4.

Sing, Bill. 1986. "Coca-Cola Acts to Cut All Ties with S. Africa." *Los Angeles Times*, September 18.

Singh, Jyotsna. 2015. "Food Industry Challenges Validity of Panel for Junk Food Sale in Schools." *DownToEarth*, August 17. https://www.downtoearth.org.in/news/food -industry-challenges-validity-of-panel-for-junk-food-sale-in-schools-42372.

Singh, P. S., Himanshu Sharma, Kwajalein S. Safari, Prafulla K. Singh, Sudhir K. Yadav, Rajesh K. Gautam, and Tony Pious. 2017. "Prevalence of Type-2 Diabetes Mellitus in Rural Population of India—a Study from Western Uttar Pradesh." *International Journal of Research in Medical Sciences* 5 (4): 1363–1367.

Singh, Rajiv. 2017. "The Resurgence of India's Fast Food Industry." *Economic Times*, December 17.

Singh, Surendra, Fisseha Tegegne, and Enefiok Ekenem. 2012. "The Food Processing Industry in India: Challenges and Opportunities." *Journal of Food Distribution Research* 43 (1): 81–89.

Skocpol, Theda, and Margaret Somers. 1980. "The Uses of Comparative History in Macrosocial Inquiry." *Comparative Studies in Society and History* 22 (2): 174–197.

Slattery, Gram, and Gabriela, Mello. 2018. "Carrefour Brasil Plans to Expand; Considers Purchases and Partnerships." *Reuters*, March 12.

Smit, N., and K. Thompson. 2010. "Junk Food's Regulations Given a Timeout."

Smith, Wesley. 1992. "Salinas Prepares Mexican Agriculture for Free Trade." *The Heritage Foundation*, no. 914, October 1. http://thf_media.s3.amazonaws.com/1992/pdf/bg914 .pdf.

Snyder, Robert, Jayant Raman, Federico Costa, Helena Lima, Juan Calcagno, Ricardo Couto, Lee Rile, Mitermyaer Reid, Albert Ko, and Guilherme Ribeiro. 2017. "Differences in the Prevalence of Non-Communicable Disease between Slum Dwellers and the General Population in a Large Urban Area in Brazil." *Tropical Medicine and Infectious Disease* 2 (3): 47. Doi:10.3390/tropicalmed2030047.

Soares, Andreia Azevedo. 2016. "Putting Taxes into the Diet Equation." *Bulletin of the World Health Organization* 94 (4): 239–240. https://www.doi.org/10.2471/BLT.16 .020416.

Soewondo, Radana, Alessandra Ferrario, and Dicky Levenus Tahapary. 2013. "Challenges in Diabetes Management in Indonesia: A Literature Review." *Globalisation and Health* 9 (63): 1–17.

Soft Drink: All Soft Drinks on the Web. n.d. "Soda in South Africa." http://www.the-soft -drinks.com/soda-south-africa.html (accessed June 24, 2020).

Song, Jiangen, Junxia Huang, Yujuan Chen, Yu Zhu, Haibo Li, Yufeng Wen, Hui Yuan, and Yali Liang. 2015. "The Understanding, Attitude and Use of Nutrition Label among Consumers." *Nutrición Hospitalaria* 31 (6): 2703–2710. https://www.doi.org/10.3305 /nh.2015.31.6.8791.

Sounak Mitra. 2017. "The Evolution of FSSAI: How the Regulatory is Upgrading Regulations and Collaborating with Food Companies to Modernize Testing Standards for Food Safety." LiveMint, October 18. https://www.livemint.com/Industry/NbljKgRz QhChgGZhtFPBoL/The-evolution-of-FSSAI.html.

South African Government. 2004. "Address of the President of South Africa, Thabo

Mbeki, to the First Joint Sitting of the Third Democratic Parliament." Streamed May 21. YouTube video, 1:18.

————. 2013. "Address by His Excellency President Jacob Zuma at the Launch of Fetsa Tlala Integrated Food Production Initiative, Kuruman, Northern Cape Province." Speech, October 24.

South African Sugar Association. N.d. "Nutrition." https://sasa.org.za/nutrition/.

Sperandio, Naiara, Cristiana Tristão Rodrigues, Sylvia do Carmo Castro Franceschini, and Silvia Eloiza Priore. 2017. "Impacto do Programa Bolsa Família no Consumo de Alimentos: Estudo Comparativo das Regiões Sudeste e Nordeste do Brasil," *Ciência and Saúde Coletiva* 22 (6): 1771–1780.

Spires, Mark, David Sanders, Philipp Hoelzel, Peter Delobelle, Thandi Puoane, and Rina Swart. 2016. "Diet-Related Non-communicable Diseases in South Africa: Determinants and Policy Response." In *South African Health Review 2016*, edited by A. Padarath, J. King, E. Mackie, and J. Casciola, 35–42. South Africa: Health Systems Trust.

Spivey, John Kirby. 2009. *Coke vs. Pepsi: The Cola Wars in South Africa during the Anti-Apartheid Era*. MA thesis, Department of History, Georgia State University.

Srivastava, Amit. 2019. "Is Coca-Cola Influencing India's Public Health Policies?" TheWire, February 6. https://thewire.in/health/coca-cola-junk-food-companies-are-influencing -indias-public-health-policies.

Stacey, Nicholas, Aviva Tugendhaft, and Karen Hofman. 2017. "Sugary Beverage Taxation in South Africa: Household Expenditure, Demand System Elasticities, and Policy Implications." *Preventative Medicine* 105: S26–S31. https://doi.org/10.1016/j.ypmed .2017.05.026.

Stacey, Nicholas, Caroline Mudara, Shu Wen Ng, Corné van Walbeek, Karen Hofman, and Ijeoma Edoka. 2019. "Sugar-Based Beverage Taxes and Beverage Prices: Evidence from South Africa's Health Promotion Levy." *Social Science and Medicine* 238: 1–8. https:// doi.org/10.1016/j.socscimed.2019.112465.

Stacey, Nicholas, Corné van Walbeek, Mashekwa Maboshe, Aviva Tugendhaft, and Karen Hofman. 2017. "Energy Drink Consumption and Marketing in South Africa." *Preventive Medicine* 105: S32–S36. https://doi.org/10.1016/j.ypmed.2017.05.011.

Stanley, Liam. 2012. "The Difference between an Analytical Framework and a Theoretical Claim: A Reply to Martin Cartensen." *Political Studies* 60: 474–482.

Statesman, The. 2018. "No Proposal to Ban Junk Food Advertisements on Television: Smriti Irani." February 8. https://www.thestatesman.com/india/no-proposal-ban -junk-food-advertisements-television-govt-1502581799.html.

Statista. 2011. "Market Share of Soft Drink Companies in South Africa 2010." August 1. https://www.statista.com/statistics/216906/market-share-of-soft-drink-companies -in-south-africa/Market.

Stevenson, Mark. 2009. "Mexican President Says Poverty Now First Priority." *San Diego Union Tribune*, November 25.

Steyn, N. P., Z. Mchiza, Z. Abrahams, and N. Temple. 2014. "Television Advertising to Children: Ethical Considerations with Regard to Advertising of Unhealthy Foods and Drinks." Policy brief. *Human Science Research Council*. Policy brief, http://hdl.handle .net/20.500.11910/2456.

Stony Brook University. N.d. "American Food in China." https://you.stonybrook.edu /americanchinesefood/conclusion/ (accessed April 10, 2020).

Stuckler, David, and Marioon Nestle. 2012. "Big Food, Food Systems, and Global Health." *PLOS Medicine* 9 (6): 1–4.

Studdert, David, Jordan Flanders, and Michelle Mello. 2015. "Searching for Public Health Law's Sweet Sport: The Regulation of Sugar-Sweetened Beverages." *PLOS Medicine* 12 (7): e1001848. https://www.doi.org/10.1371/journal.pmed.1001848.

Suryahadi, Asep, and Ridho Al Izzati. 2019. "Commentary: Indonesia Searches for that Elusive Broad-Based Growth." CAN, March 17.

Swiss Business Hub Indonesia. 2019. "Demand for Chocolate Products on the Rise in Indonesia." *Switzerland Global Enterprise*, March 14. https://www.s-ge.com/en /article/global-opportunities/20191-c7-food-indonesia-chocolate-products.

Swiss Global Enterprise. 2019. *Finished Food Products in Indonesia*. Industry report. https://www.s-ge.com/en/publication/industry-report/20182-finishedfood -indonesia.

Syahrul, Syahrul, Rumiko Kimura, Akiko Tsuda, Tanut Susanto, Ruka Saito, and Fithria Ahmad. 2016. "Prevalence of Underweight and Overweight among School-Aged Children and Its Association with Children's Sociodemographic and Lifestyle in Indonesia." *International Journal of Nursing Sciences* 3 (2): 169–177. https://doi.org /10.1016/j.ijnss.2016.04.004.

Szreter, Simon. 2003. "The Population Health Approach in Historical Perspective." *American Journal of Public Health* 93 (3): 421–431.

Tabledebates. n.d. "The New Chinese Dietary Guidelines—What Do They Really Say on Meat Consumption and Sustainability?" https://www.tabledebates.org/blog/new -chinese-dietary-guidelines-what-do-they-really-say-meat-consumption-and -sustainability.

Taneja, Sonam, and Amit Khurana. 2017. "Availability of Junk Food is Changing Children's Diet in India." DownToEarth, August 15. https://www.downtoearth.org.in/news /health/spoilt-for-choice-58417.

Tangcharoensathien, Viroj, Orana Chandrasiri, Watinee Kunkpeuk, Kamolphat Markchang, and Nattanicha Pangkariya. 2019. "Addressing NCDs: Challenges from Industry Market Promotion an Interference." *International Journal of Health Policy and Management* 8 (5): 256–260.

Tao, Yexuan, Ji Li, Martin Lo, Qingya Tang, and Youfa Wang. 2010. "Food Nutrition Labelling Practice in China." *Public Health Nutrition* 14 (3): 542–550. https://www.doi .org/10.1017/S1368980010002065.

Tapsell, Ross. 2012. "The Era of Convergent Media." Inside Indonesia, September 29. https://www.insideindonesia.org/the-era-of-convergent-media.

Taylor, Allyn L., and Michael F. Jacobson. 2016. *Carbonating the World: The Marketing and Health Impact of Sugar Drinks in Low-and Middle-Income Countries*. Washington, DC: Center for Science in the Public Interest.

Temple, Norman, Krisela Steyn, Margaret Hoffman, Naomi Levitt, and Carl Lombard. 2001. "The Epidemic of Obesity in South Africa: A Study in a Disadvantaged Community." *Ethnicity and Disease* 11: 431–437.

Thebus, Shakirah. 2019. "13% of SA Children Younger Than 5 Years Old Are Overweight-Report." IOL News, December 13.

Thekaekara, Mari Marcel. 2015. "Indian Schools Told to Junk the Junk Food." New Internationalist, May 22. https://newint.org/blog/2015/05/22/junk-food-ban.

Thore, Kelly. 2015. "Exercise Is Medicine: The Best Prescription to Advance Health." Coca-Cola, New Zealand, January 26. https://www.coca-colajourney.co.nz/stories /exercise-is-medicine-the-best-prescription-to-advance-health.

Thow, Anne Marie, Stephen Greenberg, Mafanso Hara, Sharon Friel, Andries duTOit, and David Sanders. 2018. "Improving Policy Coherence for Food Security and Nutrition in South Africa: A Qualitative Policy Analysis." *Food Security* 10 (4): 1105–1130. https:// doi.org/10.1007/s12571-018-0813-4.

Times of India. 2008. "Obesity Guidelines Released for India." November 26. https:// timesofindia.indiatimes.com/city/delhi/Obesity-guidelines-released-for-India /articleshow/3756942.cms.

TimesLIVE. 2019. "SA Children Are Overweight and Lack Vital Nutrients—Report." December 10.

Tisdell, Clem. 2009. "Economic Reform and Openness in China: China's Development Policies in the Last 30 Years." *Economic Analysis and Policy* 39 (2): 271–294. https://doi .org/10.1016/S0313-5926(09)50021-5.

Tobin, Meaghan. 2019. "Indonesia Faces a Diabetes Epidemic—and It's the Young Who Are Most Affected." *South China Morning Star*, February 6.

Tokarnia, Mariana. 2014. "Resolução do Conanda define abusos da publicidade infantil." AgênciaBrasil, July 4. https://agenciabrasil.ebc.com.br/direitos-humanos/noticia /2014-04/resolucao-do-conanda-define-os-abusos-da-publicidade-infantil.

Tomazini, Carla Guerrero, and Cristiane Kercheas da Silva Leite. 2015. "Programa Fome Zero e o Paradigma da Segurança Alimentaria: Ascensão e Queda de uma Coalizão?" *Revista de Sociologia e Política* 24 (58): 13–30.

Torkornoo, Hope, and Komla Dzigbede. 2017. "Sustainability Practices of Multinational Enterprises in Developing Countries: A Comparative Analysis of Coca-Cola Company and PepsiCo Inc." *Journal of Global Initiatives: Policy, Pedagogy, Perspective* 11 (2): 19–30. http://digitalcommons.kennesaw.edu/jgi/vol11/iss2/3.

Torres, Felipe, and Agustín Rojas. 2018. "Obesity and Public Health in Mexico: Transforming the Hegemonic Food Supply and Demand Pattern." *Problemas del Desarrollo: Revista Latinoamericana de Economía* 49 (193): 145–169.

Tourliere, Mathieu. 2016. "Incurrió Peña en 'acto immoral" al presumir que toma Coca Cola Light a diario: ONG." September 19. https://www.proceso.com.mx/nacional /2016/9/19/incurrio-pena-en-acto-inmoral-al-presumir-que-toma-coca-cola-light -diario-ong-170852.html.

Tripathi, Krishnanand. 2019. "Jan Dhan Accounts' Insurance Cover a Chimera with Less Than 10,000 Claims Paid So Far." *Financial Express*, March 9. https://www.financial express.com/economy/jan-dhan-accounts-insurence-cover-a-chimera-with-less-than -10000-claims-paid-so-far/1509849/.

Tse, Edward. 2018. "Why China Is Too Important a Market for Foreign Companies to Exit, Especially as Chinese Innovations Takes Off." *South China Morning Post*, November 19.

Tugendhaft, Aviva, and Karen Hofman. 2015. "Soft Drinks and Juices Lead the Way to Obesity in South Africa." BusinessTech, December 19.

TVCâmara, Câmara Dos Deputatos. 2017. "Seguridade Social e Família: Destímulo ao Consumidor de Bebidas Processadas." Streamed live on October 31. YouTube video, 4:33:43. https://www.youtube.com/watch?v=c2xmfvo2sds.

Undavalli, Vamsi Krishna, Satyanarayana Chowdary Ponnaganti, and Hanumanth Narni. 2018. "Prevalence of Generalized and Abdominal Obesity: India's Big Problem." *International Journal of Community Medicine and Public Health* 5 (4): 1311–1316. https://www.doi.org/10.18203/2394-6040.ijcmph20180984.

UNDP. 2015. *Converging Development Agendas: 'Napa Cita', 'RPJMN', and SDGs*. Policy report. Jakarta: UNDP Indonesia.

UNICEF. 2016. *Advertising & Marketing to Children: Global Report* (UNICEF).

———. 2019 *The State of the World's Children 2019. Children, Food and Nutrition: Growing Well in a Changing World*. New York: UNICEF.

UNICEF China. 2019. "UNICEF China and China Nutrition Society Launch the State of the World's Children (SOWC) 2019." https://www.unicef.cn/en/stories/unicef-china-and-china-nutrition-society-launch-state-worlds-children-sowc-2019.

Unilever Indonesia. 2020. "Health, Well-Being and Nutrition Pillar."

United States Department of Agriculture. 2011. *Indonesia: Food and Agricultural Import Regulations and Standards—Narrative*. FAIRS Annual Country Report. https://apps.fas.usda.gov/newgainapi/api/report/downloadreportbyfilename?filename=Food%20and%20Agricultural%20Import%20Regulations%20and%20Standards%20Report_Jakarta_Indonesia_3-18-2019.pdf.

———. 2018. *Mexico Trade & FDI*. Washington, DC: USDA.

University of North Carolina at Chapel Hill. 2012. "Child Diabetes Levels Almost Four Times Higher in China Than in the US." *Science Daily*, July 5.

Unnikrishnan, Ranjit, Ranjit Mohan Anjana, and Viswanathan Mohan. 2016. "Diabetes Mellitus and Its Complication in India." *Nature Reviews Endocrinology* 12 (6): 357–370. https://pubmed.ncbi.nlm.nih.gov/27080137/.

USAID. n.d. "South Africa: If You Can Get a Coca-Cola Product Almost Anywhere in Africa, Why Not Life-saving Medicines?" https://www.usaid.gov/sites/default/files/documents/1864/cii-pjt-last-mile-south-africa_508.pdf.

———. 2016. "USAID IUWASH PLUS." https://www.iuwashplus.or.id/?lang=en.

———. 2019. "Coca-Cola Foundation Indonesia Hands Over the Master Meter Systems for 900 Houses in Surabaya City." September 16; https://www.iuwashplus.or.id/arsip/4720?lang=en.

Utsumi, Igor. 2014. "Brazilian Soda Market." *The Brazil Business*, updated May 2.

Varadharajan, Kiruba, Tinku Thomas, and Anura Kurpad. 2013. "Poverty and the State of Nutrition in India." *Asia Pacific Journal of Clinical Nutrition* 22 (3): 326–339.

Vasconcelos, F. 2005. "Combate á Fome no Brasil: Uma Análise Histórica da Vargas a Lula." *Revista de Nutrição* 18 (4): 439–457.

Veerman, Lennert, Thow Anne Marie, and Dwirahmadi Febi. 2019. "Taxing Sugary Drinks Can Benefit Indonesia, Research Suggests." *The Conversation*, August 6.

Vermeulen, Sonja, Laura Wellesely, Sam Airey, Sudhvir Singh, Rina Agustina, Doddy

Izwardy, and Diah Saminarsih. 2019. *Healthy Diets from Sustainable Production: Indonesia*. London: Chatham House, the Royal Institute of International Affairs. https://www.chathamhouse.org/sites/default/files/2020-12/2019-01-24-healthy-diets-sustainable-production.pdf.

Victor, Jennifer Nicoll. 2007. "Strategic Lobbying: Demonstrating How Legislative Context Affects Interest Groups' Lobbying Tactics." *American Politics Research* 35 (6): 826–845. https://www.doi.org/10.1177/1532673X07300681.

Vilar-Compte, Mireya. 2018. *Using Sugar-Sweetened Beverage Taxes and Advertising Regulations to Combat Obesity in Mexico*. Case study. Global Delivery Initiative. https://www.researchgate.net/publication/335000968_Using_Sugar-Sweetened_Beverage_Taxes_and_Advertising_Regulations_to_Combat_Obesity_in_Mexico.

Villarreal, Daniel. 2018. "This Coca-Cola Campaign Turned Brazilian Homophobia Into a Symbol of Pride." The Hornet, August 18. https://hornet.com/stories/that-coke-is-a-fanta/.

Villarreal, M. Angeles. 2010. "The Mexican Economy after the Global Financial Crisis." Washington, DC: Congressional Research Service. https://apps.dtic.mil/dtic/tr/fulltext/u2/a529130.pdf.

Villarreal, M. A., and M. Cid. 2008. *NAFTA and the Mexican Economy*. Electronic version. Washington, DC: Congressional Research Service. http://digitalcommons.ilr.cornell.edu/key_workplace/565/.

Violent Capitalist. 2010. "Brazil Fast Food: A Restaurant Chain with Staying Power." Seeking Alpha, June 8. https://seekingalpha.com/article/209047-brazil-fast-food-a-restaurant-chain-with-staying-power.

Vishwanath, Apurva. 2017. "Maggi Case Still on, but FSSAI Ties Up with Nestle to Improve Own Standards." ThePrint, September 14. https://theprint.in/report/maggi-case-still-on-but-fssai-ties-up-with-nestle-to-improve-own-standards/10014/.

Vital Strategies. 2019a. "After 2 Years, South Africa's Successful Sugar Beverage Tax Is Still under Attack." Vital Stories, October 15. https://www.vitalstrategies.org/after-2-years-south-africas-successful-sugar-beverage-tax-still-under-attack/.

———. 2019b. "Will Brazil's Bolsonaro Administration Stall Food Labels that Could Reduce Obesity?" July 12. https://www.vitalstrategies.org/will-brazils-bolsonaro-administration-stall-food-labels-that-could-reduce-obesity/.

VOANews. 2009. "S. African President Unveils Anti-poverty Plan—2004-05-21." October 29. https://www.voanews.com/amp/a-13-a-2004-05-21-12-1-67348417/272845.html.

Vogel, David. 2008. "Private Global Business Regulation." *Annual Review of Political Science* 11: 261–282. https://www.doi.org/10.1146/annurev.polisci.11.053106.141706.

———. 2010. "The Private Regulation of Global Corporate Conduct: Achievements and Limitations." *Business and Society* 49 (1): 68–87. https://www.doi.org/10.1177/0007650309343407.

Walker, Edward. 2009. "Privatizing Participation: Civic Change and the Organizational Dynamics of Grassroots Firms." *American Sociological Review* 74 (1): 83–105.

Walker, Edward, and Christopher Rea. 2014. "The Political Mobilization of Firms and Industries." *Annual Review of Sociology* 40: 281–304. https://doi.org/10.1146/annurev-soc-071913-043215.

Walsh, Natalie. n.d. "This Coke is a Fanta: Coca-Cola Brazil Fights Homophobia with a New Symbol of Pride." https://nataliejwalsh.com/this-coke-is-a-fanta-coca-cola-brazil-fights-homophobia-with-a-new-symbol-of-pride.

Wan, Lester. 2018. "Indonesian Study: Insufficient Information on Sugar Intake in Relation to Health Problems." *Food Navigator Asia*, January 12.

Wang, Huijun, and Fengying Zhai. 2013. "Program and Policy Options for Preventing Obesity in China." *Obesity Reviews* 14 (2): 134–140. https://www.doi.org10.1111/obr.12106.

Wang, Jeanette. 2016. "One in Three of World's Adults with Diabetes Is in China, WHO Reports." *South China Morning Post*, April 7.

Wang, L., et al. 2017. "Prevalence and Ethnic Pattern of Diabetes and Prediabetes in China." *Journal of the American Medical Association* 317 (24): 2515–2523.

Wang, Qian, Xu Zhang, Li Fang, Qingbo Guan, Liying Guan, and Qiu Li. 2018. "Prevalence, Awareness, Treatment and Control of Diabetes Mellitus among Middle-Aged and Elderly People in a Rural Chinese Population: A Cross-sectional Study." *PLOS One* 13 (6): e0198343, https://doi.org/10.1371/journal.pone.0198343.

Wang, Sthenfeng, Yong Chen, Miao Liu, Zhiheng Hong, Dianjiany Sun, Yukun Du, Meng Su, Canqing Yu, Qingmin Liu, Yunjun Ren, Jun Lv, and Liming Li. 2011. "The Changes of Nutrition Labeling of Packaged Food in Hangzhou in China during 2008–2011." *PLOS One* 6 (12): e28443, https://doi.org/10.1371/journal.pone.0028443.

Wang, Youfa, Lu Ma, Li Zhao, Liwant Gao, Hong Xue, Liang Wang, Yixin Ding, Yixuan Li, Weidong Qu, and Suying Chang. 2019. "National Policies and Intervention Programs on Childhood Obesity Prevention in China." *Current Developments in Nutrition* 3 (1): 1946, https://doi.org/10.1093/cdn/nzz042.P22-018-19.

Wang, Zhenghe, Zhiyong Zou, Haiun Wang, Jin Jing, Jiayou Luo, Xin Zhang, Chunyan Luo, Haiping Zhao, Dehong Pan, Jun Ma, Bin Dong, and Ynghua Ma. 2018. "Prevalence and Risk Factors of Impaired Fasting Glucose and Diabetes among Chinese Children and Adolescents: A National Observational Study." *British Journal of Nutrition* 120: 813–819. https://www.doi.org/10.1017/S0007114518002040.

Wang, Zhihong, Mengying Zhai, Shufa Du, and Barry Popkin. 2008. "Dynamic Shifts in Chinese Eating Behaviors." *Asia Pacific Journal of Clinical Nutrition* 17 (1): 123–130.

Wanxian Bao. 2009. "Coca-Cola, MOH Tout 'Keeping Health Weight." *China Daily*, May 18.

Warburton, Eve. 2016. "What Does Jokowi Want for the Indonesian Economy?" *East Asia Forum*, October 30.

Watson, James. 2000. "China's Big Mac Attack." *Foreign Affairs* 79 (3): 120–134.

Watson, Katy, and Sarah Treanor. 2016. "The Mexicans Dying for a Fizzy Drink." *BBC*, February 2.

Wei, Clarissa. 2018. "Why China Loves American Chain Restaurants so Much." *Eater*, March 20, 2018.

Weissmann, Jordan. 2012. "The End of Soda?" *The Atlantic*, May 18.

West, Darrell M., Diane Heith, and Chris Goodwin. 1996. "Harry and Louise Go to Washington: Political Advertising and Health Care Reform." *Journal of Health Politics, Policy and Law* 21 (1): 35–68.

Westcott, Ben, and Serenitie Wang. 2019. "Xi Jinping is Determined to End All Poverty in China by 2020. Can He Do It?" CNN, April 20.

Wharton, University of Pennsylvania. 2017. "Can an Ethnic Beverage Brand Challenge Coca-Cola in India?" Knowledge@Wharton. January 11. https://knowledge.wharton .upenn.edu/article/can-an-ethnic-beverage-brand-challenge-coca-cola-and-pepsi/.

White, Mariel, and Simón Barquera. 2020. "Mexico Adopts Food Warning Labels, Why Now?" *Health Systems and Reform* 6 (1). https://www.doi.org/10.1080/23288604.2020 .1752063.

Whitehead, R. J. 2015a. "Food Bodies Demand Criminal Inquiry into 'Corrupt' FSSAI Practices." Food navigator-asia.com, October 5. https://www.foodnavigator-asia.com /Article/2015/10/06/Food-bodies-demand-criminal-inquiry-into-corrupt-FSSAI -practices.

———. 2015b. "'Sin Tax' of 40% Proposed to Cover Indian Soft Drinks." Food Navigator -asia.com, December 8. https://www.foodnavigator-asia.com/Article/2015/12/08 /Sin-tax-of-40-proposed-to-cover-Indian-soft-drinks#.

———. 2015c. "Soda Tax Could Cost 120,000 Indonesian Jobs." *Food Navigator Asia*, December 17.

———. 2016. "The Sugar Tax Conundrum Currently Playing Out in Asian Markets." *Food Navigator Asia*, January 19.

———. 2017. "Drinks Companies Unite to Counter India's Looming Health Policies." *Food Navigator Asia*, March 21. https://www.foodnavigator-asia.com/Article/2017/03/21 /Drinks-companies-unite-to-counter-India-s-looming-health-policies.

Whitten, Sarah. 2016. "China Sees Childhood Obesity 'Explosion' in Rural Provinces." CNBC News, April 28.

Wie, Thee Kian. 2006. *Policies for Private Sector Development in Indonesia*. Asian Development Bank, Institute discussion paper No. 46. https://think-asia.org/handle/11540 /3634.

Wie, Thee Kian, and Kunio Yoshihara. 1987. "Foreign and Domestic Capital in Indonesian Industrialisation." *Southeast Asian Studies* 24 (4): 327–349.

Wilkes, Tommy. 2015. "Coca-Cola India Warns of Factor Closure If 'Sin Tax' is Implemented." *Irish Examiner LTD*; accessed October 13, 2019. https://www.irishexaminer .com/business/arid-20371195.html.

Wilkinson, Kate, and Vinayak Bhardwaj. 2016. "SA's Proposed Sugar Tax: Claims about Calories and Job Losses Checked." *AfricaCheck*, August 31.

Wilkinson, Tracy. 2011. "Poverty Grew in Mexico to Nearly Half the Population, Study Finds." *Los Angeles Times*, July 29.

Williams, Simon. 2015. "The Incursion of 'Big Food' in Middle-Income Countries: A Qualitative Documentary Case Study Analysis of the Soft Drink Industry in China and India." *Critical Public Health* 25 (4): 455–473. https://doi.org/10.1080/09581596 .2015.1005056.

Wilson, Duff, and Adam Kerlin. 2012. "Special Report: Food, Beverage Industry Pays for Seat at Health-Policy Table." *Reuters*, October 19.

Wirdana, Ardi, 2019. "Obesity Rates in Children on the Rise Indonesia." *Indonesia Expat*, December 30.

Wisnu, Dinna, and Frans Supiarso. 2015, Jan-March. "A More Efficient Approach to Social Welfare?" *Inside Indonesia*.

World Health Organization. n.d. "Global Health Observatory Data Repository." https://www.who.int/data/gho (accessed October 2, 2019).

———. n.d. "Prevalence of Obesity among Adults." Global Health Observatory, website, accessed August 20, 2020, https://apps.who.int/gho/data/view.main.CTRY2450A?lang=en

———. 2016a. "Healthy China 2030 (from Vision to Action)." Conference promotion article. https://www.who.int/healthpromotion/conferences/9gchp/healthy-china/en/.

———. 2016b. "Rate of Diabetes in China 'Explosive': Healthy Diet and Exercise Key to Turning the Tide." April 6. https://www.who.int/china/news/detail/06-04-2016-rate-of-diabetes-in-china-explosive-.

———. 2018. "WHO Country Cooperation Strategy at a Glance: Brazil." May 1. https://www.who.int/publications/i/item/who-country-cooperation-strategy-at-a-glance-brazil.

———. 2020a. *Commission on Ending Childhood Obesity. Facts and Figures on Childhood Obesity.* https://www.who.int/end-childhood-obesity/facts/en/.

———. 2020b. "Prevalence of Obesity among Adults." Global Health Observatory, https://apps.who.int/gho/data/view.main.CTRY2450A?lang=en.

———. 2021. Prevalence of Obesity among Adults, BMI > 30, Age-Standardized Estimates by Country." Global Health Observatory Data Repository. https://apps.who.int/gho/data/node.main.A900A?lang=en.

Wu, Fei, Hiroto Narimatsu, Xiaoqing Li, Sho Nakamura, Ri Sho, Genming Zhao, Yoshinori Nakata, and Wanghong Xu. 2017. "Non-Communicable Diseases Control in China and Japan." *Globalization and Health* 13 (1): 1–11. https://doi.org/10.1186/s12992-017-0315-8.

Xin, Gu. 2015. "New Advertisement Law Prohibits Children." *China Daily*, September 1. https://www.chinadaily.com.cn/culture/2015-09/01/content_21766409.htm.

Xinhua. 2018. "Xi Stresses Unswerving Support for Development of Private Enterprises." November 2. http://english.scio.gov.cn/topnews/2018-11/02/content_69643609.htm.

———. 2019. "Chinese Cities to Introduce More Convenience Stores in 2019." Chinadaily.com.cn, June 30. https://www.chinadaily.com.cn/a/201906/30/WS5d17ee6ea3103dbf1432b055.html.

Xinhua Net. 2018. "Chinese Spent 603 Bln USD Eating Out Last Year." January 18. http://www.xinhuanet.com/english/2018-01/18/c_136905648.htm.

———. 2020. "Xinhua Headlines-Xi Focus: Xi Jinping and China's Anti-poverty War He Commands." October 17. http://www.xinhuanet.com/english/2020-10/17/c_139447664.htm.

Xinyi, Li. 2016. "PepsiCo Aims to Fight Poor Nutrition." *China Daily*, September 29. https://www.chinadaily.com.cn/cndy/2016-09/29/content_26931821.htm.

Xu, Yongjian, Siyu Zhu, Tao Zhang, Duolao Wang, Junteng Hu, Jianmin Gao, and Zhongliang Zhou. 2020. "Explaining Income-Related Inequalities in Dietary Knowledge: Evidence from the China Health and Nutrition Survey." *International Journal of Environmental Research and Public Health* 17 (2): 532. https://www.doi.org/10.3390/ijerph17020532.

Yap, Jimmy, and Daphne Tan. 2019. "A Snapshot of the Investment Laws and Regulations of Indonesia, with a Particular Focus on Those Applicable to Foreign Investments in the Food and Beverage Industry." *Mondaq*, October 18. https://www.mondaq .com/inward-foreign-investment/857824/a-snapshot-of-the-investment-laws-and -regulations-of-indonesia-with-a-particular-focus-on-those-applicable-to-foreign -investments-in-the-food-and-beverage-industry.

Yin, Junmei, Alice Kong, and Juliana Chan. 2016. "Prevention and Care Programs Addressing the Growing Prevalence of Diabetes in China." *Current Diabetes Reports* 16 (12):130. https://www.doi.org/10.1007/s11892-016-0821-8.

Yiwei, Hu. 2019. "China's Diabetes Epidemic in Charts." *CGTN News*, November 14.

Yu, Jason. 2019. "What's Driving Coca-Cola's Growth in China?" September 30. https:// www.kantarworldpanel.com/cn-en/news/Whats-driving-coca-colas-growth-in-China.

Yuan, Lu, and Terence Tsai. 2000. "Foreign Direct Investment Policy in China." *China Review*: 223–247.

Zali, Marica. 2019. "Know What You're Eating: New Food Labels in the Pipeline Aimed at South Africans Making Healthier Choices." *Health 24*, September 2. https://www .health24.com/Diet-and-nutrition/News/know-what-youre-eating-new-food-labels -in-the-pipeline-aimed-at-south-africans-making-healthier-choices-20190816.

Zama, Zanele. 2019. "Visible Warning Labels to be Compulsory on Food Packaging." *7Q2 News*, August 1.

Zhai, Fengying, Shufa Du, Zhihong Wang, Jiguo Zhang, Wenwen Du, and Barry Popkin. 2014. "Dynamics of the Chinese Diet and the Role of Urbanicity, 1991–2011." *Obesity Review* 15: 16–26. https://www.doi.org/10.111/obr.12124.

Zhang, Jiguo, Huijun Wang, Zhihong Wang, Wenwen Du, Chang Sui, Ji Zhang, Hongru Jiang, Xiaofang Jia, Feifei Huang, Yifei Ouyang, Yun Wang, and Bing Zhang. 2018. "Prevalence and Stabilizing Trends in Overweight and Obesity among Children and Adolescents in China, 2011–2015." *BMC Public Health* 18 (1): 571, https://doi.org/10 .1186/s12889-018-5483-9.

Zhang, Na, and Guansheng Ma. 2018. "Childhood Obesity in China: Trends, Risk Factors, Policies and Actions." *Global Health Journal* 2 (1): 1–13. https://doi.org/10.1016 /S2414-6447(19)30115-0.

Zhang, Qi, Shiyong Liu, Ruicui Liu, Hong Xue, and Youfa Wang. 2015. "Food Policy Approaches to Obesity Prevention: An International Perspective." *Current Obesity Reports* 3 (2): 171–182. https://www.doi.org/10.1007/s13679-014-0099-6.

Zhen, Shihan, Yanan Ma, Zhongyi Zhao, Xuelian Yang, and Deliang Wen. 2018. "Dietary Pattern is Associated with Obesity in Chinese Children and Adolescents: Data from China Health and Nutrition Survey." *Nutrition Journal* 17 (1): 68. https://doi.org/10 .1186/s12937-018-0372-8.

Zheng, Shi, Pei Xu, and Zhigang Wang. 2011. "Are Nutrition Labels Useful for the Purchase of a Familiar Food? Evidence from Chinese Consumers' Purchase of Rice." *Frontiers of Business Research in China* 5 (3): 402–421. https://www.doi.org/10.1007 /s11782-011-0137-0.

Zhou, Shengsheng, Bing Ye, Pengyu Fu, Shan Li, Pu Yuan, Li Yang, Xuan Zhan, Feng Chao, Shufang Zhang, Min Qi Wang, and Alice Yan. 2020. "Double Burden of Malnutrition:

Examining the Growth Profile and Coexistence of Undernutrition, Overweight, and Obesity among School-Aged Children and Adolescents in Urban and Rural Counties in Henan Province, China." *Journal of Obesity* 2020: 1–11. https://doi.org/10.1155/2020/2962138.

Zhou, Yijinng, Shufa Du, Chang Su, Binng Zhang, Huijun Wang, and Barry Popkin. 2015. "The Food Retail Revolution in China and Its Association with Diet and Health." *Food Policy* 55: 92–100. https://doi.org/10.1016/j.foodpol.2015.07.001.

Zhou, Zhenghua, Qinqin Diao, Nan Shao, Youke Liang, Li Lin, Yan Lei, and Lingmei Zheng. 2015. "The Frequency of Unhealthy Food Advertising on Mainland Chinese Television (TV) and Children and Adolescents' Risk of Exposure to Them." *PLOS One* 10 (7): e0128746. https://doi.org/10.1371/journal.pone.0128746.

Zhu, Zheng, Yan Tang, Jie Zhuang, Yang Liu, Xueping Wu, Yujun Cai, Lijuan Wang, Zhen-Bo Cao, and Peijie Chen. 2019. "Physical Activity, Screen Viewing Time, and Overweight/Obesity among Chinese Children and Adolescents: An Update from the 2017 Physical Activity and Fitness in China—the Youth Study." *BMC Public Health* 9: 197, https://www.doi.org/10.1186/s12889-019-6515-9.

Zhuoqiong, Wang. 2018. "Convenience Stores Expanding." *China Daily*, May 26.

———. 2019. "Snacks Continue to Be on the Upswing in Chinese Market." *China Daily*, June 12.

Zimmet, Paul Z., Assam El-Ostra, and Zumin Shi. 2017. "The Diabetes Epidemic in China Is a Public Health Emergency: The Potential Role of Prenatal Exposure." *Journal of Public Health and Emergency* 1: 80.

Zocchio, Guilherme. 2018. "Entidades cobram Candidatos por Compromisso com a Alimentação has Eleições." *O Joio e o Trigo*, August 23. https://outraspalavras.net/ojoioeotrigo/2018/08/entidades-cobram-candidatos-por-compromisso-com-alimentacao-nas-eleicoes/.

Index

Reproductive, Maternal, Newborn, and Child Health Coalition (in India), 161
restructuring society (industry policy tactic), 26, 29
Rousseff, Dilma, 90, 104

Salvador (state in Brazil), 85
Sanger-Katz, Margot, 35–36
Sanghera, Tish, 137
Sanitarista social movement, 29, 119
Savell, Emily, 17
Save the Children India, 161
SBY (Susilo Bambang Yudhoyono), 213
School Feeding Law 11.947 (in Brazil), 89
self-regulation (industry strategy), 7, 10, 17, 19, 27, 54
"shadow warriors" (unofficial, furtive lobbyists in India), 156
Shamah, Teresa, 56
"sin tax," 7, 124, 143–44, 159
South African National Health and Nutrition Examination Survey, 278
southern Western Hemisphere, 78
Srivastava, Amit, 146, 154
Strategy for the Prevention and Control of Obesity in South Africa, 280
Suharto, 182, 212–13
Sukarno, 181–82
SUN (Scaling UP Nutrition) Movement (in Indonesia), 195
Sunny Sports Program Supporting Millions of Students across China, 241
Swachh Bharat Swachh Vidyalaya (Clean India: Clean Schools) national campaign, 165, 174
Swaziland (renamed Eswatini), 272

Temer, Michel, 115–17, 118
transnational partnership, 63
tuck shops (in South Africa), 285–86

two-way street (in junk food politics), 3, 10, 113, 311, 315
type 2 diabetes, 48, 311

Uday Foundation, 157, 159
UN-Habitat, 152, 165, 174
United States, 24; city-level policy in, 322; health care policy, 14, 22; health consciousness and consumerism, 34–37, 39; industry influence on science, 58; and North American Free Trade Agreement, 42–44; and obesity, 87; and poverty as related to diet, 48; regulation of lobbying in, 156
Universal Declaration of Human Rights, 114
University of São Paulo (in Brazil), 93, 107
University of Western Cape (in South Africa), 284
Usaha Kesehatan Sekolah (UKS) (Indonesia school health program), 197
US House of Representatives, 22
US-Mexican border, 51

Verma, Rahul, 145
Vogel, David, 19, 27

Walker, J. L., 15, 21
Weissmann, Jordan, 36
Western Europe, 14, 24, 34–35, 39
Widodo, Joko "Jokowi," 8, 181, 201, 215
World Economic Forum, 68–69, 215–16
World Health Organization (WHO), 1, 189
WWF (World Wildlife Fund), 258

Xi Jinping, 10, 260–63, 265

Yudhoyono, Susilo Bambang, 8, 213

Zemin, Jian, 262
Zuma, Jacob, 301–3, 305–6